Cash CDO Modelling in Excel

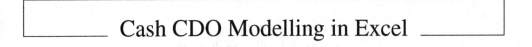

For other titles in the Wiley Finance series
please see www.wiley.com/finance

Cash CDO Modelling in Excel

A *Step by Step Approach*

Darren Smith and Pamela Winchie

A John Wiley and Sons, Ltd., Publication

This edition first published 2010
© 2010 John Wiley & Sons, Ltd

Registered office
John Wiley & Sons Ltd, The Atrium, Southern Gate, Chichester, West Sussex, PO19 8SQ, United Kingdom

For details of our global editorial offices, for customer services and for information about how to apply for
permission to reuse the copyright material in this book please see our website at www.wiley.com.

Wiley also publishes its books in a variety of electronic formats. Some content that appears in print may not be
available in electronic books.

Designations used by companies to distinguish their products are often claimed as trademarks. All brand names and
product names used in this book are trade names, service marks, trademarks or registered trademarks of their
respective owners. The publisher is not associated with any product or vendor mentioned in this book. This
publication is designed to provide accurate and authoritative information in regard to the subject matter covered. It
is sold on the understanding that the publisher is not engaged in rendering professional services. If professional
advice or other expert assistance is required, the services of a competent professional should be sought.

Library of Congress Cataloging-in-Publication Data

Smith, Darren.
  Cash CDO modelling in Excel : a step by step approach / Darren Smith and Pamela Winchie.
    p. cm.
  ISBN 978-0-470-74157-3
  1. Collateralized debt obligations–Mathematical models.   2. Credit derivatives–Mathematical models.
3. Microsoft Excel (Computer file)   I. Winchie, Pamela.   II. Title.
  HG6024.A3S566 2010
  332.63′2–dc22

                                                                                    2010005595

A catalogue record for this book is available from the British Library.

ISBN 978-0-470-74157-3

Typeset in 10/12pt Times by Aptara Inc., New Delhi, India
Printed in Great Britain by CPI Antony Rowe, Chippenham, Wiltshire

Dedicated in loving memory to Graham, Josie and Stephen

Contents

Foreword

The fixed income markets have always been centres of innovation and creativity. This much is apparent from even a cursory glance at developments in recent and not-so-recent history. However it is only in the last thirty years or so that such innovation has really been required, as economic markets changed significantly and capital started to move freely. The bond markets have been the conduit through which vital capital has been raised; continuing product development in the markets has made a significant, and irreplaceable, contribution to global economic progress. The range of products available is vast and always growing, as the needs of both providers and users of capital continually alters in response to changing conditions. This economic dynamic means that market participants observe a state of constant learning, as they must if they are to remain effective in their work. Inevitably we are required to become specialists, as each segment of the debt markets demands increasingly complex approaches in addressing its problems and requirements.

Of course, users of capital are not limited to existing products for raising finance or hedging market risk exposure. They can ask an investment bank to design an instrument specifically to meet their individual requirements, and target it at specific groups of customers. For example it is arguable whether the growth of some of the so-called "credit-card banks" in the United States could have occurred so rapidly without the securitisation mechanism that enabled them to raise lower-cost funding. Witness also the introduction of the synthetic collateralised debt obligation (CDO), allied with a credit derivative, following rapidly on the development of more conventional CDO structures and designed to meet purely credit risk management requirements. The increasing depth and complexity of the markets requires participants to be completely up-to-date on the latest analytical and valuation techniques if they are not to risk being left behind. It is clear that we operate in an environment in which there exists a long-term interest in the application of ever more accurate valuation and analytical techniques.

The arcane and specialist nature of the structured finance markets means that as a topic they are rarely reviewed in the mainstream media. This contributed to a great deal of misunderstanding amongst legislators, journalists, the general public and even some regulators in the wake of the financial crash of 2007-2008. That "CDOs" were stated by some to have been the cause of the crisis reflects the general level of ignorance at all levels. This is unfortunate. To blame the crash on financial engineering is akin to blaming cars for road deaths. Legislation in the wake of a rise in road fatalities is usually connected with making the roads safer, not banning cars. Without a doubt, heavy losses on holdings of structured credit securities were behind the trouble at some banks, but amongst the high-profile bank failures were a number of institutions that did not hold such assets, and had instead neglected their liquidity management. The simple fact is that securitisation and financial innovation have been a force for much good in the world, particularly in an era of globalisation. To take one example, one should know that the mobile phone industry is a large user of capital markets finance. To witness, as I have done, a rickshaw puller on the streets of Dhaka, average salary $1 per day, using a mobile phone is to observe the social benefits of a free market in capital, technical innovation and financial engineering coalescing in one exotic moment.

Speaking personally, I stress the importance of constantly staying at the leading edge of financial market research and development to ensure that, as bankers, we continue to deliver quality and value to our clients. Much of the innovation and product development in the markets originates from an ongoing discussion with the client base, as banks seek to meet their customer requirements.

That is why this book, from two experienced practitioners, is such a welcome publication. It is a rare beast in the universe of finance literature in actually telling one how to do something, rather than being simply an academic treatise on how one does things in a classroom. It is the authors' clarity of approach and focus that I am most excited about. They provide insight into practical techniques and applications used in the structured finance markets today. The content also sheds light on the scope and significance of these techniques in the world of finance. I am impressed by the level of detail herein on exactly how to go about building the cash flow model, something that I believe would be of use to a wide range of finance professionals, not just those concerned with structuring CDO transactions.

Another feature about this book that I personally recommend is its value for first-time practitioners. If one is working on an asset-backed security (ABS) or CDO transaction at a bank that has not previously closed such a deal, then this is a useful reference to have on the desk. Post-credit crunch, many banks that had not previously originated ABS deals sought to close "in-house" transactions to create collateral for use at the European Central Bank and Bank of England repo windows. The contents of this book would be of great interest to such bank practitioners. As such, this book deserves a wide readership.

It is a privilege to be asked to write this foreword. The authors have produced a work of the very highest quality. As focused as it is comprehensive, this is an excellent contribution to the literature and sure to become a key reference work for anyone with an interest in the securitisation and structured finance markets. My hope is that this exciting and interesting new book spurs readers on to their own research and investigation; if they follow the application and dedication evident in this work, they will not be going far wrong!

Professor Moorad Choudhry
Department of Economics
London Metropolitan University
30 March 2010

Acknowledgments

As we discovered along the way, a book is a team effort and we have many people to thank for their contributions. These include Geoff Chaplin and Moorad Choudhry for their insight, encouragement and assistance in helping us to get this book published. We would like to express our deep gratitude to Francis Richard Pereira, Dacil Acosta and Simon Chantry for being our guinea pigs. Richard is an Investment Actuary specializing in Fixed Income and Alternative Investments. Richard is highly regarded in this field and has worked for JP Morgan as an Executive Director in the Structured Alternative Investments business area. Dacil has worked as a CDO structurer for Merrill Lynch and Dresdner. Prior to that, she worked at Standard and Poor's as a CDO Ratings Analyst. Simon is a senior member of the Structured Credit team at Sumitomo Mitsui Banking Corporation's European business, focusing mainly on balance sheet structures. Prior to that, he also worked as a CDO Ratings Analyst at Standard and Poor's. All of the above people gave their personal time, and their work on the book should not be construed as an endorsement or recommendation from their employers past or present.

Darren would also like to acknowledge the following people who have helped and influenced him over the past 12 years: Pat Gallaway, Mari Kawawa, Eddie Lee, Gerrard O'Connor and Arturo Cifuentes.

Pamela would like to acknowledge the many people who have helped and inspired her over the years, including Sandra Kiss and The Honourable Mr Justice Morris Perozak.

Finally we would like to thank our families. Darren would like to thank Heather, Luke, Elizabeth and Mitchell for their patience, support and encouragement. Pamela would like to thank her parents, Terry and Diana, and her brothers, Stephen and Alexander, who have supported and encouraged her beyond words.

1
Introduction

There has been a lot written on credit derivatives during the past few years. However, much of what has been written about traditional "cash flow" collateralized debt obligations (CDOs) has been of an introductory nature. It has often been written from a research or legal point of view and there has been little discussion about the modelling and evaluation of these structures. In many books, cash CDOs are mentioned as part of a more generalized introduction to asset backed securities. According to data published by the Securities Industry and Financial Markets Association, the cash flow CDO market was over USD 400 billion in 2006. Unfortunately, the market in 2007 through 2009 was overshadowed by the "credit crunch", largely brought on by sub-prime mortgages, a major contributing factor was structured finance CDOs and their valuation. Contagion effects in the credit market virtually caused the collapse of all lending. A major theme was the mistrust in the markets that arose because of the lack of an agreed-upon valuation technique for structured finance vehicles (including CDOs). Notwithstanding these events, the authors believe that CDOs and specifically the modeling of CDOs, deserves more serious and dedicated attention.

The aim of this book is to introduce the modelling of cash flow CDOs, including construction of cash flows for both the underlying collateral and the issued notes, the evaluation of default probabilities and expected losses for rating agencies, and techniques and approaches that investors may use to value them. A newcomer to the CDO market ideally will be able to use the ideas in this book to construct her or his own models. A wider aim of this book is to encourage and promote discussion and debate about the modelling, evaluation and valuation of cash flow CDOs.

The authors acknowledge that there is not necessarily one right way to model. Every model is a compromise between several objectives including speed, flexibility, visibility, degree of automation, ease of change and verification. The book expounds the authors' views on best practice and utilizes their experiences in discussing the advantages and disadvantages of different approaches.

This book adopts a step-by-step approach to building a rudimentary model so that any reader who "sticks the course" will have a useful tool to evaluate cash flow CDOs and a template that can be built upon to suit personal taste and requirements.

1.1 TO EXCEL OR NOT TO EXCEL?

When cash CDOs were first being modelled, most modellers used spreadsheets as there was no dedicated software available. Over time, investment banks, large investors and collateral managers have developed or purchased licenses for dedicated CDO systems. These systems have varied from management tools to modelling and evaluation tools, depending on the needs of the users.

There are strengths and weaknesses to every system and tool. Microsoft Office Excel's biggest strength is that it allows for a great deal of flexibility: trivial changes to a model can be done with relative ease. However, when changes are made that are more than trivial, without a disciplined and organized approach, this ease of change can quickly become Excel's biggest weakness. One of the themes of this book is consistent application of organization to avoid the chaos that can easily creep into a workbook model making it unusable over the medium to long term. This book will discuss techniques to layer a model design, by taking advantage of the spreadsheet layout. By limiting the links between the functional parts of the model, it is easy to replace those functions in the future. The authors have replaced Collateral Sheets and Waterfall Sheets on several occasions during the time they have been using similar models without impacting the rest of the model. This is achieved by limiting links between the inputs and outputs between the functional worksheets.

Most cash flow CDOs are bespoke: although they may start from a general template, they are customized investments that are tailored to specific investor requirements. Once a modeller has created a basic model using spreadsheets, the flexibility exists with Excel to quickly model and test new CDO structures. In contrast, if software or systems are developed away from spreadsheets, extensive support from a programmer may be required to make changes or the modeller may have to learn to program in a higher-level programming language. This can significantly delay the evaluation of a new feature or structure.

Another benefit to using Excel worksheets for cash flow modelling is their origin and pedigree in auditing and accounting. Worksheets still offer one of the best frameworks on which to base an audit tool. Even rating agencies use worksheets as the basis for the tools they offer.

This book assumes a certain familiarity and working knowledge of Excel. Should the reader find their knowledge insufficient, then one of the many excellent books on Exel should help remedy the situation.

1.2 EXISTING TOOLS AND SOFTWARE

What are the alternatives to using bespoke spreadsheets to evaluate CDOs? While the authors do not advocate any one of these systems and this book is not intended to be an advertisement for any of these systems, they believe it is important for the reader to know that there are alternatives available. Generally these can be broken down into:

- CDO management systems usually provided by trustees or other third parties to enable investors and asset managers to evaluate changes to the underlying asset/risk portfolio.
- Third party data and modelling systems mainly used by investors to track their portfolios without the onerous task of updating from trustee reports. Often these systems provide little or no analysis facilities but can be extended by bespoke development, either by the supplier or the licensee.
- Rating agency supplied systems, which frequently do not deal with the underlying structure and mainly model the performance of the underlying asset portfolio according to the rating agencies, criteria. At the time of writing, the exception to this is CDOEdge, which is a tool that Moody's Investor Services sell to model cash flow transactions to their methodology.

• Analysis systems which, to be successful, typically have a mechanism to encode the priority of payments cash flows of the CDO. They will also have means to do default, interest rate or other scenario analysis either by simulation or scenarios.

These systems are often expensive and require the vendor to maintain them. The modelling explained in this book is not necessarily looking to replace these systems but complement them. Often it is useful to interface spreadsheet models to these systems to avoid duplication and maintenance of underlying data.

What are Cash CDOs?

2.1 TYPES OF CDOS

This book is intended as a guide to modelling CDOs. It is not an introductory book to all aspects of CDOs. There are many existing books that discuss the legal, accounting, regulatory and other aspects of CDOs. Nevertheless, it is worthwhile from a completeness perspective to briefly discuss what a CDO is.

The first incarnations of CDOs were CBOs (collateralized bond obligations) of high yield bonds and CLOs (collateralized loan obligations) of leveraged loans. The concept of these structures was then extended to many more asset classes, including investment grade bonds, asset backed securities, real estate investment trusts (REITs), hedge fund units, private equity shares, trust preferred bonds, derivatives (such as credit default swaps) and equity (through either shares, equity default swaps, and/or options and commodities).

CDOs can be categorized by their various different attributes in many different ways, some of which are listed below:

- cash, synthetic, or hybrid assets;
- managed or static;
- full capital structures or single tranche technology;
- cash flow (asset-liability matched) or market value;
- asset classes.

Another way to categorize CDOs is by their primary function. CDO technology may be used to achieve one or more of the following goals:

- credit risk transfer;
- funding illiquid assets;
- leveraged return on credit assets;
- regulatory and/or economic capital relief.

It should be remembered that a CDO, particularly a cash CDO, is not an asset class in its own right but a financing technique particularly suited to illiquid assets. It is therefore only as robust as the assets that are put into it. It is like a "mini-bank": it raises capital by selling debt and "equity", and invests the money raised into assets to generate an "excess" return. Cash CDOs are often called "arbitrage" CDOs as the assets are worth more repackaged than as individual securities.

2.1.1 Cash, synthetic or hybrid CDOs

Cash CDOs involve assets that are typically securities, such as bonds, but can also include bi-lateral or multi-lateral debt contracts, such as loans. The assets are transferred to a bankruptcy remote special purpose entity (SPE) as the registered owner and are paid for by the selling of liabilities (or notes). Figure 2.1 illustrates this. The assets often do not have the same terms

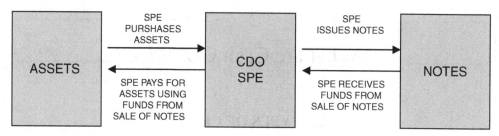

Figure 2.1 Cash CDO structure

with regard to payment dates, redemption schedules or maturity dates. Hence much of the structuring of the CDO involves matching certain characteristics of the liabilities with certain characteristics of the assets.

By contrast, synthetic CDOs are based on the transfer of risk, typically by the use of credit derivative contracts (usually using standardized terms from the International Swap Dealers Association (ISDA)). The underlying assets/contracts that they refer to may be held by a sponsor bank or other financial institution, but increasingly are sourced from the credit derivatives market. The underlying contracts usually have the same terms with regard to payment dates and maturity date, so there is little or no mismatch between the risk and the protection. Recent developments in the establishment of centralized clearing, and the "big bang" protocols which amongst other things standardized premiums, have homogenized the market further.

A cash transaction has a more complex "Priority of Payments" (colloquially called a "waterfall"), than a synthetic transaction. Synthetic CDOs or CSOs normally rely solely upon subordination to support the credit ratings of the notes, hence the reason they are sometimes referred to as "write down" structures.

Cash flow transactions typically have covenants regarding interest coverage (i.e., interest income versus interest liability servicing) and over-collateralization coverage (i.e., assets to liabilities ratio). Failure of these covenants diverts income from the assets due to the junior notes to accelerate the senior notes. These covenant tests effectively provide contingent additional subordination so that the initial subordination in a cash flow transaction is usually less than the subordination on a synthetic transaction on an equivalent portfolio. In addition, cash flow CDOs often require additional structuring to address risks that are not present in synthetic CDOs, such as interest timing mismatches, currency risks, prepayment risks and reinvestment risks.

In a synthetic (or "write-down") structure, the notes are used to support the credit protection sold. Once a claim on that credit protection is made, the notional of the note is reduced by the default amount and is written-down immediately. Recoveries (if any), when they are realized, are used to pay down the super senior swap. This payment effectively increases the detachment point of the most junior swap by the recovery amount. In contrast to a cash flow transaction, the notes are not written down until the maturity of the transaction because losses can be redeemed from excess interest proceeds (Figure 2.2).

Hybrid transactions incorporate both synthetic and cash CDO features and allow for both cash assets and synthetic securities, and cash and synthetic liabilities. Additionally, hybrid transactions allow for the ratio of cash and synthetic assets and liabilities to change. As many cash flow transactions allow for a bucket of 10 to 20 per cent synthetic securities, to be considered truly hybrid a transaction typically has more than 20 per cent synthetic securities. Additionally, many hybrid transactions allow for "short" buckets as well, which means that

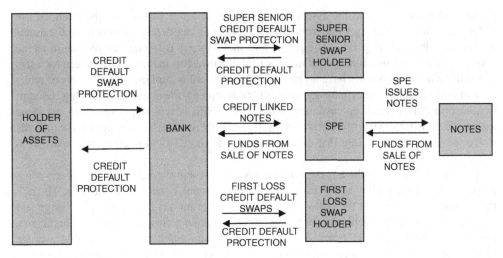

Figure 2.2 Synthetic (write-down) structure

the SPE can effectively hedge risk positions by buying protection on obligors. This also allows for "basis trades".

Basis trades are long–short positions on the same obligor risk where the "long" default risk is completely offset by a short "protection" position, ideally at a lower spread. This allows for an earned income that is independent of the underlying credit risk, although there is still, typically much lower, risk from counterparty credit.

> *Did you know?* A basis trade (also called a "negative basis trade") is where the trader or collateral manager buys an asset and buys "protection" on that asset usually from a highly credit worthy counterpart. What "protection" means is that the trader or collateral manager will enter into an agreement whereby for a portion of the interest coupon on a given asset being given to the highly credit worthy counterparty, that counterparty will agree to reimburse the trader or collateral manager should there be losses in interest or principal in the asset due to a credit event such as a default. There are known as credit default swaps ("CDSs"). The result is that the credit risk on the asset is immunised. Thus, if the trader can secure or "lock-in" a funding rate for the life of the asset that, in combination with the cost of the protection, is less than the coupon earned on the asset, then a risk free profit or arbitrage is locked in.

2.1.2 Managed or static CDOs

In a managed transaction, typically a third party asset manager is chosen to select the portfolio and to manage it during the life of transaction. Typically the manager has the ability to remove "credit impaired" and "credit improved" assets at any time and may also have a discretionary trading allowance, normally up to 15 or 20 per cent of the total portfolio balance per annum. Additionally, as the assets may prepay or amortize earlier than the intended life of the liabilities, the manager may reinvest the prepaid or amortized amounts from the assets during the reinvestment period. The purpose of the manager is to enhance the return to the equity investors and minimize the default risk to all the investors in the CDO, in return for a fee.

Static transactions usually have no provision for removal or replacement of assets or reference obligors, although they may sometimes permit replenishment of risk following redemption according to agreed replenishment criteria. The SPE is typically invested in the same assets or credits for the life of the transaction. Hence if there are rating downgrades or defaults in the assets, there is nothing that can be done inside the CDO to mitigate this apart from restructuring it.

After credit risk, often the largest issue for investors is reinvestment risk. Assets can often prepay principal depending on the interest rate and economic conditions at the time. The risk in a managed CDO during the reinvestment period is that market conditions can change and it can be difficult to find replacement investments on similar terms and/or with a similar risk profile. For example, a CDO can be structured with a covenant that the weighted average spread over LIBOR must meet a minimum threshold. After a few years into the reinvestment period, spreads in the market may have contracted and the portfolio manager will be unable to find reinvestment assets that allow the portfolio to meet the minimum weighted average spread covenant without increasing their risk appetite (i.e., lowering the credit quality). Thus, returns to investors can be damaged (particularly at the equity or first loss level) if large amounts of cash are being held in the transaction at a lower return or assets with higher default risk default more frequently than was initially expected at the closing date of the transaction. This risk is not present within static CDOs. (It should be noted, however, that from an investor's point of view, with a static CDO where principal payments are being used to pay down principal of the CDO notes, an investor must look to reinvest funds outside the CDO when principal payments are recieved. Thus the reinvestment risk is still present, but from an investor's viewpoint it has been moved outside the CDO structure and is under their control.)

2.1.3 Full capital structures versus single tranches

Cash flow CDOs tend to be full capital structure deals. This means that the issuer (or SPE) will sell a similar amount of liabilities to pay for the assets that it purchases. This is in contrast to the synthetic CDO (or CSO), where only tranches representing a small fraction of the capital structure are sold, typically the middle (or mezzanine) tranches which are often initially rated from AA to BB. The underwriting investment bank or originator will often retain the more subordinated unrated first loss (or equity) risk and the risk of the most senior tranches (commonly referred to as the "super senior" liabilities).

2.1.3.1 Cash flow (asset-liability matched) or market value

Most cash flow CDOs issue debt which matches the longest maturity of the assets so there is no refinancing risk for the CDO. An alternative approach is to deliberately mismatch the maturity between assets and liabilities by using short-term debt instruments such as commercial paper or repurchase agreements. These short-term debt instruments allow for additional yield pickup by issuing debt lower on the yield curve than the assets. The mismatch between the assets and liabilities can be typically addressed by using a combination of a liquidity provider and through market value covenants.

If the assets are not particularly liquid then a liquidity provider is needed to purchase the commercial paper or provide alternative means of financing either short term or long term if the short-term debt cannot be funded in the market. This was clearly demonstrated in the unwinding of the SIV market, where originating banks were often the liquidity providers to SIVs, and consequently they were obliged to purchase the maturing commercial paper from investors and were unable to sell it into the commercial paper market.

If the underlying assets have a sufficiently liquid market then funding can be advanced against the market value less a suitable haircut for price volatility. This is often called the "advance rate": the percentage of the market value against which funds are lent and is often only used for the most senior portion of the transaction's liabilities. The issuer may fund the rest of the asset purchases by issuing term-funded mezzanine notes and equity or capital notes. The issuer will covenant to maintain a minimum value of the portfolio with regard to the short-term debt. In the event of a breach of these covenants then several remedies can be enforced, including: (a) directing principal cash flows from the assets to pay down the principal on the senior notes; (b) preventing the issuance of more short-term debt; and (c) liquidating some or all of the assets to repay some or all of the outstanding principal of the short-term debt.

2.1.3.2 Asset types

Cash flow CDO technology has been developed for many asset types and is being continually developed and extended. At the time of writing, CDOs have been issued backed by the following asset types:

- bonds (investment grade, high yield, emerging markets);
- loans (high yield);
- asset backed securities;
- hedge funds;
- private equity;
- real estate investment trust debt (or REITS);
- trust preferred debt (insurance/bank);
- commodities.

2.2 DESCRIPTION OF A CASH FLOW CDO

A cash flow CDO commonly has some or all of the following elements:

- a bankruptcy remote special purpose entity (SPE) which purchases the assets and issues the notes;
- a security trustee holds the secured interest in the assets of the SPE on behalf of the note holders and other secured creditors;
- a custodian holds the assets usually via a clearing system such as the DTC or Euroclear/Clearstream;
- a note depository holds the physical notes so that they can be "dematerialized" and traded "book entry". This is typically the DTC or the same entity as the custodian;
- an account bank may hold cash in bank accounts, or these may be administered by the trustee in non-interest bearing cash accounts which are invested in cash or cash equivalent securities;

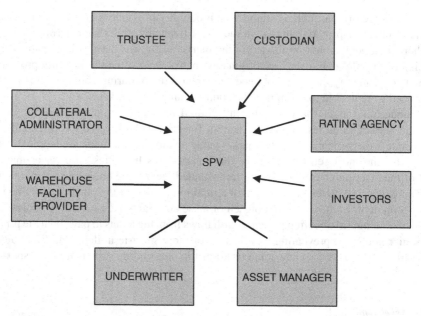

Figure 2.3 Elements of a cash flow CDO

- a collateral administrator performs the collateral tests and reporting functions as required by the transaction documents;
- the issued notes are rated by one or more rating agency;
- the SPE purchases the assets typically from a warehouse facility provider (usually a fund or bank);
- the assets are typically managed by an asset manager in exchange for fees;
- the issuance is underwritten by an investment bank that typically places (or sells) the notes to their clients.

The notes issued by the SPE will have various ratings from AAA/Aaa to lower investment grade or even speculatively sub-investment grade. The higher the rating on the notes, the lower return they will generally earn. Table 2.1 is a sample capital structure from 2006.

The notes are the SPE's liabilities and their interest coupons are paid from the interest funds received from the assets. Both interest and principal payments are received from the assets and in turn they are paid to the liabilities in accordance with the priority of payments (colloquially

Table 2.1 Sample capital structure

Class of notes	Moody's rating	S&P rating	Spread over USD LIBOR (bps)
Class A notes	Aaa	AAA	75
Class B notes	Aa2	AA	250
Class C notes	A2	A	375
Class D notes	Baa2	BBB	470
Class E notes	Ba2	BB	645
Class F notes	Not rated	Not rated	Excess cash flows

known as the "waterfall"). There are usually separate priorities of payments or waterfalls, applied to the interest and principal proceeds received from the assets. The usual reason for the existence of the priority of payments waterfalls is to ensure that the holders of senior notes are paid interest and principal before the holders of more junior notes.

Table 2.2 is an example of an Interest Waterfall where interest proceeds from the assets are applied.

Table 2.2   Interest waterfall

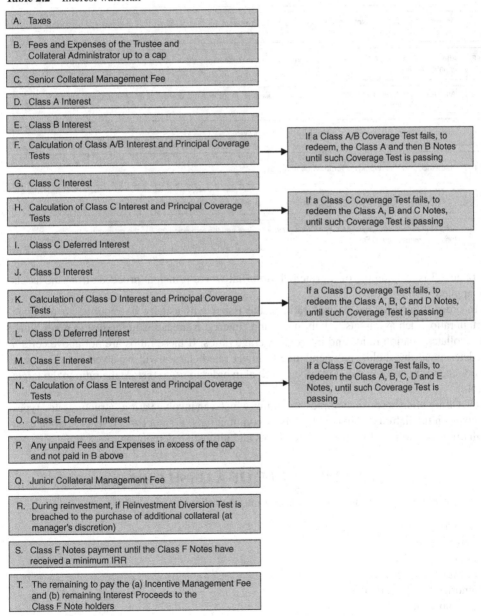

A. Taxes

B. Fees and Expenses of the Trustee and Collateral Administrator up to a cap

C. Senior Collateral Management Fee

D. Class A Interest

E. Class B Interest

F. Calculation of Class A/B Interest and Principal Coverage Tests → If a Class A/B Coverage Test fails, to redeem, the Class A and then B Notes until such Coverage Test is passing

G. Class C Interest

H. Calculation of Class C Interest and Principal Coverage Tests → If a Class C Coverage Test fails, to redeem the Class A, B and C Notes, until such Coverage Test is passing

I. Class C Deferred Interest

J. Class D Interest

K. Calculation of Class D Interest and Principal Coverage Tests → If a Class D Coverage Test fails, to redeem the Class A, B, C and D Notes, until such Coverage Test is passing

L. Class D Deferred Interest

M. Class E Interest

N. Calculation of Class E Interest and Principal Coverage Tests → If a Class E Coverage Test fails, to redeem the Class A, B, C, D and E Notes, until such Coverage Test is passing

O. Class E Deferred Interest

P. Any unpaid Fees and Expenses in excess of the cap and not paid in B above

Q. Junior Collateral Management Fee

R. During reinvestment, if Reinvestment Diversion Test is breached to the purchase of additional collateral (at manager's discretion)

S. Class F Notes payment until the Class F Notes have received a minimum IRR

T. The remaining to pay the (a) Incentive Management Fee and (b) remaining Interest Proceeds to the Class F Note holders

Table 2.3   Principal waterfall

A.	Amounts in paragraphs A to K of the Interest Waterfall to the extent not paid from Interest Proceeds
B.	During the Reinvestment Period, to acquire Additional Portfolio Assets
C.	After the end of the Reinvestment Period, to redeem the Class A Notes
D.	After the end of the Reinvestment Period, to redeem the Class B Notes, if the Class A Notes redeemed are in full
E.	After the Class A and B Notes have been redeemed, to redeem the Class C Notes including any accrued and unpaid interest
F.	After the Class A, B and C Notes have been redeemed, to redeem the Class D Notes including any accrued and unpaid interest
G.	After the Class A, B, C and D Notes have been redeemed, to redeem the Class E Notes including any accrued and unpaid interest
H.	Any unpaid amounts in sections B and P of the Interest Waterfall
I.	To the accrued and unpaid Junior Management Fee
J.	To the Class F Note holders until the Incentive Management Threshold is reached
K.	80% of the remaining proceeds to the Class F Note holders and the remaining 20% to the payment of the Incentive Management Fee

Table 2.3 is an example of a Principal Waterfall where principal proceeds from the assets are applied.

In order to achieve the desired ratings, the Issuer will usually be required to maintain certain ratios such as "assets to liabilities" and "interest from assets to interest to notes", i.e., over collateralization ratios and interest coverage ratios. If these ratios are not above certain predetermined thresholds, payments due to lower rated classes will be diverted to the most senior classes in order to pay down the principal in order to try to restore the ratio to the target level.

CDOs are often bespoke, complex structures which can involve various structures and types of notes on the liability side and all sorts of combinations of asset (or reference) pools, each with differing timings, frequency of payments and ultimate redemptions.

2.3 LIFE CYCLE OF A CASH CDO

The life cycle of a CDO can broadly be split into the following phases:

1. pre-close;
2. closing date;
3. pre-effective date;
4. reinvestment period;
5. amortization period; and
6. redemption/call

During the pre-close period, the asset manager selects the assets and instructs the warehouse provider (usually the sponsoring investment bank) to purchase the assets and hold them until the closing date. The sponsoring investment bank usually structures and manages the rating process, and markets the issued notes of the SPE. The culmination of the pre-close period is the pricing date, where investors place their orders to purchase notes on the closing date. Prior to that date, the investors typically have received the preliminary prospectus (sometimes referred to as the "red herring" or the "red" for short).

On the closing date various things happen: (a) the warehouse is typically closed; (b) the assets are transferred to the issuer; (c) the issuer (or SPE) issues the notes, which are bought by the initial purchaser, usually the underwriter; and (d) the notes are sold on to the end investors. Also at the closing, rating letters are issued by the rating agencies, but are often subject to the deal being declared "effective". Often by the closing date, the transaction has not purchased the full target amount of assets. It is typical for a transaction to close with only 70 to 90 per cent of the final transaction size of assets. If a deal closes without purchasing all of the target notional assets, the ratings issued are preliminary ratings.

A deal goes "effective" once it has purchased the assets necessary to meet the characteristics previously documented and modelled. This typically occurs at the earlier of either the purchase of the entire target notional of assets or six months (also referred to as the "ramp-up period"). On the effective date, the issuer declares that it has reached the target asset amount and that the deal, as rated on the close, is complete. The agencies affirm their ratings if the portfolio has met the target profile. If insufficient assets are purchased by the end of the ramp-up period, then the rating agency may not affirm its ratings and the transaction may have to reduce the notes outstanding by paying junior cash flows to the senior notes until the conditions necessary to maintain the initial ratings are met, unless an alternative plan is accepted by the rating agencies.

After the effective date, the transaction is typically in the reinvestment period. During this time, repayments of the principal amounts of assets are used to purchase replacement assets. The reinvestment period (if it exists) is typically three to five years, provided that the transaction is performing within the documented criteria and covenants.

At the end of the reinvestment period the transaction will start to pay down the outstanding principal of the notes, or "amortize". As principal amounts on the assets are paid, the proceeds are used to redeem the notes. Typically, CDOs amortize sequentially, paying the most senior notes first, and paying down the junior notes in order of seniority. However, in some static deals and commonly in ABS CDOs, a pro-rata amortization is allowed under certain conditions. A pro-rata amortization is where redemptions are used to pay a portion of each of the notes outstanding, usually with regard to the relevant ratio of the outstanding amount of each note, as a fraction of the total amount of outstanding notes.

A transaction is rarely envisaged to reach its maturity date. Most managed CDOs grant the equity investor or lowest class of notes the right (a call option) to terminate the transaction early. These call rights are usually conditional on the repayment of the more senior notes, and may require the issuer to pay additional payments to make the investor whole with regard to promised return hurdles, particularly for fixed rate liabilities. In addition, many CDOs have "auction call" mechanisms that automatically try to liquidate the underlying assets (as long as the notes can be repaid in full), after a predetermined period. Auction calls usually occur after the end of the reinvestment period, e.g., seven to 10 years. Other call mechanisms include "clean up" call mechanisms to redeem the transaction once the asset balance falls below a certain level, e.g., 20 to 30 per cent of the effective date portfolio size.

2.4 CONTRIBUTION TO THE "CREDIT CRUNCH"

There are many different books available on the causes and consequences of the "credit crunch", and the authors feel that it makes some sense to touch upon the subject and the role of CDOs in it.

As most readers will be aware, the root cause of the credit crunch was lending by banks and mortgage brokers to finance house purchases by borrowers with poor or non-existent credit history, in a housing market bubble. These mortgages were bought by investment banks and packaged into asset backed securities, called residential mortgage-backed securities or RMBS. These RMBS bonds were rated by the rating agencies and then sold to investors. The relatively high spread and high rating meant that these bonds were attractive investments for both CDOs and banks.

2.4.1 The role of CDOs and credit derivatives

From 2003 until 2007, CDOs, particularly structured finance CDOs, were significant buyers of both RMBS tranches and the risk (synthetically) of RMBS tranches. Often CDOs purchased the tranches that the sponsoring bank had the most difficulty selling. The buyers of the tranches of CDOs largely based their purchase decision upon the ratings on the tranches issued by the rating agencies. In addition, the development of pay-as-you-go (PAUG) credit default swaps on RMBS and CDOs allowed for banks and hedge funds to transfer risk synthetically on tranches they may or may not have held. This allowed banks to hold the senior positions of RMBS CDOs by buying protection in the form of a CDS from a bank or insurance company. This was particularly true for the mezzanine tranches of RMBS bonds and CDO tranches. Another significant factor in the poor price performance and subsequent poor credit performance was inclusion in many CDOs of a large pool of other CDOs tranches, the "CDO squared" problem. The inclusion of CDOs in troubled CDOs made valuation much more difficult and opaque.

2.4.2 The credit crunch

As the first news of poor remittance data on RMBS bonds became known, banks (both investment and commercial) began to tighten lending criteria to clients, mainly hedge funds, on RMBS and CDOs backed by RMBS. Some of these funds were highly leveraged (often 50 to 100 times) and were funded at very low rates. The new lending criteria reduced the hedge fund margins, requiring hedge funds to borrow less and pay more to borrow. This triggered the first sales by these funds to meet the margin calls. However, a lack of buyers for these securities, because of credit concerns, caused the price of these securities to effectively free-fall, as wave upon wave of margin calls resulted in more and more sales. This directly brought about the failure of several large funds as investors in those funds became nervous at the falling NAV (net asset value) of their investments and started to withdraw their funds, causing more sales. Purchases of money market securities (in particular asset-backed commercial paper) fell dramatically as the managers of money market funds, especially 2A7 funds which are supposedly very safe investments, became nervous and refused to refinance maturing asset-backed commercial paper. This initially mainly affected issuers that had large exposures to RMBS and CDOs and caused the default of several large conduits and structured investment vehicles. After this, many of these funds refused to refinance or roll any asset-backed commercial paper at all. This triggered the next phase of the credit crunch with more asset sales which eventually resulted in the collapse of the entire SIV (structure investment vehicle) market (at the time of writing all SIVs had either been consolidated by a sponsor bank or were in administration).

The failure of these large conduits effectively caused their sponsoring banks to default, which then raised the concerns of all banks in lending to other banks. Banks then started to hoard liquidity and refuse to lend to institutions that had any hint of suspect assets on their balance sheets. Central banks began to increase liquidity into the system in an attempt to avert a liquidity crisis. However, institutions without direct access to this liquidity were still vulnerable and it was this lack of liquidity that was the root cause behind the failure of Northern Rock (a mortgage bank in the UK) and Bear Stearns.

Alongside these liquidity concerns, the rating agencies began a massive downgrade programme on structured finance that was linked to the troubled RMBS vintages. This triggered more sales and forced liquidations as so-called events of default linked to ratings downgrades were triggered. Additionally, it caused the market and the agencies to review the mono-line insurers as some of the mono-lines had wrapped (or provided credit default swap protection) on the senior tranches of structured finance CDOs. Most of the mono-line insurers lost their Aaa/AAA ratings and many of them became sub-investment grade or defaulted.

2.4.3 Root causes

The lack of market agreed valuation methods and the complexity of the valuation issues of asset backed securities (including CDOs) made it difficult for counterparties to agree on values. The increase of both mark to market accounting and banks putting credit into their trading books meant that the banks took heavy write-downs as trading book losses directly fed through the income statements. Bids effectively disappeared on some products, leaving banks with valuation problems. This caused wider contagion effects as credit became more difficult for banks and brokers to buy (i.e., lend money) for the fear of taking further write-downs.

2.4.4 The role of fair value accounting

The role of fair value accounting cannot be underplayed. During the development of the credit derivatives markets, banks increased the amount of exposure on their trading books to credit, as there seemed to be a "liquid market" in credit derivatives. These positions were held relatively long term and hedged rather than traded, particularly in the credit derivative space. This treatment tended to carry over for related instruments such as CDOs. Prior to this, only relatively small amounts of credit were on trading books, for market making purposes only. The advantage of trading book treatment was that typically only a small VaR (value at risk) amount plus a counterparty add-on were required from a regulatory capital requirement. Adjustments in price, either positive or negative, fed through the income statement and affected the bank's earnings and retained reserves.

Prior to this, the majority of credit was seen as illiquid and held in banking books; this typically required more capital and was not "marked to market"or fair valued but held at purchase price with impairment reserves held against them if impaired. Adjustments were through either impairment accounts held against equity, i.e., a balance sheet adjustment, or did not directly affect the balance sheet or income at all until actual losses were incurred. Fair value accounting had a double setback effect on banks in that it initially allowed for significantly increased leverage. However, as credit became increasingly illiquid, the lack of prices increased the capital requirement significantly and reduced the banks reserves as write-downs fed through the bank's income statements. The main weakness was the lack of a mechanism to move from trading book to banking book, often forcing banks to sell assets well below an intrinsic value.

A further problem is the current treatment of credit in Basel II which requires banks to set capital according to the credit rating. As long as the credit rating is investment grade or higher, banks can allocate a fraction of their capital against the position. However, if the credit rating falls below investment grade, particularly B/B ratings, then a deduction from capital is required. The bank therefore has impairment plus the full capital against that impairment. While reasonable perhaps for corporate credit, this seems especially harsh for large or senior tranches of granular securitizations, as a significant ultimate payment may be expected, i.e., it is not all likely to completely fail, particularly if it is well diversified.

3

Introduction to Modelling

3.1 GOALS IN MODELLING

Models have to be able to satisfy many different goals for potentially different users.

Rating agencies use models to determine the credit risk and determine the credit ratings assigned to the notes that are issued. Investors use models to determine returns and note sensitivities to defaults and ratings migration. Mono-line insurers have used their own models to determine the capital requirements to maintain their ratings.

3.2 MODELLING PHILOSOPHIES AND TRADE-OFFS

The aim of any model is to optimize a number of (often contradictory) goals. These goals can include:

- speed;
- flexibility;
- visibility/audit-ability/verification;
- degree of automation;
- ease of change.

Let's discuss these aims and how balancing these will affect the approach to modelling.

3.2.1 Speed

Speed in this instance refers to the speed of execution or calculations in the model. Various things can be done to improve this and, while not all of them are recommended, if the main goal is to execute many scenarios of one transaction (or group of transactions) in as little time as possible, then they may be worth considering.

Contemplating the likely steps that Excel executes in calculation without seeing the algorithm or code, it can be surmised that Excel may use some version of a tree algorithm to determine both what it needs to calculate and the order of which to calculate it. This means that, in general, Excel will recalculate only those cells that need to be recalculated. When making changes to a cell in a worksheet, Excel will recalculate the cell that has changed and the cells that refer to or depend on that cell. However, there are functions in Excel which will recalculate every time a change is made to *any* cell in a worksheet. These functions include TODAY(), NOW(), OFFSET() and other array formulas. It is best to avoid them or use them sparingly. In addition to this, when using VLOOKUP() and HLOOKUP() with exact match utilized, the calculation time will be proportional to the number of cells required to be scanned before the solution is found.

> **Did you know?** Avoid the Clipboard! The clipboard applications purpose is to allow a very basic level of communication inter- and intra-application within the Microsoft windows environment. It is a stand alone application that predates VBA When a user types <Ctrl-C> and <Ctrl-V> (i.e. shortcuts for "copy" and "paste"), the selected data is transferred first to the clipboard and then from the clipboard to the application. Unfortunately, the communication with the clipboard takes a lot of resources as the data is formatted and packaged and then passed to the clipboard and back again. It is often a users first experience with VBA to record a macro that copies data from one point to another. By further automating that, it is very easy to fill up the clipboard. The biggest problem is that it is difficult to clear the clipboard from Excel VBA, as there is no direct VBA tool to clear the clipboard. Best practice is to avoid recording macros that use copy and paste to move data within VBA macros. It is better to use assignment within VBA and write directly to the desired range.

3.3 FLEXIBILITY

Unless the plan is to invest in or structure only one type of deal with no variation whatsoever in either collateral type or capital structure some degree of flexibility will be required. Maintaining flexibility in the model will tend to increase the size and complexity of the model and reduce the execution speed. While it is important to be flexible, the cost should not be so high as to saddle the model with too poor a performance, resulting in it taking too long to run effectively. For example, if only single currency deals are to be modelled, building in several other currencies introduces an unnecessary level of complexity and size into the model.

3.3.1 Visibility/audit-ability/verification

If the model is to be readily examined or shared among a number of users, then often it is useful to be able to quickly and easily examine the calculations and data, rather than just the inputs and outputs. For example, it may be useful to examine the construction of the interest coverage and over-collateralization coverage test ratios and the logic before altering the priority of payments. It is also quite reassuring to be able to prove that the model is verifiably accounting for all of the cash flows and is not double counting cash flows or missing cash flows. This can be particularly important to have in place after making significant changes to a model.

There are two main principles to follow in order to gain confidence in a model once changes have been made. One method is the inclusion of an audit process of some sort. The authors are rather big fans of having an "audit" or "verification" sheet. The purpose of an audit sheet is to crosscheck the inputs, outputs and verify the allocation of cash to the appropriate liabilities. While cash flow models are not necessarily very complicated from a calculation point of view, they are generally extremely detailed. Thus, a certain degree of confidence is required when changes are made. All cash must be accounted for correctly and there must be no missing cash or double counting of cash. An audit sheet is used to cross check and verify the model and can also be useful as a summary of the cash flows. The other method is by pervading the model with visible "forensics", for example, visible ratios, shortfalls and cures, thus making it easier to evaluate shortcomings in the structure.

3.3.2 Degree of automation

Modelling can be performed using Excel at a number of different levels. The authors have devised a naming system to be clear about the degree of sophistication required both for the creator and the user of such models. Generally these are complementary: the more sophisticated the model, the less sophisticated the user is assumed to be. "Level 1" applies to models that use only the functionality native to Excel, i.e., the built-in functions and the Excel engine. A "Level 2" model is mainly written using VBA and spreadsheet use is limited to providing the inputs and outputs of that model. A "Level 3" model is built using a compiled language such as C++, C# or Visual Basic to interface with in Excel, with Excel mainly used for input and output and most of the calculations internal to the compiled code.

Each level involves certain trade-offs and no one approach is necessarily right for any given situation. However, the authors believe that models should be built in such a way that they can evolve to the optimum level to solve the problems at hand.

By using solely what is available in Excel and only modelling at "Level 1", the model can be operated and understood by anyone familiar with Excel. There is no need to understand programming languages. It is also easier to debug and audit the model as all the logic and intermediate cash flows are visible and accessible. The main disadvantage is that the model tends to be larger and slower and can be tedious to use for repetitive tasks. To meet investor demands or rating agency criteria, quite often a multitude of different stress scenarios on the collateral cash flows are required to be run in the model. Without providing some degree of automation, obtaining the required, often large, number of results can be a slow and tedious procedure, and one prone to human error.

"Level 2" modelling involves delegating some or all of the calculation to logic developed in VBA using Class Modules, Functions and Subroutines. The Excel engine is mainly used to formulate inputs and outputs and does very little of the intermediate work. By using VBA, the extent of calculation can be controlled and there is less likelihood of circular references. Additionally, complicated formulae that may not easily fit into a model, such as interpolation or simulations, can be easily programmed in VBA. The downside of VBA is that it can be harder to change and less transparent to users than an Excel worksheet. Finding and correcting errors can also be tedious and it is much more of a "black-box" approach. Other than the developer, the other users do not know what is going on inside the program. However, anyone familiar with VBA can see and modify the code.

"Level 3" modelling replaces some or all of the VBA code with compiled C/C++/C# code in the form of add-ins. Add-ins can be created either using the Excel ToolKit addin or using OLE/COM/.NET (or other incarnations of Microsoft's object communication protocol). C++/C/C# replaces some of the shortfalls of using VBA alone, including persistence between calculations, and improved performance for intensive calculations and improved overall performance. However, the cost and time involved in changes to the model are more pronounced. In this instance, the code is more separate from the Excel application and would not be readily available for modification to the end user.

Each change in graduation of level in modelling requires additional degrees of knowledge and skills; with Levels 2 and 3 the skill set required is more computer science than banking. This book will concentrate on developing a "Level 1.5" model. A "Level 1.5" model is mostly implemented using the core Excel functionality and the Excel engine, but adds some limited functionality in VBA to assist in automating repetitive tasks. It has the advantages listed for a Level 1 model but aims to eliminate the tedium and the errors associated with having to manually operate it for repeated operations.

3.3.3 Ease of change

There are many ways to make it easier to make changes or adaptations to the model. For example, when creating worksheets it is always best to avoid merging cells. It is often tempting to merge "title" cells. However, if later columns or rows are added where merged cells are included, it is then more time-consuming to do so. Better practice is to go to the Format menu, choose "Cells", then choose "Alignment", then under "Horizontal" choose "Centre Across Selection".

Another general point is to try to keep the distance and navigation between related cells as short as possible. Ideally, they should be within one screen width or height of each other to allow for rapid movement back and forth between dependent cells.

In addition, taking care that the model is well organized and efficiently laid out will go a long way towards making changes more manageable.

3.4 ORGANIZATION AND LAYOUT OF A MODEL

3.4.1 Organization of a model

A well-organized approach to the design and layout of the worksheets in the model will enable its users to know where to expect to find things. It can be extremely frustrating to have to spend vast amounts of time looking for various parts of a model. It is poor modelling to not model with other users in mind (or even with the view that a particular model may not be looked at for a long period of time) and some of the original reasoning may be forgotten; why, for example, there was an input or calculation in the Excel spreadsheet "wilderness" (such as cell IR5648 on a random worksheet, or worse still, on a hidden worksheet).

Did you know? Hard-coding over calculations in formulas on your waterfall worksheet, can be a recipe for future disaster. These kinds of actions should be avoided. If absolutely necessary, they should be noted with comments or highlighted formats so that these deviations from the norm can be easily found.

By designing worksheets to have specific functions the model can be incrementally improved, modified and adapted. Our model will start with four basic worksheets:

- inputs;
- outputs;
- collateral/assets;
- waterfall.

Additional worksheets are often useful for:

- hedges;
- curves;

- look up tables;
- rating agency-specific analysis;
- simulations;
- equity/break-even analysis.

By breaking out the model into these various worksheets, it allows the modeller to quickly and efficiently make changes to the model. For example, if the modeller wants to update a ("rep line") asset sheet with actual assets, then that sheet should be relatively easy to replace with minimum impact on the rest of the model. Another example might be where rating agency methods change. If each rating agency's analysis is on a particular worksheet, then changes can be made with minimal impact on the model.

3.4.2 Layout of the model worksheets

The layout of the waterfall sheet always comes down to a choice of either (1) horizontal or (2) vertical modelling.

A horizontal waterfall sheet is one in which each successive period calculation is in the cells right to left, and the ordering of the waterfall is top to bottom. This has the advantage of clear labelling in the left-hand column as the user scrolls down.

In a vertical waterfall sheet, the waterfall goes from left to right and the periods go from top to bottom. The authors believe that this has the advantage of being easier to read. As there tend to be more rows available than columns, this has the effect of reducing the amount of navigation.

Although each layout has its advantages and disadvantages, the authors recommend a vertical layout and proceed in this book to model in this manner.

3.5 LIFE-CYCLE ISSUES: BUILDING AN ADAPTABLE MODEL

Since Excel 5.0 in 1993, Excel workbooks have been organized as a collection of worksheets in a single workbook format. This provides a sound basis for a functional organization of the model. It also allows for the model to be incrementally improved without altering and compromising the entire existing functionality. An important consideration in designing each functional part of the model is to assess the likelihood of change. By intentionally limiting the links between the different functional parts of the model, it becomes easier to replace the functional modules, as required, in the future. For example, the authors have rewritten and replaced the Collateral Sheets and Waterfall Sheets repeatedly over the time they have been using similar models and have been able to do so without seriously impacting the rest of the model. Minimizing the impact of such changes is possible by linking only the relevant inputs and outputs between the functional worksheets.

There are also some simple rules and principals that, if followed when constructing worksheets, will avoid some common problems and make the model more adaptable and manageable. These include:

- **Left to right, top to bottom**. Always try to start at the top left-hand corner of a sheet and work left to right and then return to the left-hand side. This is similar to how many cultures write on a page and therefore should be intuitive. By following this discipline, it is easier for users of the worksheet to follow its logic. Most importantly, the potential for circular references (the bane of all spreadsheet users) can be significantly reduced.

- **Separate calculations from waterfall**. By separating out the calculations from the distribution of funds, the waterfall can be dramatically shortened, avoiding overrunning the available number of columns, causing "wrap-around". "Wrap-around" should be avoided as much as possible as it dramatically reduces the "readability" of the spreadsheet and greatly increases the likelihood of circular references.
- **Named ranges and variables**. By using Excel's ability to assign a name to a collection of cells, so-called "named ranges", formulas become much easier to read and maintain. An added bonus in using named ranges is the potential to dramatically shorten long formulas and to be able to reference them from VBA code without directly referencing a cell reference. Again, this is important if amendments are made to sheets and as a consequence cells references change. Hard coding cell references in VBA will mean that the modeller will have to manually adjust cell references in the code. If, howerver, named ranges are employed instead, then Excel will automatically track the new row column reference.
- **Dynamic range formulas**. Judicious use of so-called "dynamic range formulas" to "relatively" reference rather than "absolutely" reference cells, can make alterations (particularly in crucial "priority of payment" calculations) much less painful. Using absolute referencing, inserting a column often requires extensive "knitting" together of formulas to ensure the integrity of the model, particularly in carrying forward the cash available to pay. Even more painful can be the deletion of cells, which may give rise to a plethora of "#REF!" errors throughout the model. Using relative referencing allows for the insertion and deletion of portions of the waterfall without a lot of "knitting" together, or fixing of references afterwards, by the judicious use of Excel functions such as OFFSET(), VLOOKUP(), MATCH() and SUMIF().
- **Conditional sums**. Using conditional sums to group and collect related payments for the liabilities, rather than hard coding the references from the waterfall, can greatly reduce the proclivity to errors of duplication or omission. For example, by using SUMIF() and referring to the appropriate columns with names associated with the liabilities, all the payments can be readily collected and easily identified. Contrast this to referencing each payment by cell reference; it is quite easy to reference the wrong cell, or miss or duplicate a cell.

Prerequisites to Cash Flow Modelling

Prior to beginning to describe the model, it is useful to discuss and explain some basic modelling techniques that are core to the model and will come up later. It makes sense to address them here so that those readers familiar with these concepts can proceed to the later chapters without having to endure the tedium of reviewing concepts they already know.

However, it may be a useful review for those readers who have prior knowledge of the topics but do not use that knowledge regularly.

4.1 MODELLING DATES

While it is possible to model CDOs without specific dates by using the average number of days per period (particularly for high yield and leveraged loan transactions), it is not recommended where accuracy is required. In particular, accuracy is vital where cash flows are sensitive to lower margins over the floating rate index. These types of deals usually include CDOs where the collateral consists of investment grade transactions and ABS bonds.

> **Did you know?** The basis of modelling dates in Excel is the date serial number. There are actually two formats of this number in Excel. The first and most common reflects the Gregorian day count since the 1st of January 1900. This was a carry over compatibility feature from Lotus 123 and has the same flaw. Both consider 1900 a leap year when in fact it was not. So the serial number is one larger than the actual day count. This is because the Gregorian correction for determining a leap year is that the number of the year must be divisible by four, except if it is also divisible by a hundred, in which case it is not normally a leap year unless that year is also divisible by 400. This is why 1900 was not a leap year, but by contrast, the year 2000 was a leap year. Thus, in order to counter the flaw in day count of 1900, Microsoft introduced another day count from the 1st of January 1904 which is congruent with the actual days since that time.

Modelling of dates can be arduous in Excel because of the different representations and formats in both Excel and VBA. Dates in the worksheets are commonly stored as unsigned long integers representing the elapsed number of days since a commencement date, usually 1 January 1900. However, Excel tries to interpret text (which may be in a number of different local date formats) as a date also. This can be confusing, particularly if the formatted text is being used in North America from a European-style source or vice versa, because of the transposition of the month field (i.e., the month being written first or the day being written first). This potential problem can be exacerbated when translating date information between VBA code and a worksheet, particularly if the original data was imported as text from, for example, the Bloomberg Professional system. In addition, some versions of Excel may interpret two-digit year style date formats with the year field less than 70 as being in the 20th century, rather than in the 21st century as may have been intended, i.e., 49 becomes 1949 and not 2049.

As the date is represented as a serial number in Excel, it is very easy to use standard operators such as addition and subtraction to add days or calculate the number of days between two dates. Nevertheless, it is somewhat more difficult to add whole months or years, or to add working days or determine if a date is a working day in the future. The analysis tool pack (ATP), which has been part of Excel since version 5.0, remedies some of these issues by adding more extensive date and financial instrument functions. These include EDATE() (to add months with calendar adjustment), WORKDAYS() (to add working days using a calendar), ACCRUEDINT() (to calculate the accrued interest on a bond), NEXTCPNDTE() and PREVCPNDTE() (to calculate the next and previous coupon dates for a bond given the maturity, payment frequency and settlement date).

Among the authors' most used ATP functions are EDATE() and WORKDAYS(). However, the Add-In Toolpak (ATP) is generally not loaded automatically when starting Excel and without being present, a worksheet utilizing ATP functions will show a "#NAME?" error in cells containing ATP function references. The ATP must be loaded prior to use from the Tools->Addins menu, by selecting Analysis ToolPak and Analysis ToolPak-VBA options.

4.1.1 Description of the curve and dates model

Dates are important for calculating the income from the assets and interest due on the liabilities. The complexity involved in flexibly modelling dates requires a large workbook and hence a *Curve and Dates Model* has been provided. The authors strongly recommend that this model does *not* form part of a cash flow model. This is because the dates in a cash flow model typically will not change often. Thus, combining these workbooks will result in Excel being required to perform additional calculations every time (whether required or not), which will have the effect of slowing down the performance of a cash flow model.

4.1.1.1 Model information

It is good practise to always have the following details in a model:

- **Model name**. Naming a model is a good organizational tool and it makes it clear what transaction is being modelled. This makes it clear to other users or even the original modeller if they come back to an old model after some significant time interval.
- **Model author**. This is especially useful where there are many users of a model. Knowing who created a model can be beneficial if a user has questions.
- **Last revision date**. This should be manually hardcoded in. Using the excel formula TODAY() defeats the purpose of knowing when the model was last edited.

4.1.1.2 Inputs

The following main inputs are required to generate payment and curve vectors:

Value date. The value date is usually the present day; however, other dates for valuing cash flows can be used. This may also correspond to the last date that the interest rate curve was updated.

Settlement date. This is the day from which money will change hands in the transaction, and the day from which interest will accrue. This is often also referred to as the closing date and it is usually in the future and after the Value Date.

Day count accrual. Day count conventions are important for determining how the assets and liabilities pay on payments dates and how they accrue interest between payment dates. Although there are many different conventions, for floating rate assets and liabilities the most commonly used are "actual/360" and "actual/365" and for fixed rate assets and liabilities the most common are "30/360" and "actual/actual".

Did you know? Where the day count convention is **"Actual/360"**, the period used is the sum of the actual number of days elapsed divided by 360. **"Actual/365"** is similar to Actual/360 except the period used is the sum of the number of days elapsed divided by 365 (and for a leap year, the sum of the number of days elapsed divided by 366). This day count is generally used when notes are paying British Pound Sterling LIBOR. There are two variants to this: **"Actual/365F"** where during leap years the number of days remains fixed at 365 and **"Actual/366"** in which the days in a leap year are considered to be 366 and 365 otherwise. **Actual/actual**" means the actual number of days elapsed per period over the actual days in the year. This convention is typically used for fixed rate bonds such as US Treasuries. **"30/360"** is also typically used for fixed rate bonds and it is assumed that the year is 360 days and it is made up of 12 30-day months. It is calculated as the number of days in the period divided by 360. However, if the first day of the period falls on the 31st, then this date becomes the 30th. If the last day of the period falls on the 31st, this date becomes the 30th only if the first date falls on the 30th or 31st. If the last day of the period is the last day of February, the month of February is not considered to be lengthened to a 30-day month.

Months between payments. In loan and bond transactions, the liabilities are typically paid semi-annually, and in some loan transactions and ABS transactions, the liabilities are paid quarterly. ABS CDOs with a large percentage of residential mortgage-backed securities as assets will often have at least one class of notes that pays monthly.

Business days. These reference the lists of holidays for business centres for payment on the **Holidays Sheet**. There can be more than one business centre in a transaction, especially when major parties to the transaction are located in different countries or the currency of payment is not local to the country of issue.

Date convention. This refers to the rule used to adjust the payment dates for holidays and other non-business days. The most common rules are "modified following", "following", and "preceding".

> **Did you know?**   If "Following" is used as the business day convention
> then for any payment date that falls on a day that is not a business day,
> the first following day that is a business day will be used. For example, if a
> payment date is 29 May 2010, which is a Saturday, because Monday 31
> May 2010 is a US holiday, the actual payment date will fall on Tuesday 1
> June 2010. "Modified Following" works the same a "following" with the
> exception that if that day is in the next calendar month, the date will be the
> first preceding day that is a business day. For example, if a payment date
> is 29 May 2010, which is a Saturday, because Monday 31 May 2010 is a
> US holiday, the actual payment date will fall on Friday 28 May 2010. If the
> business day convention used is "Preceding", this means that for any date
> that falls on a day that is not a business day, that date will be used will be
> the first preceding day that is a business day. For example, if a payment
> date is 29 May 2010, which is a Saturday, the actual payment date will fall
> on Friday 28 May 2010. In practise, "preceding" is rarely used for
> payment dates but is often used in the CDO world for determination dates,
> the dates by which the cash available for distribution at the next payment
> dates is determined and the amounts to be distributed on the next
> payment date are calculated.

4.1.1.3 Builder

The Builder section of the *Curve and Dates Model* is where market data is input. This data, utilizing a method commonly referred to as "bootstrapping", is used to build the zero coupon curve. In this model, a combination of USD LIBOR, USD swaps, Treasuries and USD spreads are used to create a par coupon curve, and as these are liquid products, there should not be a problem in gathering data. USD swap traders will often use futures to generate forward rates, often to at least 5 years. However, for CDO modelling purposes, it is not necessary to have that degree of precision. The *Curve and Dates Model* allows for the input of swap rates or a combination treasury (government) rates and a spread over them. If the reader has access to a source of money market and swap rates then it is easy to directly input them.

However, LIBOR and swap rates are less readily available than government yields which can often be obtained from the press or the internet. In addition, swap spreads are generally less volatile than government yields, so it is often quicker and easier to update four treasury yields (2 year, 5 year, 10 year and 30 year) than to update the whole curve.

When generating the swap curve from treasuries into an annual/360-based swap convention, it is important to remember to convert to the appropriate compounding basis and day count (i.e., semi-annual bond basis to annualized bond basis and then actual/actual to actual/360). Similarly, EURIBOR curves can be built, taking care of the appropriate day basis.

4.1.2 VBA date calculation

The dates in the *Cash Flow Model* will vary infrequently. As a result, it can be considered more optimal to generate the dates using VBA. Often, time periods for the Notes will not be evenly distributed. For example, there is usually a short or long first period, usually because after the transaction has launched, assets are still being purchased during the ramp-up period. Swaps may also often have long or short first periods, again because of the payment schedules on the referenced assets.

Therefore the *Curve and Dates Model* allows for potentially an odd first period and then generates future dates at regular intervals from the first payment date. By adding the appropriate number of months and adjusting the payment dates for the business day convention and calendars, the resultant payment dates and accural periods will be accurate.

The following VBA code is utilized in the *Curve and Dates Model*.

```vba
Sub GenerateDates()

'

' variables
'

Dim payDate As Integer       ' payment date
Dim startDate As Date        ' settlement date
Dim endDate As Date          ' maturity date
Dim firstPay As Date         ' first payment date
Dim freq As Integer          ' frequency of payment
Dim outrange As Range        ' output range for dates
Dim schedule() As Date       ' calculated array of dates
Dim noPayments As Integer    ' the number of payments in the
                               schedule
Dim nextDate As Date         ' the next payment date
Dim dy As Integer            ' day of month ordinal (1-31)
Dim mth As Integer           ' mth month ordinal (1-12)
Dim yr As Integer            ' yr year as integer current value 2007
Dim paymentdates As Range
Dim busconv As String        ' business day convention
Dim holidays As String       ' list of holidays
Dim I As Integer             ' index counter for while and for loops


' read and initialise the ranges from the spreadsheet values
startDate = Range("Settle_Date").Value
endDate = Range("End_Date").Value
firstPay = Range("First_Pay").Value
payDate = Range("Pay_Date").Value
freq = Range("freq").Value
busconv = Range("Convention").Value
holidays = Range("Calendars").Value

' get holidays
Set paymentdates = Range("Payment_Dates")    ' set output range
holidaystring = Split(holidays, ",")         ' split the number of
                                               calendars  up

noPayments = CInt((endDate - startDate) / 365) * 12 / freq + 1
ReDim schedule(1 To noPayments + 1)

schedule(1) = startDate
schedule(2) = firstPay
nextDate = firstPay

'

' now generate unadjusted forward dates and adjust them accordingly.
'

I = 3
```

```
'While nextDate <= endDate And i <= noPayments
While I <= noPayments + 1
    '
    '  so generate forward from first payment date as discussed
    '
    mth = Month(firstPay)           ' use the month from the first
                                      payment date as the normal payment
    yr = year(firstPay)             ' also reset year
    mth = mth + freq * (I - 2)      ' add the no of frequency periods
                                      from first payment date

    While mth > 12
        yr = yr + 1                 ' increment year by the whole number of
        mth = mth - 12             ' decrement mths by whole years
    Wend
'
'  as not all months have 30 or 31 dates then we have to allow for
   february, april, june, september and november
'
Select Case payDate

    Case 29, 30:
        If mth = 2 Then
            If Not isLeapYear(yr) Then
                nextDate = DateSerial(yr, mth, 28)
            Else
                nextDate = DateSerial(yr, mth, 29)
            End If
        Else
            nextDate = DateSerial(yr, mth, payDate)
        End If


    Case 31:
      If mth = 2 Then
            ' then allow for short months
            If Not isLeapYear(yr) Then
                nextDate = DateSerial(yr, mth, 28)
            Else
                nextDate = DateSerial(yr, mth, 29)
            End If
      ElseIf mth = 4 Or mth = 6 Or mth = 9 Or mth = 11 Then
            nextDate = DateSerial(yr, mth, 30)
      Else
            nextDate = DateSerial(yr, mth, payDate)
      End If


    Case Else:
            ' otherwise just create next month.
            nextDate = DateSerial(yr, mth, payDate)

    End Select
```

```
nextDate = adjustDateHols(nextDate, busconv, mth,  holidays) ' now
adjust for w/e and holidays
schedule(I) = nextDate


 I = I + 1
Wend
'
' now write them to the output range
'
For I = 1 To noPayments + 1
paymentdates.Cells(I, 1) = schedule(I)

Next I


End Sub

Function GenDates(startDate As Date, endDate As Date, firstPay As
Date, payDate As Integer, freq As Integer, busconv As String,
holidays As String) As Variant

'Function to Generate Dates
' Routine generates dates forward from the 1st payment date until
the last payment date
' taking a frequency, rolldate, rolldate convention, and list of
calendars
'Inputs:
'     startDate = beginning date
'     endDate = maturity date
'     firstpay = first payment date
'     payDate = regular day of the month for payment
'     freq = number of months between payment
'     busconv = string with business convention in it i.e.
                 Following, Preceding etc
'     holidays = calendars
'
' variables
'
Dim schedule() As Date        ' calculated array of dates
Dim noPayments As Integer     ' the number of payments in the
                                schedule
Dim nextDate As Date          ' the next payment date
Dim dy As Integer             ' day of month ordinal (1-31)
Dim mth As Integer            ' mth month ordinal (1-12)
Dim yr As Integer             ' yr year as  integer current
                                value 2007

Dim I As Integer              ' index counter for while and for loops

' work out size of array & initialise it with first 2 payments
'
```

```
noPayments = CInt((endDate - startDate) / 365) * 12 / freq + 1
ReDim schedule(1 To noPayments + 1)

schedule(1) = startDate
schedule(2) = firstPay
nextDate = firstPay

'
' now generate unadjusted forward dates and adjust them accordingly.
'
I = 3
'While nextDate <= endDate And i <= noPayments
While I <= noPayments + 1
    '
    ' so generate forward from first payment date as discussed
    '
    mth = Month(firstPay)          ' use the month from the first
                                     payment date as the normal payment
    yr = year(firstPay)            ' also reset year
    mth = mth + freq * (I - 2)     ' add the no of frequency periods
                                     from first payment date

    While mth > 12
          yr = yr + 1              ' increment year by the whole number of
            mth = mth - 12         ' decrement mths by whole years
    Wend
'
'  as not all months have 30 or 31 dates then we have to
    allow for february, april, june, september and november
'
Select Case payDate

    Case 29, 30:
        If mth = 2 Then
            If Not isLeapYear(yr) Then
                nextDate = DateSerial(yr, mth, 28)
            Else
                 nextDate = DateSerial(yr, mth, 29)
            End If
        Else
            nextDate = DateSerial(yr, mth, payDate)
        End If

    Case 31:
      If mth = 2 Then
            ' then allow for short months
            If Not isLeapYear(yr) Then
                nextDate = DateSerial(yr, mth, 28)
            Else
                 nextDate = DateSerial(yr, mth, 29)
            End If
        ElseIf mth = 4 Or mth = 6 Or mth = 9 Or mth = 11 Then
```

```
                nextDate = DateSerial(yr, mth, 30)
       Else
                nextDate = DateSerial(yr, mth, payDate)
       End If

     Case Else:
            ' otherwise just create next month.
            nextDate = DateSerial(yr, mth, payDate)

     End Select

   nextDate = adjustDateHols(nextDate, busconv, mth, holidays) ' now
adjust for w/e and holidays
   schedule(I) = nextDate

   I = I + 1
 Wend
 '
 ' now return them
 '
 GenDates = Application.WorksheetFunction.Transpose(schedule)

End Function
```

4.2 INTEREST RATE CURVE MODELLING

4.2.1 Creating a discount curve

While is it possible to use the Bloomberg Professional® FWDS function or an in-house bank's curve generator to create a forward curve, it is more portable and just as easy to create a small forward curve model. This enables the user to operate the model and, if necessary, update it away from either environment, not relying on proprietary add-ins.

To generate a forward-forward curve (the forward curve at a specific future date, based on today's par curve), the benchmark swap curve for the relevant currency needs to be "stripped" and converted into a discount or zero (coupon) curve. "Stripping" the curve removes the compounding effect in payments of instruments paying more than once. It effectively converts a par-par instrument curve into an equivalent curve of zero coupon instruments. This is achieved by "bootstrapping" from short-term rates such as money market instruments (e.g., LIBOR, bank acceptances, bank deposits, etc.) that pay only once at the end of the deposit.

Generally, money market instruments are only quoted for one to two years. The exception to this (as mentioned in the previous section) is the money market futures in some markets which may be quoted as far out as eight years. This introduces additional issues (such as convexity adjustment) which are beyond the scope of this book. Therefore it is more common to switch to quoted compound interest instruments such as bonds and swaps. Compound interest instruments pay more than once during their lifetime. This multiple payment presents an issue: the time value of those payments will not be constant, i.e., each payment has to be valued at the appropriate discount factor. This involves decompounding the payments and bootstrapping the discount curve. Using the 2-year annual swap rate as the next point on the curve as an example, it will make two payments, one at the end of each year.

The swap rate is typically for a par-par swap rate (meaning that there is no exchange or payment on the value date). In a par-par swap, the fixed rate payer pays regular fixed coupons in return for receiving floating rate payments at the prevailing rate for a standard index tenor (e.g., 3-month LIBOR, EURIBOR). The fixed leg of the swap for any maturity can be compared to a fixed rate bond (i.e., the price is the sum of the present value of the coupons plus the principal paid at the maturity of the swap).

To decompound the par rate, it is necessary to first calculate the value of money for the first year's coupon rate using the bank deposit rates. This gives the value of money in year 1, as the compound swap rate is also a given. The unknown to be calculated is the forward-forward rate (i.e., from one year to two years).

The 2-year swap can be calculated assuming exchange from the equation:

$$100 = C_1 v_1 + C_2 v_2 + 100 v_2$$

where C_1 and C_2 are the coupons paid at the rate of C (with potentially different accrual periods), and v_1 and v_2 are the discount factors.

Assume the swap is worth par today (i.e., it's a par-par swap in which the fixed payer receives the index, usually LIBOR or Euribor, in exchange for making fixed-rate interest payments).

Knowing C_1, C_2 and v_1 and rearranging the equation to solve for v_2 implies the equation:

$$v_2 = \frac{100 - C_1 v_1}{100 + C_2}$$

Thus, the real price of money can be "bootstrapped" from compound par swap instruments paying a rate of C annually for two years by deducting the value of the first year's coupon from the par rate (as the coupon rate, the accrual factor and the discount factor are known), and dividing by the value of the payment at the end of two years (which is par plus the value of the coupon for the second year).

Extending this further, the formula becomes:

$$100 = \sum C v_i \alpha_i + (100 + C v_n \alpha_n)$$

Rearranging this gives:

$$v_n = \frac{100 - C \sum \alpha_i v_i}{(100 + C v_n \alpha_n)}$$

For example, in the *Curve and Dates Model*, in cell M13 to calculate the two year Discount Factor, there is the formula:

```
"=(1-SUM($N$12:N12)*L13)/(1+L13*(K13-K12)/360)".
```

The column Swap Duration is the "αv" (Figure 4.1). The sum of each up to the period is the swap duration, i.e., the basis point sensitivity of the floating leg of a swap to the change in spread, i.e., the summation in the equation above.

4.2.1.1 Interpolation

Once a discount curve has been established, it is a simple process to calculate the present value of any future cash flow by simply multiplying it by an interpolated discount rate. There

					Builder				
Number	Time Unit	USD LIBOR	USD SWAPS	Spreads	Date	Day Count From Trade Date	Rate	Discount Factor	Swap Duration
					01/09/2009	·		1.000000	
	2 Days	0.250%			03/09/2009	2	0.250%	0.99999	
	5 Days	0.280%			10/09/2009	9	0.280%	0.99995	
	1 Month	0.256%			05/10/2009	34	0.256%	0.99982	
	2 Months	0.274%			03/11/2009	63	0.274%	0.99978	
	3 Months	0.338%			03/12/2009	93	0.338%	0.99972	
	6 Months	0.390%			03/03/2010	183	0.390%	0.99903	
	9 Months	0.479%			03/06/2010	275	0.479%	0.99878	
	1 Year	0.611%			03/09/2010	367	0.611%	0.99844	1.01231
	2 Years		0.913%	0.35	05/09/2011	734	1.252%	0.97486	0.99382
	3 Years		1.403%	0.465355	03/09/2012	1,098	1.851%	0.94516	0.95566
	4 Years		1.860%	0.4094	03/09/2013	1,463	2.251%	0.91247	0.92515
	5 Years		2.318%	0.359704	03/09/2014	1,828	2.659%	0.87311	0.88523
	6 Years		2.528%	0.4609	03/09/2015	2,193	2.970%	0.83319	0.84476
	7 Years		2.737%	0.4802	05/09/2016	2,561	3.199%	0.79433	0.81198
	8 Years		2.947%	0.4000	04/09/2017	2,925	3.329%	0.76039	0.76884
	9 Years		3.157%	0.3200	03/09/2018	3,289	3.459%	0.72566	0.73372
	10 Years		3.366%	0.2200	03/09/2019	3,654	3.569%	0.69189	0.70150
	11 Years		3.401%	0.2800	03/09/2020	4,020	3.664%	0.65913	0.67011
	12 Years		3.457%	0.3000	03/09/2021	4,385	3.740%	0.62824	0.63696
	13 Years		3.507%	0.3100	05/09/2022	4,752	3.800%	0.59903	0.61068
	14 Years		3.533%	0.3400	04/09/2023	5,116	3.857%	0.57076	0.57710
	15 Years		3.540%	0.3700	03/09/2024	5,481	3.894%	0.54513	0.55270
	16 Years		3.576%	0.3688	03/09/2025	5,846	3.929%	0.52031	0.52754
	17 Years		3.612%	0.3600	03/09/2026	6,211	3.956%	0.49704	0.50394
	18 Years		3.648%	0.3400	03/09/2027	6,576	3.973%	0.47583	0.48243
	19 Years		3.684%	0.3155	04/09/2028	6,943	3.984%	0.45579	0.46465
	20 Years		3.720%	0.2991	03/09/2029	7,307	4.004%	0.43546	0.44030
	21 Years		3.767%	0.2800	03/09/2030	7,672	4.012%	0.41731	0.42311
	22 Years		3.815%	0.2250	03/09/2031	8,037	4.025%	0.39921	0.40475
	23 Years		3.862%	0.1880	03/09/2032	8,403	4.035%	0.38198	0.38834
	24 Years		3.910%	0.1450	05/09/2033	8,770	4.040%	0.36622	0.37334
	25 Years		3.957%	0.1050	04/09/2034	9,134	4.047%	0.35070	0.35459
	26 Years		4.004%	0.0680	03/09/2035	9,498	4.058%	0.33526	0.33899
	27 Years		4.052%	0.0270	03/09/2036	9,864	4.064%	0.32095	0.32630
	28 Years		4.099%	- 0.0120	03/09/2037	10,229	4.072%	0.30687	0.31113
	29 Years		4.147%	- 0.0520	03/09/2038	10,594	4.080%	0.29346	0.29753
	30 Years		4.194%	-0.084	05/09/2039	10,961	4.095%	0.27912	0.28455

Figure 4.1 Swap Duration

are two common approaches to interpolating the discount curve: (1) linear interpolation and (2) exponential interpolation.

Additionally, it easy to generate a forward-forward index curve to index floating rate assets and liabilities from the discount curve by interpolating the discount function on the relevant payment dates.[1] While any reasonable interpolation function would do (as the differences in interpolation will be averaged out over the payment dates), the most commonly used approach is to use exponential interpolation. Exponential interpolation matches more closely the shape of the discount function, which is similar to negative exponential curve in shape (Figure 4.2).

The formula for exponential interpolation is given by:

$$v_a = v_1 {}^{\wedge} \left(\frac{d_a}{d_1}(1-\lambda) \right) v_2 {}^{\wedge} \left(\frac{d_a}{d_2}\lambda \right)$$

---

[1] Technically the date required for the interpolation is the reset date, not the payment date. The reset date typically occurs 2 business days prior to the applicable payment date. Please note this is for the next period's payment, *not* for payment at that payment date. This is typical for an index set and paid in arrears. There are some structured financial products that set and pay near the payment date.

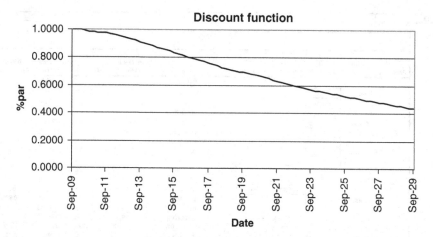

Figure 4.2 Exponential interpolation matches the shape of the discount function

where:

d_1 is the number of days from settlement date to the curve date just prior to the payment date

d_2 is the number of days from settlement date to the curve date just subsequent to the payment date

d_a is the target date for the interpolation which occurs between d_1 and d_2

v_a is the interpolated discount factor

v_1 is the discount factor on d_1

v_2 is the discount factor on d_2

λ (or lambda) is calculated by $(d_a-d_1)/(d_2-d_1)$

To implement the exponential interpolation equation, first find the discount function date prior to the payment date and its associated discount factor, and the discount function date subsequent to the payment date and its subsequent discount factor.

To find the first date prior to the payment date use the MATCH() function to find the greatest number of days in the Builder Day Count range, named "vba_days", which is less than the target date number of days. The example demonstrates this approach in the formula MATCH(S5,vba_days,1) where S5 is the target number of days, vba_days is the range of days since settlement and 1 is the type to return the largest number less than that.

> **Did you know?**
> MATCH() returns the index into an array depending on the type of match specified. In a list which is strictly increasing in value, MATCH() can find the index of largest number prior to a given number which is less than given target. Conversely in a list where the value is strictly decreasing, MATCH() can find the index of the largest number prior to a given number which is greater than the target. Additionally MATCH() can return the index of the first number equal to the target.

	AB	AC	AD	AE	AF	AG	AH
4							
5			Interpolation Exploded				
6		6	0.999718	93	0.00000	1.00	0.99972
7		7	0.999026	183	1.00000	0.51	
8							

Figure 4.3 Interpolation exploded

Use this MATCH() result to return the date (d_1) and the appropriate discount factor (v_1) by using the INDEX() function. The INDEX() function returns values from a range organized like a matrix by using a row and column offset into the range.

The named range "vba_df" is used to locate the *Builder Discount Factors*. Therefore to get d_1, the formula INDEX(vba_days,AC5) is used and the formula INDEX(vba_df,AC5) is used to find v_1.

Implementing the formula above as:

```
Cell AH5 contains "=AD5^(AG5*(1-AF5))*AD6^(AG6*AF5)"
```

where:

$AD5 = v_1$
$AG5 = d_a/d_1$
$AF5 = \lambda$ (lambda)
$AD6 = v_2$
$AG6 = d_a/d_2$

The final formula can be quite daunting. For example in cell V6 there is a formula,

```
"=INDEX(vba_df,MATCH(S6,vba_days,1))^(S6/INDEX(vba_days,MATCH(S6,
vba_days,1))*(1-(S6-INDEX(vba_days,MATCH(S6,vba_days,1)))/(INDEX(vba_
days,MATCH(S6,vba_days,1)+1)-INDEX(vba_days,MATCH(S6,vba_days,1)))))*
INDEX(vba_df,MATCH(S6,vba_days,1)+1)^((S6-INDEX(vba_days,MATCH(S6,
vba_days,1)))/(INDEX(vba_days,MATCH(S6,vba_days,1)+1)-INDEX(vba_days,
MATCH(S6,vba_days,1)))*S6/INDEX(vba_days,MATCH(S6,vba_days,1)+1))".
```

(see Figure 4.4)

	V	W
4	Discount Factor (Using Cell Names)	Rate
5	0.99999	
6	0.99972	0.1059%
7	0.99903	0.2771%
8	0.99878	0.0972%
9	0.99844	0.1318%
10	0.99461	1.5232%

Figure 4.4 Discount factor when using cell names in the formula

X	Y
Discount Factor (Not Using Cell Names)	**Rate**
0.99999	
0.99972	0.1059%
0.99903	0.2771%
0.99878	0.0972%
0.99844	0.1318%
0.99461	1.5232%

Figure 4.5 Discount factor when not using cell names in the formula

This is less so than if named ranges were not used. For example cell X6 contains the formula

```
"=INDEX($N$5:$N$42,MATCH(S6,$L$5:$L$42,1))^(S6/INDEX($L$5:$L$42,MATCH
(S6,$L$5:$L$42,1))*(1-(S6-INDEX($L$5:$L$42,MATCH(S6,$L$5:$L$42,1)))/
(INDEX($L$5:$L$42,MATCH(S6,$L$5:$L$42,1)+1)-INDEX($L$5:$L$42,MATCH
(S6,$L$5:$L$42,1)))))*INDEX($N$5:$N$42,MATCH(S6,$L$5:$L$42,1)+1)^((S6
-INDEX($L$5:$L$42,MATCH(S6,$L$5:$L$42,1)))/(INDEX($L$5:$L$42,MATCH(S6,
$L$5:$L$42,1)+1)-INDEX($L$5:$L$42,MATCH(S6,$L$5:$L$42,1)))*S6/INDEX
($L$5:$L$42,MATCH(S6,$L$5:$L$42,1)+1))".
```

(see Figure 4.5).

A way to build this complex and complicated formula out is to address each part of piece by piece, for example by replacing AA5 with:

```
"INDEX($M$4:$M$41,MATCH(S5,$K$4:$K$41,1))"
```

and replacing AA6 with:

```
"INDEX($M$4:$M$41,MATCH(S5,$K$4:$K$41,1)+1)".
```

This continues by replacing the d_1 variable with:

```
"S5/INDEX($M$4:$J$41,MATCH(S5,$K$4:$K$41,1)"
```

until the desired final formula is achieved.

Once all of the appropriate discount factors have been interpolated for the relevant dates it is easy to generate the forward-forward rates from:

$$r_{n,m} = (v_n/v_m - 1)(360/(d_m - d_n))$$

where:

$r_{n,m}$ is the rate from period n to m
v_n is the discount factor at the beginning of the period
v_m is the discount factor at the end of the period
d_n is the date (or days from settlement) at the beginning of the period
d_m is the date (or days from settlement) at the end of the period

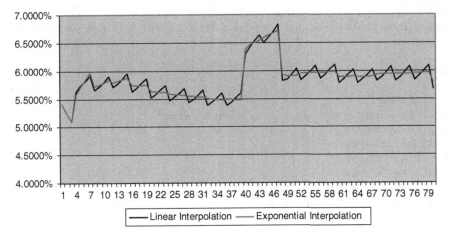

Figure 4.6   Exponential interpolation used in forward-forward rates

By comparison if liner interpolation is used:

$$v_a = v_1 \left(\frac{(d_2 - d_a)}{(d_2 - d_1)} \right) + v_2 \frac{(d_a - d_1)}{(d_2 - d_1)})$$

Again, if d_n, d_m and v_n and v_m are used as before and linear interpolation is used to find the discount factors, the result tends to be "choppy" forward, as one period tends to overestimate the discount factor and the other underestimates it. Figure 4.6 shows why most practitioners tend to prefer exponential interpolation when generating forward-forward rates.

Alternatively it also possible to write a VBA function to perform interpolation. The advantage of this is that it is more readable and can be called from a VBA subroutine to generate values rather than formulas. Interest rate curves tend to change relatively slowly and therefore do not impact structures greatly in the short term, particularly if there are hedges in place. It is more important to have an accurate curve if swaps are embedded in the transaction as the cost of terminating a swap either in part or in whole can be quite significant. The tendency for interest rates curves to remain stable means that they only require infrequent generation and updating. At least two approaches exist for doing this:

- calculating the forward-forward curve and linking it to the main cash flow model;
- generating the forward-forward curve in VBA and cutting and pasting the forwards as values.

Using a separate curve model, values will only be updated when the *Curve and Dates Model* is opened. In the interim, the model will cache the values for calculation purposes. The user has the option when opening the model to open and update the values or use the last stored values. This reduces the calculation time for the forwards and discount factors as they are only calculated when updating and not in every calculation cycle. The main disadvantage of having a separate model is that a separate curve model is generated for every transaction. Using VBA to generate and paste values is also a valid and reasonable approach. However, its main disadvantage is reduced transparency.

```
Function MyexpInterp(da As Integer, dtes As String, crv As String)
  As Double

' variables

  Dim r1 As Range                  ' the crv range
  Dim r2 As Range                  ' date range
  Dim d1 As Integer
  Dim d2 As Integer
  Dim df1 As Double
  Dim df2 As Double
  Dim lambda As Double
  Dim oneminuslambda As Double
  Dim I As Integer

  ' set range

  Set r1 = Range(crv)
  Set r2 = Range(dtes)
' assumes range is laid out with days,rates and discount
  factors as the first 3 columns
'
  I = Application.WorksheetFunction.Match(da, r2, 1)
  d1 = Application.WorksheetFunction.Index(r2, I)
  d2 = Application.WorksheetFunction.Index(r2, I + 1)
  lambda = (da - d1) / (d2 - d1)
  df1 = Application.WorksheetFunction.Index(r1, I, 3)
  df2 = Application.WorksheetFunction.Index(r1, I + 1, 3)

  oneminuslambda = 1# - lambda
'
  MyexpInterp = df1 ^ (da / d1 * oneminuslambda) * df2 ^ (da / d2 *
  lambda)

End Function
```

4.2.1.2 Obtaining LIBOR, USD swaps and spreads

If using Bloomberg Professional, it is possible to use the *Bloomberg Current Rates Model* which has automatic updating charts for sourcing the latest rates and spreads from Bloomberg Professional. To look this information up on Bloomberg Professional, type in the codes in the left-hand column of each of the table and press "GO". For example, typing in "CT02" and pressing <Govt> <GO> will bring up the latest bid/ask yield for US Treasuries.

If using the Internet to obtain information, USD interest rate swaps can be obtained at http://www.thefinancials.com/free/EX_Interest_Swaps.html. To estimate BBA LIBOR USD Fixings go to http://www.bba.org.uk/bba/jsp/polopoly.jsp?d=141. Information for estimating USD Treasury Bonds can be found at http://www.federalreserve.gov/releases/h15/update/ or at http://www.bloomberg.com/markets/rates/.

It can be difficult to find USD swap spreads on the Internet. A way of estimating swap spreads, although in no way perfect, is to subtract relevant USD Treasury rates from the respective USD interest rate swaps. While not ideal, it can give a good indication of the USD swap spreads.

Did you know? Swap rates reflect the "riskless" rate of Treasuries plus the credit risk associated with the financial sector. Because swap yields are conventionally quoted as spreads over Treasuries, thus to estimate the swap spread you can calculate the difference between the benchmark swap rate and the specific treasury rate.

After locating the appropriate input data, it is possible to use interpolation to estimate the **USD Swaps** and **Spreads** that the data reference has not provided. For example, to calculate the estimated 5-year **USD Swap** in cell G16 calculate:

$$sr_5 = \left(1 - \left(\frac{y_5 - y_4}{y_{10} - y_4}\right)\right) \times sr_4 + \left(\frac{y_5 - y_4}{y_{10} - y_4}\right) \times sr_{10}$$

where:

sr_5 is the 5-year swap rate
y_4 is the 4th year
y_5 is the 5th year
y_{10} is the 10th year
sr_4 is the 4-year swap rate
sr_{10} is the 10-year swap rate (Figure 4.5).

Thus, $sr_5 = (1-((5-4)/(10-4)))*0.0534+((5-4)/(10-4))*0.052 = 5.3167\%$

To calculate the **Dates** in the **Builder**, start with the **Value Date** or **Settlement Date** in the first cell. In the subsequent cells add the specified number of months using EDATE(). If required, adjust for business days using the holiday and the business day convention. Continue down the cells until date calculated is greater than or equal to the maturity date.

Calculate and use the **Day Count From Value Date** when determining the **Discount Factor**.

The **Rate** is used when calculating the **Discount Factor Using Linear Interpolation**. As previously discussed, in the model, linear interpolation is not the preferred method of interpolation.

The **Discount Factor** is calculated for example, for the 12 month Discount Factor as:

$$df_{12} = df_1/(1 + (Rate_{12} \times (Date_{12} - Date_1)/360)$$

where df_1 is the value or settlement discount factor and $Date_1$ is the value date.

4.3 PRESENT VALUE MODELLING

When modelling cash flows it is useful to be able to calculate and convey the value of a future stream of promised cash flows when discounted at a yield or a spread to an index.

It is also often useful to measure the sensitivity of changes in the price of a CDO note when there is a change in the yield or discount margin, i.e., to calculate duration. Additionally, the yield or internal rate of return of a series of cash flows, particularly under various different

	E	F	G	H
4	**Number**	**Time Unit**	**USD LIBOR**	**USD SWAPS**
5				
6	2	Days	0.250%	
7	5	Days	0.280%	
8	1	Month	0.256%	
9	2	Months	0.274%	
10	3	Months	0.338%	
11	6	Months	0.390%	
12	9	Months	0.479%	
13	1	Year	0.611%	
14	2	Years		0.913%
15	3	Years		1.403%
16	4	Years		1.860%
17	5	Years		2.318%
18	6	Years		2.528%
19	7	Years		2.737%
20	8	Years		2.947%
21	9	Years		3.157%
22	10	Years		3.366%

Figure 4.7   Interpolation for USD swaps and spreads

default assumptions for the assets, is often required by both the rating agencies and the end investors. Both weighted average life and duration are also used to determine expected loss thresholds in some rating agency approaches, which in turn will determine the ultimate rating.

In the *Prerequisites Model* there are various worksheets showing the calculations for present value, yield, internal rate of return, weighted average life and duration.

4.3.1 Present value

Present value calculations are most often used in CDO modelling when pricing the liabilities which are not sold at par (100%) and also for measuring potential loss relative to promised interest rates. Discounting at a fixed yield is usually used for fixed income (i.e., fixed coupon) securities, while discount margin (or DM) is often used for floating rate securities which are set from an index such as LIBOR or EURIBOR. While DM is often quoted, it is technically more often the Z-spread that is actually given. A true DM is calculated using a fixed rate for the future LIBOR rates, whereas a z-spread or zero-volatility option adjusted spread adds a spread to the forward-forward index rates, and discounts using the combined rate.

> **Did you know?** The z-spread is essentially the difference between the present value of the future cash flows using spot rates and the price that is quoted in the market. The z-spread thus is considered to encompass the credit risk, liquidity and other factors.

	O	P	Q
3	Net Present Value (using NPV)	Discount Factor	Net Present Value
4	10,000,000.00	1.00	10,000,000.00
5	10,000,000.00	0.97	10,000,000.00
6	10,000,000.00	0.95	10,000,000.00

Figure 4.8   Calculating net present value (NPV) of a floating rate bond

The **NPV (Floating Rate) Sheet** shows a floating rate note paying a spread of 6-month LIBOR + 50 bps on an actual/360 basis. The dates are unadjusted in the example as it is solely focussed on the NPV function. There are two named variables (ranges):

spread is the coupon spread which is added to LIBOR
dm is added to LIBOR in order to discount the cash flows

Often these may be the same, which would result in a par price or no losses. If the discount margin rate is higher than the spread, the price will be below par. If it is lower than the spread, the price will be above par.

The discounted per period net present value (NPV) is generated by using the function NPV, with the first argument being the per period discount rate obtained by multiplying the annualized discount rate by the number of days in the period divided by 360, and the second argument being the previous periods NPV and payments.

A similar result can be obtained by generating per period discount factors and multiplying the latest discount factor and dividing by the earlier discount factor, i.e., using the earlier notation. This is another reason to use the *Curve and Dates Model* other than to simply generate forward rates and it makes it easy to calculate net present values (NPV) (Figure 4.8).

If the only result required is the NPV (and per period NPVs are not required), then the use of the SUMPRODUCT() formula is also useful (Figure 4.9).

4.3.2 Internal rate of return

With residual cash flows cash to the equity, or lowest class of notes, it is often necessary to determine an internal rate of return calculation. Excel provides two functions to assist with this task: IRR() and XIRR().

IRR() assumes equal intervals of payment and calculates the period return; XIRR() has the date schedule as well and is useful for calculating internal rate of return when the date periods are uneven. XIRR() returns an annualized internal rate of return rather than a per-period rate of return and is therefore independent of the payment frequency.

	A	B	C	I
7				
8		NPV	10,000,000	
9		Price	100.00%	
10		Loss	0.00	
11				

Figure 4.9   Using SUMPRODUCT() to calculate NPV

To convert yields from one compounding frequency return to another use the following formula:

$$r_m = m((1 + r/n)^{n/m} - 1)$$
$$r_1 = 1((1 + r/2)^{2/1} - 1)$$
$$r_1 = ((1 + r/2)^2 - 1)$$

where:

r is the rate;
n is the frequency of payment;
m is the desired compounding frequency rate.

The example on the **IRR Sheet** is created using random payments for the note and uses three methods to determine the IRR, annualized IRR(), XIRR() and the discount factor method. An important note is that all methods effectively solve for a zero net present value (see the **Discount Factor Check**). Either the initial investment (i.e., payment to purchase the note) is of a negative sign relative to the note receipts (which is normal for an investment) or vice versa for a loan (i.e., a mortgage). NPV() basically solves for a zero present value given an initial outflow or investment against the future inflows or returns. An initial negative number representing the outflow is required, otherwise the formula will not resolve. Hence, the first payment in the **Total Payments** column is a negative number.

The IRR cell has the per-period internal rate of return for the **Total Payments** column. The **Annualized IRR** converts this from a per-period rate to an annualized rate by the application of the above formulas. XIRR() takes the **Total Payments** and all of the **Payment Dates** as the inputs.

The minor difference between the results for annualized IRR() and XIRR() is due to the discounting method. XIRR() uses ratio of accrued days divided by 365 as the method of dividing up the year, so it will typically not be divided evenly; whereas IRR() assumes even division of the interval for payment.

	A	B	C	D
7				
8		IRR	4.8318%	
9		Annualised IRR	9.8970%	
10		XIRR	9.8931%	
11		Discount Factor Check	0	
12				

Figure 4.10   Three methods to determine internal rate of return

An alternative to using internal functions is to use the discount factor method. Again with reference to the **IRR Sheet** a column of semi annual fixed rate **Discount Factors** is created by using the **Bond Equivalent Yield**. Any initial value will do, and it is quite traditional to use 7% as an initial value. Using the SUMPRODUCT() formula with the **Total Payments** column and the **Discount Factors** will result in a positive number (if the discount rate is below the internal rate of return) or a negative number (if the discount rate is above the internal rate of return) for the **Discount Factor**, by using "Goal Seek" from the Tools menu. This effectively replicates the method used internally by the various IRR() and YIELD() functions. The sum of the present value of the (negative) cost of purchase and the discounted future receipts should equal zero when the discount yield is equal to the IRR. Hence, in the worksheet, H4 is the net present value (targeted to be zero) and D2 is the discount yield.

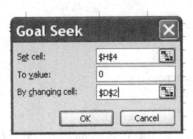

Figure 4.11 Goal seek

In this instance, because of the payment frequency a **Bond Equivalent**, i.e., semi annual yield, is generated. To convert this to an annualized yield, apply the formulas described earlier. This result is almost identical to the annualized IRR calculation.

4.3.3 Future value

A future value is often required in determining the return threshold in excess of "high water marks" so that the manager can participate in incentive payments. In the example on IRR(2) **Sheet**, the manager receives an **Incentive Fee Share** of 20% of the return once it exceeds a **Return Threshold** of 12% and the investor receives the excess beyond that. To calculate the future value, multiply the current value by 1+ **Return Threshold** yield per period and deduct the payment received, then only once this future value has been reduced to zero will the manager be entitled to receive anything. The **Balance** has the balance of the investment at the threshold yield and the **Future Value** is the future value at the threshold yield. The **Payments up to Return Threshold** holds the payments up to the threshold and the **Excess** has the money in excess of the **Payments up to Return Threshold**. The **Paid to Manager** has the manager's 20% share and the **Excess Payment to Note holders** has the payment to the equity. Finally, the **Closing Balance** is calculated at the threshold yield.

4.3.4 Weighted average life

Weighted average life (WAL) is used for amortizing or sinking fund bonds to measure the point where half the principal is returned to the investor. It is important for two main reasons: (a) investors like to know the effective maturity of their investments; and (b) to estimate loss thresholds when establishing a Moody's rating. To calculate it (without applying any potential

	N	O	P	Q	R	S
3	Future Value	Return Threshold	Excess	Paid to Manager	Payment to note holders	Closing Balance
4						
5	10,600,000.00	94,486.62	0.00	0.00	0.00	10,505,513.38
6	11,135,844.18	594,394.11	0.00	0.00	0.00	10,541,450.07
7	11,173,937.07	235,992.11	0.00	0.00	0.00	10,937,944.97

Figure 4.12

losses) is given by:

$$WAL = \frac{\sum_{i=1}^{n} p_i \, t_i}{N}$$

where:

p_i is the principal payments in period i;
t_i is the time to the payment;
N is the original nominal amount.

In the **WAL Sheet**, to calculate the WAL, simply use SUMPRODUCT to multiply the **Period** numbers by the **Principal** payments and divide by the **Opening Balance**. The result given in **WAL (period)** is the WAL number of periods; to convert to years it needs to be divided by the payment frequency which in this case is semi annual. That result is given in **WAL years (estimate)**. Alternatively, use the time in each period to generate a slightly more accurate result in **WAL (accurate)**, by using the time to the **Accrual Period** interval instead of the **Period** number. This also can be used in a more general case for uneven payment periods, for example, if there is a long or short first or last coupon payment.

Where there are losses and thus not all the principal is returned, dividing by the original notional will result in the duration appearing to get shorter as losses increase. To compensate for losses, add back the shortfall (i.e., the amount lost) in the last period of the transaction so the duration will extend if payment is not in full. The need for this will become more apparent later in Chapter 8 where the *Cash Flow Model* is addressed more fully.

4.3.5 Duration

Duration covers a number of different types and names of measures of sensitivity of price versus yield and/or spread. The most well known is the Macaulay duration, which is calculated by summing the cash flows multiplied by their time to payment and dividing by the price.

Another type of duration is modified duration, which is related to Macaulay duration by:

$$ModDuration = \frac{MacaulayDuration}{\left(1 + \frac{yield}{n}\right)}$$

Modified duration is also related to the first derivative of the price versus yield for a fixed income instrument. It is always important to remember that duration and modified duration are a measure of relative price or percentage price sensitivity to change in spread or yield. To calculate the actual change in price, multiply the duration by the price and the change in yield. Multiplying the modified duration by the price is defined as the dollar or price duration. Thus,

$$DollarDuration = ModDuration x Price x \Delta yield$$

This is the real change in price and is often used as a risk measure for hedging.

This difference is best demonstrated by the duration of a zero coupon bond. The duration of a zero coupon bond will be its maturity, as it only has one payment at maturity. Its modified duration will be its maturity divided by 1 plus its yield per period, which will be very similar to its maturity. However, its dollar duration will be typically much smaller because of its price. For example, a 30-year zero will have a duration of 30 years. If the yield is 6% on a bond equivalent basis, the modified duration will be 29.21. The dollar duration, however, is much lower as the price of a 30-year zero would be only $16.97 per $100 of notional value. The dollar duration is therefore much lower at –4.94. This is easily verified by recalculating the yield at 5.99% and seeing a dollar price change of 4.95 cents as the price becomes $17.02.

Excel has functions DURATION() and MDURATION() to calculate the Macaulay duration and modified duration. Unfortunately, they are not much use for amortizing bonds or floating rate bonds as they only allow for a bullet maturity and fixed rate assets. The provided examples demonstrate the calculations of duration for amortizing and floating rate notes.

The **Duration (1) Sheet** calculates the duration of a fixed rate amortizing bond. Firstly calculate the NPV as described earlier. Then determine each **Period Contribution** by multiplying the **Accrual Period** by the **Total Payments** by the **Discount Factor**. The **Classic Macaulay Duration** is then the sum of the **Period Contributions** divided by the **NPV**. Convert this into a **Classic Modified Duration** by dividing by the yield, and convert to a **Classic Dollar Duration** by multiplying by the price.

The veracity of the calculation can be checked by calculating the sensitivity of the price to a basis point change in yield. Column M holds the **Discount Factors** at the original yield and the price for the original yield is cell M3 and is calculated as before using SUMPRODUCT().

Generate discount factors for two new yields, **Yield 1** and **Yield 2**, respectively. The discount factors for **Yield 1** which is a basis point higher in yield than the original **Yield** are in the **Discount Factors 1** column and **Price (using df1) (%)** is calculated again using SUMPRODUCT(). **Discount Factors** and **Price** are also calculated for **Yield 2**, which is the original **Yield** less one basis point.

Under the **Quick Check Calculations**, the **Dollar Duration** compares very favourably with the **Classic Dollar Duration** calculation. Converting back to **Modified Duration** by dividing by the price gives a result which compares very favourably with the **Classic Modified Duration**. Finally, recalculate for the **Macaulay Duration** by multiplying the **Modified Duration** by one plus the yield per period, which can be seen to be equivalent with the **Classic Macaulay Duration** result.

On the **Duration (2) Sheet**, a floating rate duration calculation is examined. In this worksheet, the bond yields LIBOR plus 1% and is discounted at LIBOR+1.5%. The calculations are as described above for the sensitivity although in this case the discount factors are generated from the LIBOR rates plus the discount margin. The main difficulty in converting the durations is to understand the average yield over the life and the **Average Yield** as calculated from the discount factors.

	N
1	
2	**Price (%)**
3	95.07
4	**Discount Factor**
5	1.0000
6	0.9685
7	0.9380
8	0.9085
9	0.8799

Figure 4.13   Discount factor

	A	B	C
4			
5		Coupon	6%
6		Yield	6.50%
7		Yield 1	6.51%
8		Yield 2	6.49%
9		Opening Balance	10,000,000
10			
11		Classic Calculations	
12		Classic Dollar Duration	-	9.5123
13		Classic Modified Duration	-	10.0051
14		Classic Macaulay Duration	-	10.3303
15			
16		Quick Check Calculations	
17		Dollar Duration	-	9.5144
18		Modified Duration	-	10.0073
19		Macaulay Duration	-	10.3326
20			

Figure 4.14   Yield and duration calculations

The **Swap Duration** is calculated from the accrual periods multiplied by the nominal outstanding multiplied by the discount factors. Where does this come from? It is a rearrangement of a simple par bond pricing formula where:

$$P = C \sum \alpha_i n_i v_i + \sum v_i p_i$$

P is the presentvalue
C is the coupon
α is the accrual
n is the periodnotionalbalance
v is the perioddiscountfactor
p is the principalpayment

If it is priced at par and solving for C:

$$C = \frac{\left(100 - \sum v_i p_i\right)}{\sum \alpha_i n_i v_i}$$

In this equation, the denominator is the swap duration. This was seen also in the stripping of the yield curve in Section 4.2.

In the **IRR(3) Sheet**, these calculations are extended to equity cash flows. Solving for IRR (using the discount factors or generating them from the IRR() or XIRR() payment) then it is easy to come up with the Macaulay duration as before.

5
Getting Started

5.1 CREATE THE INPUT SHEET

By opening the ***Cash Flow Model***, the reader can follow using the description below.

5.1.1 Model inputs

	A	B	C
2			
3		**Model Inputs**	
4		Model Name	Cash Flow 1.0
5		Model Author	C. Flow
6		Transaction Name	CDO 1
7		Last Revision Date	01-Sep-09
8			

Figure 5.1 Model inputs

Model Name (cell C4): It is always wise to name the model so that it is always clear what is being referred to.

Model Author (cell C5): It is helpful for other users of the model to know who created it and who to go to if they have questions (or want to blame someone!).

Transaction Name (cell C6): Always change the transaction name when starting a new deal to prevent confusion when working on more than one deal at a time.

Last Revision Date (cell C7): Keeping track of when the last amendments were made to a model can be helpful if there have been changes to the market or the deal since that time. It is best practise to hard code in this date as using the function TODAY() defeats the purpose.

5.1.2 CDO tranche inputs

Tranche Number (cells C10 to H10): It is good to number the tranches simply to keep track of them and the order they are in. Adding more tranches to the structure is addressed later.

CDO Class Name (cells C11 to H11): These are the names of each of the tranches, i.e., Class A, Class B, Class C, etc.

Amount (cells C12 to H12): This is the issuance amount of each of the tranches. It is assumed at this point that the notes are issued at par (100% of the face value).

Price (cells C13 to H13): This is the percentage of par at which the notes are issued. This is also used later to determine the discount margin of the security.

	A	B	C	D	E	F	G	H
9			CDO Tranche Inputs					
10		Tranche Number	1	2	3	4	5	6
11		CDO Class Name	Class A	Class B	Class C	Class D	Class E	Class F
12		Amount	278,000,000	34,000,000	20,000,000	16,000,000	22,000,000	30,000,000
13		Price	100.00%	100.00%	100.00%	100.00%	100.00%	80.00%
14		Proceeds	278,000,000	34,000,000	20,000,000	16,000,000	22,000,000	24,000,000
15		Moody's Desired Rating	Aaa	Aa2	A2	Baa2	Ba2	NR
16		S&P Desired Rating	AAA	AA	A	BBB	BB	NR
17		Spread (bps)	40	75	125	225	600	NA
18		Discount Margin (bps)	40	75	125	225	600	800
19		PIKable? (1=Yes, 0=No)	0	0	1	1	1	NA
20		Credit Enhancement	30.50%	22.00%	17.00%	13.00%	7.50%	NA
21		OC Test	NA	115.1%	111.8%	108.0%	104.3%	NA
22		OC Result	142.4%	126.92%	119.28%	0	0	0
23		OC Cushion	NA	11.82%	7.48%	108.00%	104.30%	NA
24		IC Test	NA	120.0%	114.0%	110.0%	100.0%	NA
25		IC Result	NA	120.00%	114.00%	110.00%	91.34%	NA
26		IC Cushion	NA	0.00%	0.00%	0.00%	-8.66%	NA
27		SP Recovery Rate	55.00%	59.00%	62.00%	65.00%	68.00%	NA
28		Covenanted Minimum Recovery Rate	45.00%	45.00%	45.00%	45.00%	45.00%	NA

Figure 5.2   CDO tranche inputs

Proceeds (cells C14 to H14): This is the amount of each of the notes multiplied by the price. It is useful for ensuring that the total proceeds, i.e., the sum of all the notes proceeds, is greater than or equal to the amount paid for the collateral, including upfront fees.

Moody's Desired Rating (cells C15 to H15): Usually the ratings hoped to be achieved will range from Aaa to B3.

S&P Desired Rating (cells C16 to H16): The expected S&P rating usually ranges from AAA to B−.

Spread (bps) (cells C17 to H17): The spread refers to the amount that is paid on the notes above the floating rate, which in our example is USD LIBOR. Here, the spread is expressed in basis points (one one-hundredth of one percent).

> ***Did you know?***   London Interbank Offered Rate (LIBOR) is the interest rate at which banks borrow funds from other banks. The British Bankers' Association (BBA) fixes LIBOR each morning at 11 a.m. London time. To learn more about the BBA and LIBOR see www.bba.org.uk.
>
> EURIBOR or the Euro Interbank Offered Rate is the interest rate at which euro interbank term deposits within the Euro zone are offered between prime banks. To learn more visit www.euribor.org.

Discount Margin (bps) (cells C18 to H18): This is the effective holding yield relative to a floating rate index (e.g., LIBOR or EURIBOR), that the note holder receives.

PIKable? (**1 = Yes, 0 = No**) (cells C19 to H19): PIKable denotes whether the tranche is able to defer interest, i.e., not pay timely interest. Many subordinate tranches have the ability to defer interest and effectively pay-in-kind (or PIK) by capitalizing the current interest due. It is important to make this distinction as it changes both the potential cash flows and the analysis of the cash flows.

Credit Enhancement (cells C20 to H20): The percentage of the sum of the amounts of the CDO issuance below the current tranche, divided by the total note issuance, is the credit enhancement. Indicative general credit enhancement levels (using pre-2008 criteria) for various types of deals are illustrated below.

CLOs (with sizes ranging from 275 million to 800 million): Senior AAA/Aaa: 23% to 40%; Junior AAA/Aaa: 24% to 32%; AA/Aa: 17% to 26%; A/A: 12% to 19%; BBB/Baa: 8% to 13% and BB/Ba: 6% to 10%.

TRUPs (with sizes ranging from 350 million to 800 million): Senior AAA/Aaa: 30% to 47%; Junior AAA/Aaa: 34% to 37%; AA/Aa: 19% to 27%; A/A: 9% to 15%; BBB/Baa: 3% to 8% and BB/Ba: 3% to 8%.

High Grade ABS CDOs (with sizes ranking from 1000 million to 2000 million): Senior AAA/Aaa: 6.0% to 11.4%; Junior AAA/Aaa: 3.5% to 5.4%; AA/Aa: 2.1% to 4.5%; A/A: 1.3% to 2.5%; BBB/Baa: 0.8% to 1.5% and BB/Ba: 0.6% to 0.8%.

Mezz ABS CDOs (with sizes ranging from 300 million to 950 million): Senior AAA/Aaa: 22% to 42%; Junior AAA/Aaa: 17% to 37%; AA/Aa: 8% to 34%; A/A: 6% to 24%; BBB/Baa: 3% to 19% and BB/Ba: 3% to 5%.

OC Test (cells C21 to H21): The over-collateralization hurdles that must be passed are generally different depending on the ratings and type of assets in the deal. For example, where a transaction size ranges from 300 million to 550 million, OC Tests can generally be seen in the area of the following levels: Junior AAA OC Tests 123%; AA OC Tests 114%; A OC Tests 109%; BBB OC Tests 105%; and BB OC Tests 103%. For deals that range from 1 billion to 2 billion, OC Tests are likely to be found near the following levels: Junior AAA OC Tests 103%; AA OC Tests 102%; A OC Tests 101%; BBB OC Tests 100.5%; and BB OC Tests 100.3%.

OC Result (cells C22 to H22): This is the result at the effective date for the transaction. OC Ratios are measurements of the total principal amounts of the assets of the CDO divided by the outstanding liabilities at and above the level of the relevant test.

OC Cushion (cells C23 to H23): This is the difference between the OC Result and the OC Test. The higher the OC Cushion, the more protection the CDO has against losses.

IC Test (cells C24 to H24): There will be a hurdle percentage that the IC Result must pass. The hurdles for these tests are generally different depending on the size of the deal and the individual tranche sizes. For example, for a deal with an issuance size between 300 million to 550 million, IC Tests typically range at the following levels: Junior AAA IC Tests 125%; AA IC Tests 118% to 120%; A IC Tests 113% to 115%; BBB IC Tests 108% to 110%; and BB IC Tests 103% to 105%. For deals that range from 1 billion to 2 billion, IC Tests are typically set in the following ranges: Junior AAA IC Tests 102% to 106%; and AA IC Tests 101% to 103%.

IC Result (C25 to H25): This is the minimum of all of the results over the life of the transaction.

Did you know? Class A OC ratio and Class B OC ratios would generally be calculated as follows:

The Class A OC ratio is the percentage obtained by dividing:
(a) the sum of the balances of:
    (i) the collateral (excluding defaulted and downgraded collateral);
    (ii) the Unused Proceeds Account and the Principal Collection Account;
    (iii) all Eligible Investments;
    (iv) for each defaulted asset, the sum of the lower of (i) the product of (A) the lowest rating agency assumed recovery rate and (B) the balance of each defaulted portfolio asset; and (ii) the market value of each defaulted portfolio asset; and
    (v) for each downgraded asset, the aggregate of the product of (A) the balance of each downgraded asset and (B) any "haircut" that may apply to such asset;
by
(b) the sum of principal amount of the Class A Notes outstanding.

Similarly, the Class B OC ratio is the percentage obtained by dividing:
(a) the sum of the balances of:
    (i) the collateral (excluding defaulted and downgraded portfolio assets);
    (ii) the Unused Proceeds Account and the Principal Collection Account;
    (iii) all Eligible Investments;
    (iv) for each defaulted asset, the sum of the lower of (i) the product of (A) the lowest rating agency assumed recovery rate and (B) the balance of each defaulted asset; and (ii) the market value of each defaulted portfolio asset; and
    (v) for each downgraded asset, the aggregate of the product of (A) the balance of each downgraded asset and (B) any "haircut" that may apply to such asset;
by
(b) the sum of principal amount of the Class A Notes and the Class B Notes outstanding.

What is a "haircut"? Haircuts are discounts that apply when calculating OC ratios to the notional outstanding for an asset that has been downgraded.

Where a downgraded asset has more than one rating, the lowest such rating usually applies in determining the relevant percentage.

Did you know? The "Class A Interest Coverage Ratio" in general means the ratio obtained by dividing:
(a) (i) the sum of all of the interest payments received and expected to be received in the Payment Period minus (ii) the fee and expenses payable which are senior to the Class A interest in the Interest Proceeds waterfall and due and payable
by:
(b) the interest on the Class A Notes payable on such Payment Date.

The "Class B Interest Coverage Ratio" in general means the ratio obtained by dividing:
(a) The sum of (i) all of the interest payments received and expected to be received in the Payment Period minus (ii) the fee and expenses payable which are senior to the Class A interest in the Interest Proceeds waterfall and due and payable
by:
(b) the sum of the interest on the Class A Notes and the Class B Notes payable on such Payment Date.

IC Cushion (cells C26 to H26): This is the difference between the IC Result and the IC Test.

5.1.3 Fees and expenses

Upfront Fees (cell C31): Fees are usually charged to the Issuer and taken from the deal either on the closing date or over the life of the deal on a running basis. These fees usually include the structuring fees that the investment bank charges, the ratings agencies fees for rating the notes, legal counsel fees and expenses, upfront trustee fees, fees and expenses to set up the SPE, registration and listing fees, upfront costs for any swaps, options or other hedges and, if there are bonds in the collateral, the cost of the purchased accrued.

Running Taxes (USD per Period) (cell C32): This is the amount of estimated taxes in the currency of the deal assumed to be payable each period.

Running Trustee/Admin Fees and Expenses (bps) (cell C33): Trustee and Administrative Fees and Expenses are often assumed to be anywhere from 1 to 5 basis points per annum. In large deals of USD 1.5 billion or more, often 1 basis point is assumed. For smaller deals of perhaps USD 300 million, often 5 or 6 basis points may be assumed, particularly for loan deals that require active due diligence and loan agents.

Fixed Costs/Trustee/Admin (cell C34): Many trustee/administrators charge a fixed minimum amount. This becomes particularly important when the transaction begins to de-lever, typically after the end of the reinvestment period.

Senior Trustee Fees and Expenses Cap (cell C35): Often there is a cap on the fees paid at this level of the waterfall. Usually this cap is assumed to be from USD 60 000 to USD 200 000. Fees in excess of this cap are then paid lower in the priority of payments.

Running Senior Management Fee (bps) (cell C36): This fee is in basis points per annum and is applied to the outstanding collateral in each period. The senior management fee can run in most USD 300 million to 550 million size CDOs or CLOs at 15 bps, whereas for larger deals of USD 1 billion or more, from 3 basis points to 5 basis points might be assumed.

Running Junior Management Fee (bps) (cell C37): The junior management fee can run in most USD 300 million size CDOs or CLOs at 10 to 30 basis points, whereas for larger deals of USD 1 billion or more, anywhere from 2 to 6 basis points are more normal. Often it is the combined senior and junior management fees that are most important. Overall, larger deals of 1 billion or more will see total management fees of 8 to 10 basis points per annum. Smaller deals of 300 to 550 million will see total management fees of 30 to 50 basis points bps per annum.

Interest on Unpaid Management Fees? (1 = Yes, 0 = No) (cell C38): Sometimes interest on unpaid management fees will be structured into the CDO. If this is the case, the input should be one, otherwise it should be zero.

A	B	C
29		
30	**Fees and Expenses**	
31	Upfront Fees	4,000,000
32	Running Taxes (USD per Annum)	-
33	Running Trustee/Admin Fees and Expenses (bps)	3.50
34	Fixed Costs Trustee/Admin	150,000
35	Senior Trustee Fees and Expenses Cap	200,000
36	Running Senior Management Fee (bps)	10
37	Running Junior Management Fee (bps)	40
38	Interest on Unpaid Management Fees? (1 = Yes, 0 = No)	1
39	Interest Spread on Unpaid Management Fees (bps)	10
40	Incentive Management Fee	20%
41	Incentive Management Fee Hurdle	12%
42		

Figure 5.3 Fees and expenses

Interest Spread on Unpaid Management Fees (bps) (cell C39): As the name describes, this is the interest payable on unpaid management fees. This can be the same as the management fee plus (usually) the index. The conventions vary from transaction to transaction and in many cases may only be paid at the index flat, i.e., without a spread at all.

Incentive Management Fee (cell C40): This is usually a fee payable in any period to the collateral manager where the return to the equity or preference shares exceeds a threshold or high water mark. It is usually a percentage of the amounts available for distribution to the equity tranche after the threshold or Incentive Management Fee Hurdle return to the equity has been paid. Usually this fee ranges from 10% to 30% of the available proceeds. Alternatively, it can take the form of additional fixed fees.

Incentive Management Fee Hurdle (cell C41): This is is generally defined as the internal rate of return threshold that the equity notes must have received for the period from the launch of the deal until the relevant payment period in order for an Incentive Management Fee to be paid. Typical threshold value range from 8% to 15%.

5.1.4 Collateral inputs

Collateral Amount (cell C44): This is the total amount of collateral that the CDO will have purchased when it is issued/ramped up.

Collateral Currency (cell C45): It is important to state the currency that the collateral will be in. This ensures that the collateral and the associated curves are aligned and becomes even more significant in multicurrency transactions.

Moody's Weighted Average Rating (cell C46): This is taken from the *Warehouse Model*, as the alphanumeric rating interpolated from the numeric weighted average rating factor (WARF) by performing a lookup in the Moody's idealized loss table.

Weighted Average Life (cell C47): This is the typically covenanted expected weighted average life that the collateral manager will typically attempt to manage to, and *not* the initial weighted average life of the collateral portfolio. It is usually the reinvestment period plus an anticipated amortization of the pool in line with the initial pool. That is to say, it is usually similar to the amortization of the current pool shifted by the reinvestment period. This number is typically used in conjunction with the WARF to determine the inputs to the Moody's BET analysis.

Initial Weighted Average Spread (bps) (cell C48): A weighted average margin over the floating interest rate is applied to the initial pool of collateral.

Reinvestment Weighted Average Spread (bps) (cell C49): Similar to the initial weighted average spread, a weighted average margin over the floating interest rate is applied to the reinvested collateral.

Weighted Average Spread Vector (cell C50): Rather than run the model at a covenanted minimum weighted average spread, it may be useful, and in some cases required, to examine the likelihood of spread compression. It is particularly so at either end of the transaction, i.e., during ramp-up and as it begins to redeem. Spread compression tests are particularly important if the distribution of spreads in the portfolio is widely dispersed.

Reinvestment WAS Vector (cell C51): This is as discussed above but applied to the reinvestment portfolio only. Reinvestment risk is a concern for the rating agencies but of even more concern for the potential equity and other junior tranche buyers. This vector can

	A	B	C
42			
43		**Collateral Inputs**	
44		Collateral Amount	396,000,000
45		Collateral Currency	USD
46		Moody's Weighted Average Rating	B2
47		Weighted Average Life	9
48		Initial Weighted Average Spread (bps)	285
49		Reinvestment Weighted Average Spread (bps)	285
50		Weighted Average Spread Vector	Initial_Sprd
51		Reinvestment WAS Vector	Reinvest_Sprd
52		Reinvestment Period End	20
53		Ramp Vector	Ramp_1
54		Mandatory Liquidation of Collateral Period End	80
55		Liquidation Price	100%
56		Interest on Interest Proceeds (bps)	-25
57		Timing of Interest on Interest Proceeds	0.5
58		Amortization Vector	Base
59		Reinvestment Amortization Vector	Base_1
60		Shift Reinvestment	FALSE
61		Prepayment Rate	0%
62		Reinvest Prepayment Rate	0%
63		Prepayment End Period	20
64		Constant Default Rate Used? (1 = Yes, 0 = No)	0
65		Constant Default Rate	0%
66		Cumulative Default Rate	0%
67		Default Vector	YR2_25/25/25/25
68		Default Original (1) Or Outstanding Balance (0)	1
69		Anticipated Recovery Rate	45%
70		Default Reinvestment (1 = Yes, 0 = No)	-
71		Recovery Rate	45%
72		Recovery Lag Periods	4
73		Cohorts? (1 = Yes, 0 = No)	1
74		Hedges (Swaps) (1 = On, 0 = Off)	0
75		Principal Cures	1
76		Epsilon	1.00E-10
77			

Figure 5.4   Collateral inputs

be used to investigate the effects of spread compression or expansion of the reinvestment spread over time.

Reinvestment Period End (cell C52): This is the period in which the reinvestment period comes to an end. After this, the collateral manager can no longer purchase assets to add to the collateral portfolio and if an asset pays principal after the reinvestment period end date, the proceeds are used to pay principal on the CDO liabilities.

Ramp Vector (cell C53): This is the name of the vector applied to the Collateral Amount and is used to model the assumed rate of purchase of collateral per period after the deal has launched.

Mandatory Liquidation of Collateral Period End (cell C54): This is the period in which the outstanding aggregate principal amount of the collateral is deemed to be sold in its entirety. It is normally set to the maturity date of the transaction or when examining the yield to call for the equity holders, i.e., the equity call date.

Liquidation Price (cell C55): This is a dirty price assumption for the liquidation of the portfolio that is applied at the mandatory liquidation or collateral period end.

Interest on Interest Proceeds (bps) (cell C56): A margin above (or below) the Collateral Floating Interest Rate Vector is applied to the interest proceeds received from the collateral intra-period. If interest is assumed to be received at the end of the period, there will be no interest on interest proceeds.

Timing of Interest on Interest Proceeds (cell C57): As there is some discrepancy between the payment dates of the liabilities and the assets, there is potential for the transaction to earn interest on the interest collections. The rating agencies allow the model to assume that the majority of cash is paid in the middle of the period. However, this number can be adjusted to stress the impact of this assumption.

Amortization Vector (cell C58): This is the name of the vector applied for the percentage of principal of the total original collateral being repaid.

Reinvestment Amortization Vector (cell C59): This vector is typically selected so that the amortization profile of the reinvestment pool is at or close to the covenanted weighted average life of the transaction. Depending on the type of underlying assets it can be a sinking fund (for ABS and potentially loans) or a bullet maturity for bonds.

Shift Reinvestment (cell C60): This Boolean input allows for the amortization profile to be either fixed (i.e., when the input is false) or be shifted in line with the advancement of time to reflect the reduction in the maturity of assets that the manager can purchase.

Prepayment Rate (cell C61): Many assets, but in particular loans and ABS, have a legal final maturity which is not the same as the expected maturity because of early prepayment by the obligor. This input allows for a specified prepayment rate to be used, and is typically not used in rating agency analysis.

Reinvest Prepayment Rate (cell C62): This is as above but solely for the reinvestment pool.

Prepayment End Period (cell C63): In some cases the assumptions for prepayment are only extended out for a number of periods. This is typically to the end of the reinvestment period as it reflects effectively the likely turnover of the collateral portfolio. It is usually more conservative to assume that the transaction will take longer to mature post the end of the reinvestment period, i.e., assume there is no prepayment post expiry of the reinvestment period.

Constant Default Rate Used? (1 = Yes, 0 = No) (cell C64): Two types of default analysis are usually presented when analysing CDOs: cumulative defaults and constant defaults. Cumulative defaults reflect the total defaults applied over the life of the transaction and usually require some form of timing vector. Constant defaults are usually applied to the outstanding balance of the portfolio as a steady rate when analysing breakeven default rates and equity returns. It is a Boolean input with 1 for Yes and 0 for No.

Constant Default Rate (cell C65): This is the annual percentage rate of defaults that is applied to the collateral.

Cumulative Default Rate (cell C66): As discussed above in the Constant Default Rate Used? description, it is more common to use a total or cumulative default rate when performing a rating agency analysis. Typically, this is only applied to the original pool and the default rate represents the cumulative amount of default applied to the original portfolio balance.

Default Vector (cell C67): A vector of varying defaults that can be applied to the collateral over the life of the deal. The reader is referred to Chapters 7, 9 and 10 for discussions on applying defaults to the cash flows, and rating agency modelling.

Default Original (1) Or Outstanding Balance (0) (cell C68): This is a Boolean input set in conjunction with the Cumulative Default Rate analysis (when it is set to 0), or the Constant Default Rate analysis (when it is set to 1).

Anticipated Recovery Rate (cell C69): If recovery delays are utilized in the model, then there are some periods post a default when a recovery is expected but not yet received. In order to credit this amount to the collateral tests (particularly the over-collateralization tests), an expected recovery rate is selected. Often this is the lowest of either Moody's or S&P's recovery covenants.

Default Reinvestment (1 = Yes, 0 = No) (cell C70): Another Boolean input commonly used set in conjunction with the "Default Original or Outstanding Balance", and is usually set similarly, i.e., 1 for Outstanding Balance or 0 if defaulting the original balance.

Recovery Rate (cell C71): A percentage of recoveries from defaults is applied to the amount of defaults in a particular period.

Recovery Lag Periods (cell C72): A number of periods will usually pass after a default before recoveries will be applied to the collateral. The amount of time assumed for recovery lags will depend on the type of collateral in the transaction. This ranges from 0 periods (thus, immediate recoveries are assumed), to as much as 3 years. Often 1 year is assumed.

Cohorts? (1 = Yes, 0 = No) (cell C73): The reinvestment pool is modelled two separate ways, as a single homogeneous pool or as a group of heterogeneous pool, or cohorts. By selecting one, the cohort approach is used.

Hedges (Swaps) (1 = No, 0 = Off) (cell C74): This input is basically a switch that enables the swaps to be either in the waterfall or not. It is used to examine the cost or gain in terms of returns or spread.

Principal Cures (cell C75): This input is a switch that will turn on and off cures of coverage tests from principal proceeds in the waterfall.

Epsilon (cell C76): In many instances an absolute precision in Excel is neither warranted nor required. In many cases it is useful to compare a near zero result to a very small number rather than absolute zero. Additionally, adding a number very close to zero to the denominator of ratio tests, such as the Over-collateralization tests, makes it very unlikely to divide by zero, or have the "#DIV/0!" error occur. By having a constant number, it is easy to adjust the effect of it in one place.

5.1.5 Date inputs

Value Date (cell C79): The value date usually the current date. It is used for many calculations including present values.

Settlement Date (cell C80): This is the date when the CDO is expected to commence. This is also known as the "closing date".

Pay Date (cell C81): The "roll" date is the date on which the CDO Notes will normally pay without considering adjustments for holidays and other non-business days.

	A	B	C
77			
78		**Date Inputs**	
79		Value Date	1-Sep-09
80		Settlement Date	3-Sep-09
81		Pay Date	3
82		Day Count	Act/360
83		Payment Frequency	4
84		Floating Interest Rate Vector	Forward
85		Date Convention	Modified Following
86		Calendars	LDN,NYO
87			

Figure 5.5 Date inputs

Day Count (cell C82): As previously described in Chapter 4, Day Count refers to the day count fraction. There are many types of day count fractions that are commonly used, including actual/365, actual/360 and actual/actual.

Payment Frequency (cell C83): The number of payments per year.

Floating Interest Rate Vector (cell C84): This is the name of the floating rate interest vector that will be used in the cash flows. In some cases this will be taken from the *Curve and Dates Model* in Chapter 4.

Date Convention (cell C85): As discussed in Chapter 4, this is the method used for adjusting any relevant date to take into account days that are not business days. As previously discussed, there are in general three types of date conventions: "Following", "Modified Following" and "Preceding".

Calendars (cell C86): Every country has its own holidays. In some cases, regions within a country will have different holidays, as is the case for Germany.

5.1.6 Model Notes

It is always helpful to note certain things in the model which make the current deal different from other deals (cells B88 to C95).

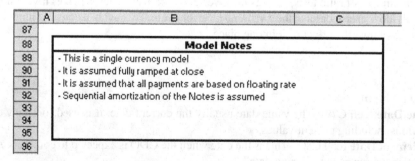

	A	B	C
87			
88		**Model Notes**	
89		- This is a single currency model	
90		- It is assumed fully ramped at close	
91		- It is assumed that all payments are based on floating rate	
92		- Sequential amortization of the Notes is assumed	
93			
94			
95			
96			

Figure 5.6 Model Notes

5.2 THE VALUE OF LABELLING

Every input cell has been named in the *Cash Flow Model* because, when creating cash flows, it is much easier and more transparent to look in a formula and know to what it is referring without having to trace the cell reference back to the value or input. Additionally, it is easier to find the cell in Excel and reference it from VBA for automation purposes without having to be concerned that changes to the sheet have not moved the reference.

In order to name a cell or range, first click on the cell which is to be named. Go to the menu bar and under "Insert", choose "Name", then choose "Define" and enter in the name for the cell. Conversely, a name can readily be looked up by hitting the "F5" or "go to" button.

6

Modelling Assets

6.1 INITIAL ASSET POOL: REP LINE MODELLING VS. ACTUAL ASSETS

Most of the modelling work carried out with a cash flow model will be done using rep lines. What is a rep line? A rep line represents a pool of collateral with similar characteristics and it is used in order to simplify the modelling of assets. Typically, it is described by the nominal amount, the interest payment, amortization amount, default amount and a recovery amount. Rep lines are most commonly used in the early stages of modelling before a pool has been identified. Firstly, the basic pool characteristics need to be identified, including:

- weighted average coupon/spread;
- weighted average recovery rate;
- amortization profile;
- rating/default probability;
- correlation/diversity.

Rep lines are typically used to aggregate collateral by a predominant type or characteristic, e.g., loans by order of senority (i.e., senior, subordinated, etc.) or by currency (USD, EUR, GBP) for multicurrency transactions.

Usually a portfolio model is then created which tracks the "ramp up" and this has a cash collator that converts the actual projected asset pool principal cash flows into a "rep line" amortization curve so that it can be incorporated into the **Vectors Sheet** of the *Cash Flow Model*.

Some advantages of rep line modelling are:

- the cash flow model is substantially smaller;
- it is useful where the final asset pool is not known;
- it is easier to model defaults.

Some disadvantages include:

- it is less realistic for actual monitoring of assets;
- it is easier to miss concentration issues in the portfolio;
- it is easier to miss basis issues.

6.2 THE COLLATERAL SHEET IN THE CASH FLOW MODEL

The **Collateral Sheet** is organized as follows:

- Hyperlinks at the top of the Collateral Sheet
- Starting at row 100: Collateral Summary
- Starting at row 200: Original Collateral Pools
- Starting at row 300: Rep Line Reinvestment Collateral Pools
- Starting at row 400: Cohorts Reinvestment Summary
- Starting at row 500: Individual Reinvestment Cohorts

	K	L	M	N	O	P	Q	R	S
101									
102					Aggregate Original Pools				
103	Beginning of Period Balance	Purchased Amount	Defaulted Amount	Anticipated Recovery	Recovery Amount	Amortization Amount	Prepay Amount	Sold Amount	End of Period Balance
104	396,000,000								396,000,000
105	396,000,000	-	-	-	-	-	-	-	396,000,000
106	396,000,000	-	-	-	-	-	-	-	396,000,000

Figure 6.1 Aggregate Original Pools

6.2.1 Collateral Summary

The Collateral Summary (at row 100) is a summary of the Original Collateral and the Reinvestment Collateral. All of the calculations used on the waterfall page will use the information contained in the Collateral Summary.

The reason for creating a Collateral Summary section is that if a user wishes to add other pools of collateral, it is possible to do so within the **Collateral Sheet** and it is not necessary to change references used on the **Waterfall Sheet** or other sheets. Adding other pools of collateral or, conversely, splitting the collateral into smaller subpools is sometimes required when assets that form part of the collateral may perform differently, or which the modeller desires to stress differently, e.g., through the use of other default rates or profiles, interest curves, or recoveries.

The Period, Dates, and Day Count (starting in cells B103, C103 and D103) are repeated for ease of reference. The Vectors for the Interest Rate, Ramp, Amortization, Default and Recovery (beginning in cells F103 to J103) are also reproduced for reference.

In the **Aggregate Original Pools** the following are provided (Figure 6.1):

- Beginning of Period Balance (cells K104 to K184)
- Purchased Amount (cells L104 to L184)
- Defaulted Amount (cells M104 to M184)
- Anticipated Recovery (cells N104 to N184)
- Recovery Amount (cells O104 to O184)
- Amortization Amount (cells P104 to P184)
- Prepay Amount (cells Q104 to Q184)
- Sold Amount (cells R104 to R184)
- End of Period Balance (cells S104 to S184)

Then, in the Original Pool Aggregate Interest (Figure 6.2), the Interest Collections (cells U104 to U184), Interest on Interest (cells V104 to V184), and the Total Interest Collections (cells W104 to W184) are calculated.

The **Interest Collections** (cells U104 to U184) are simply calculated as the *product of*:

- the *sum of*
  - the Beginning of Period Balance *plus*
  - the Purchased Amount *less*
  - the Defaulted Amount
- the applicable Collateral Interest Rate Vector *plus* the Initial weighted average spread
- the Day Count

	U	V	W	
101				
102	**Original Pool Aggregate Interest**			
103	**Interest Collections**	**Interest on Interest**	**Total Interest Collections**	
104		-	-	
105	2,958,889	-	2,958,889	
106	3,095,785	105	3,095,889	
107	2,982,566	-	2,982,566	

Figure 6.2 Original Pool Aggregate Interest

For example, cell U105 contains the formula

```
"=(K105+L105-M105)*(HLOOKUP(Interest_Vector,Interest_Rate_Vectors,
$B105+2,FALSE)+(HLOOKUP(Init_WAS_Vector,Interest_Rate_Vectors,$B105+2,
FALSE)/10000))*(D105)".
```

Similarly, for the **Interest on Interest** (cells W104 to W184) calculation, it is the *maximum of*:

- Interest Collections
- *multiplied by* the applicable Collateral Interest Rate Vector *plus* the Initial weighted average spread
- *multiplied* the Day Count
- *multiplied by* the Interest on Interest Timing
- and zero

The Interest on Interest timing is, as described in Chapter 5, the proportion of the payment period in which interest on the income is assumed to be accruing.

For example, for Period 1, cell V105 has the formula

```
"= (V105
*(HLOOKUP(Coll_Interest_Vector,Interest_Rate_Vectors,$B105+2,FALSE)
+(Int_on_Int_Spread/10000))*(D105))
*Int_On_Int_Timing"
```

The **Total Interest Collections** (cells W104 to W184) are simply:

- Interest Collections
- *plus* the Interest on Interest

Similarly to the Aggregate Original Pools, in the **Aggregate Reinvestment Pool** the following are provided (Figure 6.3):

- Beginning of Period Balance (cells Y104 to Y184)
- Reinvested Amount (cells Z104 to Z184)
- Defaulted Amount (cells A104 to A184)
- Anticipated Recovery (cells AB104 to AB184)

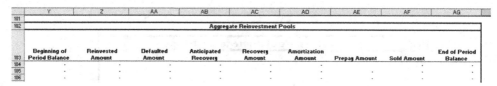

Figure 6.3   Aggregate Reinvestment Pools

- Recovery Amount (cells AC104 to AC184)
- Amortization Amount (cells AD104 to AD184)
- Prepay Amount (cells AE104 to AE184)
- Sold Amount (cells AF104 to AF184)
- End of Period Balance (cells AG104 to AG184)

In the Reinvestment Pool Aggregate Interest (Figure 6.4), the Interest Collections (cells AI104 to AI184), the Interest on Interest (cells AJ104 to AJ184), and the Total Interest Collections (cells AK104 to AK184) are calculated as they were calculated in the Aggregate Original Pool calculation described above.

The final **Aggregate Interest Collections** (cells AO104 to AO184) are the *sum of*:

- the Total Interest Collections for the Original Pool and
- the Total Interest Collections for the Reinvestment Pool

Thus, AO105 contains the formula "=W105+AK105".[1]

The final **Principal Proceeds** (cells AQ104 to AQ184) are sums of:

- Original Pool Recovery Amount
- Original Pool Amortization Amount
- Original Pool Prepay Amount
- Original Pool Sold Amount
- Reinvestment Pool Recovery Amount
- Reinvestment Pool Amortization Amount
- Reinvestment Pool Prepay Amount
- Reinvestment Pool Sold Amount

	AI	AJ	AK
101			
102	**Reinvestment Pool Aggregate Interest**		
103	**Interest Collections**	**Interest on Interest**	**Total Interest Collections**
104			
105	.	.	.
106	.	.	.

Figure 6.4   Reinvestment Pool Aggregate Interest

---

[1] The formula in cell AP105 will be "W105+AM105+AK105", once the Hedges/Swaps are added as described in Chapter 11.

	K	L	M	N	O	P	Q	R	S
201									
202					Collateral: Original Pool1				
203	Beginning of Period Balance	Purchased Amount	Defaulted Amount	Anticipated Recovery	Recovery Amount	Amortization Amount	Prepay Amount	Sold Amount	End of Period Balance
204	396,000,000								396,000,000
205	396,000,000	-	-	-	-	-	-	-	396,000,000
206	396,000,000	-	-	-	-	-	-	-	396,000,000

Figure 6.5 Collateral: Original Pool 1

For example, cell AQ105 contains `"=O105+P105+R105+Q105+AC105+AD105+AF105+AE105"`.

6.2.2 Original Collateral Pools

In the Original Collateral Pools section, which starts at row 200, the Period, Dates and Day Count (cells B204 to D184) and Vectors for Interest Rate, Ramp, Initial Pool Amortization, and Default (cells F204 to I184) are again repeated for convenience.

The following items appear in the Collateral: Original Pool 1 (Figure 6.5):

- Beginning of Period Balance (cells K204 to K284)
- Purchased Amount (cells L204 to L284)
- Defaulted Amount (cells M204 to M284)
- Anticipated Recovery (cells N204 to N284)
- Recovery Amount (cells O204 to O284)
- Amortization Amount (cells P204 to P284)
- Prepay Amount (cells Q204 to Q284)
- Sold Amount (cells R204 to R284)
- End of Period Balance (cells S204 to S284)

Each calculation will be explained in detail in the following section.

For Period 0, the **Beginning of Period Balance** is equal to the Collateral Amount Input such that cell L204 contains `"=Collateral_Amount"`.

After Period 0, the Beginning of Period Balance is equal to the End of Period Balance for the previous period. For Period 1, cell K205 reads `"= S204"`.

The **Purchased Amount** is calculated as:

- the Collateral Amount
- *multiplied by* one *minus* the applicable Ramp Vector input.

Hence for Period 1, cell L205 has the formula `"= Collateral_Amount*(1-G205)"`.

6.3 MODELLING DEFAULTS AND RECOVERIES

Modelling default risk can be performed in many ways. For general structuring and rating purposes it is usual to default the rep line.

While the expected loss of a portfolio can be fairly accurately estimated from its price or rating, the actual timing of the losses, i.e., whether they occur in the first year or the last year, is more difficult to estimate. While the shape of the loss distribution and the unexpected loss, effectively the variance of loss, can be calculated by estimating the codependence or correlation between the assets within the portfolio, calculating the default distribution by the use of a single extraneous variable such as correlation is fraught with issues:

- it is unlikely to be constant;
- it does not bear any relationship with observable data;
- it may measure other risks than default (i.e., liquidity).

However it is the distribution of losses that will determine the variance around the mean or expected loss, which is required for tranching and ratings. Ratings are typically based upon the probability of exceeding a certain standard deviation of loss with regard to the mean or expected loss. Hence a distribution is required. While the exact distribution is not known, by stressing the assumptions, the need for accuracy with regard to the distribution is significantly reduced. This is discussed in more depth in Chapters 9 and 10 in which rating agency criteria are explored.

Timing of defaults is another issue. While it can be expected that more risky assets are likely to default first, it is also likely that obligors in a related industry sector are likely to experience similar industry stresses. However, it is not possible to be sure which assets might default first. Hence there is a case for simulating the time to default for a pool of obligors.

6.3.1 Rep line modelling

Given the above constraints, it has been common for both rating agencies and investors to use deterministic default patterns to assess the sensitivity of returns and losses of the tranches of a CDO. These are generally applied to a rep line of the collateral in question. When modelling defaults and losses in a rep line, the following parameters are commonly required:

- default rate;
- recovery rate;
- recovery delay;
- anticipated recovery.

Default Rate is the rate applied to the rep line beginning of Period Principal Outstanding. Typically, this rate will apply to the whole pool. However, there are occasions where pool-specific default rates may be required, for example, when modelling heterogeneous pools of assets where the default risk or recovery is bar-belled rather than reasonably distributed around a single mean.

Default rates can be constant (per period) or cumulative (over the life of the transaction) and can apply to the outstanding or original balance. Constant default rates are typically applied to the outstanding collateral balance and are used to determine sensitivity to loss and/or return.

The Default Rate Vector is reproduced at cell I203 of the **Collateral Sheet** and the Constant/Cumulative Default Rates are found on the **Inputs Sheet**.

The Defaulted Amount is determined as the *minimum* of:

- Default Rate *multiplied by* either the Original Principal or the Outstanding Principal (depending on the Depending Original or Outstanding switch); or
- Beginning of Period Balance *plus* the Purchased Amount.

Thus, for the Period 1, Defaulted Amount in cell M205 is represented by the formula

```
"=MIN(I205*IF(Default_Original_or_Outstanding,K$104,K205),K205+
L205)".
```

Recovery Rate is the expected recovery rate when the obligor has worked out their debt. This is in reality a random variable which is strongly negatively correlated to the number of defaults in the relevant industry as well as the type of industry. As with the default distribution, though, it is more about estimating the impact against variance of a rate about a expected mean than modelling for a random recovery. The actual recovery will depend on the type of asset and the jurisdiction of the contract law.

Recovery Delay: it is unlikely that a creditor experiencing anything other than trivial problems will be able to resolve its problems in a short time frame. Real life workout periods can be anything from a few months to years. However, as a rule, the shorter the workout period assumed, the lower recoveries will be. It is therefore typical to model a delay before recovery (i.e., Recovery Lag) of anything between 6 months to 3 years, depending on the asset type and experience of the manager.

In modelling recovery delays there are two approaches:

1. assume a full recovery at the end of the delay, i.e., a simple delay; or
2. allow for partial recoveries during the period. Multi-year recoveries can often assume partial recovery in the interim. This can be modelled using a recovery vector.

Rating agency criteria for recovery amounts and timing are discussed further in Chapters 9 and 10.

6.3.2 Recovery amount using simple delay

Modelling for a simple delay in recoveries is simple but there are two main considerations: one addresses defaults at the beginning of the transaction, the second is at the end of the transaction. Ordinarily, it is a simple matter to use the offset function to look back at the prior defaults and apply the recovery rates. Cell O205 isolates the simple delay for recoveries as

```
"=IF(B205-Recovery_Lag>0,OFFSET($M$204,B205-Recovery_Lag,0)*Recovery_
Rate,0)".
```

Prior to the Recovery Lag, the recovery will be zero and after the Recovery Lag the applied recovery will be the recovery of the default in the applicable prior period. For example, if the transaction pays quarterly and there is a default at 1 year (period 4) and a recovery occurs one year later (period 8), then the recovery in period 8 will be for the default in period 4. The reader will recall that Recovery Lag is an Input as described in Chapter 5.

An important issue to be considered is the recoveries for defaults occurring at the end of the transaction, i.e., the concept that delayed recoveries potentially could occur after the final legal maturity date of the transaction. There are two main approaches to this issue: one is to try and avoid it altogether and the second is to discount the post-maturity recoveries at some predetermined rate back to the maturity date of the transaction.

6.3.3 Recovery amount using recovery vector

A flexible approach to modelling recoveries is to use a Recovery Vector to determine partial recoveries over a period. To use this technique, first create a Recovery Vector, the length of which will depend on the number of periods over which the recovery can be applied. For example, for a 3-year period of recovery on a quarterly paying transaction a horizontal vector of a length of 12 periods is created.

A fully calculated Recovery Amount formula is:

- if the current period is less than or equal to the Recovery Lag, the Recovery Amount will be zero;
- once the Recovery Lag is greater than the current period, the Recovery Amount will be the relevant Recovery Vector Rate *multiplied by* the Recovery Vector Rate.

This has not been incorporated into the **Cash Flow Model** but it can be added by the reader if desired.

6.3.4 Anticipated Recovery

For the purpose of determining collateralization ratios, it is customary to assume a minimum recovery rate that will happen in the future, i.e., it is considered unreasonable that defaulted assets will have a zero value prior to recovery. It is therefore reasonable to calculate that in the rep line.

The input for the **Anticipated Recovery Rate** is taken from the **Inputs Sheet**. The Anticipated Recovery is a cumulative recovery amount that is determined as:

- the *product of* the *sum of* Defaulted Amounts from the Period 0 to the current Period and the Anticipated Recovery Rate;
- *less* the *product of* the *sum of* Recovery, and the Anticipated Recovery Rate *divided by* the Recovery Rate.

For cell N205, in the Period 1 Anticipated Recovery is written as the formula

```
"=SUM(M$204:M205)*Anticipated_Recovery_Rate-
SUM(O$204:O205)*Anticipated_Recovery_Rate/Recovery_Rate".
```

6.3.5 Timing of defaults and recoveries

Timing of both default and recovery intra period should be considered. It is usual to assume that defaults occur at the beginning of a payment period and that no interest income is received on a defaulted security.

The default rate can be applied to the original balance or to the outstanding balance as a rate. For rating agency criteria it is often applied to the original balance while for some investor runs it may be applied to the outstanding balance. As one can deduce, defaulting the outstanding balance will usually result in lower defaults.

Timings of defaults are determined by standardized patterns, the most common of which is a spike in one year, and a steady rate for rest. The default stresses are usually applied over the first five or six years. In order to model this, vectors of default patterns are typically used and applied according to the outstanding balance.

For each pool there are, as before, columns for:

(a) Payment Date
(b) Opening Balance
(c) Interest Rate
(d) Interest Paid
(e) Principal Paid, and
(f) Closing Balance.

To that, columns are now added for:

1. Default Rate (per period)
2. Default Amount
3. Anticipated Recovery, and
4. Recovery.

Typically 1 and 2 above sit between (c) and (d) in the rep line above, and 3 and 4 sit between (d) and (e).

6.4 AMORTIZATION

The **Amortization Vector** input selects the lookup for the percentage amortization per period. There are typically two types of amortization vectors:

- A vector that amortizes each period with respect to an original outstanding notional principal of 100%, i.e., an absolute amount.
- A vector that is relative to the outstanding notional principal at the beginning of the period.

It is relatively easy to convert from one type to the other using summation, i.e., absolute percentage = relative percentage * (1 – sum of all the prior period percentages), where the percentages are percentages of nominal.

The advantages of using absolute amortization is that it is easy to calculate the average life and easy to ensure that 100% of the pool is amortized. However, it is easier to use relative amortization within the **Collateral Sheet** to accommodate additional amortizations and losses from defaults in the modelling.

> **Did you know?** Epsilon, as used here, is simply a device to avoid guarding for dividing by zero, i.e. rather than testing for zero, the bottom line is not zero, just very close to it.

The calculation for the **Amortization Amount** in the *Cash Flow Model* is determined by the Amortization Rate for the Period (the absolute amortization):

- *divided by* the conversion of the absolute amortization back into a relative amortization *plus* Epsilon (currently input at 0.0000000001)
- *multiplied by the sum of*
  o the Beginning of Period Balance and the Purchased Amount
  o *less* the Defaulted Amount

The formula in cell Q205 is given by

```
=H205/((1-IF(B205>1,SUM(OFFSET($H$205,0,0,B205-1,1)),0)+Epsilon))*
(K205-M205)".
```

Another approach, used by some of the rating agencies, is to deduct the total default amount in period one, and amortize using the original profile. **Amortization Vectors** depend on the collateral modelled and the characteristics of that collateral:

- Leveraged loans, typically have a bullet mandatory repayment, but usually do not incur prepayment penalties. It is therefore typical to either add an additional prepayment factor or to construct a vector to capture the prepayments.
- High yield bonds also have a bullet maturity profile but often have prepayment penalties for early redemption, thus a prepayment penalty curve may be sensible to build in. Additionally, unlike leveraged loans in which only part of the capital needs to be repaid, high yield bonds are typically all or nothing with regards to redemption.
- ABS bonds typically amortize like a sinking fund and are sold to investors at a "pricing speed". When modelling these assets, the "base" prepay speed for recently originated assets is considered the pricing speed at closing. Then a "fast" prepay speed of 150% of the base speed is assumed, and a "slow" prepay speed of 50% of the base case is modelled. For "seasoned" assets, i.e., more than six months after issue, it is typical to use 6-month average of actual prepays as the base rate.

6.4.1 Prepay Amount

As discussed above, leveraged loan borrowers typically have the option of prepaying their loans without penality at any time, usually as a result of refinancing more preferential terms. The rate of prepayment cannot be covenanted to and thus it is not modelled for rating agency purposes. However, a modeller will often assume a certain level of prepayments when conducting analysis for potential investors.

If the current period is less than or equal to the Prepayment End Date, the Prepay Amount is calculated as:

- Prepay Rate *divided by* Payment Frequency *multiplied by:*
  - ○ the Beginning of Period Balance
  - ○ *less* the Default Amount
  - ○ *less* the Amortization Amount

For example, in cell Q205 there is the formula

```
"=IF(B205>=Prepay_End,(Prepayment_Rate/Pay_Freq)*(Collateral!K205-
Collateral!M205-Collateral!P205),0)".
```

6.4.2 Sold Amounts

The Sold Amount is treated as the "clean up" in the *Cash Flow Model*. Thus, if the current period is less than the Collateral Liquidation Period Input then the Sold Amount is zero. Where the current period is greater than or equal to the Collateral Liquidation Period Input then the amount sold will equal the *sum of*:

- Beginning of Period Balance
- *plus* Purchased Amount
- *less* Defaulted Amount
- *less* Amortized Amount

multiplied by the Collateral Liquidation Price Input.

For Period 1, the Sold Amount on cell R205 will have the formula:

`"=IF(B205<Coll_Liquidation,0,(K205+L205-M205-Q205)*Coll_Liq_Price)"`

6.4.3 End of period balances

The End of Period Balance is simply:

- Beginning of Period Balance
- *plus* Purchased Amount
- *less* Defaulted Amount
- *less* Amortized Amount
- *less* Prepay Amount
- *less* Sold Amount *divided by* the Collateral Liquidation Price

Therefore, for period 1, the End of Period Balance calculation in cell S205 will be

`"=K205+L205-M205-P205-Q205-R205/Coll_Liq_Price"`.

6.5 MODELLING REINVESTMENT

Most managed CDOs have a reinvestment or revolving period in which the manager can invest in new assets using the redemption or sales proceeds of the original pool. The reinvestment period is typically five years or less and may be shortened by poor performance of the transaction or extended at the option of the note holders. There are significant potential risks to the transaction from reinvestment, including inability to meet asset criteria such as:

- target spread or yield;
- target credit quality;
- target weighted average recovery criteria.

Additionally, the default risk of the new investments purchased over the life of the transaction may mean larger losses than originally expected.

There are two main approaches to modelling reinvestment:

- an additional rep line;
- a cohorts approach.

6.5.1 Rep line reinvestment collateral pools

The rep line approach for reinvestment is similar to the method used for the Original Pool as it introduces a single separate pool(s) for new investments corresponding to the pool(s) of original collateral. Usually there is a single overall amortization profile and new asset purchases are added to the pool in accordance with the priority of payments or waterfall. Therefore, rows 300–399 are added for Rep Line Reinvestment Collateral Pools.

Similar to the rep line modelling for the Original Pool, the Reinvestment Pool has the following columns:

- Beginning of Period Balance
- Reinvested Amount

- Defaulted Amount
- Anticipated Recovery
- Recovery Amount
- Amortization Amount
- Prepayment Amount
- Sold Amount
- End of Period Balance

The major difference between the Reinvestment Pool and the Original Pool is that Reinvested Amount is used instead of "Purchased Amount".

The **Beginning of Period Balance** is the End of Period Balance for the Previous Period. Hence, for Period 1 the formula in cell K305 is `"=S304+L305"`.

The **Reinvested Amount** is simply a LOOKUP in the Principal Waterfall for the amounts going **To Reinvestment** based on whether the Cohorts switch is on. The formula for Period 1 in cell L305 is `"=IF(Cohorts?,0,G504)"`.

The **Defaulted Amount** during the period is modelled in Column M, in a similar fashion to the Original Pool, except the switch for Default Reinvestment needs to be checked in order to default the Reinvestment Pool, such that if reinvestment is to be defaulted, the relevant amount is the *minimum of*:

- Default Rate *multiplied by* the Beginning of Period Balance;
- Beginning of Period Balance *plus the* Reinvested Amount.

In cell M305, the formula is

`"=IF(Default_Reinvestment,MIN($I305*K305,K305+L305),0)"`.

As the reader can likely gather, not defaulting reinvestment pool(s) will result in a lower overall default rate and hence better results. However, it is normal only to default the reinvestment pool if defaulting the original pool on the outstanding balance. Defaulting both the original pool at the original balance and reinvestment will give a too severe result.

Recovery Amount and **Anticipated Recovery** arising from the defaults are modelled as previously. For example, in cell N305 the Anticipated Recovery is

```
"=SUM(M$304:M305)*Anticipated_Recovery_Rate-
SUM(O$304:O305)*Anticipated_Recovery_Rate/Recovery_Rate",
and in cell "O305", the formula found is:
"=IF(B305-Recovery_Lag>0,
OFFSET($M$304,B305-Recovery_Lag,0)
*Recovery_Rate,0)"
```

The **Amortization Amount** during the period, also modelled as previously, i.e., cell P305 is

```
"=H305/((1-IF(B305>1,SUM(OFFSET($H$305,0,0,B305-1,1)),0)+Epsilon))*
(K305-M305)".
```

The **Prepayment Amount** is calculated in a similar fashion to that in the Original Pool. For example in cell Q305 there is

```
"=IF(B305<Prepay_End,(Reinvest_Prepay/Pay_Freq)*(Collateral!K305-
Collateral!M305-Collateral!P305),0)".
```

Sold Amount, as in the Original Pool, is added to provide for modelling the value of a call on the transaction by the equity. Most transactions grant the right to collapse or call the transaction early if the note holders can be repaid in full. This is modelled in cell R305 as

```
"= IF(B305<Coll_Liquidation,0,(K305+L305-M305-P305-
Q305)*Coll_Liq_Price)".
```

The **End of Period Balance** is calculated as the sum of:

- Beginning of Period Balance
- *less* the Default Amount
- *less* Amortization Amount
- *less* Prepayment Amount
- *less* Sold Amount

For example, cell S305 has the formula

```
"=K305+L305-M305-P305-Q305-R305/Coll_Liq_Price".
```

While modelling reinvestment with a single reinvestment line is simple and effective it is not particularly flexible and may not be realistic, particularly with the amortization and default profile of the new assets. For example, if a fixed amortization profile is used, then all investments are amortized at the same time regardless of the time of their origination and/or purchase.

6.6 REINVESTMENT COHORTS

A more generic and flexible approach is to use a cohort approach. In a cohort approach, the proceeds available for reinvestment are modelled separately from each other. An overall rep line which gathers all the cohorts is fed back into the model. Hence it is relatively easy to realistically alter the amortization or default profile.

A consideration is the layout: horizontal or vertical. In considering the layout, the main considerations are: the number of reinvestment periods, which is determined by the payment frequency and the length of the reinvestment; and the number of periods in the transaction.

Unless you are using Excel 2007 or later, then the worksheet dimensions are very restricted in the number of columns compared to the number of rows (256 versus 65356).

Each cohort will be modelled with the following data:

- Initial Balance
- Reinvested Amount
- Percentage Default
- Defaulted Amount
- Anticipated Recovery
- Recovery Amount
- Amortization Percentage
- Amortization Amount
- Interest Rate
- Interest Amount

- Prepayment Amount
- Sold Amount
- Final Balance

Eight to 10 rows or columns are usually required. For a quarterly paid loan transaction with a 5-year reinvestment period, this implies 20 periods of reinvestment, and 200 rows or columns to model. In addition, a set of summary rows or columns is required. Therefore, using a column layout without gaps between each cohort will limit the number of reinvestment periods to 25 before requiring a "wraparound". Another consideration is the total number of transaction periods. A loan transaction is typically modelled for 10 to 15 years and is paid quarterly; hence 40 to 45 periods are required. However, an ABS transaction is typically 30 to 40 years in length and often pays monthly. Hence the total number of periods is between 360 and 480 and the number of reinvestment periods is typically 60. Thus, modelling an ABS transaction with monthly payments and five years' reinvestment would most likely require a "wraparound" no matter which orientation is used.

The *Cash Flow Model* addresses a loan transaction, and as such the orientation can be vertical with each cohort going from right to left. The 10 columns will be the summary columns. Label each cohort in the first column of the cohort with an ordinal, starting from 1, and use the label to index into the reinvestment proceeds to model each period of reinvestment.

Starting at row 400 there is a Cohorts Reinvestment Summary where each group of data from each of the individual cohorts is summed. Then, starting at row 500, are the Individual Reinvestment Cohorts.

As the reader will notice, the calculations for the cohorts follow along the same line as the calculations used for the rep lines.

6.7 ACCOUNTS

Prior to the Issuance Date there are various accounts that must be established with the appointed account bank. These will include:

- Principal Collection Account
- Interest Collection Account
- Payment Account
- Expense Reimbursement Account
- Unused Proceeds Account

Usually funds in these accounts are invested by the Collateral Manager in what is known as "Eligible Investments". These commonly are:

- cash;
- commercial paper or short-term securities;
- certificates of deposit or bankers' acceptances;
- market funds which allow for daily liquidation.

Eligible Investments typically are required to have maturities not later than the last day of each payment period.

6.7.1 Principal Collection Account

The Principal Collection Account acts much as the name implies. Normally the following amounts are paid into this account:

- principal payments from the collateral received at maturity, scheduled amortizations, mandatory prepayments or mandatory sinking fund payments;
- unscheduled principal repayments on collateral assets;
- amounts received upon the sale of collateral assets;
- amendment and waiver fees, late payment fees and other fees and commissions received in connection with any defaulted or non-defaulted collateral;
- recoveries on defaulted collateral;
- accrued interest purchased with principal proceeds at the time collateral is acquired;
- where the full ramp-up of the collateral has not occurred on or before the effective date, the funds in the Unused Proceeds Account;
- the unused proceeds on the effective date;
- redemption amounts of eligible investments originally acquired using funds in the Principal Collection Account;
- all other amounts to be paid to the issuer which are not required to be paid into any of the other accounts.

The following amounts are generally paid out of the Principal Collection Account:

- on payment dates, all principal proceeds to the Payment Account to the extent required for disbursement in the Principal Waterfall;
- during the reinvestment period, to the acquisition of collateral;
- at any time, to the acquisition of eligible investments;
- all earnings accrued and received, if any, on the investment of funds in the Principal Collection Account to the Interest Collection Account

Figure 6.6 provides a succinct look at the payments in and out of the Principal Collection Account.

6.7.2 Interest Collection Account

The following amounts are commonly set out to be paid into an Interest Collection Account:

- interest (excluding accrued interest purchased with principal proceeds at the time collateral is acquired) in respect of collateral and eligible investments;
- the accrued interest portion of any sale proceeds from collateral;
- recoveries over 100% of the principal amount on defaulted collateral;
- earnings accrued and received, if any, on the investment of funds in other Accounts;
- where acquired using funds in the Interest Collection Account, eligible investment redemption amounts.

From an Interest Collection Account the following payments will usually be made:

- on each payment date, all interest proceeds to the Payment Account to the extent required for disbursement in the Interest Waterfall;
- at any time, to the acquisition of eligible investments.

Figure 6.7 on page 75 illustrates the general workings of an Interest Collection Account.

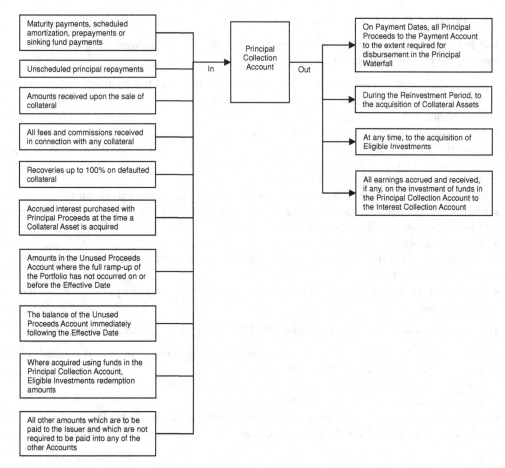

Figure 6.6 Payments in and out of Principal Collection Account

6.7.3 Expense Reimbursement Account

The following amounts are customarily paid into an Expense Reimbursement Account:

- on issuance of the CDO, amounts for the upfront fees and expenses which for various reasons (including failing to receive an invoice on or prior to the issue date) were not paid on the issuance date;
- on each payment date, usually in a rather senior payment priority of the waterfall, an amount that will bring an Expense Reimbursement Account to a stated minimum credit balance.

Payments made out of an Expense Reimbursement Account will normally include:

- at any time prior to the first payment date, any upfront fees and expenses that were not paid on the issuance date;
- at any time, in payment of any fees and expenses that have accrued and become due and payable prior to any payment date, upon receipt of invoices;

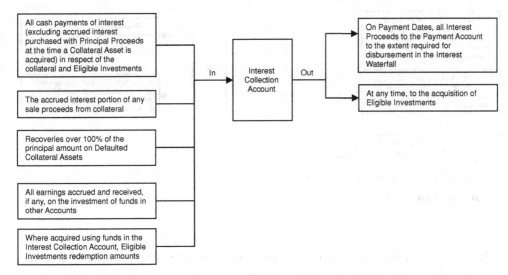

Figure 6.7 Payments in and out of an Interest Collection Account

- on each payment date, all amounts in the Expense Reimbursement Account (other than any upfront fees and expenses to the payment account for disbursement in the Interest Waterfall;
- at any time, in the acquisition of eligible investments;
- all earnings accrued and received, if any, on the investment of funds in the Expense Reimbursement Account to the Interest Collection Account.

6.7.4 Payment Account

The Payment Account acts like a clearing account. Monies are deposited into this account for the purpose of payment out according to the Interest and Principal Waterfalls. Thus, on each payment date the following are deposited into the Payment Account:

- principal proceeds to the extent required for disbursement in the Principal Waterfall;
- interest proceeds to the extent required for disbursement in the Interest Waterfall;
- amounts in the Expense Reimbursement Account (other than any upfront fees and expenses).

Payments out of the Payment Account on payment dates are disbursed in accordance with the Waterfalls. This is the only time that funds can usually be withdrawn from the Payment Account, with the exception of any earnings received on the investment of funds in eligible investments in the Payment Account. These funds are then credited to the Interest Collection Account. Figure 6.8 illustrates this.

6.7.5 Unused Proceeds Account

On issuance the proceeds of issue of the Notes remaining after the payment of the following are generally paid into the Unused Proceeds Account:

- upfront fees and expenses;
- all amounts payable for the purchase of collateral.

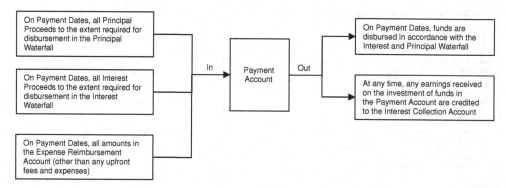

Figure 6.8   Payment Account

Payment of the following is commonly made out of the Unused Proceeds Account up to the effective date (or end of the ramp-up period):

- purchase of collateral;
- in the event that the Issuer fails to purchase the required minimum amount of collateral by the effective date, all amounts standing to the credit of the Unused Proceeds Account are usually transferred to the Principal Collection Account;
- the balance of the Unused Proceeds Account the day after the effective date; less any amount required to be paid by the issuer for any collateral agreed to be purchased prior to the effective date but where payment for such collateral is scheduled to take place after the effective date, is transferred to the Principal Collection Account;
- at any time, to the acquisition of eligible investments;
- all earnings accrued and received, if any, on the investment of funds in the Unused Proceeds Account to the Interest Collection Account.

6.8 TIMING MODELS VS. ACTUAL TIMING

6.8.1 Interest calculation periods

Interest calculation periods are used when calculating the interest due for the relevant issued Notes. The interest calculation period is modelled as it is defined: from one payment date (or the issue date) (inclusive) to the next payment date (exclusive) (Figure 6.9).

6.8.2 Payment dates

Suppose the CDO pays interest on the Notes quarterly. Each payment date will usually be a set day in each quarter (e.g., the 3rd day of February, May, August and November). The first payment date will be at some point after the issuance date.

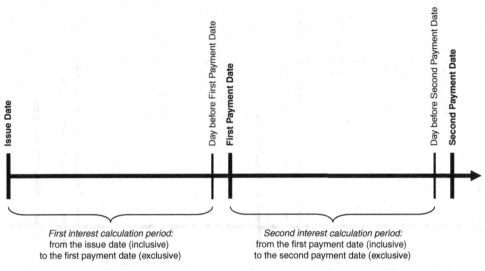

Figure 6.9

> **Did you know?** The maturity date and each redemption date will also be payment dates. Maturity date means the legal final maturity date of the Notes. Redemption dates will usually include:
> - optional redemption dates on any payment date after the expiry of the non-call period at the written request of a majority of the equity note holders
> - clean-up call redemption on any payment date where the aggregate principal amount of all /notes outstanding is less than, for example, 30% of the total amount issued
> - mandatory redemption on payment dates upon the breach of one or more coverage tests
> - redemption upon the occurrence of certain taxation events
> Redemptions following expiry of the reinvestment period as principal proceeds are received and are then applied in accordance with the Waterfall.

6.8.3 Payment periods

Payment periods are used when calculating fees and expenses such as:

- taxes;
- fees and expenses for among other things, trustees, paying agents, custody and agencies;
- senior management fees;
- junior management fees.

The payment period is defined as from one payment date (or the issue date) (inclusive) to the next payment date (exclusive) (Figure 6.10).

Unlike the definition, the payment periods are not generally modelled as they are defined. They are generally modelled as the Interest Calculation Period definition above: from one payment date (or the issue date) (inclusive) to the next payment date (exclusive).

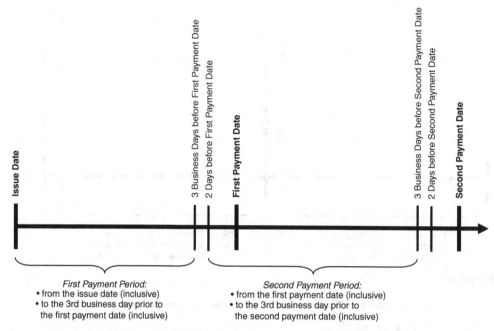

Figure 6.10

6.8.4 Timing for other calculations

For the calculation of the Incentive Management Fee, the time for calculating the Incentive Management Fee Threshold can be from the issue date (inclusive) to the applicable payment date (inclusive). This is because this involves calculating the value of the cumulative cash flow paid to the equity note holders.

6.9 SIMPLE WAREHOUSE MODELLING

Collateral models can be helpful for determining the characteristics of the collateral and tracking the collateral as it may change. There are other reasons for developing and maintaining collateral models, which are discussed further in Chapters 9, 10 and 13, where rating agency requirements, accrued interest and cash collation are examined.

The authors encourage the reader to maintain their collateral model as a separate model from their **Cash Flow Model**. This is because combining the models will often result in a large, unwieldy workbook that will have reduced performance.

Collateral models are often referred to as warehouse models. This is because the assets for a CDO are colloquially held in a "warehouse" prior to being transferred into the SPE for the CDO. The "warehouse" can be on the origination bank's balance sheet or in a separate (pre-CDO) SPE which is funded by the bank and/or first loss providers. First loss providers are generally investors who, in exchange for superior returns, will take on the obligation of losses in a warehouse in the first instance usually up to a limit.

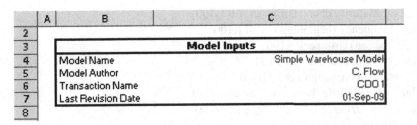

Figure 6.11   Model Inputs

A warehouse model can generally start with the following worksheets:

- an **Inputs and Portfolio Sheet** which describes the characteristics of the individual assets;
- a **Summary Sheet** to record the actual portfolio characteristics against the target portfolio characteristics.

6.9.1 The Portfolio Sheet

Looking at the *Simple Warehouse Model*, the **Inputs and Portfolio Sheet** starts in cells B3 to C7 with a basic "Model Inputs" section where the following are provided (Figure 6.11):

- Model Name (cell C3)
- Model Author (cell C4)
- Transaction Name (cell C5)
- Last Revision Date (cell C6)

Although this basic information is often overlooked, it is vital for preventing confusion when there are several versions of the same model.

An **Inputs and Portfolio Sheet** usually has the following fields for each of the assets:

- No. (an index ordinal starting in cell B100)
- Asset/Borrower Name (beginning in cell C100)
- Tranche (from cell D100)
- Identifier (CUSIP, ISIN or internal identifier code) (beginning in cell E100)
- Asset Class (starting in cell F100)
- Asset Subclass (beginning in cell G100)
- Currency (commencing in cell H100)
- Notional Amount (starting in cell I100)
- Price (at which the asset was transferred into the warehouse starts from cell J100)
- Purchased Amount (which is generally calculated as the notional amount multiplied by the price is found starting in cell K100)
- Current Balance (tracks the outstanding principal amount of the asset and begins in cell L100)
- Floating or Fixed (this refers to whether the asset pays a floating or fixed interest rate and commences in cell M100)
- Par Spread (the actual spread or coupon rate paid on the asset, starting in cell N100)
- Previous Payment Date (beginning in cell O100)
- Next Payment Date (from cell P100)

- Final Legal Maturity date (starting in cell Q100)
- Payment Frequency (beginning in cell R100)
- Index (if floating) (from cell S100)
- Roll Day (commencing in cell T100)
- Roll Convention (starting in cell U100)
- Weighted Average Life (beginning in cell V100)
- Bullet or Amortizing indicator (from cell W100)
- Country (starting in cell X100)

It also may be helpful to the modeller to have the following other information, depending on the type of assets in the collateral:

- PIKable? (starting in cell Y100)
- Synthetic? (commencing in cell Z100)
- Drawn Amount (from cell AA100)
- Undrawn Amount (beginning in cell AB100)
- Total Commitment (from cell AC100)
- Notes (starting in cell AD100)

6.9.2 Summary Sheet

The **Summary Sheet** in the *Simple Warehouse Model* provides a very simple summary of the key characteristics of the portfolio. General Characteristics are summarized in cells B4 to E11 (Figure 6.12).

These include:

- Portfolio Size (cell C6): This is simply the sum of the Notional Values from the **Portfolio Inputs Sheet**. Thus, the formula found in this cell is `"=SUM('Portfolio Inputs'!I101:I399)"`. The target amount for the portfolio size is input in cell D6.
- Number of Assets (cell C7): This calculation is a count of the number of non-empty cells in the Asset/Borrower Name column of the **Portfolio Inputs Sheet**. The formula is `"=COUNTA('Portfolio Inputs'!C101:C399)"`
- Number of Obligors (cell C8): This counts the number of unique obligors in in the Asset/Borrower Name column of the **Portfolio Inputs Sheet** using the rather long formula

```
"=SUM(IF(FREQUENCY(IF(LEN('Portfolio Inputs'!C101:C399)>0,MATCH
   ('Portfolio Inputs'!C101:C399,'Portfolio Inputs'!C101:C399,0),
   ""),IF(LEN ('Portfolio Inputs'!C101:C399)>0,MATCH('Portfolio
   Inputs'!C101:C399,'Portfolio Inputs'!C101:C399,0),""))>0,1))".
```

	Characteristic	Portfolio Level	Constraint/Covenant	Pass/Fail?
	General Characteristics			
	Portfolio Size	390,000,000	400,000,000	
	Number of Assets	100		
	Number of Obligors	85		
	Weighted Average Spread	2.85%	2.80%	PASS
	Weighted Average Life	4.28		
	Weighted Average Price	95.12%		

Figure 6.12   General Characteristics

- Weighted Average Spread (cell C9): This is calculated from the **Portfolio Inputs Sheet** as the sum of the product of each of the Par Spreads (in column N) and the Notionals (in column I) all divided by the sum of the total notional amount of the portfolio. This is expressed as

```
"=SUMPRODUCT('Inputs and Portfolio'!N101:N399,'Inputs and Portfolio
   '!I101:I399)/SUM('Inputs and Portfolio'!I101:I399)".
```

It should be noted that if there are fixed assets in the portfolio, a separate column should be created along with a "floating/fixed" options for each asset so that a similar calculation can be done to determine the weighted average coupon. In cell D9 the covenanted minimum weighted average spread is input such that in cell E9 the portfolio level is assessed to determine whether the covenant is in compliance. Cell E9 contains the formula

```
"=IF(C9>=D9,"PASS","FAIL")".
```

- Weighted Average Life (cell C10): This is calculated again from the **Portfolio Inputs Sheet** as the sum of the product of each of the Weighted Average Life amounts (in column V) and the Notionals (in column I) all divided by the sum of the total notional amount of the portfolio. The formula in cell C10 reflects this as

```
"=SUMPRODUCT('Inputs and Portfolio'!V101:V399,'Inputs and Portfolio
   '!I101:I399)/SUM('Inputs and Portfolio'!I101:I399)"
```

- Weighted Average Price (cell C11): This is calculated from the **Portfolio Inputs Sheet** as the sum of the product of each of the asset Prices (in column J) and the Notionals (in column I) all divided by the sum of the total notional amount of the portfolio. The formula is thus similar to the above calculations for the other weighted averages,

```
"=SUMPRODUCT('Inputs and Portfolio'!J101:J399,'Inputs and Portfolio
   '!I101:I399)/SUM('Inputs and Portfolio'!I101:I399)"
```

An analysis of Country Concentrations can be found in cells B14 to E44 (Figure 6.13). The Portfolio Levels in cells C16 to C43 are determined by summing the notional amounts of the assets grouped by country by the total amount of the notional assets. For example, the concentration for Australian assets in the portfolio is calculated in cell C16 by the formula

```
"=SUMIF('Inputs and Portfolio'!$X$101:$X$399,Summary!B16,'Inputs and
Portfolio'!$I$101:$I$399)/SUM('Inputs and Portfolio'
!$I$101:$I$399)".
```

The Constraint/Covenants are provided in cells D16 to D43 and an assessment of compliance of "PASS" or "FAIL" is provided in cells E16 to E43.

In the final row of the Country Concentrations section is a Total (check). The authors strongly recommend as a way to help prevent perpetuating errors. The calculation in cell C44 is simply the sum of the concentrations above in cells C16 to C43.

It should be noted that it may be quicker to determine concentrations in a portfolio by using the Pivot Table tool in Excel. While the authors have certainly used this tool on many

	Country Concentations			
Country	Portfolio Level	Constraint/Covenant	Pass/Fail?	
Australia	0.00%	0.00%	PASS	
Austria	0.00%	0.00%	PASS	
Belgium	0.00%	0.00%	PASS	
Canada	0.00%	0.00%	PASS	
Denmark	0.00%	0.00%	PASS	
Finland	0.00%	0.00%	PASS	
France	0.00%	0.00%	PASS	
Germany	0.00%	0.00%	PASS	
Greece	0.00%	0.00%	PASS	
Iceland	0.00%	0.00%	PASS	
Ireland	0.00%	0.00%	PASS	
Italy	0.00%	0.00%	PASS	
Japan	0.00%	0.00%	PASS	
Korea	0.00%	0.00%	PASS	
Liechtenstein	0.00%	0.00%	PASS	
Luxembourg	0.00%	0.00%	PASS	
The Netherlands	0.00%	0.00%	PASS	
New Zealand	0.00%	0.00%	PASS	
Norway	0.00%	0.00%	PASS	
Portugal	0.00%	0.00%	PASS	
South Africa	0.00%	0.00%	PASS	
Singapore	0.00%	0.00%	PASS	
Spain	0.00%	0.00%	PASS	
Sweden	0.00%	0.00%	PASS	
Switzerland	0.00%	0.00%	PASS	
Taiwan	0.00%	0.00%	PASS	
UK	0.00%	0.00%	PASS	
US	100.00%	100.00%	PASS	
Total (Check)	100.00%			

Figure 6.13 Country Concentrations

occasions, it is not recommended for long-term use on the **Summary Sheet** as neglecting to specifically update a pivot table can lead to incorrect concentrations being assumed. This is especially true once the model encompasses increasing amounts of information.

The Basis Concentrations (in cells B47 to E51), Currency Concentrations (in cells B54 to E59) and Asset Concentrations (in cells B62 to E67) (Figure 6.14) are all determined in the

	Basis Concentrations			
Basis	Portfolio Level	Constraint/Covenant	Pass/Fail?	
Floating	100.00%	100.00%	PASS	
Fixed	0.00%	0.00%	PASS	
Total (Check)	100.00%			

	Currency Concentrations			
Currency	Portfolio Level	Constraint/Covenant	Pass/Fail?	
USD	100.00%	100.00%	PASS	
EUR	0.00%	0.00%	PASS	
GBP	0.00%	0.00%	PASS	
Total (Check)	100.00%			

	Asset Concentrations			
Asset Type	Portfolio Level	Constraint/Covenant	Pass/Fail?	
Senior Secured Loan	91.64%	90.00%	PASS	
Second Lien Loan	3.31%	10.00%	PASS	
Structured Finance Bond	5.05%	10.00%	PASS	
Total (Check)	100.00%			

Figure 6.14 Basis Concentrations, Currency Concentrations and Asset Concentrations

	A	B	C	D	E	
69						
70		Largest Obligor Concentrations				
71		Obligor	Portfolio Level	Constraint/Covenant	Pass/Fail?	
72		Largest Obligor	2.21%	5.00%	PASS	
73		Second Largest Obligor	2.18%	4.00%	PASS	
74		Third Largest Obligor	2.15%	3.00%	PASS	
75		Fourth Largest Obligor	2.08%	3.00%	PASS	
76		Fifth Largest Obligor	2.08%	3.00%	PASS	
77						

Figure 6.15 Largest Obligor Concentrations

	A	B	C	
78				
79		Obligor Concentrations		
80		Corporate Borrower 1	1.05%	
81		Corporate Borrower 2	1.46%	
82		Corporate Borrower 3	1.51%	

Figure 6.16 Obligor Concentrations

same way as the Country Concentrations; by summing the notional amounts of the assets that meet the criteria of the desired characteristic, by the total amount of the notional assets. Again, the Contraints/Covenants are input in column D and assessed in column E.

The Portfolio Levels in the Largest Obligor Concentrations in cells C70 to E76 are ascertained using the LARGE() function (Figure 6.15). For example, the largest obligor is established in cell C72 using the formula

"=LARGE($C$80:$C$378,1)".

Similarly, the second largest Moody's Industry in cell C73 is determined with the formula

"=LARGE($C$80:$C$378,2)".

The concentrations in this section are referring to the Obligor Largest Concentrations in cells B80 to C378. Finally, covenant/constraints are input in column D and compliance with these tests is measured in column E of the table.

The Obligor Concentrations (cells B80 to B378) (Figure 6.16) are calculated, as in the sections above, in the **Summary Sheet** by summing the notional amounts of the assets grouped by industry by the total amount of the notional assets. The Asset/Borrower Names are used starting in cell C100 of the **Inputs and Portfolio Sheet**.

There are various portfolio statistics that can be determined in the **Summary Sheet**. The types of statistics that are sought will depend on the types of assets in the portfolio.

7

Basic Waterfall Modelling

7.1 BASIC WATERFALLS

This chapter will introduce the heart of any cash flow CDO model, "the Priority of Payments" or, colloquially, "the waterfall", so called because of the "trickle down" of cash to the liabilities of the CDO in order of priority.

Most CDOs have at least two waterfalls: the "Interest Priority of Payments", or "Interest Waterfall", and the "Principal Priority of Payments", or "Principal Waterfall". As the names suggest, they deal with payments made from asset interest collections and assets principal collections respectively. Occasionally transactions may have more than two waterfalls, usually in order to facilitate different priorities of payment for a change in circumstances; e.g., for unwind or enforcement proceedings. CDOs have also been issued that only have one combined collections waterfall for both interest and principal proceeds; however, these are exceedingly rare.

The waterfalls are legal descriptions that form part of the terms and conditions of the notes. They are usually found in the indenture or trust deed for the CDO and are also reproduced in the prospectus or offering memorandum. They describe how to apply collections of interest and principal from the collateral and assign them in order of priority within the transactions. Contractual covenants or promises (i.e., coverage tests) are tested in the transaction, and their compliance or otherwise will determine the priority of payments. Usually failure to meet a test will direct cash collections to the most senior investor in order to protect that investor from deteriorations in credit quality and ultimately credit losses within the portfolio. These tests are generically called the over-collateralization ("OC") tests and the interest coverage ("IC") tests; and can be directly compared to covenants in corporate loan transactions, particularly those senior secured loans lent to highly leveraged companies ("leveraged loans").

Section 7.1.1 shows an example of a typical sequential paying interest and principal waterfall (pre-enforcement) for a CLO that would be typically found in a prospectus (the inputs required to model it are found in Chapter 5).

7.1.1 Priority of payments for interest proceeds (the interest waterfall)

In this section, the application of Interest Proceeds from the Interest Collection Account is discussed. The reader is referred back to Chapter 6 for a refresher on the names and uses of the various cash accounts within a CDO. Interest Proceeds are those amounts in the Interest Collection Account that are available for distribution on payment dates. A typical CLO will have Interest Proceeds applied for each payment period on the relevant payment date to the sequential payment of:

A. any taxes;
B. accrued and unpaid fees and expenses up to a cap;
C. the Senior Collateral Management Fee due and payable and any Senior Collateral Management Fee not paid on any prior payment date (including any Collateral Management Fee Interest thereon);

D. interest due and payable on the Class A Notes;

E. interest due and payable in respect of the Class B Notes;

F. if the Class A/B OC Test is breached, to redeem the outstanding Class A Notes and, following their redemption, to redeem the outstanding Class B Notes, to the extent necessary to cause the Class A/B OC Test to be met if recalculated following such redemption. If the Class A Interest Coverage ("IC") Test is breached, to redeem the outstanding Class A/B Notes and, following their redemption, to redeem the outstanding Class B Notes, to the extent necessary to cause the Class A IC Test to be met if recalculated following such redemption;

G. interest due and payable on the Class C Notes (including any interest on Class C Deferred Interest);

H. if the Class C OC Test is breached, to redeem the outstanding Class A Notes and, following their redemption, to redeem the outstanding Class B Notes, and following their redemption, to redeem the outstanding Class C Notes, to the extent necessary to cause the Class C OC Test to be met if recalculated following such redemption. If the Class C IC Test is breached, to redeem the outstanding Class A Notes and, following their redemption, to redeem the outstanding Class B Notes and, following their redemption, to redeem the outstanding Class C Notes, to the extent necessary to cause the Class C IC Test to be met if recalculated following such redemption;

I. Class C Deferred Interest which has been capitalized;

J. interest due and payable on the Class D Notes (including any interest on Class D Deferred Interest);

K. if the Class D OC Test is breached, to redeem the outstanding Class A Notes and, following their redemption, to redeem the outstanding Class B Notes, and, following their redemption, to redeem the outstanding Class C Notes, and following their redemption, to redeem the outstanding Class D Notes, to the extent necessary to cause the Class D OC Test to be met if recalculated following such redemption. If the Class D IC Test is breached, to redeem the outstanding Class A Notes and, following their redemption, to redeem the outstanding Class B Notes and, following their redemption, to redeem the outstanding Class C Notes and, following their redemption, to redeem the outstanding Class D Notes, to the extent necessary to cause the Class D IC Test to be met if recalculated following such redemption;

L. Class D Deferred Interest which has been capitalized;

M. interest due and payable on the Class E Notes (including any interest on Class E Deferred Interest);

N. if the Class E OC Test is breached, to redeem the outstanding Class A Notes and, following their redemption, to redeem the outstanding Class B Notes and following their redemption, to redeem the outstanding Class C Notes and, following their redemption, to redeem the outstanding Class D Notes. their redemption, to redeem the outstanding Class E Notes, to the extent necessary to cause the Class E OC Test to be met if recalculated following such redemption. If the Class E IC Test is breached, to redeem the outstanding Class A Notes and, following their redemption, to redeem the outstanding Class B Notes and, following their redemption, to redeem the outstanding Class C Notes and, following their redemption, to redeem the outstanding Class D Notes, and, following their redemption, to redeem the outstanding Class E Notes, to the extent necessary to cause the Class E IC Test to be met if recalculated following such redemption;

O. Class E Deferred Interest which has been capitalized;

P. any unpaid fees and expenses to the extent not paid in paragraph B above;

Q. the Junior Collateral Management Fee due and payable on such payment date and any Junior Collateral Management Fee not paid on any prior payment date including any Collateral Management Fee Interest thereon;

R. during the reinvestment period, if the reinvestment diversion test is breached, some or all of the funds that otherwise would be paid in paragraphs S and T below may be diverted at the collateral manager's discretion to purchase additional assets;[1]

S. payment to the Class F Notes until the aggregate paid to the Class F Note holders exceeds the original principal amount of the Class F Notes and the Class F Note holders have received an Internal Rate of Return of 12% for the period from the Issue date to such payment date; and

T. 20% of all remaining interest proceeds after taking account of amounts payable under paragraphs A to S above to the payment of the Incentive Management Fee and (ii) 80% of all remaining interest proceeds after taking account of amounts payable under paragraphs A to S above as interest on the Class F Notes.

As described above there are effectively three general classes of notes:

- Senior Notes;
- Deferrable Mezzanine Notes;
- Residual, Junior or Equity Notes or Interests.

Senior notes are structured to pay timely interest and principal to their investors. Deferrable mezzanine notes are structured to provide credit enhancement to the transaction by providing for the diversion of interest due and payable to mezzanine and junior notes, to pay principal to the senior notes. These notes are often described as PIK-able, or payable-in-kind notes. That is to say, interest due but currently not paid is added to the principal of the note outstanding in a similar fashion to a negative amortization feature on option ARMs. Usually the current interest on a PIK-able note is paid prior to its associated coverage test, including the interest on deferred interest. The deferred and past due interest is usually repaid after the coverage test and before the current interest of a more junior note. Junior notes typically receive the excess interest income after paying all the interest, expenses and coverage test breaches above them.

7.1.2 Priority of payments for principal proceeds or principal waterfall

The contents and purpose of the Principal Collection Account were described in Chapter 6. Principal proceeds are those amounts in the Principal Collection Account that are available for distribution on payment dates. Principal proceeds would commonly be applied for each payment period on the relevant payment date to the sequential payment of:

A. to the payment of the following amounts to the extent not paid in the Interest Waterfall:
   1. any taxes;
   2. accrued and unpaid fees and expenses up to a cap;
   3. the Senior Collateral Management Fee due and payable and any Senior Collateral Management Fee not paid on any prior payment date including any Collateral Management Fee Interest thereon;

---

[1] Reinvestment diversion tests are found in some CLOs. It should be noted that this is not usually modelled in a cash flow model as it is discretionary.

4. interest due and payable on the Class A Notes;

5. interest due and payable in respect of the Class B Notes;

6. where the Class A/B OC Test is breached, to redeem the outstanding Class A Notes, and following their redemption, to redeem the outstanding Class B Notes, to the extent necessary to cause the Class A/B OC Test to be met if recalculated following such redemption and if the Class A/B IC Test is breached, to redeem the outstanding Class A Notes and following their redemption in full, to redeem the outstanding Class B Notes, to the extent necessary to cause the Class A/B IC Test to be met if recalculated following such redemption;

7. if the Class C OC Test is breached, to redeem the outstanding Class A Notes and following their redemption, to redeem the outstanding Class B Notes and following their redemption, to redeem the outstanding Class C Notes, to the extent necessary to cause the Class C OC Test to be met if recalculated following such redemption and if the Class C IC Test is breached, to redeem the outstanding Class A Notes and following their redemption, to redeem the outstanding Class B Notes and following their redemption, to redeem the outstanding Class C Notes, to the extent necessary to cause the Class C IC Test to be met if recalculated following such redemption;

8. if the Class D OC Test is breached, to redeem the outstanding Class A Notes and following their redemption, to redeem the outstanding Class B Notes and following their redemption, to redeem the outstanding Class C Notes and following their redemption, to redeem the outstanding Class D Notes, to the extent necessary to cause the Class D OC Test to be met if recalculated following such redemption. If the Class D IC Test is breached, to redeem the outstanding Class A Notes and, following their redemption, to redeem the outstanding Class B Notes and, following their redemption, to redeem the outstanding Class C Notes and, following their redemption, to redeem the outstanding Class D Notes, to the extent necessary to cause the Class D IC Test to be met if recalculated following such redemption;

B. during the reinvestment period, all remaining Principal Proceeds shall be applied to the acquisition of collateral;

C. on and after the last day of the reinvestment period, to redeem the outstanding Class A Notes;

D. on and after the last day of the reinvestment period, to redeem the outstanding Class B Notes;

E. if the Class A Notes and the Class B Notes have been redeemed, that element of the principal of the Class C Notes that represents Class C Deferred Interest which has been capitalized, only to the extent not paid in paragraph I of the Interest Waterfall and to redeem the outstanding Class C Notes;

F. if the Class A Notes, the Class B Notes and the Class C Notes have been redeemed, the interest due and payable on the Class D Notes (including any interest on the Class D Deferred Interest), only to the extent not paid in paragraph J in the Interest Waterfall and to redeem the outstanding Class D Notes;

G. if the Class A Notes, the Class B Notes, the Class C Notes and the Class D Notes have been redeemed, the interest due and payable in respect of the Class E Notes (including any interest on the Class E Deferred Interest), only to the extent not paid in paragraph M of the Interest Waterfall and to redeem the outstanding Class E Notes;

H. any unpaid Fees and Expenses to the extent not paid in paragraphs B and P in the Interest Waterfall;

I. the Junior Collateral Management Fee due and payable and any Junior Collateral Management Fee not paid on any prior payment date including any Collateral Management Fee Interest thereon, to the extent not paid in paragraph R in the Interest Waterfall;

J. on and after the last day of the reinvestment period, to the Class F Note-holders until the Incentive Management Fee Threshold has been reached; and

K. on and after the last day of the reinvestment period, (i) 20% of the principal proceeds remaining after taking account of payments pursuant to paragraphs A to J above of the Principal Waterfall to the payment of the Incentive Management Fee and (ii) 80% of the principal proceeds remaining after taking account of payments pursuant to paragraphs A to J of the Principal Waterfall the Class F Noteholders.

7.1.3 Post enforcement priority of payments

There may also be a Post Enforcement Priority of Payments to allocate collections in a different priority following an event of default.

The events of default for a CDO will generally include:

- the issuer failing to pay any due and payable interest or principal after allowing for a small grace period of a few business days (to allow for delays of a technical nature) on any:
  - Class A Notes, or following their redemption,
  - Class B Notes, or following their redemption,
  - Class C Notes, or following their redemption,
  - Class D Notes, or following their redemption,
  - Class E Notes, or following their redemption,
  - Class F Notes;
- if the issuer does not perform or comply with certain of its covenants, warranties or other agreements under the Notes or the transaction documents (other than the failure to meet any coverage tests);
- changes in the legal status of the issuer, e.g., if the issuer were to become subject to registration as an investment company for the purposes of the United States Investment Company Act;
- changes in the tax status of the issuer, i.e., the issuer becomes domiciled "on-shore" for tax purposes;
- if insolvency proceedings are initiated against the issuer;
- if it becomes illegal or unlawful for the issuer to perform or comply with its material obligations under the Notes;
- in some CDOs, if there are breaches of minimum coverage ratios at or below a critical threshold (usually the senior attachment point). In some instances, and often controversially, the principal balances in the calculation of these ratios are haircut for downgraded assets.

7.1.4 Acceleration

Where an event of default occurs, at the option of the most senior class of notes outstanding, usually all the Notes are immediately due and payable at their "redemption prices" together

Did you know? Post-Enforcement Priorities of Payment: The net proceeds from enforcement of the security interest over the collateral or upon its realisation, is often distributed with the following priorities to the payment of:

a)   fees, costs, charges, expenses and liabilities incurred by the trustee or any receiver in connection with the enforcement of the security or the early redemption of the Notes;
b)   accrued and unpaid fees and expenses;
c)   any Senior Collateral Management Fee due and payable (plus any Collateral interest thereon);
d)   interest due and payable on the Class A Notes;
e)   redemption of the Class A Notes;
f)   interest due and payable on the Class B Notes (including any Class B Deferred Interest);
g)   redemption of the Class B Notes;
h)   interest due and payable on the Class C Notes (including any Class C Deferred Interest);
i)   redemption of the Class C Notes;
j)   interest due and payable on the Class D Notes (including any Class D Deferred Interest);
k)   redemption of the Class D Notes;
l)   interest due and payable on the Class E Notes (including any Class E Deferred Interest);
m)   redemption of the Class E Notes;
n)   accrued and unpaid fees and expenses to the extent not paid under paragraph (b) above;
o)   any amount payable to the collateral manager comprising, resulting from or referable to, any tax liability;
p)   any junior collateral management fee due and payable (plus any interest thereon); and
q)   the balance, if any, to the Class F Notes.

with accrued interest up to the date of redemption.[2] This is known as "acceleration" of the Notes.[3]

For the Class A to Class E Notes, "redemption prices" are usually 100% of the principal outstanding, and for the Class F Notes, the aggregate proceeds of liquidation of the collateral or realization of the security remaining in accordance with the Post-Enforcement Priorities of Payment described below.

Once the Notes become subject to acceleration the collateral can be liquidated to pay down the Notes, so long as the redemption prices are paid for all the notes.

7.2 LAYOUT AND DESIGN

As discussed in Chapter 3, the layout of the **Waterfall Sheet** in the *Cash Flow Model* is vertical and left to right (Figure 7.1). It is designed to have a summary at the top and various components starting at each of 100, 200, 300, etc. Thus, the following sections have been created:

- Row 100: Liabilities Cash Flows
- Row 200: Fees and Expenses Cash Flows
- Row 300: Interest Waterfall
- Row 400: Interest Waterfall (Available Funds After Payment)
- Row 500: Interest Waterfall Calculations

---

[2] The exception to this is where an event of default occurs due to insolvency proceedings: in this case there is an automatic acceleration of maturity of the Notes.

[3] Acceleration can generally be withdrawn, where the event(s) of default has been cured or waived, the senior-most class of note holders agree, and where the Issuer has deposited with the Trustee a sum sufficient to pay:

(A) all overdue payments of interest and principal on the Notes;
(B) all due but unpaid taxes owing by the issuer;
(C) all unpaid fees and expenses;
(D) the total amount of any unpaid senior collateral management fee; and
(E) all amounts due and payable under any hedge agreements.

Liabilities Cash Flows

Periods			Vectors		Principal Beginning Period Balance	Interest Due
Period	Dates	Day Count	Interest Rate			
0	03/09/2009	0.00	0.00%		278,000,000	
1	08/12/2009	0.27	4.23%		278,000,000	3,432,373

Fees and Expenses Cash Flows

Periods			Vectors		Taxes Due	Taxes Paid
Period	Dates	Day Count	Interest Rate			
0	03/09/2009	0.00	0.00%		-	-
1	08/12/2009	0.27	4.23%		-	-

Interest Waterfall

Periods			Vectors		Taxes Paid	Trustee/Admin Fees Paid
Period	Dates	Day Count	Interest Rate			
0	03/09/2009					
1	08/12/2009	0.27	4.23%		-	36,927

Interest Waterfall (Available Funds After Payment)

Periods			Interest Proceeds Available		Taxes Paid	Trustee/Admin Fees Paid
Period	Dates	Day Count				
0	03/09/2009	0.00	-		-	-
1	08/12/2009	0.27	7,508,679		7,508,679	7,471,752

Interest Waterfall Calculations

Periods			Vectors		Taxes Due	Trustee/Admin Fee Due
Period	Dates	Day Count	Interest Rate			
0	03/09/2009	0.00	0.00%		-	-
1	08/12/2009	0.27	4.23%		-	36,927

Principal Waterfall

Periods					Taxes Paid	Trustee/Admin Fees Paid
Period	Dates	Day Count				
0	03/09/2009	0.00				
1	08/12/2009	0.27			-	-

Principal Waterfall (Available Funds After Payment)

Periods			Principal Proceeds Available		Taxes Paid	Trustee/Admin Fees Paid
Period	Dates	Day Count				
0	03/09/2009	0.00	-		-	-
1	08/12/2009	0.27	716,055		716,055	716,055

Principal Waterfall Calculations

Periods					Taxes Due	Trustee/Admin Fee Due
Period	Dates	Day Count				
0	03/09/2009	0.00			-	-
1	08/12/2009	0.27				

Over Collateralization Tests

Periods					Class A & Class B OC Coverage		
Period	Dates	Day Count	Over-collateralization Coverage Numerator	Over-collateralization Coverage Denominator	Over-collateralization Coverage Ratio	Interest Over-collateralization Coverage Shortfall
0	03/09/2009	0.00	396,000,000	312,000,000	126.92%	-
1	08/12/2009	0.27	396,000,000	312,000,000	126.92%	-

Interest Coverage Tests

Periods					Class A & Class B Interest Coverage		
Period	Dates	Day Count	Interest Coverage Numerator	Interest Coverage Denominator	Interest Coverage Ratio	Interest Coverage Shortfall
0	03/09/2009	0.00				
1	08/12/2009	0.27	7,366,248	3,883,893	189.66%	-

End

Figure 7.1   Waterfall Sheet

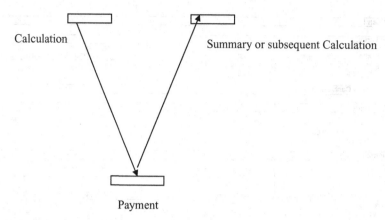

Figure 7.2 Basic cell referencing.

- Row 600: Principal Waterfall
- Row 700: Principal Waterfall (Available Funds After Payment)
- Row 800: Principal Waterfall Calculations
- Row 900: Over-Collateralization Tests
- Row 1000: Interest Coverage Tests

A detailed explanation of each section is given later in this chapter.

As mentioned previously, calculations should flow left to right and top to bottom to avoid the possibility of circular references. That is to say, the precedents for a particular cell (as disclosed by the auditing toolbars) should be to the left and/or above a cell. To state this another way, a cell above can reference a cell below but that cell should be to the left of it.

Figure 7.2 shows the basic ordering of cell references recommended in order to avoid circular references.

Ideally these basic design rules should be followed as closely as possible. Comparing this with Figure 7.3, it can be seen that an alternative scheme, i.e., no scheme at all, invites the problem of circular references, which are the scourge of any modeller's existence.

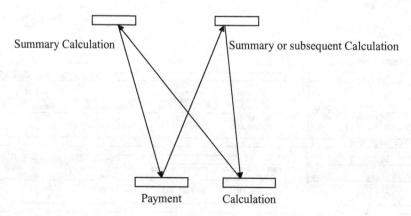

Figure 7.3 Circular references

7.3 AVOIDING NEGATIVE VALUES

The basis behind all the waterfall calculations is to compare the available funds with the due payment and pay the minimum. A simple method is to use the MIN() function, which takes the minimum of list of number and returns the lowest. An issue with just using MIN() is one of negative numbers. Negative numbers are usually indicative of an error in the model, as generally there is no provision to borrow as would be the case indicated by a negative number. A design question for a modeller is whether or not to guard for them. It is quite a common practice to use a combination of the MIN() and MAX() functions to provide a zero guard, for example, guarding the MIN() calculation with MAX() using MAX(MIN(a,b),0). However, an alternative approach may be to use the MEDIAN() function. e.g., MEDIAN(Available Funds, Calculations of Funds Due, 0), thus returning the middle number.

> **Did you know?** MEDIAN() is a statistical function that returns middle number when numbers are ranked from lowest to highest. If the number of observations are odd it will return the middle number, however if the number observations is even it will average the middle two values. Also if negative numbers appear it may return 0, masking the error in the model.

7.4 TIMING MODELLED VS. ACTUAL TIMING

As explained in Chapter 6, Interest Calculation Periods and payment periods for the purposes of modelling are from one payment date (or the issue date) (inclusive) to the next payment date (exclusive).

7.5 LIABILITIES CASH FLOWS

This section describes the actual Excel formulas used in the **Waterfall Sheet**. Starting in Row 100, the following is provided from left to right:

- Periods:
  - Periods
  - Dates
  - Day Count

  The **Dates** and **Day Count** are taken from the "Dates" section of the **Vectors Sheet**

- Vectors:
  - Interest Rate

The **Interest Rate** is a lookup from the **Floating Interest Rate Vector** input from the **Input Sheet** to the **Vectors Sheet**, Interest Rate Vectors section, and indexed to the relevant Period. In order to index the per period index interest rate from the interest vector, the HLOOKUP() function is used. For example, in cell F105 on the **Waterfall Sheet**, the formula is

```
"=HLOOKUP(Tranches_Interest_Vector, Interest_Rate_Vectors,
$B105+2,FALSE)"
```

A section is provided for each Class of Note containing the following columns:

- Principal Beginning Period Balance
- Interest Due[4]
- Interest Paid
- Interest Past Due[5]
- Interest Past Due Paid
- Principal Paid
- Principal End Period Balance
- Total Payments

Using the Class A Note as an example, the **Principal Beginning Period Balance** in Period 0 is equal to the Class A Issuance Amount, which in the *Cash Flow Model* is shown cell H104, `"= Tranche_1_Amount"`

After Period 1, the **Principal Beginning Period Balance** is equal to the previous period's **Principal End of Period Balance**. Hence, cell H105 contains the formula `"= M104"`

The **Interest Due** is calculated as the

- *sum of* the Principal Beginning Period Balance and the Interest Past Due
- *multiplied by* the Interest Rate plus the spread
- *multiplied by* the Day Count
- *plus* the Interest Past Due if the tranche is not PIKable.

For example for Period 1, in cell I105 there is the formula:

`"=(H105+K104)*($F105+(Tranche_1_Spread/10000))*$D105+K104*NOT`
`(Tranche_1_PIK?"`

The **Interest Paid** for the tranche is calculated as the *sum of*:

- the Interest Paid in the Interest Waterfall and
- the Interest Paid in the Principal Waterfall

Again for Period 1, the Class A Interest Paid is in cell J105, as `"= L305+L605"`

Interest Past Due is simply determined as:

- Interest Due
- *less* Interest Paid
- *plus* previous period's Interest Past Due where the tranche is PIKable.

Cell K105, contains the formula for period 1, i.e., `"= I105-J105+K104*Tranche_1_PIK?"`

The **Principal Paid** is calculated the sum of:

- Principal Paid in the Principal Waterfall
- *plus* the Interest Cures in the Interest Waterfall
- *plus* the Principal Cures in the Principal Waterfall.

Cell L105 has the formula for period 1 as `"=S605+AK305+AL605"`.

---

[4] Interest Due is not included for the equity notes.
[5] Interest Past Due is not included for the equity notes.

The **Principal End Balance** is calculated simply:

- Principal Beginning Period Balance
- *less* Principal Paid

Referring, for example to the first period, cell M105, this contains `"=H105-L105"`.

For period 0, the **Total Payments** is the investor's outlay, i.e., the negative value of the Principal Beginning Period Balance. Thereafter, it is the per period:

- Interest Paid
- *plus* Principal Paid

as evidenced in cell N105, as `"=J105+L105"`.

These calculations are then repeated for each of the other tranches, except the equity notes. As the equity notes are paid with the residual cash flows, the Interest Due and the Interest Past Due are not applicable. For Class C, D and E Notes, Past Due Interest Due and Past Due Interest Paid to the Class C, Class D and Class E Notes must be included in the calculations.

7.6 FEES AND EXPENSES CASH FLOWS

The Fees and Expenses Due are those fees, expenses and indemnity amounts that will be paid during the life of the deal (as opposed to the upfront fees paid at the issuance or closing of the CDO). They may include fees for the trustee, agent, collateral administrator, accountant, legal, corporate administrator, rating agency, stock exchange, listing agent, liquidation agent and any other persons' fees and expenses in relation to the CDO Notes or collateral.

The section for ongoing fees and expenses starts in Row 20, and covers:

- taxes;
- trustee/administration fees;
- senior management fee;
- junior management fee.

The **Taxes Due** (if any) are usually fixed amounts, due and payable per annum, and are calculated as the Taxes input multiplied by the Day Count. For Period 1, by way of example, cell H205 contains `"= Taxes*D205"`. The **Taxes Paid** are calculated as the *sum of*

- Taxes Paid senior in the Interest Waterfall
- Taxes Paid senior in the Principal Waterfall

Again for period 1, cell I205 contains the following formula, `"=H305+Y305+H605+AA605"`.

While some fees are fixed and independent of the asset balances (i.e., rating agency monitoring fees, corporate administration fees, etc.), other costs are linked to the asset balances held by the trustee and custodian. These fees include the custody fees, trustee fees/collateral administrator fees, and management fees. These fees can be based upon:

(a) beginning of the period balance;
(b) end of period balance; or
(c) average balance over the period.

There are even variations in how the average balance is calculated; whether it is a simple average of balance on the first and last days versus a weighted average balance for the entire period. As the difference between either approach from a modelling perspective will typically not significantly affect the ratings or the equity cash flows, the ***Cash Flow Model*** demonstrates the simple average approach.

Trustee/Admin Fees Due is calculated by first calculating:

- the average of the beginning and the end balance in the original collateral pool *plus* the average of the beginning and end balance of the reinvestment collateral pool
- *multiplied by* the Running Trustee/Admin Fees Input (and dividing this by 10 000 because the input is expressed in basis points) and
- *multiplied by* the day count.

Accordingly, for the first period, the formula in cell J205 applies and is reproduced below as

```
"=(AVERAGE(Collateral!$K105,Collateral!$S105)+AVERAGE(Collateral!
$Y105,Collateral!$AG105))*(Running_Trustee_Admin_Fees/10000)*$D205".
```

It is usually a rating agency requirement to subject these expenses to a cap relating to the extent they are paid senior in the Waterfall, to ensure that the amounts can be pre-determined and will not affect the payments to the notes. Payments in excess of the cap are paid junior in the Waterfall, after the rated notes but usually before the equity. It is usual to run the model at the cap even though this is typically in excess of the anticipated regularly incurred expenses. The Senior Fees and Expenses Cap are factored in when the Fees and Expenses Paid are determined in the Interest Waterfall

The **Trustee/Admin Fees Paid** is determined by the *sum of*:

- Trustee/Admin Fees Paid senior in the Interest Waterfall
- Trustee/Admin Fees Paid junior in the Interest Waterfall
- Trustee/Admin Fees Paid senior in the Principal Waterfall
- Trustee/Admin Fees Paid junior in the Principal Waterfall

Hence, for example for the first period, cell K205 contains `"=I305+Z305+I605+AB605"`.

The **Senior Collateral Management Fee Due** is usually defined as an annual percentage fee payable each payment date to the Collateral Manager. It is based on the sum of the average of beginning- and end-of-period balances of (i) Collateral (generally excluding defaulted collateral) and (ii) cash in the Principal Collection Account and Unused Proceeds Account (and may also sometimes include the Interest Proceeds Account). It is typically calculated using the day count fraction for the CDO liabilities

In the **Waterfall Sheet**, the **Senior Collateral Management Fee Due** for each period is calculated in a similar fashion as the **Trustee/Admin Expenses**:

- the *sum* of the average amount at the beginning of period and the end of period of the principal balances in both the original collateral pool(s) and reinvestment collateral pool(s)
- *multiplied by* the Senior Management Fee Input (and again dividing this by 10 000 because the input is expressed in basis points)
- *multiplied by* the day count.

Therefore for Period 1, the calculation can be expressed as the following Excel formula in cell L205:

```
"=(AVERAGE(Collateral!$K105,Collateral!$S105)+AVERAGE(Collateral!
$Y105,Collateral!$AG105))*(Sr_Mgt_Fee/10000)*$D205+(L204-M204)+(L204-
M204)*$D205*(F205+Int_On_Unpaid_Mgt_Fees*10000)".
```

The **Senior Management Fee Paid** is the *sum of*:

- Senior Management Fee Paid in the Interest Waterfall
- Senior Management Fee Paid in the Principal Waterfall

For Period 1, cell M205 contains `"=K305+K605"`.

The **Junior Collateral Management Fee Due** is usually defined in a comparable way as the Senior Collateral Management Fee. That is, an annual percentage fee payable each payment date to the Collateral Manager based on the average of the beginning- and end-of-period (i) Collateral balances (usually excluding defaulted collateral) and (ii) balances in the Principal Collection Account and Unused Proceeds Account. It is calculated based on the day count fraction for the CDO notes.

The **Junior Collateral Management Fee Due** for each period is calculated as:

- the average amount of the beginning-of-period and the end-of-period balances in the original collateral pool(s)
- *plus* the average amount of the beginning-of-period and end-of-period balance of the reinvestment collateral pool
- *multiplied* by the Junior Management Fee Input (divided by 10 000 because the fee input is expressed in basis points) and
- *multiplied* by the day count.

For example, the period 1 fee is calculated in cell N205, and includes any of the Junior Collateral Management Fees not paid on any prior Payment Date and any interest thereon is also added to the calculation,

```
"=(AVERAGE(Collateral!$K105,Collateral!$S105)+AVERAGE(Collateral!
$Y105,Collateral!$AG105))*(Jr_Mgt_Fee/10000)*$D205+(N204-O204)+(N204-
O204)*D205*(F205+Int_On_Unpaid_Mgt_Fees/10000)".
```

The Junior Management Fee Paid is the *sum of*:

- Junior Management Fee Paid in the Interest Waterfall
- Junior Management Fee Paid in the Principal Waterfall.

So, for Period 1, cell O205 holds `"=AA305+AC605"`.

7.7 INTEREST WATERFALL

The payments made in the Interest Waterfall are set out in the section starting at Row 300. The calculations in the payment section are calculated using the MEDIAN() function to return the smallest number bounded by zero and the lesser of the available funds and the payment due, i.e.:

- the Available Funds;
- the Calculation of Funds Due;
- zero

For the **Taxes Paid** the calculation will be the *median of*:

- Interest Proceeds Available in the Interest Waterfall (Available Funds after Payment)
- Taxes Due from the Interest Waterfall Calculations.
- zero

For Period 1, cell H305 contains `"= MEDIAN(F405,H505,0)"`, where F405 is the available funds, and H505 is the amount to be paid.

The **Trustee/Admin Fees Paid** calculation has the Senior Trustee/Admin Fees Cap built in, and as such it is determined by the *median of*:

- Available Funds after Payment of the Taxes Paid
- the *minimum of*:
  o the annual Senior Trustee/Admin fees Expense Cap *multiplied by* the Day Count, or
  o Trustee/Admin Fee Due from the Interest Waterfall Calculations
- zero.

Cell I305 contains the Period 1 calculation, i.e., `"=MEDIAN($H405,MIN(Sr_Tee_Fees_Exp_Cap*D305,I505),0)"`, where H405 is the available funds, D305 is the accrual period, and I505 is the amount to be paid. Currently, hedge payments are not being considered. For a discussion of hedging in CDOs see Chapter 11.

In each case, for the Senior Management Fee Paid, the Interest Paid and the Deferred Interest Paid for the various classes, the Junior Taxes Paid, the Junior Trustee/Admin Fees and the Junior Management Fee Paid, the calculation is similar to that of the Taxes Paid, in that it is the median of:

- the Interest Proceeds Available after the payment of the preceding Interest Waterfall liability
- the payment due from the Interest Waterfall Calculations
- zero.

To illustrate the Senior Management Fee Paid for Period 1, see cell K305 where the calculation is expressed as `"= MEDIAN(J405,K505,0)"`, where J405 is the available funds, and K505 is the calculated amount.

Next is the Class A and Class B interest. As these are non-PIKable or non-deferrable tranches, that is to say they must pay their interest current, they appear before any coverage tests.

Class A Interest Paid is calculated by taking the MEDIAN() of the available funds and the **Class A Interest Due**, and zero. For the first period this is illustrated in cell L305, as the formula `"=MEDIAN(K405,L505,0)"`, where K405 is the available funds and L505 is the calculated interest due.

Class B Interest Paid is calculated in a similar fashion. By way of example, for the first period, see cell M305, which has the formula `"=MEDIAN(L405,M505,0)"`, with L405 being the available funds and M505 the calculated interest due.

The **Class A/B Coverage Shortfall to Principal Paydown** is determined by the *median of*:

- the Interest Proceeds Available after the payment of the preceding Interest Waterfall liability
- the *maximum of*:
  o the OC Coverage Shortfall from the Over-Collateralization Tests Section
  o the Interest Coverage Shortfall from the Interest Coverage Section
  o zero.

Illustrating the calculation using Period 1 as an example, cell O305 holds `"=MEDIAN(N405,MAX(I1005,I905,0),0)"`, where N405 is the available funds, I1005 is the interest shortfall calculation and I905 is the principal shortfall calculation.

The current **Class C Interest Due** is paid prior to the Class C Coverage Test. As Class C is a PIK-able tranche, only the current and not the deferred interest is paid. For the first period, the interest due is calculated in cell P505, and the available funds to pay are in O405; as before the actual interest paid is given by the equation in cell P305, as `"=MEDIAN(O405,P505,0)"`.

Similarly, the Class **C Coverage Shortfall to Principal Paydown** is calculated as the *median of*:

- the Interest Proceeds Available after the payment of the preceding Interest Waterfall liability, the Class B Interest Paid
- the *maximum of*:
  - ○ OC Coverage Shortfall from the Over-Collateralization Tests Section
  - ○ IC Shortfall from the Interest Coverage Section
  - ○ zero
- zero

The Excel formula for Period 1, shown in cell Q305, `"=MEDIAN(P405,MAX (MAX(Q1005,R905,0),0),0)"`, where P405 is the available funds, Q1005 is the interest shortfall calculation, R905 is the principal shortfall calculation.

In an Interest Waterfall, deferred interest is typically paid after the associated test. The **Class C Deferred Interest** is the interest not paid from previous periods, which is effectively capitalized to the outstanding Class C notional. The formula required to pay the **Class C Deferred Interest Paid** amount is shown in cell R305, utilizing the formula `"=MEDIAN(Q405,R505,0)"`, where Q405 is the available funds and R505 is the deferred and unpaid interest from the previous period; which in this case is stored in cell AA104.

The current **Class D Interest Paid** is next in the waterfall and, like the Class C Interest, is only the current due and payable interest, and excludes any deferred interest from previous periods. The formula for the payment is similar to other payments in the waterfall, and is, for example in the first period, given by the formula in cell S305, i.e. `"=MEDIAN(R405,S505,0)"`, where R405 is the available funds and S505 is the calculated amount.

The **Class D Coverage Shortfall to Principal Paydown** is similarly the *median of*:

- the Interest Proceeds Available after the payment of the preceding Interest Waterfall liability, the Class D Interest Paid
- the *maximum of*:
  - ○ OC Coverage Shortfall from the Over-Collateralization Tests Section
  - ○ IC Shortfall from the Interest Coverage Section
  - ○ zero
- zero.

Cell T305 contains the formula for the Period 1 as, `"=MEDIAN(S405,MAX(MAX (Y1005,AA905,0),0),0)"`, where S405 is the available funds, Y1005 is the interest shortfall, AA905 is the principal shortfall.

The **Class D Deferred Interest Paid**, like the Class C Deferred Interest, is paid after the Class D Coverage test. The formula again is the MEDIAN() of the available funds and the calculated amount due which is shown for the first period in cell U305, and contains the following formula: `"=MEDIAN(T405,U505,0)"`.

The current **Class E Interest Paid** is paid prior to the Class E coverage tests in the waterfall, and similarly to the Class C and Class D Interest, it is only the current interest. The formula for the payment is similarly formed, and is given, for example in the first period, by the formula in cell V305, i.e, `"=MEDIAN(U405,V505,0)"`, where U405 is the available funds and V505 is the calculated amount.

Finally, the **Class E Coverage Shortfall to Principal Paydown** is similarly calculated as the *median of*:

- the Interest Proceeds Available after the payment of the preceding Interest Waterfall liability, the Class E Interest Paid
- the maximum of:
  - OC Coverage Shortfall from the Over-Collateralization Tests Section
  - IC Shortfall from the Interest Coverage Section
  - zero
- zero.

Using as before the Period 1 calculation to illustrate, cell W305 contains the following Excel formula, `"=MEDIAN(V405,MAX(MAX(AG1005,AJ905,0),0)"` where V405 is the available funds, AG1005 is the interest shortfall calculation, AJ905 is the over-collateralization test shortfall.

The **Class E Deferred Interest** Paid is paid subsequent to the test but prior to any junior expenses and or equity payments. The payment is the minimum of the available funds and the calculated due payment, illustrated for the first period in cell X305 by the formula `"=MEDIAN(W405,X505,0)"`, where W405 is the available funds and X505 is the calculated due amount.

Junior Expenses are paid next and see above for the calculation.

The **Incentive Fee Paid** and the **Class F Interest Paid** as "left-over" payments are calculations as the *maximum of*:

- Payment Due from the Interest Waterfall Calculations
- zero.

Therefore, the Period 1 Incentive Fee Paid is, cell AB305 holds `"=MAX(AC505,0)"` and for the Period 1 Class F Interest Paid, cell AC305 contains `"=MAX(AB405,0)"`.

7.7.1 Interest check

At the end of the Interest Waterfall section in AE303, AF303 and AG303 is a small audit check, checking that all the cash coming into the transaction from the assets is allocated to the liabilities. If there are no errors or omissions, the difference between the Interest Cash In and the Interest Cash Out should always equal 0.

The **Interest Cash In** is the Aggregate Interest Collections from the **Collateral Sheet** in the Collateral Summary Section.

The **Interest Cash Out** is the sum of all of the payment of interest proceeds out in this Interest Waterfall Section.

The **Difference** calculation is equal to the **Interest Cash In** *minus* the **Interest Cash Out.** To highlight any discrepencies and make them easy to see, the cell has conditional formatting to highlight the font in red when a value appears which is not equal to zero.

7.7.2 Interest cures

Cures Paid are the *sum of* the following amounts in the Interest Waterfall in cells AJ305:AP384:

- Class A/B Coverage Shortfall to Principal Paydown
- Class C Coverage Shortfall to Principal Paydown
- Class D Coverage Shortfall to Principal Paydown
- Class E Coverage Shortfall to Principal Paydown

Such that, for the Period 1, cell AJ305 contains `"=O305+T305+Q305+W305"`.

7.7.3 Interest due but not paid current (interest waterfall)

The Interest Due But Not Paid Current in the Interest Waterfall is determined by:

- Interest Due
- less Interest Paid
- less the Deferred Interest Paid.

Using the Class C Interest Due but Not Paid Current as an example, for Period 1, cell AT305 has the formula `"=P505-P305-R305"`.

7.8 INTEREST WATERFALL (AVAILABLE FUNDS AFTER PAYMENT)

This section starts in Row 400 and contains the calculations for the remaining Interest Proceeds after the payment of each step in a period, and in each period of the Interest Waterfall. It starts with the Interest Proceeds Available for Distribution, which is taken directly from the **Collateral Sheet**. After each step in the Interest Waterfall is paid, the remaining amount of interest proceeds available for distribution after payment of the referenced liability/obligation is calculated. At the end of the Interest Waterfall in each period, there should be zero Interest Proceeds available for further distribution.

For example, for Period 1, the Funds Available after Payment of Taxes Paid is calculated in cell H405 as `"=F405-H305"`.

The reader will note that the Taxes Paid in the Interest Waterfall is lined up in the same column as the Funds Available after Taxes Paid. The authors believe it is good practice as it allows the user to easily scroll through calculations to determine if incorrect references or errors have been made and avoids circular references. It is also easier to insert new columns and calculations.

7.9 INTEREST WATERFALL CALCULATIONS

The Interest Waterfall Calculations are found in the section starting in row 500. This section provides an individual look at each of the amounts due (but not necessarily paid) according to the Interest Waterfall, but excluding the calculations for the OC ratios and IC ratios which are calculated further down in the **Waterfall Sheet**.

The **Taxes Due**, **Trustee/Admin Fee Due** and **Senior Management Fee Due** are each taken from the Fees and Expenses Cash Flows section starting in Row 200.

The **Class A Interest Due**, **Class B Interest Due**, **Class C Interest Due**, **Class D Interest Due** and **Class E Interest Due** are each taken from the Liabilities Cash Flows section found in Row 100.

The **Class C Deferred Interest Due**, **Class D Deferred Interest Due** and **Class E Deferred Interest Due** are each calculated as the *product of*:

- Interest Due and Not Paid in the Interest Waterfall
- Tranche PIK switch.

As an example, the Class C Deferred Interest Due in Period 1, calculated in cell R505, as `"=(AA104-AB104)*Tranche_3_PIK?"`, where AA104 is the calculated overdue interest, AB104 is the past due interest paid, and Tranche_3_PIK? is a flag to determine whether the interest is to be paid current (FALSE) or can defer (TRUE).

The **Junior Taxes Due** and **Junior Trustee/Admin Fee Due** are both calculated as the *maximum of*:

- the Senior Taxes or Trustee/Admin Fee Paid *less* the Taxes or Trustee/Admin Fee Due
- zero.

For example, in cell Y505, the formula `"=MAX(H505-H305,0)"` is used.

The Incentive Fee Hurdle Amount is calculated as:

- the outstanding Class F at the beginning of the period
- *multiplied by* the 1+ Incentive Management Fee Hurdle
- *multiplied by* the Day Count
- *less* the payments made during the period.

That is to say the Incentive Fee Hurdle is the outstanding future value of the Class F notes/preferences projected at the Incentive Management Hurdle Rate.

For the first period, cell AB505 refers to cell BA104, which contains the formula `"=MAX(BA104*(1+Incent_Mgt_Fee_Hurdle*Waterfall!D105)-MIN(AZ105, BA104),0)"`.

The **Incentive Fee Due** is determined by:

- Available Funds After Payment of the Junior Management Fee in excess of the Incentive Fee Hurdle Amount;
- *multiplied by* the Incentive Management Fee percentage.

Hence, for Period 1, the formula in cell AC505 contains the following calculation:

`"=IF(AA405-AB505>0,(AA405-AB505)*Incent_Mgt_Fee,0)"`.

The Class F Interest Due is:

- Available Funds After Payment of the Incentive Management Fee

Therefore, for Period 1, cell AD505 contains `"=AB405"`.

7.9.1 Summary of the principal outstanding of the notes

In cells AK503 to AP503 is a Summary of the Principal Outstanding of the Notes. This is used for the calculations of the Interest Cures. In keeping with the Layout and Design Guidelines described above, the amounts of Principal Outstanding are reproduced in the Interest Cures in an effort to follow good modelling practices and avoid circular references. Also for more sophisticated pay down schemes, such as a pro-rata curing scheme, then some form of percentage allocation can be used here.

7.10 PRINCIPAL WATERFALL

Row 600 is the section beginning the Principal Waterfall. As with the calculations in the Interest Waterfall, the MEDIAN() function is used to return the middle number of:

- the Principal Proceeds Available;
- the Calculation of Amounts Due;
- zero.

For the **Taxes Paid** the calculation will be the *median of*:

- Principal Proceeds Available in the Principal Waterfall (Available Funds after Payment)
- Taxes Due from the Principal Waterfall Calculations.
- zero.

For Period 1, cell H605, the Taxes Paid is given by the following formula "=MEDIAN(F705,H805,0)", where F705 is the available funds and H805 is the amount due.

The Principal Waterfall typically only pays the senior expenses to the extent that they were not paid senior in the Interest Waterfall. Consequently, the **Trustee/Admin Fees Paid amount** in the Principal Waterfall is only paid to the extent it was not paid in the Interest Waterfall and is again subject to the extent of the cap.

Therefore, for Period 1, cell I605 shows the required calculation as "=MEDIAN(H705,I805,0)", where H705 is the available funds, I805 is the amount due, and is given by the calculation "=MAX(MIN(Sr_Tee_Fees_Exp_Cap*D805,I505)-I305-Z305,0)". In other words, the shortfall, if any, is only the amount unpaid in the Interest Waterfall up to the cap.

The calculations for the Senior Management Fee Paid, the Interest Paid and Deferred Interest Paid for the various classes, the Junior Taxes Paid, the Junior Trustee/Admin Fees and the Junior Management Fee Paid, use similar formulas to that used in the Interest Waterfall, and the calculation is the *median of*:

- the Principal Proceeds Available after the payment of the preceding Principal Waterfall liability/obligation
- the payment due from the Principal Waterfall Calculations (which will be the shortfall from the Interest Waterfall)
- zero.

To illustrate, for Period 1, the **Senior Management Fee Paid** is calculated in cell K605 as "=MEDIAN(J705,K805,0)", where J705 is the available funds and K805 is the shortfall from the Interest Waterfall, calculated as "=MAX(K505-K305,0)". The Class A Interest Paid and the Class B Interest Paid are calculated in cells L605, and K605 respectively. Each is the median of available cash and any interest shortfall from the interest waterfall.

The Class A/B Coverage Shortfall to Principal Paydown is determined by the *median of*:

- the Principal Proceeds Available after the payment of the preceding Interest Waterfall liability
- the Class A/B Coverage Shortfall to Principal Paydown paid in the Interest Waterfall
- *less the maximum of*:
  - o the OC Coverage Shortfall from the Over-Collateralization Tests Section
  - o the IC Shortfall from the Interest Coverage Section
  - o zero
- zero.

Using the Period 1 as an example, cell O605 holds the formula, `"=MEDIAN(N705, O805,0))"`, where N705 is the available funds and O805 is the calculation. The calculation in O805 depends on the type of cures used. Similarly the Class C and Class D Coverage Tests are paid. Not all transactions require all the tests to be met before reinvestment.

The amount to be paid **To Reinvestment** depends on whether the current **Period Number** is less than the **Reinvestment Period End**. If it is less than the current **Reinvestment Period End**, then the remaining Proceeds available are paid into the Reinvestment Collateral Pool on the **Collateral Sheet**. Where the current period is greater than or equal to the current **Reinvestment Period End**, the amount available **To Reinvestment** is zero.

For example, for Period 1, cell R605 contains the following Excel formula, `"=MEDIAN(Q705,R805,0))"`, where Q705 is the available funds and R805 is the calculated amount for reinvestment. After the Reinvestment period, the money in the Principal account is used to pay down the principal of the Notes in order of priority, including any accrued and unpaid interest and PIK interest.

The **Incentive Fee Paid** pays the minimum of the available funds and the excess of the available funds over the Incentive Fee threshold amount taking into account any payments made in the Interest Waterfall.

Hence for Period 1, the calculation is given by `"=MEDIAN(Z705,AA805,0)"`, in cell AA605.

The **Class F Interest Paid** is a "left-over" payment and calculations as the *maximum of*:

- Available Funds, and
- zero.

Therefore, the Period 1 the Class F Interest Paid, is calculated in cell AB605, as `"=MAX(AA705,0)"`.

7.10.1 Principal check

At the end of the Principal Waterfall section in AG603, AH603 and AI603 is a small audit check to ensure that the sum of all of the Principal Waterfall outputs can be compared to the principal payments and recoveries on the assets. If there are no errors or omissions, the difference between the two should always equal 0. As with the Interest Check at the end of the Interest Waterfall, conditional formatting is used to highlight any difference from zero by changing the font to red in the associated cell.

The **Principal Cash In** is the Aggregate Principal Collections for the **Collateral Sheet** in the Collateral Summary Section, i.e., cell AG605 contains `"=Collateral!AQ105"`.

The **Principal Cash Out** is the sum of all of the payment of principal proceeds out in the Principal Waterfall Section, i.e., cell AH605 contains the following formula `"=SUM(H605:AE605)"`.

The **Difference** calculation is equal to the **Principal Cash In** *minus* the **Principal Cash Out** and uses conditional formatting to highlight in red when a value appears which is not equal to zero.

Hence cell AI605 calculates the check as `"=AG605-AH605"`.

7.10.2 Principal cures

Cures Paid are simply the Class A/B Coverage Shortfall to Principal Paydown plus the Class C Coverage Shortfall to Principal Paydown plus the Class D Coverage Shortfall to Principal Paydown and the Class E Coverage Shortfall to Principal. Such that, for Period 1, cell AK605 refers simply to O605+P605+Q605, i.e., is formulated as `"=O605+P605+Q605"`.

The Principal Cures are calculated as the *median of*:

• Principal Outstanding for the relevant class
• Cures Available in the Principal Waterfall (Available Funds after Payment)
• zero.

Thus, for example, in cell AI605, the Class A pay down is formulated by `"=MEDIAN(AL805,AK705,0)"`.

7.11 PRINCIPAL WATERFALL (AVAILABLE FUNDS AFTER PAYMENT)

The Principal Waterfall (Available Funds after Payment) section begins in Row 700, and contains the calculations for the remaining Principal Proceeds after the payment of each liability/obligation in each step of the Principal Waterfall, and for each period of the Principal Waterfall. It is often quite useful to observe the patterns of payment in this section to see why certain classes perhaps pay off at the expense of others.

This section starts with the Principal Proceeds Available for Distribution, which is referenced directly from the **Collateral Sheet**. After each liability/obligation in the Principal Waterfall is paid, the amount of proceeds available for further distribution after such payment of the referenced liability/obligation for subsequent is shown. At the end of the Principal Waterfall there should be zero Principal Proceeds available for distribution.

For Period 1, the **Principal Funds Available** after **Payment of Taxes Paid** is shown in cell H705 as `"=F705-H605"`, where F705 is the available funds, and H605 is the payment from the waterfall. All calculations for each step of the waterfall are similarly calculated.

As with the Interest Waterfall, the Taxes Paid in the Principal Waterfall are lined up in the same column as the Funds Available after Taxes Paid, allowing the user to easily scroll through calculations to determine if incorrect references or errors have been made.

7.12 PRINCIPAL WATERFALL CALCULATIONS

Row 800 contains the section for the Principal Waterfall Calculations. Here the calculations are performed for amounts due (but not necessarily paid because of the potential for insufficient proceeds) from the application of Principal Waterfall.

The **Taxes Due** are those that are due but were not paid in full in the Interest Waterfall. The due amount is calculated as the *maximum of*:

- the Taxes Due as determined in the Interest Waterfall Calculations *less* the Taxes Paid in the Interest Waterfall
- zero.

Hence for Period 1, cell H805 holds the formula `"=MAX(Y505-Y305,0)"`, where Y505 is the amount due and Y305 is the amount paid in the Interest Waterfall.

Similarly the **Trustee/Admin Fees** due for Period 1 – which are still subject to the cap at the senior part of the waterfall – are calculated, for example in the first period, in cell I805 as `"=MAX(MIN(Sr_Tee_Fees_Exp_Cap*D805,I505)-I305-Z305,0)"`.

Also the **Senior Collateral Management Fee** that is due but was not paid in full in the Interest Proceeds Waterfall, in Period 1 is calculated in cell K805 as `"=MAX(K505-K305,0)"`.

The **Interest Due** for the various tranches in the Principal Waterfall refers to the interest that was not paid in the Interest Waterfall. Thus, the **Class A Notes Interest Due** is that interest which was not paid in full in the Application of Interest Proceeds. It is taken as equalling the Interest Due but not paid current in the Interest Waterfall (cells AR303 to AV303).

It follows that the Class A Interest Due for Period 1 in the Principal Waterfall is given in cell L805 as `"=AR305"`.

Similarly, the formula for **Class B Interest Due** for Period 1 in cell M805, is `"=AS305"`.

The **Class A/B Coverage Shortfall to Principal Paydown** calculation is given in cell O805, as `"= MAX(MAX(L905,K1005),0)"`.

The **Class C Coverage Shortfall to Principal Paydown** calculation is given in cell P805, for example, as `"= MAX(MAX(U905,S1005),0)"`.

The **Class D Coverage Shortfall to Principal Paydown** calculation as calculated for period 1, is shown in cell Q805, as `"=MAX(MAX(AD905,AA1005),0)"`.

7.12.1 Available for reinvestment

During the Reinvestment Period, all available remaining Principal Proceeds are used for the acquisition of additional Collateral.

If the current Period in the model is less than the Reinvestment Period End date (as specified on the **Inputs Sheet**), then the Proceeds After the payment of the Class B Notes Interest Due, but not paid in the full in the Interest Waterfall, are put into the Unused Proceeds account for reinvestment in the Reinvestment Collateral Pool.

This is accomplished in the model using the following Excel Formula in cell R805, as `"=IF(B805<Reinvest_End,Q705,0)"`.

One point to take care of is whether the end of the Reinvestment Period is inclusive or exclusive. The formula above shows an exclusive end date. To change it to an inclusive date, the test should be changed from "equals" to "less than or equals". Typically, reinvestment can occur only if the deal is in compliance with its coverage tests and potentially also collateral quality tests, in other words, the Reinvestment Period may terminate early after a Coverage Test breach, or if losses in the Portfolio exceed a threshold.

7.12.2 Principal due

Principal Proceeds shall be applied on and after the Reinvestment Period (or if Reinvestment Criteria or other conditions are not met), to redeem the outstanding **Class A Notes**. This is calculated as the *median of*:

- the outstanding Principal Proceeds *less* the Interest Cures in the Interest Waterfall
- the Principal Proceeds available after Reinvestment is paid
- zero.

For example for the A Notes, cell S805 calculates the principal due as `"=MEDIAN(H105-AK305,R705,0)"`, where H105 is the start of period balance, AK305 is the amount paid from interest cures, and R705 is the available funds in the principal account. Similarly for the Class B Principal Due in Period 1, in T805, is `"=MEDIAN(P105-AL305,S705,0)"`. For the Class C Principal Due in period 1, cell U805 holds the formula `"=MEDIAN(X105-AM305,T705,0)"`. For the Class D Notes, cell W805, `"=MEDIAN(AG105-AN305,U705,0)"`. Finally for the Class E Notes, cell Y805 is calculated as `"=MEDIAN(AP105-AO305,V705,0)"`. In addition for the Notes that can PIK, the past due interest is required to be paid. For example for the C Notes is cell V605 is `=MEDIAN(T705,U805,0)`.

7.12.3 A note on deferred interest

The deferred interest due on PIK-able tranches is usually paid after the reinvestment. The authors have provided various "Not Used" columns where deferred interest calculations can be moved depending on the deal type.

7.12.4 Trustee/admin fees

The **Trustee/Admin Fees Due** and not paid in the Interest Waterfall, and senior in the Principal Waterfall are calculated as, for Period 1, in cell AB805 as `"=MAX(Z305-Z505-I605,0)"`, where Z305 is the trustee/admin fees due but not paid in the Interest Waterfall, less the amount paid in the Interest Waterfall (Z505) less the amount to the cap paid in the Principal Waterfall (I605).

The Junior Collateral Management Fee that is due but was not paid in full in the Interest Waterfall, is calculated as a *maximum of*:

- the Junior Collateral Management Fee Due in the Interest Waterfall Calculations *less* the Junior Collateral Management Fee Paid in the Interest Waterfall
- zero.

For the first period, the calculation is in cell AC805, given by the formula `"=MAX(AA305-AA505,0)"`, where AA305 is the calculated amount in the Interest Waterfall and AA505 is the amount paid.

7.12.5 Incentive fee and equity due

As in the Interest Waterfall Calculations, the **Incentive Fee Due** is determined by (if positive):

- the Available funds

  less

- the Principal Beginning of Period Balance
- *multiplied by* the Incentive Management fee Hurdle
- *multiplied by* the Day Count

  less payments made in the Interest Waterfall.

  Hence the Excel formula for Period 1 in cell AA805 is `"=IF(AC705-AB505+AC305>0,`
`MAX((AC705-AB505)*Incent_Mgt_Fee,0),0)"`.

7.13 ADDING OVER-COLLATERALIZATION TESTS

The Over-Collateralization Test calculations start in Row 900. In this section of the **Waterfall Sheet**, the ratios and results for the OC tests are calculated on a period-by-period basis. This differs from the OC Result on the **Inputs Sheet**, which only provides the OC Test Result on the Effective Date.

7.13.1 Using interest to cure breaches vs. using principal to cure breaches

The failure of an OC test will have the effect of directing interest and potentially principal cash flows to pay principal on the CDO Notes.

There are three main types of OC calculations to address the different sources of cash to reduce the liabilities:

1. interest only calculation;
2. principal only calculation; and a
3. combined interest and principal calculation.

An interest only calculation assumes that the cure will be paid solely from interest income and consequently is effectively "extra money" from a principal perspective, as can be seen from the calculation:

$$Roc = \frac{P_A}{L_A}$$

where R_{OC} is the actual OC ratio, P_A is the actual principal balance and L_A is the actual liability balance.

Let R_T be the target OC ratio for the covenant to be met. Then

$$R_{OC} \geq R_T$$

describes the transaction operating normally.

However, if the condition above is not satisfied then it must be cured by either reducing the amount of liabilities or increasing the asset notional. It would be theoretically possible potentially to do either; however, as increasing the number of assets would also increase the risk in the pool, it is normally the case that a breach in the ratio is attempted to be cured by reducing the number of liabilities. So

$$Roc = \frac{P_A}{L_A} < R_T$$

describes the situation when the transaction is in breach.

$$Roc' = \frac{P_A}{(L_A - \Delta L)} = R_T$$

Rearranging for ΔL,

$$\Delta L = L_A - \frac{P_A}{R_T}$$

Factoring out the liabilities, the cure can be further expressed as:

$$\Delta L = L_A \left(1 - \frac{Roc}{R_T}\right)$$

If the available cash in the Interest Waterfall is sufficient to afford the payment of ΔL, then the transaction will again be in compliance. If there are insufficient collections available in the Interest Waterfall it is then common to apply principal proceeds in order to restore the transaction to compliance. Two approaches are common:

1. paying the shortfall between the interest-only cure and the available interest proceeds with principal proceeds; and
2. recalculating the ratio to take into consideration the prior payment from interest proceeds and take into consideration that a payment of principal proceeds actually reduces both the numerator and denominator of the OC ratio.

In using approach 1, there is no recalculation of the OC test and only the shortfall is applied. This conveniently ignores the fact that the numerator of the test will be reduced by the same amount. It is therefore impossible to "cure" an "interest-only" OC breach calculation using principal during a single period.

Looking at what is implied in a principal cure, as before P_A is the actual principal balance of the assets. Splitting P_A into P_A'' and P_A'', the asset balance and the cash balance (in the Unused Proceeds account) respectively, and adapting the formula above to:

$$Roc' = \frac{(P_A - \Delta L)}{(L_A - \Delta L)} = \frac{(P_A' +'' P_A'' - \Delta L)}{(L_A - \Delta L)} = R_T$$

Rearranging and solving for ΔL as before gives:

$$\Delta L = \frac{(R_T L_A - P_A)}{(R_T - 1)}$$

With the limit of ΔL being the available cash P_A'', i.e.,

$$\Delta L = \min\left(\frac{(R_T L_A - P_A)}{(R_T - 1)}, P_A''\right)$$

It is possible to calculate a combined principal and interest cure that looks more like a "principal-only" cure but which typically includes the excess spread of the Interest Waterfall as an asset (i.e., the interest income in excess of the amount needed to pay the interest on the class). This can be employed in either a combined Principal and Interest Waterfall or sequentially as before. However, as it contemplates payment from both interest and principal, it does not require recalculating. Denoting the income in excess of the amount to meet the interest on the liabilities as I_e, the above then becomes:

$$Roc = \frac{(P_A + I_e)}{L_A} = \frac{(P'_A +'' P''_A + I_e)}{L_A}$$

The modified cure is similar to that of a principal cure but with the excess income considered part of the principal:

$$Roc' = \frac{(P_A + I_e - \Delta L)}{(L_A - \Delta L)} = \frac{(P'_A +'' P''_A + I_e - \Delta L)}{(L_A - \Delta L)} = R_T$$

Solving as above:

$$\Delta L = \frac{(R_T L_A - P_A - I_e)}{(R_T - 1)}$$

This cure can be calculated once and paid from interest first and principal second without resulting in a recalculation and providing a cure in the same period if there are sufficient proceeds. It is limited by I_e in the Interest Waterfall and by P''_A in the Principal Waterfall. While often more severe when triggered, the impact of the excess interest in the numerator will be to slightly delay the onset of a breach.

In conclusion, the most common practice for calculating OC tests is to do one of the following:

(a) cure a shortfall from interest proceeds first, not recalculate the OC Test after these interest proceeds have been exhausted and just apply the cure;

(b) cure a shortfall from interest proceeds first, recalculate and apply a principal cure as above; or

(c) occasionally, either a principal-only cure or a principal cure followed by an interest-only cure. This is typical in transactions where the underlying assets pay very high levels of income and it is designed along with several other measures to prolong the flow of cash to the equity.

To use a simple example to illustrate the above, assume a transaction has a collateral principal balance of €100 (including some cash in the Principal Collections Account) and a Class A Note of €75. The initial OC Ratio will be €100/€75 = 133%. If the OC Test is set at 125% and there is a loss of €10 in the Collateral Principal Balance, and assuming there is €1 available from Interest Proceeds and €4 available from Principal Proceeds to cure the breach, the following will be the outcome in (a), (b) and (c) above:

(a) The OC ratio is calculated as €90/€75 = 120%. The shortfall to cure will be calculated as €75 – (€90/125%) = €3. The OC ratio will only be calculated once and €1 will be used from Interest Proceeds and €2 will be used from Principal Proceeds to pay the shortfall. However, as some of the "assets" have been used to pay the OC shortfall, the subsequent post-test OC becomes €88/€72, or 122.2%. This is still short of the desired 125% but would be considered "cured" in this period. However, unless there is a change in the assets and liabilities going forward through trading activity, it will still be in breach in the next period. Hence it may take several periods until the deficit is cured solely from Interest Proceeds until the test is back in compliance.

(b) The OC ratio is calculated as €90/€75 = 120% as before. The shortfall to cure will be calculated as €75 – (€90/125%) = €3. From Interest Proceeds available, €1 will be used for the shortfall. Then the OC ratio will be recalculated as €90/€74 = 122%. The shortfall to cure from Principal Proceeds will be (125% × €74 – €90)/(125% –1) = €10. Thus, all €4 of Principal Proceeds will be used as a shortfall pay down. In this instance the post-cure ratio will be €86/€70, or 122.86%. This is still short of the desired amount but neither is it considered "cured". However, if the required €10 was available in the Principal Proceeds and was used to pay down the Class A note, the post-cure ratio would be €80/€64, or 125%, i.e., "cured".

(c) The OC ratio is calculated as (€90 + €1)/€75 = 121.33%. The shortfall to cure from Principal Proceeds will be (125% × €75 – €90 – €1)/(125% – 1) = €11. Thus, all €4 of Principal Proceeds will be used as shortfall pay down. Because the shortfall to cure is greater under this calculation, the senior note holders are provided with greater protection but, of course, at the expense of the subordinate note holders. The advantage to the subordinated note holders is that if the Principal Proceeds are applied first, then the likelihood of interruption to interest flows will be reduced.

Again, however, if €11 of Principal Proceeds are available then the ratio post the Principal Proceeds cure would be €80/€64, but there would still be €1 available to pay the subordinate note holders. These sorts of structures occur more often in distressed transactions which may be significantly overcollateralized from a principal perspective.

An alternative use of this style of calculation is to do a "single style" of calculation, and pay in the normal order. In this case any shortfall from the Interest Waterfall can be topped up from the Principal Waterfall and, if satisfied in the Principal Waterfall post the cure, the OC ratio test would be satisfied.

7.13.2 Class A/B OC coverage

Class A/B OC Ratio is the percentage ratio obtained by the Principal Balance defined as the *sum of*:

- the outstanding notional amount of the Collateral (excluding defaulted Collateral and often downgraded Collateral below a certain rating and/or above a certain threshold amount);
- the *sum of*:
  o all of the amounts in the Principal Proceeds, Unused Proceeds Account and may or may not include the Interest Proceeds Account
  o the notional amount of each Eligible Investment (attributable to Principal Proceeds)
- the sum of the *lower of* the *product of*:
  o the lowest applicable rating agency assumed recover rate and
  o the Principal Balance of each Defaulted Collateral Asset; and
  o the current market value of all of the defaulted collateral.
- the sum of the product of (i) the notional outstanding principal of each downgraded asset and (ii) the downgraded asset's "Haircut" if applicable or less the excess of the CCC/Caa bucket over the CCC/Caa threshold amount

divided by

- the aggregate principal amount of the Class A and Class B Notes Outstanding.

The Class A/B OC Test needs to be satisfied as long as there are Class A and Class B Notes outstanding, and is satisfied as long as the Class A/B OC Ratio is at least equal to the Class A/B OC Test threshold (as entered into the model on the **Inputs Sheet**).

Most transactions use a single value threshold for the test; however, there have been transactions in which a step-up threshold is used, typically based upon the level of defaults, losses or perceived increases in credit risk via rating factors.

In order to calculate and evaluate this test the following four columns are utilized:

- OC Coverage Numerator;
- OC Coverage Denominator;
- OC Coverage Ratio;
- OC Coverage Shortfall (if any).

The **Class A/B OC Coverage Numerator**, or **Principal Balance**, is calculated as the current period sum of the:

- Original Collateral Pool Anticipated Recovery (for those Defaulted Collateral Assets which have yet to be worked out)
- Original Collateral Pool Recovery Amount (for workouts)
- Original Collateral Pool Amortization Amount
- Original Collateral Pool Sold Amount
- Original Collateral Pool End of Period Balance
- Reinvestment Collateral Pool Anticipated Recovery
- Reinvestment Collateral Pool Recovery Amount
- Reinvestment Collateral Pool Amortization Amount
- Reinvestment Collateral Pool Sold Amount
- Reinvestment Collateral Pool End of Period Balance and, depending on the calculation
- Excess Interest Proceeds.

The Class A/B OC Coverage Numerator for the first period is calculated in cell F905 as `"=SUM(Collateral!N105:S105,Collateral!AB105:AG105)"`.

There are certain factors of the OC Coverage Numerator that may be required to be modelled, depending upon how complex the structure is required to be. This may include haircuts to the principal balance for assets in the collateral pool that have been either downgraded by one or more of the rating agencies below certain thresholds or have balances in excess of minimum rating requirements.

The **Class A/B OC Coverage Denominator** is calculated as the beginning of period Class A Notes Outstanding *plus* the beginning of period Class B Notes Outstanding.

By way of example, the formula for the first period in cell G905 is `"=H105+P105"`.

The Class A/B OC Coverage Ratio is simply:

- the Class A OC Coverage Numerator *divided by* the Class A OC Coverage Denominator.

The formula is qualified to test that if the OC Denominator is greater than zero to avoid divide by zero (`#DIV/0!`) errors. If the denominator is greater than zero, the ratio is calculated, otherwise the OC Test threshold (Tranche_2_OC_Test) as given on the **Inputs Sheet** is returned.

The formula for the ratio in the first period is given in cell H905, as `"=IF(G905>0, F905/G905,Tranche_2_OC_Test)"`.

Alternatively, a so-called "guard number" can be added to the denominator to prevent it ever reaching exactly zero. This will have the effect of creating a very high rather than an infinite divide by zero or `"#DIV/0!"` error in Excel. If chosen to be small enough, the "guard number" will have no material impact on the calculations, and the model will execute slightly more quickly as the test will become unconditional. For example, the formula in cell H905 becomes `"= F904/(G904+epsilon)"`. The reader will recall that epsilon is defined in the Inputs as 1e-8, or 0.00000001.

The **Class A/B OC Coverage Shortfall** (interest-only type cure) is calculated as the *maximum of*:

- the product of:
  - o the Class A and Class B beginning of the period and
  - o one *less* the quotient of Class A/B OC Coverage Ratio divided by the Class A/B OC Coverage Test
- zero.

The test needs then to be either qualified by the condition that the OC Coverage Test input be greater than zero for the calculation to occur or the result has to be guarded as mentioned before with an epsilon number, to avoid a `#DIV/0!` error.

For example, the formula for the OC test given in cell I905, as `"=IF(Tranche_2_OC_Test>0,MAX((H105+P105)-F905/Tranche_2_OC_Test,0),0)"`, when using a conditional formula or `"=MAX((H105+P105)-F905/(Tranche_2_OC_Test+Epsilon)"`, when using a guard number.

Where there is a Class A/B OC Coverage Shortfall, Interest Proceeds are used to first cure the amount of the shortfall in the Interest Waterfall before the current Class C Interest (as opposed to deferred or past due interest) is paid. If the Interest Proceeds available for distribution are insufficient to pay the shortfall amount in full, Principal Proceeds are then used to pay any remaining shortfall, prior either to purchasing additional collateral during the **Reinvestment Period** or paying down the notes after the **Reinvestment Period**.

As discussed above, simply topping up an "interest-only" calculation shortfall in the Principal Waterfall does not cure to the OC Test level in this period. A principal-based OC Test would be required to do that. However, it is quite common in CLO transactions to do just that, i.e., only top up an "interest-only" calculation shortfall by paying the shortfall in the Principal Waterfall.

The **Prior Cures** are taken from the Cures Paid in the Interest Waterfall. Thus, in J905 there is the formula `"=AJ305"`.

The **New Ratio** is determined as:

- the Over-collateralization Coverage Numerator
- *divided by Over-collateralization Coverage Denominator*
- *less* Prior Cures
- *plus* Epsilon.

For example, K905 contains the formula `"=F905/(G905-J905+Epsilon)"`.

The **Class A/B Principal Over-collateralization Coverage Shortfall** is determined, if the Principal Cure switch is "1", as the maximum of:

- the Class A/B OC Test
- *multiplied by* the Over-collateralization Coverage Denominator

- *less* the Interest Over-collateralization Coverage Shortfall
- *less the Over-collateralization Coverage numerator*
- *divided by* the Class A/B OC Test less one plus epsilon and zero;

otherwise, the Interest Over-collateralization coverage shortfall is less the Prior Cure.

Therefore, in cell L905 there is the formula `"=IF(Prin_Cures,MAX((Tranche_2_OC_Test*(Waterfall!G905-Waterfall! J905)-Waterfall!F905)/(Tranche_2_OC_Test-1+Epsilon), 0),MAX(I905-J905,0))"`.

7.13.3 Class C OC test

This is very similar to the Class A/B OC Ratio but adds the Class C liability balance to the denominator. As the Class C is also a PIK-able tranche, it will add any accrued but deferred interest that has been capitalized. Consequently the **Class C OC Ratio** is the percentage ratio obtained by:

- the Principal Balance (as defined in the Class A/B OC ratio)
- *divided by* the aggregate principal amount of the Class A, Class B and Class C Notes Outstanding (including any PIK interest).

The **Class C OC Test** needs to be satisfied as long as there is any Class C Notes Outstanding and is satisfied so long as the Class C OC Ratio is at least equal to the Class C OC Test threshold (as entered into the model on the **Inputs Sheet**).

The **Class C OC Coverage Numerator** is the Principal Balance as defined in the Class A/B OC Ratio.

The **Class C OC Coverage Denominator** is calculated as the beginning of period Class A Notes Outstanding, Class B Notes Outstanding and Class C Notes Outstanding (plus any accrued and unpaid deferred interest (if PIK-able). For example for the Period 1, O905 holds the Class C OC Coverage Denominator, and calculates it with the following Excel formula as `"=H105+P105+X105+AA104"`.

The **Class C OC Coverage Ratio** is simply the Class C OC Coverage Numerator divided by the Class C OC Coverage Denominator. The formula is qualified such that if the OC Coverage Denominator is greater than zero, the ratio is calculated, otherwise the OC Coverage Test threshold (Tranche_3_OC_Test) given on the **Inputs Sheet** is used. Alternatively, a guard number can be used as before (see the Class A/B OC Coverage Ratio above).

Using a conditional formula, cell P905 becomes `"=IF(O905>0,N905/O905,Tranche_3_OC_Test)"`

The **Prior Interest Cures** are equal to the Class A/B Coverage Shortfall to Principal Paydown in the Interest Waterfall. For example, cell Q905 contains the formula `"O305"`.

The **Class C OC Coverage Shortfall** (again as an interest-only cure) is calculated as the maximum of (a) the product of (i) the Class A, Class B and Class C (including any PIKed Interest) beginning of the period times; (ii) one (1) *less* the Class C OC Coverage Ratio divided by the Class C OC Coverage Test, and (b) zero. The test is then qualified by the condition that the OC Test is greater than zero for the calculation to occur, otherwise the result is a zero shortfall.

Cell R905 has the conditional calculation `"=IF(Tranche_3_OC_Test>0,MAX(MAX(O905-Q905,0)-N905/ Tranche_3_OC_Test,0),0)"`.

This number needs to be reduced by the payments already made to restore the Class A/B coverage test (if any).

The **Prior Cures** after the Interest Shortfall are taken from the Cures Paid in the Interest Waterfall. Thus, in S905 there is the formula `"=J905+O805"`.

The **New Ratio** is determined as:

• the Over-collateralization Coverage Numerator

divided by

• Over-collateralization Coverage Denominator
• *less* Prior Cures
• *plus* Epsilon.

For example, T905 contains the formula `"=(N905-(S905-AJ305)*Prin_Cures)/(O905-S905+Epsilon)"`.

The **Class C Principal Over-Collateralization Coverage Shortfall** is determined, if the Principal Cures switch is "1", the maximum of:

• the Class C OC Test

multiplied by:

• the Over-collateralization Coverage Denominator
• less Prior Cures

less:

• the Over-collateralization Coverage Numerator
• divided by the Class C OC Test less one plus epsilon

and zero,
otherwise, the Interest Over-collateralization coverage shortfall less the Prior Cures.
Therefore, in cell U905 there is the formula `"=IF(Prin_Cures,MAX((Tranche_3_OC_Test*(Waterfall!O905-Waterfall!S905)-Waterfall!N905-(S905-AJ305)*Prin_Cures))/(Tranche_3_OC_Test-1+Epsilon), 0),MAX(R905-S905,0))"`.

7.13.4 Class D OC and Class E OC tests

No prizes will be given to those readers who correctly guessed that Class D OC and Class E OC Tests are very similar to the Class C OC Test. We just have to add the outstanding Class C Notional, including any accrued but deferred interest, to the denominator, the numerator being the same as that for the Class A/B OC Test and Class C OC Test, i.e., the Principal Balance.

The **Class D OC Coverage Denominator** is calculated as the sum of:

• the beginning of period Class A Notes Outstanding
• the beginning of period, Class B Notes Outstanding
• the beginning of period, Class C Notes Outstanding including any accrued and unpaid deferred interest
• the beginning of period Class D Notes Outstanding including accrued and unpaid deferred interest.

By way of example cell X905 contains the calculation for the first period by utilizing the following Excel formula, `"=H105+P105+X105+AG105+AA104-AB104+AJ104-AK104"`.

As with the Class A/B and Class C OC Coverage Ratios, the **Class D OC Coverage Ratio for Period 1** is given in cell Y905 by the formula `"=IF(X905>0,W905/X905,Tranche_4_OC_Test)"`.

The **Prior Interest Cures** are equal to the Class A/B Coverage Shortfall to Principal Paydown in the Interest Waterfall. For example, cell Z905 contains the formula `"O305+Q305"`.

Cell AA905 contains the following formula to calculate the Period 1 **Class D OC Coverage Shortfall**:

`"=IF(Tranche_4_OC_Test>0,MAX(MAX(X905-Z905,0)-W905/Tranche_4_OC_Test,0),0)"`.

The **Prior Cures** after the Interest Shortfall are taken from the Cures Paid in the Interest Waterfall. Thus, cell AB905 refers to `"=S905+P605"` and in S905 there is the formula `"=J905+O605"`.

The **New Ratio** is determined as:

- the Over-collateralization Coverage Numerator
- *divided by* Over-collateralization Coverage Denominator
- *less* Prior Cures
- *plus* Epsilon.

For example, AC905 contains the formula `"=(W905-(AB905-AJ305)*Prin_Cures)/(X905-AB905+Epsilon)"`.

The **Class D Principal Over-collateralization Coverage Shortfall** is determined, if the Principal Curse switch is "1", as the maximum of:

- the Class D OC Test
- *multiplied by the Over-collateralization Coverage Denominator*
- *less* Prior Cures

less:

- the Over-collateralization Coverage Numerator
- *divided by* the Class D OC Test less one plus epsilon

and zero;

otherwise, the Interest Over-collateralization Coverage Shortfall less the Prior Cures.

Therefore, in cell AD905 there is the formula `"=IF(Prin_Cures,MAX((Tranche_4_OC_Test*(Waterfall!X905-Waterfall!AB905-MAX(AB905-AJ305,0)*Prin_Cures)-Waterfall!W905)/(Tranche_4_OC_Test-1+Epsilon),0),MAX(AA905-AB905,0))"`.

By now the reader should be able to check for themselves that the Class E OC formulas are very similar to the Class D OC Test, adding again the outstanding Class E Notional, including any accrued but deferred interest, to the Denominator.

7.14 ADDING INTEREST COVERAGE TESTS

In Row 1000, the Interest Coverage ("IC") Tests are analysed. As in the OC Test section of the **Waterfall Sheet**, the ratios and results for the IC Tests are calculated on a period-by-period basis. This differs from the IC Result on the **Inputs Sheet**; give the IC Test Result as the minimum of all of the IC results over the life of the transaction.

7.14.1 Class A/B IC test

The purpose of an IC Test covenant in the transaction is to help maintain a higher income earned from the Collateral Assets than is expended in the servicing cost of the CDO debt. A breach of this covenant will, like a breach in an OC covenant, result in a diversion of cash away from the interest to pay down the senior-most note.

It is more common to have IC tests for only the more senior notes. The theory and calculations for the conventional interest coverage tests are shown below.

Let I_N be the Interest Income, let E_S be the expenses senior to the Notes, and I_A be the interest for the Class A Note and L_A is the nominal outstanding for the Class A note. Let r_A be the interest rate for the liability. Let R_T be the Ratio threshold as before, in normal operation.

$$I'_N = I_N - E_S$$

$$I'_N - R_T I_A > 0$$

$$R_{IC} = \frac{I'_N}{I_A}$$

$$I_A = r_A L_A$$

$$R_{IC} = \frac{I'_N}{r_A L_A}$$

$$I'_N - R_T r_A (L_A - \Delta L) = 0$$

$$\Delta L = L_A - \frac{I'_N}{R_T r_A}$$

$$\Delta L = L_A - \frac{I'_N L_{A-}}{R_T r_A L_A}$$

$$\Delta L = \left(1 - \frac{R_{IC}}{R_T}\right) L_A$$

Class A/B IC Ratio is the percentage ratio of the *sum of*:

- the interest payments on the collateral that are expected to be received in the Payment Period, *excluding*:
  - accrued and unpaid interest on defaulted collateral
  - amounts expected to be withheld at source or deducted for taxes
  - interest payments on collateral that the Issuer or the Collateral Manager knows will not be made
- all amounts in the Interest Collection Account and the Expense Reimbursement Account; and
- the interest on the balances in the Principal Collection Account, the Interest Collection Account, the Unused Proceeds Accounts and the Payment Account to be received in the Payment Period

minus the following amounts payable senior in the Interest Waterfall:

- the taxes owed by the Issuer
- the accrued and unpaid Fees and Expenses up to the Senior Fees and Expenses Cap

- the Senior Collateral Management Fee due and payable and any Senior Collateral Management Fee not paid prior (including any interest thereon), defined as the Net Interest Amount

divided by the interest on the Class A Notes and Class B Notes payable.

The Class A/B IC Test will be required to be satisfied as long as any of the Class A or Class B Notes remain outstanding, and will be satisfied if the Class A/B IC Ratio is at least equal to the threshold Class A/B IC Test Input (on the **Inputs Sheet**).

As with the OC Tests, in order to calculate the following four columns are utilized:

- IC Numerator;
- IC Denominator;
- IC Ratio;
- IC Shortfall.

The IC Numerator is equal to the Aggregate Interest Collections less the senior expenses for the application period, the net Interest Amount or Collections.

The IC Numerator is calculated for the first period, in F1005. The formula is `"=Collateral!AP105-SUM(H505:K505)"`, where `SUM(H505:K505)` is the expenses senior to the Class A Interest Due.

The IC Denominator is modelled as the Class A Interest Due and the Class B Interest Due. For example cell G1005 contains the `"=L505+M505"`

The IC Ratio is a very simple calculation of the IC Numerator divided by the IC Denominator. However, to avoid the possibility of a tranche in the model not being used, the formula is qualified such that the ratio is calculated if the IC Denominator is greater than zero, otherwise the IC Test threshold (Tranche_2_IC_Test) given on the Inputs Sheet is used.

For Period 1, cell H1005 contains the following calculation `"=IF(G1005>0,F1005/G1005,Tranche_2_IC_Test)"`.

Again this can also be alternatively accomplished by using a "guard number" in the denominator.

The **Interest Coverage Shortfall** is calculated as the maximum of (one minus the IC Ratio divided by the IC Test, and zero) multiplied by the Class A and Class B Outstanding Principal. The test is then qualified by the condition that the IC Test be greater than zero for the calculation to occur (to avoid `#DIV/0!`), otherwise the result returned is a zero shortfall.

Thus, I1005 contains the following formula, `"=IF(Tranche_2_IC_Test>0,MAX(1-H1005/Tranche_2_IC_Test,0)*(H105+P105),0)"`.

The Class A/B IC Test **Prior Cures** are equal to the Interest Waterfall Cures Paid. Hence, for example for period one, the formula in cell J1005 is `"=AJ305"`.

The **New Shortfall** is equal to the *maximum of*:

- the Interest Coverage Shortfall *less* the Prior Cures
- zero.

The period 1 New shortfall in cell K1005 is `"=MAX(I1005-J1005,0)"`.

7.14.2 Class C IC

Similarly the Class C IC can be constructed in a similar manner as the Class A/B IC.

"Class C IC Ratio" is the percentage ratio of:

- the net Interest Amount (as defined the Class A/B IC Ratio)
- *divided by* the interest on the Class A, Class B and Class C Notes payable.

The Class C IC Test is satisfied as long as any of the Class C Notes remain Outstanding, and if the Class C IC Ratio is at least equal to the Class C Interest Test threshold.

As with the Class A/B IC Test, the **Class C IC Numerator** is equal to the Aggregate Interest Collections for the application period less the expenses senior to the Class A Interest Note.

For Period 1, M1005 contains the following calculation `"=Collateral!AP105 - SUM(H505:K505)"`.

The **Class C IC Denominator** is calculated as the sum of the Class A Interest Due, the Class B Interest Due and the Class C Interest Due.

Therefore, for the first period, cell N1005 contains the formula `"=L505+M505+P505."`.

As with the Class A/B IC calculations, the **Class C IC Ratio** is simply the IC Numerator divided by the IC Denominator. Again, the formula is qualified such that the ratio is calculated if the IC Denominator is greater than zero, otherwise the IC Test threshold (Tranche_3_IC_Test) given on the **Inputs Sheet** is used.

For period 1, cell O1005 contains the formula `"=IF(N1005>0,M1005/N1005, Tranche_3_IC_Test)"`.

The **Prior Cures** equal the Class A/B Coverage Shortfall to Principal Paydown from the Interest Waterfall. For example, cell P1005 contains `"=O305"`.

The **Class C IC Shortfall** is calculated as the maximum of (one minus the IC Ratio divided by the IC Test, and zero) multiplied by the Class A, Class B and Class C Outstanding Principal (including accrued and unpaid interest), less the Prior Cures. Again, the test is then qualified by the condition that the IC Test is greater than zero for the calculation to occur, otherwise the result is zero shortfall. Again, for the first period, Q1005 contains the following calculation `"=IF(Tranche_3_IC_Test>0,MAX(MAX(1-O1005/Tranche_3_IC_Test,0)*(H105+ P105+X105+AA104)-P1005,0),0)"`.

Prior Cures after the Shortfall equals the Prior Interest Proceeds Cures *plus* the Class A/B Coverage Shortfall to Principal Paydown from Principal Proceeds. Therefore, in cell R10005 there is the formula `"AJ305+O805"`.

Principal Payment Due is equal to the *maximum of*:

• Interest Coverage shortfall *less* the Prior Cures
• zero

7.14.3 Class D and Class E IC tests

Although the Class D and Class E IC Tests have not been included in the example that is being worked though in this chapter, it is the authors' view that best modelling practice is to build all levels of the tests. Hence, the Class D and Class E IC Tests have been built into the model in a similar fashion to the Class A/B and C IC Tests above.

7.15 TECHNICAL ISSUES WITH COVERAGE TESTS

7.15.1 Notes on setting ratios

Ratios are typically set to trigger from the bottom up, and pay from the top down.

As cumulative losses in a portfolio accumulate, the OC tests will trigger progressively from the Class E through to the Class A. The margin between the original OC ratio (at the Effective Date) and the trigger or test level also tends to increase the higher up the capital structure the tranche is (Table 7.1).

For example a typical $400 million CLO having the following capital structure would purchase approximately $390 million of collateral at close. The difference between the issuance

Table 7.1   Margin between OC ratio and trigger level

Tranche	Size	Percentage	Initial OC	Test Level	Loss Amount (mm)	Margin
A	270	67.5%	146.1%			
B	50	12.5%	123.3%	111.6%	37.4	11.7%
C	16	4.0%	117.4%	108.3%	30.6	9.1%
D	20	4.0%	110.8%	104.8%	21.4	6.0%
E	16	4.0%	106.0%	103.1%	11.0	2.9%
F	30	8.0%	98.1%			

is typically down to fees and expenses at the close and the purchase of above par priced collateral.

The margin between the Initial OC level and the Test level will increase, as the seniority of the tranche increases. Similarly, the IC tests are set with suitable margins to trigger from the bottom up and pay from the top down. However, there have been some cases of IC tests triggering from the bottom up and also paying the more junior classes of Notes from the bottom up. These so-called "reverse triggers" may make some sense for equity-friendly deals and deals with high junior costs of funds. That is, on triggering a junior interest coverage test and paying down the senior (usually cheaper) funding, the interest coverage problem may be exacerbated as the average cost of funds will be increasing. Subject to other constraints, such as passing the OC triggers, paying the D note for a breach of a D IC trigger may make more sense, particularly from an E note holder's perspective.

7.15.2 Collateral par tests

Often in CLO transactions there are so called soft triggers – Collateral Par tests that are placed between the junior management fee and the equity payments in order to rebuild collateral principal payments in the event of a loss. At the start of a transaction, as seen from Table 7.1, there is usually a margin between the test level and the trigger level. However, once the test level is breached, the remedy usually only cures to the trigger. The transaction can therefore be very sensitive to minor losses, and the payments can become "choppy", i.e., junior notes and equity paying one period and not the next, and then the period after that. To avoid this problem there can be a soft trigger that diverts income due to the equity to rebuild the collateral amount by purchasing more collateral. This will tend to rebuild the margin over the test levels and provide for a steady payment frequency to the junior tranches. As an alternative to a contractual collateral par test some transactions provide for diversion of payments to the equity or preference shares to the purchase of additional collateral, at the collateral manager's discretion.

7.15.3 Curing OC breaches in the principal waterfall

As you will recall from above:

$$\Delta L = \min\left(\frac{(R_T L_A - P_A)}{(R_T - 1)}, P_A''\right)$$

which is the cure amount, if paid from the Principal Waterfall, required to cure to the trigger level. Eagle-eyed readers will spot a problem as the required ratio, R_T, approaches 1. That is right: the cure amount tends to be infinite! The upshot is that it is impossible to cure an OC trigger level of 100% within a Principal Waterfall. Additionally, as the trigger level tends to 100%, the more unlikely it is that there will be sufficient proceeds to cure.

Additional considerations with regard to restrictions on payments in the Principal Waterfall to expenses and interest due, but not paid, which require such payments only to be made if they were not to breach a coverage test. This can also be very problematic for deals with test ratios close to 100%.

In particular, most transactions trigger a default if the senior-most note, the Class A note typically, does not receive full and timely interest. Therefore most CDO transactions unconditionally allow for "leakage" from principal to pay at least the Class A note (sometimes the Class B note also). However, occasionally the authors have seen this senior payment subject to not causing a breach in triggers. This seemingly innocuous condition can make payment to the Class A notes in full unlikely and trigger a default on the transaction, in extreme default scenarios.

This additional constraint necessitates an increase in the cure by the "additional liability" of paying the interest, so effectively an "over-cure" is required in order to allow for the interest "leakage" coming after.

Effectively the equation becomes:

$$\Delta L = \min \left(\frac{(R_T L_A + I - P_A)}{(R_T - 1)}, P_A'' \right),$$

where I is the interest to be paid. To incorporate these restrictions throughout, there has to be a running calculation of available monies to be paid, which will tend to $I + \Delta L = P_A''$, the available principal proceeds. The interest available to be paid is therefore restricted to $I = (P_A'' - \Delta L) * (R_{T-1})$.

These points are addressed in more detail in Chapter 11.

8
Outputs Sheet

8.1 PURPOSE OF THE OUTPUTS SHEET

Once the logic for the waterfall has been determined, the performance of the liabilities under various input scenarios needs to be assessed to ascertain the potential ratings and to demonstrate the value of the tranches for investors. Rather than incorporate the **Outputs Sheet** as part of the waterfall, the authors prefer a separate worksheet as part of a modular design for the following reasons:

- it provides a buffer between the ratings and investor analysis, and the logic of the waterfall; and
- it allows for changes to other parts of the model, i.e., the waterfall, while it limits the impact of these changes on the rest of the model, thus assisting in maintaining the model over its life cycle.

The **Output Sheet** summarizes the outputs for the liabilities. The main uses of the **Output Sheet** are to calculate:

(a) the net present value of the liabilities;
(b) the tranche losses;
(c) pricing for discount securities;
(d) analytical information such as the weighted average life and the various durations.

8.2 COLLATING WATERFALL OUTPUTS

The **Outputs Sheet** is arranged such that in the first section, rows 1 to 99, there are the following calculations for each class of notes:

- General Calculations (Figure 8.1):
  - Internal Rate of Return
  - Weighted Average Life
- Calculations at Par Spread (Figure 8.2):
  - Par Spread
  - Net Present Value
  - Loss
  - Loss Percentage
  - Swap Duration
  - Average Rate
  - Macaulay Duration
  - Modified Duration
  - Dollar Duration
  - Price

	I	J
4		
5	**General Calculations**	
6	Internal Rate of Return	3.28%
7	Weighted Average Life	5.517
8		

Figure 8.1   General Calculations

	L	M
4		
5	**Calculations at Par Spread**	
6	Par Spread (bps)	40
7	Net Present Value	278,000,000
8	Loss	-
9	Loss Percentage	0.00%
10	Swap Duration	5.20
11	Average Yield	3.19%
12	Macaulay Duration	5.24
13	Modified Duration	5.20
14	Dollar Duration	5.20
15	Price	100.00%
16		

Figure 8.2   Calculations at Par Spread

- Calculations at Discount Margin (Figure 8.3):
  - Par Spread
  - Net Present Value
  - Loss
  - Loss Percentage
  - Swap Duration
  - Average Rate
  - Macaulay Duration
  - Modified Duration
  - Dollar duration
  - Price

Below this, in the section starting in Row 100, are the Output Calculations. Creating this part of the worksheet is the first step. The collation of the data from the various other worksheets occurs in this section.

First, in cells B104 to F184, the Vectors are reproduced for reference (Figure 8.4). Column B holds the Period ordinal, Column C holds the Payment Dates, Column D is the Accrual in days per day count in the period. Column E is the cumulative accrual since the issuance date and Column F holds the applied floating index values (e.g., LIBOR, EURIBOR) for each period.

After this, for each class of note (excluding the equity notes), the following amounts are produced (Figure 8.5):

- Coupon Rate
- Interest Paid

	O	P
4		
5	**Calculations at Discount Margin**	
6	Discount Margin (bps)	100
7	Net Present Value	269,468,657
8	Loss	(8,531,343)
9	Loss Percentage	-3.07%
10	Swap Duration	5
11	Average Yield	3.78%
12	Macaulay Duration	5.24
13	Modified Duration	5.19
14	Dollar Duration	5.03
15	Price	96.93%
16		

Figure 8.3   Calculations at Discount Margin

- Principal Paid
- Total Paid
- Discount Rate at Par Spread
- Period Contribution at Par Spread
- Swap Duration Contribution at Par Spread
- Discount Rate at Discount Margin
- Period Contribution at Discount Margin
- Swap Duration Contribution at Discount Margin

The **Coupon Rate** is calculated as the LIBOR rate in column F plus the spread for the relevant note.

For the Period 1, the Class A Coupon Rate in cell H105, the calculation is `"=F105 + $M$6/10000"`.

The **Interest Paid** is taken from the **Waterfall Sheet** in the "Vectors and Liabilities Cash Flows" section in Rows 100 to 199.

The formula in cell I105 for the Period 1 Class A Interest Paid is `"='Waterfall'!J105"`.

The **Principal Paid** in Period 0 is the negative value of the Tranche Amount Input from the **Inputs Sheet**. After Period 0, the Principal Paid references the **Waterfall Sheet** in the "Vectors and Liabilities Cash Flows" section in Rows 100 to 199.

Again, for the Period 1 Class A Notes, the calculation, in cell J105, is `"=Waterfall!L105"`.

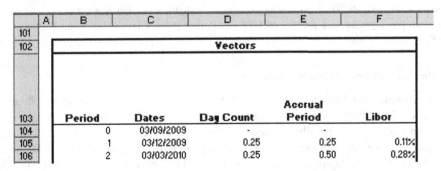

A	B	C	D	E	F
101					
102			Vectors		
103	Period	Dates	Day Count	Accrual Period	Libor
104	0	03/09/2009	-	-	
105	1	03/12/2009	0.25	0.25	0.11%
106	2	03/03/2010	0.25	0.50	0.28%

Figure 8.4   Vectors

	H	I	J	K	L	M	N	O	P	Q
16										
100					Output Calculations					
101										
102										
103	Class A Coupon Rate	Class A Interest Paid	Class A Principal Paid	Class A Total Paid	Class A Discount Rate at Par Spread	Class A Period Contribution at Par Spread	Class A Swap Duration Contribution at Par Spread	Class A Discount Rate at Discount Margin	Class A Period Contribution at Discount Margin	Class A Swap Duration Contribution at Discount Margin
104			(278,000,000)	(278,000,000)	100.00%			100.00%		
105	0.51%	355,530	-	355,530	99.87%	89,755	0.25	99.87%	89,755	0.25
106	0.68%	470,553	-	470,553	99.70%	235,882	0.25	99.70%	235,882	0.25

Figure 8.5 Output Calculations

The **Total Paid** is simply calculated as:

- Interest Paid
- *plus* Principal Paid

Hence in cell K105 there is the formula `"=I105 + J105"`.

8.3 PRESENT VALUE

For the **Discount Rates at Par Spread**, a discount factor for each period is calculated as described in Chapter 4. The discount factors are constructed using the same interest rate as the interest payments due on the tranche, and are a combination of the Day Count vector in Column D and the Coupon Rate.

That is:

$$df_n = \frac{df_{n-1}}{(1 + r_n t_n)}$$

where:

df_n – is the current Discount Rate;
df_{n-1} – is the Discount Rate for the previous period;
r_n – is the current Coupon Rate;
t_n – is the current Day Count.

Starting with a value of 100% in Period 0, the Discount Factors at the Par Spread are calculated for each period. For example, for the Class A Discount factor at Par Spread for Period 1, found in cell L105, the formula is `"=L104/(1 + H105*D105)"`.

The **Discount Factors at Discount Margin** is calculated in the same manner, with the exception being that the **Discount Margin** is used instead of the Par Spread.

For example, starting with a value of 100% in Period 0, the Class A Discount Factor at Discount Spread for Period 1 in cell O105 is `"=O104/(1 + (F105 + $P$6/10000)*D105)"`.

8.3.1 Par Spread and Discount Margin

The **Par Spread** and **Discount Margin (DM)** are referenced on the **Outputs Sheet** for convenience. This sheet is designed in such a way that if a modeller wishes to make a quick analysis on this sheet it is possible to hard-code over these references and view the change in the outputs, i.e., value, duration, etc., with a change in either the Par Spreads or DMs. It is always best practice to highlight in another colour and record a comment when hard-coding over a formula or reference so that it is easy to find and correct later.

8.3.2 Net present value

The net present value or NPV of the tranche is obtained by taking the sumproduct of the payments and the discount factors.

$$\sum_{n}^{i=1} TP_i \, df_i$$

where:

TP$_i$ = is the Total Paid in Period i
df$_i$ = is the Discount Factor in Period i.

Thus, the **Class A Net Present Value at Par Spread** (in cell M7, named Tranche_1_Par_NPV) is calculated as `"=SUMPRODUCT(K105:K184,L105:L184)"`.

The Class A Net Present Value at Par Spread should equal the initial nominal value of the tranche, i.e., nominal par under a zero loss scenario.

The **Net Present Value at Discount Margin** is calculated the same as above, with the exception that as the Discount Rate vector at the Discount Margin is different to the Discount Rate at Par Spread, the NPV will also differ.

For example, the Class A Net Present Value at Discount Margin (cell P7, named Tranche_1_DM_NVP) is determined by `"=SUMPRODUCT(K105:K184,O105:O184)"`.

8.3.3 Loss

The **Loss at Par Spread** will be calculated as the Par NPV *less* the Tranche Amount at issuance. Thus, for example, the Loss at Par Spread for the Class A Notes (cell M8, named Tranche_1_Par_Loss) is `"=Tranche_1_Par_NPV-Tranche_1_Amount"`.

Similarly, the **Class A Notes Loss at Discount Margin** (cell P8, named Tranche_1_DM_Loss) is `"=Tranche_1_DM_NPV-Tranche_1_Amount*Tranche_1_Price"`.

8.3.4 Loss Percentage

The **Loss Percentage** is simply the Loss *divided by* the Issuance Amount of the Tranche. That is, the Class A Par Spread Loss Percentage in cell M9, named Tranche_1_Par_Loss_Pct is `"=Tranche_1_Par_Loss/Tranche_1_Amount"`.

The **Discount Margin Loss Percentage** in cell P9, named Tranche_1_DM_Loss_Pct is `"=Tranche_1_DM_Loss/Tranche_1_Amount"`.

8.4 DURATION

It is also useful to calculate the duration for the tranche: Macaulay Duration, Modified Duration and Dollar Duration. See Chapter 4 for an explanation of these calculations.

As discussed before, while Excel has built in functions for duration these are designed for fixed rate bullet securities paying either annually or semi-annually, they do not support either floating rates, amortizing securities or more frequent payments.

8.4.1 Macaulay Duration

The **Par Spread Macaulay Duration**, in cell M12, is calculated as the sum of the Period Contributions at Par Spread divided by the Par NPV. Therefore, for the Class A1 Notes, the Par Spread Macaulay Duration is `"=SUM(M105:M184)/(Tranche_1_Par_NPV+Epsilon)"`.

The **Period Contributions at Par Spread** are the per period calculations required to determine the Macaulay Duration. It is determined for each period as the *product of*:

- Cumulative **Accrual Period** for that period
- **Total Paid** for the period
- **Discount Rate at Par Spread** for that period.

For example, the Class A Period Contribution at Par Spread for Period 1 in cell M105 is `"=E105*K105*L105"`.

The **Discount Margin Macaulay Duration**, in cell P12, is calculated in the same way, with the exception that the DM is used instead of the Par Spread. Hence the formula `"=SUM(P105:P184)/(Tranche_1_DM_NPV + Epsilon)"`.

8.4.2 Modified Duration

Modified Duration is calculated as the Macaulay Duration divided by the sum of one plus the Yield multiplied by the average Accrual Period (assumed as the first Accrual Period). The Class A Par Spread Modified Duration in cell P13 contains `"=Tranche_1_Par_Mac_Dur/ (1 + Tranche_1_Par_Yield*E105 + Epsilon)"`.

8.4.3 Average Yield

The **Average Yield** is one minus sum of the discounted principal redemptions divided by the total principal amount and divided by the swap duration. For example, the Class A Par Spread Average Yield in cell M11 is `"=(1-SUMPRODUCT(J105:J184,L105:L184)/Tranche_ 1_Amount)/Tranche_1_Par_Swap_Dur"`.

As before, the **Discount Margin Average Yield** is one minus sum of the discounted principal redemptions, using the **Discount Rate at Discount Margin**, divided by the total principal amount and divided by the **Swap Duration at Discount Margin**. In cell P11 there is the formula `"=(1-SUMPRODUCT(J105:J184,O105:O184)/Tranche_1_Amount)/ Tranche_1_DM_Swap_Dur"`.

8.4.4 Swap Duration

As discussed in Chapter 4, the **Swap Duration** is the basic sensitivity to a change in the index for a floating rate. For an amortizing liability, the **Swap Duration Contribution** per period needs to be weighted by the balance of the liabilities outstanding at the beginning of the period.

For Period 1, the total tranche liability is used as the weighting, but for subsequent periods the weighting is the outstanding nominal of the tranche, i.e., the original nominal *minus* the principal payments from all the previous periods.

For example, the Class A Swap Duration Contribution at Par Spread for Period 1 in cell N105 is calculated as `"=($D105*(Tranche_1_Amount))/Tranche_1_Amount*L105"`, and the Class A Swap Duration Contribution at Par Spread for Period 2 in cell N106 is `"=($D106*(Tranche_1_Amount-SUM(J$105:J105)))/Tranche_1_Amount*L106"`.

8.4.5 Dollar Duration

The **Dollar Duration or Price Duration** (for non-dollar investors) is probably the most useful number as it gives an indication of the change in the price of the note for a change in the yield, rather than the percentage change as given by Modified Duration. The Dollar Duration is determined by multiplying the Modified Duration by the Price.

> *Did you know?* A rough check of the accuracy of the calculation can be done by changing the Par Spread in M5 by plus one basis point and minus one basis point and taking the difference in Price. If this difference in Price is the divided by 2 basis points, the result should be very close to the same value as the modified duration in cell M12.

Thus, the Class A Par Spread Dollar Duration in cell M14 is determined by `"=Tranche_1_Par_Mod_Dur*Tranche_1_Par_Price"`.

8.4.6 Price

When issuing a CDO it is often a necessity to "price" the tranche. Issuing the liabilities at a discount to par is common. Additionally, when valuing a tranche after issuance it may be useful to be able to price at a discount, that is, represent the potential change in new issue spreads and/or the bid-offer. To accomplish this is quite simple, and only requires generating the discount factors at the new spread and calculating the present value or price of the cash flows using those discount factors.

In cell M15, the Par Price is calculated as `"=Tranche_1_Par_NPV/Tranche_1_Amount"`.

Similarly, the cell P14, the Price at Discount Margin is `"=Tranche_1_DM_NPV/Tranche_1_Amount"`.

8.5 WEIGHTED AVERAGE LIFE AND INTERNAL RATE OF RETURN

8.5.1 Internal Rate of Return

The Internal Rate of Return (IRR) is calculated using the XIRR() function using the **Dates** in column C and the relevant **Total Paid** amounts.

For example, the Class A IRR, in cell J6, is determined by `"=XIRR(K104:K184, C104:C184)"`.

8.5.2 Weighted Rverage Life

The **Weighted Average Life** (WAL) is the average time to repayment of half of the principal of the Note. It is usually calculated using SUMPRODUCT of the time to payment in column E and the payments in column J *divided by* the tranche notional.

> ***Did you know?*** *A more precise measurement of WAL is to use Actual/365 or 30/360 rather than the accrual time. For greater accuracy an additional vector can be added to the Outputs Sheet for the purpose of the WAL calculation.*

However, there is an additional part to determining the Weighted Average Life: dealing with shortfalls in the case of losses. If losses are not considered, the WAL will shorten under extreme losses and may even disappear. This is counter-intuitive as the Weighted Average Life should be increasing and technically becoming infinite if a noteholder receives no principal back. The way to deal with this conundrum is to effectively add the loss/unpaid principal back at the maturity of the transaction. This will have the desired effect of lengthening the average life as losses increase.

Thus, for the Class A Weighted Average Life in cell J7, the calculation is `"=(SUMPRODUCT($E105:$E184,J105:J184)/Tranche_1_Amount+SUM(J104:J184)*$E184/Tranche_1_Amount)*360/365"`.

As discussed here and in Chapter 9, both WAL and Duration are used to assess the thresholds of expected loss permissible for particular ratings. In some instances a probability WAL is used, i.e., average life under losses in the portfolio weighed by the probabilility of such losses.

8.6 EQUITY ANALYSIS

While the above analysis is repeated for each liability tranche, the requirements for analysis of the equity tranches are slightly different. Payments to the equity tranche are usually residual cashflows and consequently the equity tranche does not usually have a stated promised return. It should be noted, however, that it is sometimes possible to rate an equity tranche to a lower promise of payment: either a lower promised coupon or to the return of principal only.

It is most common to analyse the equity tranche using the following measures:

- IRR;
- Duration.

Less commonly, measures of the WAL and discount margin are used.

The IRR is usually calculated using the native EXCEL functions such as IRR(), MIRR() or XIRR(). This is slightly incongruous as the residual tranche is typically linked to the floating index with a levered spread. It is also possible to use discount factors and the "goal seek" function within Excel to solve for a discount margin or a fixed yield. The choice of the IRR() function can make quite a difference with regard to the value of the internal rate of return calculation.

The IRR() function calculates a "per period" internal rate of return assuming even periods. This differs from XIRR() which provides an internal rate of return assuming that the schedule of cash flows is not necessarily on even periods and is based on an annualized rate using actual/365.

The difference when compounding or decompounding the rate can be quite noticeable given the high rates that are generally calculated. For example, using the standard compounding/decompounding formulas shown in Chapter 4, the difference between a semi-annual and an annualized rate, when for example the calculated semi-annual rate is 20% (i.e., bond basis), is 100 basis points or one whole percentage point. This can vary further depending on the payment frequency and day count convention.

Given this, it should therefore not be surprising to know that many offering documents actually quote the Excel XIRR() function as the basis for calculation for determining incentive fees or for quoted indicative returns.

8.7 BASIC AUDITING

While cash flows CDOs are not necessarily excessively complicated from a calculation perspective, they can encompass a large amount of detail in which it is possible for the new or unwary modeller to get lost. The size and the extent of detail can be intimidating. How does a modeller know if the model is error free, particularly after changes? While there are several techniques that can be used to fault find a model (see Chapter 12), basic checks can help to give confidence to a modeller.

The **Outputs Sheet** acts as a basic audit worksheet to catch obvious and avoidable errors. For example, if there is an Equity IRR of 90% when it is clear that the structure and pricing make this impossible, it is then clear that there is a fault in the model. As another example, if the Net Present Value at Par Spread for a tranche is not equal to the initial nominal value of the tranche where there are no defaults or losses and the price is 100%, then barring a very uncommon structure, there is probably a fault in the modelling.

It should be noted that this simple method of auditing will not catch logic errors with regard to misallocation of cash flows between tranches. The authors believe an Audit Sheet is indispensable for this and such a sheet is described in more detail in Chapter 11.

8.7.1 Conditional formatting

It is noteworthy that, as a matter of good practice, the authors use conditional formatting to highlight in red text any negative numbers in the *Cash Flow Model*. This will always aid a modeller in "seeing" the negative numbers. As will become obvious as a cash flow model is constructed, there is a large amount of information and calculations. Hence, failing to see a negative value can occur quite easily. Using every means possible to guard against this and/or readily identify negative values is the most prudent course.

Moody's Rating Agency Methodology

9.1 INTRODUCTION TO AGENCY METHODOLOGIES

At this point, prior to starting the discussion on rating agency methodologies, the authors believe the following "health" warning is required. The following chapters discussing the methodologies of Moody's and S&P summarize the authors' views, experience and understanding of the methodologies. It is a summary of how to adapt a cash flow model to these methodologies and should therefore be viewed as supplemental to, and not a replacement for, the agencies' own published papers and/or their analysts' views. The authors' experience may not be the same as the reader's, and also the agencies reserve the right to modify and/or supplement their methodologies at any time, especially during rating committees, and therefore should be expected to differ.

Another warning is also required before the agency methodologies are delved into. A certain basic level of statistical knowledge is assumed in this chapter and Chapter 10. Where possible, the authors have attempted to provide "Did you know?" information boxes. Unfortunately, it is outside the scope of this book to provide more information, and the reader is encouraged to seek this out elsewhere. That said, it is possible to model a CDO for rating purposes without such knowledge, albeit with gaps in the reader's understanding of the criteria.

9.1.1 Two-stage modelling process

Rating agencies typically use a two-stage process when analysing the modelling aspects of rating a cash flow CDO:

- first, the collateral portfolio is assessed to determine the credit risk of each of the obligors individually and the portfolio as a whole;
- second, the distribution of cash flows to the note holders as described in the legal documentation for the CDO is modelled and examined under various stress scenarios.

For the first stage, the rating agencies often use a proprietary "black box" model to assess the credit risk in the underlying portfolio. For the second stage, the cash flow modelling of the CDO is examined and stressed. Among other potential modelling and stress assumptions, an agency will commonly determine, and provide to the modeller, the levels of default rates and respective timings, and recovery rates and respective timings appropriate to the transaction. In addition, because of concerns over potential differences in asset and liability interest rates and potentially associated interest rate swaps, there are usually additional requirements to stress the interest rates over the life cycle of the transaction. Also, in transactions where assets and liabilities are denominated in more than one currency, additional currency stresses may be required to assess foreign exchange risk.

9.1.2 Moody's approach

Moody's rates structured finance obligations on a scale from Aaa to C; however, Moody's has announced[1] its intention to supplement the rating of these obligations by the suffix "(sf)" from

---

[1] "Announcement: Moody's announces plans for structured ratings indicator", Moody's Investors Service, 27 October 2009.

the second quarter, 2010, to comply with the anticipated regulatory requirements from the European Union. The ratings reflect the expected credit loss which might occur on or before the final legal maturity in relation to the defined promise of payments. The ratings incorporate Moody's assessment of the default probability and loss severity of the obligations.[2]

> **Did you know?**
>
> Moody's structured finance ratings range from "Aaa" to "C". "Aaa" is the rating assigned to obligations with minimal credit risk and determined to be of the highest quality. In contrast, "C" rated obligations are the lowest rated and are commonly in default with low expectation of recovery of principal or interest. Moody's also uses the numbers 1, 2 and 3 and the end of ratings between Aa and Caa to indicate subclasses within the ratings where 1 is the highest ranking and 3 is the lowest within each subclass.

At the time of writing, Moody's main approach to cash CLOs is based upon the Binomial Expansion Technique or "BET". Several different variants of this approach have been or are being used. These include the double binominal technique, Moody's alternative BET approach and the correlated binomial technique. This chapter will mainly address the original BET approach which is currently used for leveraged loan CDOs.

9.2 THE BET APPROACH

Moody's approach to rating corporate credit CDOs (which are subject to a complex waterfall) is to generate expected loss estimates for the CDO tranches using the "BET". The seminal paper on BET was first published by Moody's in 1996 and the approach has only been modified moderately since then.[3]

The basic premise of the methodology is that a portfolio of heterogeneous obligors (with respect to rating, size, industry, recovery rate and correlation) can be approximated as a homogeneous collection of "D" independent obligors with the same default probability, recoveries and maturity profile, where D is the diversity number or score. The core inputs to this approach are:

- Moody's Weighted Average Rating Factor (colloquially known as "WARF");
- Moody's Diversity Score;
- Weighed Average Life (or "WAL");
- Moody's Weighted Average Recovery Rate (or "WARR").

As discussed above, the diversity score ("D") reduces the actual number of interdependent obligors in the actual portfolio into an idealized portfolio of "D" number of homogeneous, uncorrelated or indepenent obligors. The concept of independent obligors is important in that, by asserting independence, the default of one obligor has no influence on the default performance of the rest of the obligors that make up the portfolio. In other words, the probability of two defaults is the product of their individual probabilities, and the cumulative probability of n defaults from a pool of m obligors, is the sum of the total combinations of selecting

---

[2] "Moody's Rating Symbols & Definitions", Moody's Investors Service, June 2008, page 12.

[3] "Moody's Rating Symbols & Definitions", Moody's Investors Service, June 2008, page 12.

"n" defaults from "m" total obligors with "m-n" survivors – the so-called binomial formula (discussed further below).

The diversity score, "D", number of assets is then used to calculate the expected loss distributions. There are $D + 1$ default scenarios (0 defaults, 1 default... to D defaults) and the binomial formula is used to determine the probability of each default scenario. Once the losses under each of the default scenarios are determined, the losses and the default probabilities from the binomial distribution are then used to create estimates of the portfolio and tranche loss distributions. These distributions are then used to determine the tranche ratings.

> **Did you know?** *"Expected loss" is calculated as "expected value" is calculated in basic statistics. The expected value of a probability distribution is the sum of:*
> * *each value*
> * *multiplied by the probability of each respective value occurring.*

At the time of writing, this method is still being used for CLO ratings.[4] Below are listed the outline steps for applying the current method, which is applied to each tranche:

Step 1: Calculate the diversity score
Step 2: Assess the weighted average rating factor and weighted average recovery rate
Step 3: Determine the weighted average life
Step 4: Calculate the default rate
Step 5: Determine the cumulative binomial probabilities
Step 6: Determine the losses for each of the 0 to D defaults and weight the resultant average or expected loss by the probability of default

Before starting on the analysis of the above steps, various Moody's variables should be built into a collateral model.

9.3 EVALUATING THE COLLATERAL

In Chapter 6, the *Simple Warehouse Model* was discussed. In this chapter, this model is expanded to create the *Standard Warehouse Model*.

As mentioned previously, a warehouse model at its most basic level will usually contain the following worksheets:

* a Portfolio Sheet which describes the characteristics of the individual assets;
* a Summary Sheet to record the portfolio characteristics as a whole;
* a Reference Sheet with the relevant rating agency tables and other reference material.

---

[4] In 2006, Moody's published a Request for Comment proposing an initiative to move from using the BET to using the correlated BET when analysing US cash flow CLOs. In February 2007, Moody's further stated that a Request of Comment regarding this was expected to be published later in 2007. As of the time of writing, this has not yet occurred. See "Moody's Approach to Adapting U.S. Cash-Flow CLO Rating Methodology to PDR/LGD Initiative", 21 February 2007, page 2.

9.3.1 The Portfolio Sheet

Looking at the *Standard Warehouse Model*, the **Inputs and Portfolio Sheet** covers each of the assets fields from the index ordinal (in cell B100) to the bullet/amortizing indicator (in cell W100).

Additional fields usually used at the time of writing for Moody's attributes include:

- Moody's Borrower/Issuer Rating (cell X100)
- Moody's WARF (cell Y100)
- Moody's Facility/Tranche Rating (cell Z100)
- Country (cell AB100)
- Moody's Country Rating (cell AC100)
- Moody's Industry (cell AE100)
- Moody's Industry No. (cell AF100)
- Moody's Difference in Rating: Borrower/Issuer vs. Tranche (cell AI100)
- Moody's Asset Type for Recovery Rate Purposes (cell AJ100)
- If Structured Finance, Type and Thickness of Tranche (AK100)
- Moody's Recovery Rates (cells AL100 to BC100)

Most of these fields are discussed in further detail below.

With respect to Moody's ratings, where there are no Moody's public ratings for the assets in the portfolio, analysis will be based on credit estimates, a bank's internal ratings or another agency's ratings. In general, Moody's will make a two-notch downward adjustment to the rating of S&P-rated loans, a one-notch downward adjustment for S&P-rated investment grade bonds, and a two-notch downward adjustment for S&P-rated speculative grade bonds (and while this was explicit in the December 2008 paper it was less clear in the August 2009 paper, see below).[5]

With respect to corporate assets which are on review for upgrade or downgrade by Moody's, for the purposes of analysis within the CDO, it is the authors' experience that these assets will be treated as if they have already been downgraded or upgraded by one notch if on watch negative or positive as applicable for investment grade assets, and by two notches for credits on review for downgrade.[6] This also will apply for assets whose credit ratings are inferred from another agency where that agency has placed the asset on review for downgrade or upgrade. For structured credit assets, it is the authors' experience that the adjustment will be at least two notches for assets that are on review for downgrade and potentially more at the discretion of the analyst/rating commitee.[7]

9.3.2 The Reference Sheet

There are three sections to the **Reference Sheet**:

- Moody's reference tables (beginning in row 100)
- S&P reference tables (starting in Row 400), which will be explored in Chapter 10
- SIC Codes tables (commencing in Row 600)

---

[5] "Moody's Approach to Rating Collateralized Loan Obligations", Moody's Investors Service, 31 December 2008, pages 4–5.

[6] "Moody's Approach to Rating Collateralized Loan Obligations", Moody's Investors Service, 12 August 2009, pages 4–5.

[7] See "Moody's Approach to Rating Collateralized Loan Obligations", Moody's Investors Service, 12 August 2009, page 5.

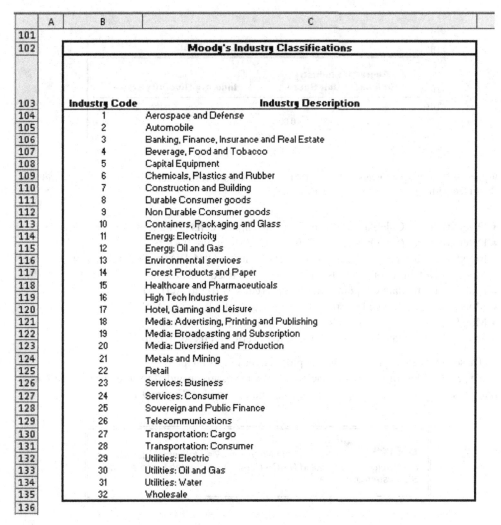

Figure 9.1 Moody's Industry Classifications, © Moody's Investors Service, Inc. and/or its affiliates. Reprinted with permission. All Rights Reserved.

The Moody's section includes:

- Industry Classifications table[8] (cells B102 to C135, named "M_Industries"). This was updated in 2009 to only 32 industries, as shown in Figure 9.1
- Diversity Score Table (cells E102 to F304) (Figure 9.2)

---

[8] For Moody's Industry Classifications including descriptions, see "Moody's Approach to Rating Collateralized Loan Obligations", Moody's Investors Service, 31 December 2008, Appendix 6, page 42. For Moody's Industry Classifications including descriptions, see "Moody's Approach to Rating Collateralized Loan Obligations", Moody's Investors Service, 12 August 2009, Appendix 6, page 44.

	E	F
101		
102	**Moody's Diversity Score Table**	
103	**Aggregate Industry Equivalent Unit Score**	**Industry Diversity Score**
104	0.0000	0.0000
105	0.0500	0.1000
106	0.1500	0.2000
107	0.2500	0.3000

Figure 9.2 Moody's Diversity Score Table, © Moody's Investors Service, Inc. and/or its affiliates. Reprinted with permission. All Rights Reserved.

- Diversity Score Calculations From Portfolio Inputs (cells H102 to K304) (Figure 9.3)
- Diversity Score Calculator (cells M102 to O135) (Figure 9.4)
- Moody's Rating Factors (cells Q102 to R123, named "M_WARFs") (Figure 9.5)
- Moody's Notching Table (cells T102 to U123, named "M_Notching") (Figure 9.6)
- Moody's Immediate Corporate Recoveries (cells W102 to AO126)
- Moody's 1 Year Lagged Corporate Recoveries (cells W133 to AO133)
- Moody's 2+ Year Corporate Recoveries (cells W156 to AO180)
- Moody's Immediate structured finance Recoveries (cells AQ102 to BG117)

These tables are reproduced and explored later in this chapter.

The SIC Codes Tables (commencing in Row 600), are provided for the purposes of potentially assisting in determining rating agency industry codes (Figure 9.7).

> **Did you know?** In 1997, the North American Industry Classification System (commonly called NAICS Codes) was created to replace the SIC system over time.

One of the most widely accepted categorization schemes of industry groups is the United States Standard Industrial Classification Manual in which there are Standard Industry Classifications, commonly known as SIC Codes. The SIC Codes are organized first by Divisions:

- Division A: Agriculture, Forestry, And Fishing
- Division B: Mining
- Division C: Construction
- Division D: Manufacturing
- Division E: Transportation, Communications, Electric, Gas, and Sanitary Services
- Division F: Wholesale Trade
- Division G: Retail Trade
- Division H: Finance, Insurance, and Real Estate
- Division I: Services
- Division J: Public Administration
- Division K: Nonclassifiable Establishments

	H	I	J	K
101				
102	Diversity Score Calculations From Portfolio Inputs			
103	Obligor	Amount for Obligor	Unit Score	Industry
104	Corporate Borrower 1	4,100,000	0.89	10
105	Corporate Borrower 2	5,700,000	1.00	13
106	Corporate Borrower 3	5,900,000	1.00	23

Figure 9.3   Diversity Score Calculations from Portfolio Inputs

	M	N	O
101			
102	Diversity Score Calculator		
103	Asset Code	Capped Industry Totals	Industry Diversity Score
104	1	2.92	1.95
105	2	1.07	1.05
106	3	2.00	1.50

Figure 9.4   Diversity Score Calculator

	Q	R
101		
102	Moody's Rating Factors	
103	Rating	Rating Factor
104	Aaa	1
105	Aa1	10
106	Aa2	20
107	Aa3	40
108	A1	70
109	A2	120
110	A3	180
111	Baa1	260
112	Baa2	360
113	Baa3	610
114	Ba1	940
115	Ba2	1350
116	Ba3	1766
117	B1	2220
118	B2	2720
119	B3	3490
120	Caa1	4770
121	Caa2	6500
122	Caa3	8070
123	Ca	10000
124		

Figure 9.5   Moody's Rating Factors, © Moody's Investors Service, Inc. and/or its affiliates. Reprinted with permission. All Rights Reserved.

	T	U
101		
102	**Notching Table**	
103	**Rating**	**Ordinal No.**
104	Aaa	1
105	Aa1	2
106	Aa2	3
107	Aa3	4
108	A1	5
109	A2	6
110	A3	7
111	Baa1	8
112	Baa2	9
113	Baa3	10
114	Ba1	11
115	Ba2	12
116	Ba3	13
117	B1	14
118	B2	15
119	B3	16
120	Caa1	17
121	Caa2	18
122	Caa3	19
123	Ca	20
124		

Figure 9.6 Notching Table

Within the Divisions, there are Major Groups, which run from 01 to 99. Then within the Major Groups there are Industry Groups, from 011 to 999. Finally, within the Industry Groups there are Industry Codes from 0111 to 9999.

Where a modeller is unsure of the rating agency industry code, it is possible to make an educated guess by determining the SIC Code of an organization and matching this up to a potential coordinating Moody's Code, an estimate of which the authors have included adjacent to each SIC Code.

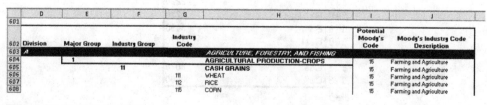

	D	E	F	G	H	I	J
601							
602	Division	Major Group	Industry Group	Industry Code		Potential Moody's Code	Moody's Industry Code Description
603	A				*AGRICULTURE, FORESTRY, AND FISHING*		
604		1			AGRICULTURAL PRODUCTION-CROPS	15	Farming and Agriculture
605			11		CASH GRAINS	15	Farming and Agriculture
606				111	WHEAT	15	Farming and Agriculture
607				112	RICE	15	Farming and Agriculture
608				115	CORN	15	Farming and Agriculture

Figure 9.7 SIC Codes Table

There are several possible ways to determine what the SIC Code is for a corporate obligor. There are several websites that, at the time of writing, provide SIC Codes including:

- www.investorwords.com (free service)
- www.webstersonline.com (free service)
- www.ratingsdirect.com (an S&P subscription service)

9.3.3 The Summary Sheet

The **Summary Sheet** provides a summary of the key characteristics of the portfolio. What has been provided in the ***Standard Warehouse Model*** is a simple sheet. The summary includes the constraints/covenants, or maximum/minimum bucket limits for the collateral and highlights breaches of any of these constraints/covenants.

General characteristics are summarized in cells B3 to E25. This includes the Moody's measurements shown in Figure 9.8.

The Weighted Average Rating Factor (Moody's) (cell C9) is determined by taking from the **Portfolio Inputs Sheet** the sum of the product of each of the Moody's WARFs (in column Y) and the Notionals (in column I) and dividing this by the sum of the total notional amount of the portfolio. Thus, the formula is "=SUMPRODUCT('Inputs and Portfolio'!Y101:Y399, 'Inputs and Portfolio'!I101:I399)/Portfolio_Size_Notional".

The Weighted Average Moody's Rating (cell C10) is determined by looking up the Rating from the Moody's WARF table on the **Reference Sheet**. Hence, the formula is "=INDEX(M_WARFs,MATCH(Summary!C9,Reference!$R$104:$R$123,1),1)".

The Moody's Diversity Score (cell C12) is taken as the sum of the Industry Diversity Scores on the **Reference Sheet**. Thus, cell C12 contains the formula "=SUM(Reference!O104:O135)". The calculation of this score is described further below.

Moody's Recovery Rates are determined in cells C13 to C18.

A	B	C	D	E
	General Characteristics			
	Characteristic	**Portfolio Level**	**Constraint/Covenant**	**Pass/Fail?**
	Portfolio Size	390,000,000	400,000,000	
	Number of Assets	100		
	Number of Obligors	85		
	Weighted Average Spread	2.85%	2.80%	PASS
	Weighted Average Rating Factor (Moody's)	2067	2090	PASS
	Weighted Average Moody's Rating	Ba3	Ba3	
	Weighted Average Life	4.42		
	Moody's Diversity Score	51.32	50	PASS
	Weighted Average Moody's Aaa Recovery Rate (1 Year Lag)	49.25%	43%	PASS
	Weighted Average Moody's Aa2 Recovery Rate (1 Year Lag)	49.00%		
	Weighted Average Moody's A2 Recovery Rate (1 Year Lag)	53.90%		
	Weighted Average Moody's Baa2 Recovery Rate (1 Year Lag)	58.13%		
	Weighted Average Moody's Ba2 Recovery Rate (1 Year Lag)	63.03%		
	Weighted Average Moody's B2 Recovery Rate	62.52%		
	Weighted Average S&P AAA Recovery Rate	67.98%	65%	PASS
	Weighted Average S&P AA Recovery Rate	70.75%	68%	PASS
	Weighted Average S&P A Recovery Rate	73.52%	70%	PASS
	Weighted Average S&P BBB Recovery Rate	77.03%	73%	PASS
	Weighted Average S&P BB Recovery Rate	80.29%	76%	PASS
	Weighted Average S&P B Recovery Rate	80.54%	78%	PASS
	Weighted Average Price	95.12%		

Figure 9.8   General Characteristics

As the reader is likely aware, corporations may issue more than one level of debt. Moody's provides probability-of-default ratings ("PDRs") to corporate obligor families as a whole. A PDR is an indication of the likelihood that any obligor within a corporate family will default on any of its debt issuance. Moody's further provides loss-given-default assessments, represented by a six-point scale, and point estimates ("PEs") for speculative grade corporate debt issuances. Both PDRs and PEs are available on the Moody's website.[9]

The "Moody's Borrower/Issuer Rating" on the **Inputs and Portfolio Sheet** in column X is where the PDR is input. As the PDR represents the rating for an obligor's corporate family and the likelihood of default of any of its debt issuance, it is the values in column X which are used to calculate the WARF in column Y, as described previously.

The "Moody's Facility/Tranche Rating" in column Z on the **Inputs and Portfolio Sheet** is where the Moody's rating for the specific debt obligation is input.

The Moody's Recovery Rate analysis is done in columns AI to BC of the **Inputs and Portfolio Sheet**.

In column AI, the "Moody's Difference in Rating: Borrower/Issuer vs. Tranche" is determined by looking up the difference in the notches for the Moody's Tranche rating versus the Moody's Borrower/Issuer. For example, in AI101 there is the formula "=VLOOKUP(Z101, M_Notching,2,0)-VLOOKUP(X101,M_Notching,2,0)". "M_Notching" is a table in the **Reference Sheet** in cells T102 to U123.

"Moody's Asset Type for Recovery Rate Purposes" and "If Structured Finance, Type and Thickness of Tranche" in columns AJ and AK are used when looking up the recovery rates in columns AL to BC of the **Inputs and Portfolio Sheet**.

The Recovery Rates for US corporate debt are found on the **Reference Sheet** in cells W102 to AO180.

The corporate debt recovery rates for immediate recoveries are shown in Figure 9.9. The corporate debt recovery rates for 1-year lagged recoveries are shown in Figure 9.10. The corporate debt recovery rates for 2+ year lagged recoveries are shown in Figure 9.11.

The structured finance recovery rates are shown in Figure 9.12.

Immediate Corporate Recoveries

Rating	Bonds −3 or less (−3)	−2 notch (−2)	−1 notch (−1)	0 notch (0)	1 notch (1)	2+ or more (2)	Senior Unsecured Loans −3 or less (−3)	−2 notch (−2)	−1 notch (−1)	0 notch (0)	1 notch (1)	2+ or more (2)	Senior Secured Loans −3 or less (−3)	−2 notch (−2)	−1 notch (−1)	0 notch (0)	1 notch (1)	2+ or more (2)
Aaa	2.00%	10.00%	15.00%	30.00%	35.00%	40.00%	10.00%	15.00%	30.00%	40.00%	42.50%	45.00%	20.00%	30.00%	40.00%	45.00%	50.00%	60.00%
Aa1	2.00%	10.00%	15.00%	30.00%	35.00%	40.00%	10.00%	15.00%	30.00%	40.00%	42.50%	45.00%	20.00%	30.00%	40.00%	45.00%	50.00%	60.00%
Aa2	2.00%	10.00%	15.00%	30.00%	35.00%	40.00%	10.00%	15.00%	30.00%	40.00%	42.50%	45.00%	20.00%	30.00%	40.00%	45.00%	50.00%	80.00%
Aa3	2.10%	10.30%	15.50%	31.00%	36.20%	41.70%	10.30%	15.50%	31.00%	41.70%	44.20%	46.70%	20.70%	31.00%	41.70%	46.70%	51.70%	61.70%
A1	2.20%	10.70%	16.00%	32.00%	37.30%	43.30%	10.70%	16.00%	32.00%	43.30%	45.80%	48.30%	21.30%	32.00%	43.30%	48.30%	53.30%	63.30%
A2	2.30%	11.00%	16.50%	33.00%	38.50%	45.00%	11.00%	16.50%	33.00%	45.00%	47.50%	50.00%	22.00%	33.00%	45.00%	50.00%	55.00%	65.00%
A3	2.40%	11.40%	17.10%	34.10%	39.80%	46.70%	11.40%	17.10%	34.10%	46.70%	49.20%	51.70%	22.80%	34.10%	46.70%	51.70%	56.70%	66.70%
Baa1	2.50%	11.70%	17.60%	35.20%	41.10%	48.30%	11.70%	17.60%	35.20%	48.30%	50.80%	53.30%	23.50%	35.20%	48.30%	53.30%	58.30%	68.30%
Baa2	2.60%	12.10%	18.20%	36.30%	42.40%	50.00%	12.10%	18.20%	36.30%	50.00%	52.50%	55.00%	24.20%	36.30%	50.00%	55.00%	60.00%	70.00%
Baa3	2.70%	12.50%	18.80%	37.50%	43.90%	51.70%	12.50%	18.80%	37.50%	51.70%	54.20%	56.70%	25.00%	37.50%	51.70%	56.70%	61.70%	71.70%
Ba1	2.80%	12.90%	19.40%	38.80%	45.50%	53.30%	12.90%	19.40%	38.80%	53.30%	55.80%	58.30%	25.90%	38.80%	53.30%	58.30%	63.30%	73.30%
Ba2	2.90%	13.30%	20.00%	40.00%	47.00%	55.00%	13.30%	20.00%	40.00%	55.00%	57.60%	60.00%	26.70%	40.00%	55.00%	60.00%	65.00%	75.00%
Ba3	3.00%	14.00%	20.00%	40.00%	47.00%	55.00%	14.00%	20.00%	40.00%	55.00%	57.60%	60.00%	26.70%	40.00%	55.00%	60.00%	65.00%	75.00%
B1	3.00%	14.00%	20.00%	40.00%	47.00%	55.00%	14.00%	20.00%	40.00%	55.00%	57.60%	60.00%	26.70%	40.00%	55.00%	60.00%	65.00%	75.00%
B2	3.00%	14.00%	20.00%	40.00%	47.00%	55.00%	14.00%	20.00%	40.00%	55.00%	57.60%	60.00%	26.70%	40.00%	55.00%	60.00%	65.00%	75.00%
B3	3.00%	14.00%	20.00%	40.00%	47.00%	55.00%	14.00%	20.00%	40.00%	55.00%	57.60%	60.00%	26.70%	40.00%	55.00%	60.00%	65.00%	75.00%
Caa1	3.00%	14.00%	20.00%	40.00%	47.00%	55.00%	14.00%	20.00%	40.00%	55.00%	57.60%	60.00%	26.70%	40.00%	55.00%	60.00%	65.00%	75.00%
Caa2	3.00%	14.00%	20.00%	40.00%	47.00%	55.00%	14.00%	20.00%	40.00%	55.00%	57.60%	60.00%	26.70%	40.00%	55.00%	60.00%	65.00%	75.00%
Caa3	3.00%	14.00%	20.00%	40.00%	47.00%	55.00%	14.00%	20.00%	40.00%	55.00%	57.60%	60.00%	26.70%	40.00%	55.00%	60.00%	65.00%	75.00%
Ca	3.00%	14.00%	20.00%	40.00%	47.00%	55.00%	14.00%	20.00%	40.00%	55.00%	57.60%	60.00%	26.70%	40.00%	55.00%	60.00%	65.00%	75.00%
C	3.00%	14.00%	20.00%	40.00%	47.00%	55.00%	14.00%	20.00%	40.00%	55.00%	57.60%	60.00%	26.70%	40.00%	55.00%	60.00%	65.00%	75.00%

Figure 9.9 Corporate debt recovery rates for immediate recoveries, © Moody's Investors Service, Inc. and/or its affiliates. Reprinted with permission. All Rights Reserved.

---

[9] See "Moody's Approach to Adapting U.S. Cash-Flow CLO Rating Methodology to PDR/LGD Initiative", 21 February 2007, page 2 and for Moody's website see www.moodys.com.

1 Year Lagged Corporate Recovery Gross Up Caps

Rating	Bonds						Senior Unsecured Loans						Senior Secured Loans					
	-3 or less	-2 notch	-1 notch	0 notch	1 notch	2+ or more	-3 or less	-2 notch	-1 notch	0 notch	1 notch	2+ or more	-3 or less	-2 notch	-1 notch	0 notch	1 notch	2+ or more
	-3	-2	-1	0	1	2	-3	-2	-1	0	1	2	-3	-2	-1	0	1	2
Aaa	2.20%	10.80%	16.10%	32.30%	37.60%	43.00%	10.80%	16.10%	32.30%	43.00%	45.70%	50.00%	21.50%	32.30%	43.00%	50.00%	55.00%	64.00%
Aa1	2.20%	10.80%	16.10%	32.30%	37.60%	43.00%	10.80%	16.10%	32.30%	43.00%	45.70%	50.00%	21.50%	32.30%	43.00%	50.00%	55.00%	64.00%
Aa2	2.20%	10.80%	16.10%	32.30%	37.60%	43.00%	10.80%	16.10%	32.30%	43.00%	45.70%	50.00%	21.50%	32.30%	43.00%	50.00%	55.00%	64.00%
Aa3	2.30%	11.10%	16.70%	33.30%	38.90%	44.80%	11.10%	16.70%	33.30%	45.00%	47.50%	52.00%	22.30%	33.30%	45.00%	52.00%	57.00%	65.70%
A1	2.40%	11.50%	17.20%	34.40%	40.10%	46.50%	11.50%	17.20%	34.40%	47.00%	49.20%	54.00%	22.90%	34.40%	47.00%	54.00%	59.00%	67.30%
A2	2.50%	11.80%	17.70%	35.50%	41.40%	48.40%	11.80%	17.70%	35.50%	49.00%	51.10%	56.00%	23.70%	35.50%	49.00%	56.00%	61.00%	69.00%
A3	2.60%	12.30%	18.40%	36.70%	42.80%	50.20%	12.30%	18.40%	36.70%	50.70%	52.90%	57.70%	24.50%	36.70%	50.70%	57.70%	63.00%	71.00%
Baa1	2.70%	12.60%	18.90%	37.80%	44.20%	51.90%	12.60%	18.90%	37.80%	52.30%	54.60%	59.30%	25.30%	37.80%	52.30%	59.30%	65.00%	73.00%
Baa2	2.80%	13.00%	19.60%	39.00%	45.60%	53.80%	13.00%	19.60%	39.00%	54.00%	56.40%	61.00%	26.00%	39.00%	54.00%	61.00%	67.00%	75.00%
Baa3	2.90%	13.40%	20.20%	40.30%	47.20%	55.60%	13.40%	20.20%	40.30%	56.00%	58.30%	63.00%	26.90%	40.30%	56.00%	63.00%	68.70%	76.70%
Ba1	3.00%	13.90%	20.90%	41.70%	48.90%	57.30%	13.90%	20.90%	41.70%	58.00%	60.00%	65.00%	27.80%	41.70%	58.00%	65.00%	70.30%	78.30%
Ba2	3.10%	14.30%	21.50%	43.00%	50.50%	59.10%	14.30%	21.50%	43.00%	60.00%	61.90%	67.00%	28.70%	43.00%	60.00%	67.00%	72.00%	80.00%
Ba3	3.20%	15.10%	21.50%	43.00%	50.50%	59.10%	15.10%	21.50%	43.00%	60.00%	61.90%	67.00%	28.70%	43.00%	60.00%	67.00%	72.00%	80.00%
B1	3.20%	15.10%	21.50%	43.00%	50.50%	59.10%	15.10%	21.50%	43.00%	60.00%	61.90%	67.00%	28.70%	43.00%	60.00%	67.00%	72.00%	80.00%
B2	3.20%	15.10%	21.50%	43.00%	50.50%	59.10%	15.10%	21.50%	43.00%	60.00%	61.90%	67.00%	28.70%	43.00%	60.00%	67.00%	72.00%	80.00%
B3	3.20%	15.10%	21.50%	43.00%	50.50%	59.10%	15.10%	21.50%	43.00%	60.00%	61.90%	67.00%	28.70%	43.00%	60.00%	67.00%	72.00%	80.00%
Caa1	3.20%	15.10%	21.50%	43.00%	50.50%	59.10%	15.10%	21.50%	43.00%	60.00%	61.90%	67.00%	28.70%	43.00%	60.00%	67.00%	72.00%	80.00%
Caa2	3.20%	15.10%	21.50%	43.00%	50.50%	59.10%	15.10%	21.50%	43.00%	60.00%	61.90%	67.00%	28.70%	43.00%	60.00%	67.00%	72.00%	80.00%
Caa3	3.20%	15.10%	21.50%	43.00%	50.50%	59.10%	15.10%	21.50%	43.00%	60.00%	61.90%	67.00%	28.70%	43.00%	60.00%	67.00%	72.00%	80.00%
Ca	3.20%	15.10%	21.50%	43.00%	50.50%	59.10%	15.10%	21.50%	43.00%	60.00%	61.90%	67.00%	28.70%	43.00%	60.00%	67.00%	72.00%	80.00%
C	3.20%	15.10%	21.50%	43.00%	50.50%	59.10%	15.10%	21.50%	43.00%	60.00%	61.90%	67.00%	28.70%	43.00%	60.00%	67.00%	72.00%	80.00%

Figure 9.10 Corporate debt recovery rates for 1-year lagged recoveries, © Moody's Investors Service, Inc. and/or its affiliates. Reprinted with permission. All Rights Reserved.

2+ Year Lagged Corporate Recovery Gross Up Caps

Rating	Bonds						Senior Unsecured Loans						Senior Secured Loans					
	-3 or less	-2 notch	-1 notch	0 notch	1 notch	2+ or more	-3 or less	-2 notch	-1 notch	0 notch	1 notch	2+ or more	-3 or less	-2 notch	-1 notch	0 notch	1 notch	2+ or more
	-3	-2	-1	0	1	2	-3	-2	-1	0	1	2	-3	-2	-1	0	1	2
Aaa	2.30%	11.60%	17.30%	34.70%	40.40%	46.20%	11.60%	17.30%	34.70%	47.00%	49.10%	56.00%	23.10%	34.70%	47.00%	56.00%	62.00%	68.00%
Aa1	2.30%	11.60%	17.30%	34.70%	40.40%	46.20%	11.60%	17.30%	34.70%	47.00%	49.10%	56.00%	23.10%	34.70%	47.00%	56.00%	62.00%	68.00%
Aa2	2.30%	11.60%	17.30%	34.70%	40.40%	46.20%	11.60%	17.30%	34.70%	47.00%	49.10%	56.00%	23.10%	34.70%	47.00%	56.00%	62.00%	68.00%
Aa3	2.40%	11.90%	17.90%	35.80%	41.80%	48.20%	11.90%	17.90%	35.80%	49.00%	51.10%	58.30%	23.90%	35.80%	49.00%	58.30%	64.00%	70.00%
A1	2.50%	12.40%	18.50%	37.00%	43.10%	50.00%	12.40%	18.50%	37.00%	51.00%	52.90%	60.70%	24.60%	37.00%	51.00%	60.70%	66.00%	72.00%
A2	2.70%	12.70%	19.10%	38.10%	44.50%	52.00%	12.70%	19.10%	38.10%	53.00%	54.90%	63.00%	25.40%	38.10%	53.00%	63.00%	68.00%	74.00%
A3	2.80%	13.20%	19.80%	39.40%	46.00%	54.00%	13.20%	19.80%	39.40%	55.00%	56.90%	65.00%	26.30%	39.40%	55.00%	65.00%	70.00%	75.70%
Baa1	2.90%	13.50%	20.30%	40.70%	47.50%	55.80%	13.50%	20.30%	40.70%	57.00%	58.70%	67.00%	27.20%	40.70%	57.00%	67.00%	72.00%	77.30%
Baa2	3.00%	14.00%	21.00%	41.90%	49.00%	57.80%	14.00%	21.00%	41.90%	59.00%	60.70%	69.00%	28.00%	41.90%	59.00%	69.00%	74.00%	79.00%
Baa3	3.10%	14.40%	21.70%	43.30%	50.70%	59.70%	14.40%	21.70%	43.30%	61.00%	62.60%	71.00%	28.90%	43.30%	61.00%	71.00%	76.00%	81.00%
Ba1	3.20%	14.90%	22.40%	44.80%	52.60%	61.60%	14.90%	22.40%	44.80%	63.00%	64.50%	73.00%	29.90%	44.80%	63.00%	73.00%	78.00%	83.00%
Ba2	3.40%	15.40%	23.10%	46.20%	54.30%	63.60%	15.40%	23.10%	46.20%	65.00%	66.60%	75.00%	30.90%	46.20%	65.00%	75.00%	80.00%	85.00%
Ba3	3.50%	16.20%	23.10%	46.20%	54.30%	63.60%	16.20%	23.10%	46.20%	65.00%	66.60%	75.00%	30.90%	46.20%	65.00%	75.00%	80.00%	85.00%
B1	3.50%	16.20%	23.10%	46.20%	54.30%	63.60%	16.20%	23.10%	46.20%	65.00%	66.60%	75.00%	30.90%	46.20%	65.00%	75.00%	80.00%	85.00%
B2	3.50%	16.20%	23.10%	46.20%	54.30%	63.60%	16.20%	23.10%	46.20%	65.00%	66.60%	75.00%	30.90%	46.20%	65.00%	75.00%	80.00%	85.00%
B3	3.50%	16.20%	23.10%	46.20%	54.30%	63.60%	16.20%	23.10%	46.20%	65.00%	66.60%	75.00%	30.90%	46.20%	65.00%	75.00%	80.00%	85.00%
Caa1	3.50%	16.20%	23.10%	46.20%	54.30%	63.60%	16.20%	23.10%	46.20%	65.00%	66.60%	75.00%	30.90%	46.20%	65.00%	75.00%	80.00%	85.00%
Caa2	3.50%	16.20%	23.10%	46.20%	54.30%	63.60%	16.20%	23.10%	46.20%	65.00%	66.60%	75.00%	30.90%	46.20%	65.00%	75.00%	80.00%	85.00%
Caa3	3.50%	16.20%	23.10%	46.20%	54.30%	63.60%	16.20%	23.10%	46.20%	65.00%	66.60%	75.00%	30.90%	46.20%	65.00%	75.00%	80.00%	85.00%
Ca	3.50%	16.20%	23.10%	46.20%	54.30%	63.60%	16.20%	23.10%	46.20%	65.00%	66.60%	75.00%	30.90%	46.20%	65.00%	75.00%	80.00%	85.00%
C	3.50%	16.20%	23.10%	46.20%	54.30%	63.60%	16.20%	23.10%	46.20%	65.00%	66.60%	75.00%	30.90%	46.20%	65.00%	75.00%	80.00%	85.00%

Figure 9.11 Corporate debt recovery rates for 2+ year lagged recoveries, © Moody's Investors Service, Inc. and/or its affiliates. Reprinted with permission. All Rights Reserved.

Moody's Recovery Rates for Structured Finance

Tranche as % of capital	Rating of the Tranche															
	Aaa	Aa1	Aa2	Aa3	A1	A2	A3	Baa1	Baa2	Baa3	Ba1	Ba2	Ba3	B1	B2	B3
Diversified >70%	85%	80%	80%	80%	70%	70%	70%	60%	60%	60%	50%	50%	50%	40%	40%	40%
Diversified <=70%,>10%	75%	70%	70%	70%	60%	60%	60%	50%	50%	50%	40%	40%	40%	30%	30%	30%
Diversified <=10%	70%	65%	65%	65%	55%	55%	55%	45%	45%	45%	35%	35%	35%	25%	25%	25%
Residential >70%	85%	80%	80%	80%	65%	65%	65%	55%	55%	55%	45%	45%	45%	30%	30%	30%
Residential <=70%,>10%	75%	70%	70%	70%	55%	55%	55%	45%	45%	45%	35%	35%	35%	25%	25%	25%
Residential <=10%,>5%	65%	55%	55%	55%	45%	45%	45%	40%	40%	40%	30%	30%	30%	20%	20%	20%
Residential <=5%,>2%	55%	45%	45%	45%	40%	40%	40%	35%	35%	35%	25%	25%	25%	15%	15%	15%
Residential <=2%	45%	35%	35%	35%	30%	30%	30%	25%	25%	25%	15%	15%	15%	10%	10%	10%
Undiversified >70%	85%	80%	80%	80%	65%	65%	65%	45%	45%	45%	35%	35%	35%	30%	30%	30%
Undiversified <=70%,>10%	75%	70%	70%	70%	55%	55%	55%	45%	45%	45%	35%	35%	35%	25%	25%	25%
Undiversified <=10%,>5%	65%	55%	55%	55%	45%	45%	45%	35%	35%	35%	25%	25%	25%	15%	15%	15%
Undiversified <=5%,>2%	55%	45%	45%	45%	35%	35%	35%	30%	30%	30%	20%	20%	20%	10%	10%	10%
Undiversified <=2%	45%	35%	35%	35%	25%	25%	25%	20%	20%	20%	10%	10%	10%	5%	5%	5%

Figure 9.12 Structured finance recovery rates, © Moody's Investors Service, Inc. and/or its affiliates. Reprinted with permission. All Rights Reserved.

For each of the Recovery Rates in columns AL to BC of the **Inputs and Portfolio Sheet** there are lookup formulas to find the relevant recovery rate based on the Asset Type (and where structured finance, type and thickness of tranche) and for the rating of the CDO tranche in row 100. For example, in cell AL101 there is the following formula: `"=IF($AJ101="Senior Secured Loan",VLOOKUP(AL$100,M_Immediate_Corp _Recovery_Rates,17+$AI101,0),IF($AJ101="Second Lien/Senior Unsecured Loan",VLOOKUP(AL$100,M_Immediate_Corp_Recovery_Rates,10+$AI101,0), IF($AJ101="Corporate Bond",VLOOKUP($AJ101,M_Immediate_Corp_Recovery _Rates,5+$AI101,0),VLOOKUP($AK101,M_SF_Recovery_Rates,MATCH(AL$100, Reference!$AQ$104:$BG$104,0),0))))"` It should be noted that where a portfolio contains both corporate and structured finance assets, the Aa2 weighted average recovery rate may be slightly lower than the Aaa weighted average recovery rate due to the structured finance assets that have thinner tranches with decreasing recovery rates as the rating decreases.

Where a debt instrument is not rated by any agency, a credit estimate of default probability and recovery rate must be obtained from Moody's. If the specific debt instrument is not rated by Moody's but there is a Moody's rating for another debt issuance in the same corporate family, then there will be a PDR and the recovery rate will be determined using Moody's current loss given default assumptions. Where the debt instrument is (a) rated by Moody's but there is no PDR or PE or (b) not rated by Moody's but rated by S&P, the PE and the Recovery rate will be derived from the following relationship: Default Probability = Expected Loss Factor ÷ Loss Severity (or LGD).

These recovery rates in cells C13 to C18 of the **Summary Sheet** in the *Standard Warehouse Model* are used in the *Cash Flow Model* to determine the initial ratings to the CDO notes. Moody's will want to have the maximum covenanted allocations possible in those asset classes with the lowest recoveries. Hence, the usual practice is to use the weighted average recovery rates achieved for each tranche in the portfolio and add a reasonable cushion between this and the minimum recovery rate. The minimum recovery rates generated from the *Standard Warehouse Model* are applied to the *Cash Flow Model*.

The Moody's Rating Concentrations in cells B28 to C46 of the **Summary Sheet** are determined by summing the notional amounts of the assets which are of the desired rating by the total amount of the notional assets. For example, the Moody's rating concentration for Aaa-rated asset in the portfolio is calculated in cell C30 by the formula `=SUMIF('Inputs and Portfolio'!Z101:Z399,Summary!B30,'Inputs and Portfolio'!I101: I399)/SUM('Inputs and Portfolio'!I101:I399)"`.

In the final row of the Moody's Rating Concentrations section is a Total (check) (Figure 9.13). The authors strongly recommend using this as a way to help protect against errors. The calculation in cell C46 is simply the sum of the concentrations above in cells C30 to C45.

As was mentioned in Chapter 6, although it is often quicker to determine concentrations in a portfolio by using the Pivot Table tool in Excel, the authors do not recommend it for long-term use on the **Summary Sheet**. Neglecting to specifically update a pivot table can lead to incorrect concentrations being assumed.

To the right of the Moody's Rating Concentrations section is a section for the Moody's Major Ratings Concentrations (cells E28 to H36). This table (see Figure 9.14) is simply a summary of each of the Moody's Ratings Concentrations, the applicable constraint/covenant and an assessment of whether the portfolio level is passing or failing the constraint. The Aa concentration, for example, is simply the sum of the Aa1, Aa2 and Aa3 concentrations in cells C31 to C33.

A	B	C
27		
28	**Moody's Rating Concentrations**	
29	**Rating**	**Portfolio Level**
30	Aaa	0.00%
31	Aa1	0.00%
32	Aa2	0.00%
33	Aa3	0.00%
34	A1	0.00%
35	A2	0.00%
36	A3	0.00%
37	Baa1	0.00%
38	Baa2	1.13%
39	Baa3	0.87%
40	Ba1	9.38%
41	Ba2	13.46%
42	Ba3	32.46%
43	B1	17.67%
44	B2	20.15%
45	B3	4.87%
46	Total (Check)	100.00%
47		

Figure 9.13 Moody's rating concentrations

E	F	G	H
27			
28	**Moody's Major Ratings Concentrations**		
29	**Rating**	**Portfolio Level**	**Constraint/Covenant**	**Pass/Fail?**
30 Aaa	0.00%	100%	PASS
31 Aa	0.00%	100%	PASS
32 A	0.00%	100%	PASS
33 Baa	2.00%	100%	PASS
34 Ba	55.31%	100%	PASS
35 B	42.69%	50%	PASS
36 Total (Check)	100.00%		
37			

Figure 9.14 Moody's major ratings concentrations

Moody's Largest Industry Concentrations (Figure 9.15) are ascertained using the LARGE() function. For example, the largest Moody's Industry is established in cell C128 using the formula "=LARGE($C$136:$C$169,1)". Similarly, the second largest Moody's Industry in cell C129 is determined with the formula "=LARGE($C$136:$C$169,2)". The concentrations in this section refer to the Moody's Industry Concentrations in cells B136 to B169.

The Moody's Industry Concentrations (cells B136 to C169, see Figure 9.16)) are calculated as in earlier sections above in the **Summary Sheet** by summing the notional amounts of the assets from the desired industry by the total amount of the notional assets. Finally, at the end in cell C170 there is a Total (Check) to ensure no assets have been mistakenly disregarded.

Having reviewed the basics of the *Standard Warehouse Model* as it will apply to the Moody's evaluations, the various steps in the criteria for rating can now be examined.

	A	B	C	D	E
125					
126		Moody's Largest Industry Concentrations			
127		Industry	Portfolio Level	Constraint/Covenant	Pass/Fail?
128		Largest Industry	5.51%	15.00%	PASS
129		Second Largest Industry	5.33%	11.00%	PASS
130		Third Largest Industry	5.08%	6.00%	PASS
131		Fourth Largest Industry	5.00%	6.00%	PASS
132		Fifth Largest Industry	4.62%	6.00%	PASS
133					

Figure 9.15 Moody's largest industry concentrations

	A	B	C
134			
135		Moody's Industry Concentrations	
136		Aerospace and Defense	4.03%
137		Automobile	1.26%
138		Banking, Finance, Insurance & Real Estate	3.44%

Figure 9.16 Moody's industry concentrations

9.3.4 Step 1: Calculating the diversity score

The diversity score is incorporated into the **Standard Warehouse Model**, as will be described further below. However, to begin with, the **Moody's Diversity Score Example Model** is used as a simple description.

The approach to determining a diversity score is to first assign an appropriate industry category to each of the assets in the portfolio. Next, an average size for each obligor is calculated. Holdings from the same obligor, or with the same parent company or guarantor, are counted together. The holdings in excess of the average are capped at the average. A lookup table is provided to convert the holdings from obligor count to a diversity score and numbers between the scores are interpolated. The diversity score table is reproduced in Figure 9.17.[10] Some industries are considered as only local although, as of the time of writing, these have recently been drastically reduced, from 12 to three. Obligors in these industries, but domiciled on different continents, count as separate industries for the purposes of diversity calculation.

The greater the number of assets in a portfolio, the higher the diversity score will be. Similarly, the more widely distributed the assets across various industries, the lower the correlation and hence the higher the diversity score. Finally, the more evenly distributed the par (notional) amounts of the assets and hence the higher the diversity score, the less the probability of extreme losses.[11]

In the **Moody's Diversity Score Example Model** an illustration is provided where there are 85 obligors in a portfolio with a total amount of $300 million of assets and 32 industries are represented (Figure 9.18). The portfolio obligors, amounts and industry codes are set out in cells B8 to D109. Each obligor is then isolated in column F and the total amounts for each

---

[10] See "Moody's Approach to Rating Collateralized Loan Obligations", Moody's Investors Service, 12 August 2009, appendix 4, pages 42–43.

[11] See "Moody's Approach to Rating Collateralized Loan Obligations", Moody's Investors Service, 12 August 2009, Section 2.3.2.1, page 9–9.

Aggregate Industry Equivalent Unit Score	Industry Diversity Score	Aggregate Industry Equivalent Unit Score	Industry Diversity Score	Aggregate Industry Equivalent Unit Score	Industry Diversity Score	Aggregate Industry Equivalent Unit Score	Industry Diversity Score
0.0000	0.0000	4.9500	2.6667	9.9500	4.0000	14.9500	4.5000
0.0500	0.1000	5.0500	2.7000	10.0500	4.0100	15.0500	4.5100
0.1500	0.2000	5.1500	2.7333	10.1500	4.0200	15.1500	4.5200
0.2500	0.3000	5.2500	2.7667	10.2500	4.0300	15.2500	4.5300
0.3500	0.4000	5.3500	2.8000	10.3500	4.0400	15.3500	4.5400
0.4500	0.5000	5.4500	2.8333	10.4500	4.0500	15.4500	4.5500
0.5500	0.6000	5.5500	2.8667	10.5500	4.0600	15.5500	4.5600
0.6500	0.7000	5.6500	2.9000	10.6500	4.0700	15.6500	4.5700
0.7500	0.8000	5.7500	2.9333	10.7500	4.0800	15.7500	4.5800
0.8500	0.9000	5.8500	2.9667	10.8500	4.0900	15.8500	4.5900
0.9500	1.0000	5.9500	3.0000	10.9500	4.1000	15.9500	4.6000
1.0500	1.0500	6.0500	3.0250	11.0500	4.1100	16.0500	4.6100
1.1500	1.1000	6.1500	3.0500	11.1500	4.1200	16.1500	4.6200
1.2500	1.1500	6.2500	3.0750	11.2500	4.1300	16.2500	4.6300
1.3500	1.2000	6.3500	3.1000	11.3500	4.1400	16.3500	4.6400
1.4500	1.2500	6.4500	3.1250	11.4500	4.1500	16.4500	4.6500
1.5500	1.3000	6.5500	3.1500	11.5500	4.1600	16.5500	4.6600
1.6500	1.3500	6.6500	3.1750	11.6500	4.1700	16.6500	4.6700
1.7500	1.4000	6.7500	3.2000	11.7500	4.1800	16.7500	4.6800
1.8500	1.4500	6.8500	3.2250	11.8500	4.1900	16.8500	4.6900
1.9500	1.5000	6.9500	3.2500	11.9500	4.2000	16.9500	4.7000
2.0500	1.5500	7.0500	3.2750	12.0500	4.2100	17.0500	4.7100
2.1500	1.6000	7.1500	3.3000	12.1500	4.2200	17.1500	4.7200
2.2500	1.6500	7.2500	3.3250	12.2500	4.2300	17.2500	4.7300
2.3500	1.7000	7.3500	3.3500	12.3500	4.2400	17.3500	4.7400
2.4500	1.7500	7.4500	3.3750	12.4500	4.2500	17.4500	4.7500
2.5500	1.8000	7.5500	3.4000	12.5500	4.2600	17.5500	4.7600
2.6500	1.8500	7.6500	3.4250	12.6500	4.2700	17.6500	4.7700
2.7500	1.9000	7.7500	3.4500	12.7500	4.2800	17.7500	4.7800
2.8500	1.9500	7.8500	3.4750	12.8500	4.2900	17.8500	4.7900
2.9500	2.0000	7.9500	3.5000	12.9500	4.3000	17.9500	4.8000
3.0500	2.0333	8.0500	3.5250	13.0500	4.3100	18.0500	4.8100
3.1500	2.0667	8.1500	3.5500	13.1500	4.3200	18.1500	4.8200
3.2500	2.1000	8.2500	3.5750	13.2500	4.3300	18.2500	4.8300
3.3500	2.1333	8.3500	3.6000	13.3500	4.3400	18.3500	4.8400
3.4500	2.1667	8.4500	3.6250	13.4500	4.3500	18.4500	4.8500
3.5500	2.2000	8.5500	3.6500	13.5500	4.3600	18.5500	4.8600
3.6500	2.2333	8.6500	3.6750	13.6500	4.3700	18.6500	4.8700
3.7500	2.2667	8.7500	3.7000	13.7500	4.3800	18.7500	4.8800
3.8500	2.3000	8.8500	3.7250	13.8500	4.3900	18.8500	4.8900
3.9500	2.3333	8.9500	3.7500	13.9500	4.4000	18.9500	4.9000
4.0500	2.3667	9.0500	3.7750	14.0500	4.4100	19.0500	4.9100
4.1500	2.4000	9.1500	3.8000	14.1500	4.4200	19.1500	4.9200
4.2500	2.4333	9.2500	3.8250	14.2500	4.4300	19.2500	4.9300
4.3500	2.4667	9.3500	3.8500	14.3500	4.4400	19.3500	4.9400
4.4500	2.5000	9.4500	3.8750	14.4500	4.4500	19.4500	4.9500
4.5500	2.5333	9.5500	3.9000	14.5500	4.4600	19.5500	4.9600
4.6500	2.5667	9.6500	3.9250	14.6500	4.4700	19.6500	4.9700
4.7500	2.6000	9.7500	3.9500	14.7500	4.4800	19.7500	4.9800
4.8500	2.6333	9.8500	3.9750	14.8500	4.4900	19.8500	4.9900
						19.9500	5.0000

Figure 9.17 Diversity score table, © Moody's Investors Service, Inc. and/or its affiliates. Reprinted with permission. All Rights Reserved.

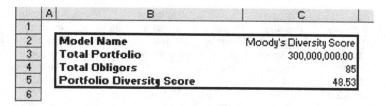

	A	B	C
1			
2		Model Name	Moody's Diversity Score
3		Total Portfolio	300,000,000.00
4		Total Obligors	85
5		Portfolio Diversity Score	48.53
6			

Figure 9.18 Moody's diversity score example model

obligor are determined in column G. In column H, the Industry Codes for each obligor are summarized so that each Unit Score can be determined in column I such that the *minimum of*:

- one, and
- the total obligor amount divided by the notional amount divided by the number of obligors.

For example, in cell I10 the formula is "`=MIN(1,G10/($C$3/$C$4))`".

For each industry in column K, the capped industry total concentrations are determined in column L. From these sums a lookup is done in the Moody's Diversity Table (cells O8 to P210) to determine each Industry Code's Diversity Score (cells M10 to M43). The sum of each of these numbers provides the Portfolio Diversity Score in cell C5.

The Diversity Score concept can easily be added to the **Warehouse Model**. As was previously described, the Moody's Diversity Score calculation in cell C12 of the **Summary Sheet** is taken as the sum of the Industry Diversity Scores on the **Reference Sheet**. By way of example, cell C12 contains the formula "`=SUM(Reference!O104:O137)`".

The Obligor Names (in column C), the Notional Amounts (in column I) and Moody's Industry Numbers (in column AF) on the **Inputs and Portfolio Sheet** are all used as the starting entries for the "Diversity Score Calculators From Portfolio Inputs" in cells H102 to K304 of the **Reference Sheet**.

The Obligors are collated in cells H102 to H304 of the **Reference Sheet**. For example, in cell H104 there is the formula "`=IF(COUNTIF('Inputs and Portfolio'!C$101:C$399, 'Inputs and Portfolio'!C101)=1,'Inputs and Portfolio'!C101,IF( 'Inputs and Portfolio'!C101<>'Inputs and Portfolio'!C100,'Inputs and Portfolio'!C101,0))`".

The corresponding total notional amounts for each obligor are determined in cells I102 to I304 of the **Reference Sheet**. In cell I104 the total notional amount for Corporate Borrow 1 is determined by "`=SUMIF('Inputs and Portfolio'!$C$101:$C$399,Summary !L136,'Inputs and Portfolio'!$I$101:$I$399)`".

The Unit Score is calculated as the *minimum of*:

- one
- and the total obligor amount
  - Portfolio Size
  - *divided by* the Number of Obligors

Therefore in cell J104 the Unit Score is determined by "`=MIN(1,I104/(Summary!$C$5/ Summary!$C$7))`".

The Industries in cells K102 to K304 are looked up in the **Inputs and Portfolio Sheet** based on the Obligor. In cell K104 there is the formula "`=IF(J104>0,VLOOKUP(H104,'Inputs and Portfolio'!$C$101:$AF$200,30,0),0)`".

In the **Reference Sheet** the Capped Industry Totals in cells N104 to N137 are calculated by summing the Unit Scores. For example, in cell N104 there is the formula `"=SUMIF($K$104:$K$304,M104,$J$104:$J$304)"`.

The Industry Diversity Scores in cells J104 to J138, look up the values in the Capped Industry totals and provide the applicable Industry Diversity Score. For example, in cell O104 the formula reads `"=IF(N104>0,VLOOKUP(N104,$E$104:$F$304,2),0)"`.

This then leads us in a full circle back to the Moody's Diversity Score calculation in cell C12 of the **Summary Sheet** where the Industry Diversity Scores on the **Reference Sheet** are aggregated.

9.3.5 Step 2: Assessing the weighted average rating factor

The weighted average rating factor (or "WARF") can be calculated from the idealized expected loss table. Most cash CDOs use the 10-year rating factor (or "RF"). What is the Rating Factor? It is the relative increase over the expected loss for an Aaa-rated obligor. For example, the Rating Factor for an Aaa obligation is 1, i.e., the relative factor to the loss of an Aaa is 1. By way of comparison, the Rating Factor for an Aa1 obligation is 10, i.e., the idealized expected loss of an Aa1 security is 10 times that of an Aaa.

The reader will find Idealized Expected Loss Rates, Idealized Default Rates and Rating Factors in the *Cash Flow Model*, on the **Rating Agency Reference Sheet** in the Moody's section starting in row 200. That said, Figure 9.19 shows the Moody's 10-Year Idealized Expected Loss Rate, Default Rate and Rating Factors and so the reader can

10-Year Idealized Expected Loss Rates, Default Rates and Rating Factors			
Rating	Idealized Expected Loss Rates	Idealized Default Rates	Rating Factor
Aaa	0.005500%	0.01%	1
Aa1	0.055000%	0.10%	10
Aa2	0.110000%	0.20%	20
Aa3	0.220000%	0.40%	40
A1	0.385000%	0.70%	70
A2	0.660000%	1.20%	120
A3	0.990000%	1.80%	180
Baa1	1.430000%	2.60%	260
Baa2	1.980000%	3.60%	360
Baa3	3.355000%	6.10%	610
Ba1	5.170000%	9.40%	940
Ba2	7.425000%	13.50%	1,350
Ba3	9.713000%	17.66%	1,766
B1	12.210000%	22.20%	2,220
B2	14.960000%	27.20%	2,720
B3	19.195000%	34.90%	3,490
Caa1	26.235000%	47.70%	4,770
Caa2	35.750000%	65.00%	6,500
Caa3	44.385000%	80.70%	8,070
Ca	55.000000%	100.00%	10,000
C	100.000000%	100.00%	10,000

Figure 9.19 Moody's 10-year idealized expected loss rate, © Moody's Investors Service, Inc. and/or its affiliates. Reprinted with permission. All Rights Reserved.

appreciate how the Rating Factors are relative to the increase over the expected loss for an Aaa rating.[12]

The Rating Factors in the *Standard Warehouse Model* are assigned in the *Standard Warehouse Model* in column Y. The Moody's Borrower/Issuer Rating in column X is looked up in the Moody's WARF table in the **Reference Sheet**. For example, in cell Y101 there is a formula `"=IF(X101=" ",0,(VLOOKUP(X101,M_WARFs,2,0)))"`.

An overall WARF is calculated by multiplying the par amount of each portfolio asset by its applicable Rating Factor and dividing by the total portfolio nominal amount. As explained previously, the Weighted Average Rating Factor (Moody's) in cell C9 of the **Summary Sheet** is determined by taking from the **Inputs and Portfolio Sheet** as the sum of the product of each of the Moody's WARFs (in column Y) and the Notionals (in column I) and dividing this by the sum of the total notional amount of the portfolio.

A cushion will usually be added to the WARF from the *Warehouse Model* and the minimum covenanted WARF is then used for Moody's rating purposes in the *Cash Flow Model*, which is discussed further below.

9.3.6 Step 3: Determining the weighted average life

The weighted average life (WAL) is taken as the par (notional) weighted average life of the portfolio. On the **Summary Sheet** in the *Standard Warehouse Model* in cell C11 this is calculated from the formula `"=SUMPRODUCT('Inputs and Portfolio'!V101:V399,'Inputs and Portfolio'!I101:I399)/SUM('Inputs and Portfolio'!I101:I399)"`, as described previously.

Where a CDO has a reinvestment period, often the average life is covenanted after the expiry of the reinvestment period. The value at the end of the reinvestment period will typically be the longest average life. For example, if the reinvestment period is 5 years and the average life at the end of the reinvestment period is 4 years, then the average life of the portfolio used for rating purposes will be 9 years. This covenanted WAL will be used when selecting the idealized benchmarks for determining the WARF.

9.3.7 Step 4: Calculating the default rate

With the minimum covenanted WARF and the minimum covenanted WAL determined, a default rate for the pool can be determined by looking it up in the Moody's Idealized Default Rates[13] table (Figure 9.20). A two-way interpolation based upon the WARF and WAL will give an idealized default rate for the portfolio.

For example, if a portfolio has a WAL of 8.5 and a WARF of 2220, the idealized default rate for the portfolio would be 20.735% (interpolating between the 8 and 9 year idealized default rate at a WARF of 2220).

Once the idealized portfolio default rate is determined, the default rate for each tranche of the CDO is calculated by multiplying the tranche stress by the portfolio default rate. These stressed tranche default rates are then used in the binomial probability calculations for each "D +1" default scenarios. As of February 2009, Moody's announced it will increase the portfolio default rate by 30%.

---

[12] See "Moody's Approach to Rating Collateralized Loan Obligations", Moody's Investors Service, 12 August 2008, appendix 2, page 34.

[13] See "Moody's Approach to Rating Collateralized Loan Obligations", Moody's Investors Service, 12 August 2009, appendix 1, page 33.

Moody's Idealized Default Probability Rates									
Year	1	2	3	4	5	6	7	8	9	10
Aaa	0.00005%	0.00020%	0.00070%	0.00180%	0.00290%	0.00400%	0.00520%	0.00660%	0.00820%	0.01000%
Aa1	0.00057%	0.00300%	0.01000%	0.02100%	0.03100%	0.04200%	0.05400%	0.06700%	0.08200%	0.10000%
Aa2	0.00136%	0.00800%	0.02600%	0.04700%	0.06800%	0.08900%	0.11100%	0.13500%	0.16400%	0.20000%
Aa3	0.00302%	0.1900%	0.05900%	0.10100%	0.14200%	0.18300%	0.22700%	0.27200%	0.32700%	0.40000%
A1	0.00581%	0.03700%	0.11700%	0.18900%	0.26100%	0.33000%	0.40600%	0.48000%	0.57300%	0.70000%
A2	0.01087%	0.07000%	0.22200%	0.34500%	0.46700%	0.58300%	0.71000%	0.82900%	0.98200%	1.20000%
A3	0.03885%	0.15000%	0.36000%	0.54000%	0.73000%	0.91000%	1.11000%	1.30000%	1.52000%	1.80000%
Baa1	0.09000%	0.28000%	0.56000%	0.83000%	1.10000%	1.37000%	1.67000%	1.97000%	2.27000%	2.60000%
Baa2	0.17000%	0.47000%	0.83000%	1.20000%	1.58000%	1.97000%	2.41000%	2.85000%	3.24000%	3.60000%
Baa3	0.42000%	1.05000%	1.71000%	2.38000%	3.05000%	3.70000%	4.33000%	4.97000%	5.57000%	6.10000%
Ba1	0.87000%	2.02000%	3.31000%	4.20000%	5.28000%	6.25000%	7.06000%	7.89000%	8.69000%	9.40000%
Ba2	1.56000%	3.47000%	5.18000%	6.80000%	8.41000%	9.77000%	10.70000%	11.66000%	12.65000%	13.50000%
Ba3	2.81000%	5.51000%	7.87000%	9.79000%	11.86000%	13.49000%	14.62000%	15.71000%	16.71000%	17.66000%
B1	4.68000%	8.38000%	11.58000%	13.85000%	16.12000%	17.89000%	19.13000%	20.23000%	21.24000%	22.20000%
B2	7.16000%	11.67000%	15.55000%	18.13000%	20.71000%	22.65000%	24.01000%	25.15000%	26.22000%	27.20000%
B3	11.62000%	16.61000%	21.03000%	24.04000%	27.05000%	29.20000%	31.00000%	32.58000%	33.78000%	34.90000%
Caa1	17.38160%	23.23416%	28.63861%	32.47884%	36.31374%	38.96665%	41.38538%	43.65696%	45.67182%	47.70000%
Caa2	26.00000%	32.50000%	39.00000%	43.88000%	48.75000%	52.00000%	55.25000%	58.50000%	61.75000%	65.00000%
Caa3	50.99020%	57.00877%	62.44998%	66.24198%	69.82120%	72.11103%	74.33034%	76.48529%	78.58117%	80.70000%

Figure 9.20 Moody's idealized default probability rates, © Moody's Investors Service, Inc. and/or its affiliates. Reprinted with permission. All Rights Reserved.

Did you know? Binomial distribution is often used when a random variable has only two mutually exclusive and collectively exhaustive possible outcomes p and 1 – p, and each event is independent. A commonly used example of this is coin tossing. Each time a coin is tossed there are two possible outcomes: heads or tails, and each result of every coin toss is independent of any other coin toss.

9.3.8 Step 5: Determining the binomial probabilities

Once the diversity score has been calculated, and the default rate to be applied (including any stress multiplier) has been determined, then the probability of each diverse default is calculated using the binomial distribution.

The cumulative probability of "x" defaults in the portfolio is calculated as:

$$P_x = \frac{D!}{x!(D-x)!}p^x(1-p)^{D-x}$$

where:

- D is the diversity score
- x is number of default events
- D! is factorial D (i.e., the product of all the numbers from 1 to D). Excel provides a FACT() function to calculate factorial. Hence to calculate the number of ways, for example, to pick 1 object from 5 different objects, divide 5 factorial by the product of factorial 1 and factorial 4. Hence you would have 5 different choices to select 1 thing from 5 things. Luckily, Excel also provides a function to assist in calculating the probability, BINOMDIST(), so this function does not need to be expanded.
- p denotes the probability of an event occurring and $1-p$ is the probability of an event not occurring.

The cumulative probability at each number of defaults, or value of x, is the number of ways or combinations that x defaults can be selected from a finite set of D independent obligors, multiplied by the probability of default (as discussed above), the probability of default raised to the number of defaults, multiplied by the survival probability for those obligors not defaulting, i.e., $(1-p)$ to the number of surviving obligors.

Each of these probabilities for each number of defaults for each tranche is found in each of the Block Curves in row 132 on the **Moody's Sheet** of the *Cash Flow Model*. This is described further below. The expected loss of the CDO portfolio is then calculated as:

$$EL = \sum_{i=1}^{D} P_i L_i$$

where:

- P is the probability of i defaults;
- L is the loss in the i-th default.

The expected loss for each tranche is calculated by defaulting each of the diverse obligors in the collateral rep line and applying the appropriate recovery rate. The expected loss can be calculated by again using the SUMPRODUCT() function to sum the products of the default probabilities generated by the BINOM() function and the losses for each default.

9.4 CREATING THE MOODY'S SHEET AND RELATED REFERENCES IN THE CASH FLOW MODEL

Two new sheets are added at this stage of the *Cash Flow Model*:

- **Moody's Sheet**: for the Moody's specific inputs and calculations; and
- **Rating Agency Reference Sheet**: for reference tables of each rating agency used in the *Cash Flow Model*.

The **Moody's Sheet** is divided into two sections and further subsections:

- Moody's inputs:
  - Moody's inputs
  - rated CDO tranches
  - interest rate curves
  - default rate curves

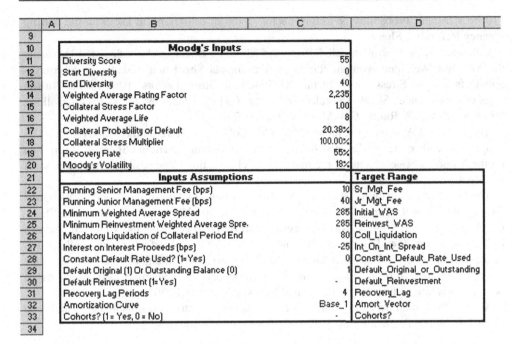

	A	B	C	D
9				
10		**Moody's Inputs**		
11		Diversity Score	55	
12		Start Diversity	0	
13		End Diversity	40	
14		Weighted Average Rating Factor	2,235	
15		Collateral Stress Factor	1.00	
16		Weighted Average Life	8	
17		Collateral Probability of Default	20.38%	
18		Collateral Stress Multiplier	100.00%	
19		Recovery Rate	55%	
20		Moody's Volatility	18%	
21		**Inputs Assumptions**		**Target Range**
22		Running Senior Management Fee (bps)	10	Sr_Mgt_Fee
23		Running Junior Management Fee (bps)	40	Jr_Mgt_Fee
24		Minimum Weighted Average Spread	285	Initial_WAS
25		Minimum Reinvestment Weighted Average Spre.	285	Reinvest_WAS
26		Mandatory Liquidation of Collateral Period End	80	Coll_Liquidation
27		Interest on Interest Proceeds (bps)	-25	Int_On_Int_Spread
28		Constant Default Rate Used? (1= Yes)	0	Constant_Default_Rate_Used
29		Default Original (1) Or Outstanding Balance (0)	1	Default_Original_or_Outstanding
30		Default Reinvestment (1= Yes)	-	Default_Reinvestment
31		Recovery Lag Periods	4	Recovery_Lag
32		Amortization Curve	Base_1	Amort_Vector
33		Cohorts? (1 = Yes, 0 = No)	-	Cohorts?
34				

Figure 9.21 Moody's inputs, inputs assumptions and target range

- Moody's results
  - blocks 1 to 5
  - blocks 1A to 5A
  - block curves

There follows an examination of each of the subsections (see also Figure 9.21).

9.4.1 Moody's inputs

The Moody's Inputs box aggregate cells are named "M_Inputs".

As throughout the *Cash Flow Model*, those cells in blue font are inputs and those in black font contain formulas.

On the **Moody's Sheet**, the Diversity Score (cell named "M_Diversity_Score") is where the diversity score result is entered into the model (cell C11).

The Start Diversity (cell C12 named "M_Diversity_Start") is where the default analysis, outlined in more detail below, will begin. This cell is usually set at zero.

The End Diversity ("M_Diversity_End" in cell C13) is the default level at which the last scenario will be run. The use of the CRITBINOM() function is discussed below, as a way of calculating the critical point, beyond which the probabilities of default are no longer significant to the calculation. Using this function can result in a lower value being used in this cell, thus speeding up the calculation analysis by ignoring those calculations that are not contributing to the expected loss.

The Weighted Average Rating Factor is an input determined by taking the Moody's Weighted Average Rating on the **Inputs Sheet** and looking up its equivalent rating factor in the

"10 Year Default Probability & Rating Factor" table in cells B268 to D289 on the **Rating Agency Reference Sheet**.

Collateral Stress Factor in cell C15 on the **Moody's Sheet** is also calculated by taking the Moody's Weighted Average Rating on the **Inputs Sheet** and looking up its equivalent Default Rate Stress Factor in the "Default Rate Stress Factors" table on the **Rating Agency Reference Sheet** in cells B291 to C311. Thus, "M_Stress_Factor_Coll = VLOOKUP(M_WA_Rating_Coll,M_Stress_Factors,2,0)".

The Weighted Average Life, named "M_WAL_Coll" in cell C16 on the **Moody's Sheet**, is simply a reference to the Weighted Average Life entered on the **Inputs Sheet**. It is repeated on the **Moody's Sheet** to enable the modeller to change this value easily for the purpose of the Moody's analysis only.

The Collateral Probability of Default is also a formula lookup of the Moody's Weighted Average Rating on the **Inputs Sheet** to the "Moody's Idealized Default Probability Rates" table in cells B224 to R244 on the **Rating Agency Reference Sheet** using the Weighted Average Life input on the **Moody's Sheet** plus one. The probability of default for the collateral is broken down in cells F17 to K21 on the **Moody's Sheet**, with the final solution referenced in cell C17, repeated from cell K21. Since the announcement in February 2009 as discussed below, this is now required to be multiplied by a stress factor of 130%.

Most of the remainder of the **Moody's Sheet** inputs are entries that enable the modeller to easily manipulate the data for the purposes of the Moody's analysis:

- Collateral Stress Multiplier ("M_Def_Prob_Coll_Mult" in cell C18)
- Recovery Rate ("M_Rec_Rate_Coll" in cell C19)
- Moody's Volatility ("M_Volatility" in cell C20)
- Running Senior Management Fee (bps) ("M_Sr_Mgt_Fee" in cell C22)
- Running Junior Management Fee (bps) ("M_Jr_Mgt_Fee" in cell C23)
- Minimum Weighed Average Spread ("M_Initial_WAS" in cell C24)
- Minimum Reinvestment Weighted Average Spread ("M_Reinvest_WAS" in cell C25)
- Mandatory Liquidation of Collateral Period End ("M_Coll_Liquidation" in cell C26)
- Interest on Interest Proceeds (bps) ("M_Int_On_Int_Spread" in cell C27)
- Constant Default Rate Used? (1=Yes) ("M_Constant_Default_Rate_Used" in cell C28)
- Default Original (1) Or Outstanding Balance (0) ("M_Default_Original_or_Outstanding" in cell C29)
- Default Reinvestment? (1=Yes) ("M_Default_Reinvestment" in cell C30)
- Recovery Lag Periods ("M_Recovery_Lag" in cell C31)
- Amortization Curve ("M_Amort_Curve" in cell C32)
- Cohorts? (1=Yes, 0 = No) (in cell C33)

For Moody's analysis, the authors usually set the Cohorts? (1=Yes, 0 = No) input to zero. Often a profile is used that matches the covenanted WAL profile, without redemptions during the reinvestment period, as this is the most conservative since there is no reliance on principal cash flows to service interest shortfalls. However, if a reinvestment profile is selected, it is in the authors' experience acceptable to use the simpler rep-line approach to modelling reinvestment, rather than the cohorts approach, as Moody's generally require a covenanted WAL from the end of the reinvestment period to the end of the deal. It is relatively simple for the modeller to create a rep-line that meets the covenanted profile.

	1	2	3	4	5	6	7
			Rated CDO Tranches				
Tranche Number	1	2	3	4	5	6	7
CDO Class Name	Class A	Class B	Class C	Class D	Class E	Class F	Combo Note
Amount	278,000,000	34,000,000	20,000,000	16,000,000	22,000,000	30,000,000	21,000,000
Moody's Desired Rating	Aaa	Aa2	A2	Baa2	Ba2	NR	B2
Moody's Stress Factor	1.5	1.4	1.31	1.23	1.15	0	1
Moody's Default Probability	30.57%	28.53%	26.69%	25.06%	23.434240%	0.00%	20.38%
Covenanted Minimum Recovery Rate	45.37%	45.09%	49.12%	53.16%	57.24%	NA	56.69%
Rate This?	N	N	N	N	Y	N	N
Output Range?	M_Block_1	M_Block_2	M_Block_3	M_Block_4	M_Block_5	M_Block_6	M_Block_7
Loss	0.00%	0.00%	0.01%	0.08%	3.53%	0.00%	8.41%
WAL (Duration for Combo Note Tranche 7)	5.569	7.220	7.728	7.979	8.593	-	6.873
Expected Loss Threshold	0.0019%	0.0640%	0.4382%	1.5624%	6.7358%	0.0000%	
Result	PASS	PASS	PASS	PASS	PASS	FAIL	

Figure 9.22   Rated CDO tranches

9.4.2 Rated CDO Tranches

The box for Rated CDO Tranches is named "M_Tranches" and is found in cells B36 to I46 of the **Moody's Sheet** (Figure 9.22).

The Tranche Numbers (cells B37 to I37), CDO Class Names (cells B38 to I38), Amounts (cells B39 to I39) and Moody's Desired Ratings (cells B40 to I40) on the **Moody's Sheet** are simply taken from the **Inputs Sheet**. They are repeated in the **Moody's Sheet** both for reference and for ease of potential targeted manipulation when structuring.

In addition to the 130% collateral stress multiplier, a tranche multiplier is used to stress default probability. These multipliers, or stress factors, are intended to take into account the tails of the loss distributions of the liabilities, therefore providing for a higher amount of stress for higher rated liabilities.[14] Figure 9.23 shows multipliers[15] reproduced in cells B291 to C311 of the **Rating Agency Reference Sheet** in the *Cash Flow Model*.

As this is applied in the *Cash Flow Model*, each tranche's Moody's Stress Factor is determined by a lookup of the rating for the tranche in the Moody's Stress Factors in the **Rating Agency Reference Sheet**, while also guarding against a "#N/A" for "NR" (where the tranche is not rated). For example, for the first tranche in cell C41 of the **Moody's Sheet**, the Moody's Stress Factor formula is "=IF(M_Tranche_1_Rating="NR",0,VLOOKUP (C39,M_Stress_Factors,2,0))".

Moody's Default Probabilities for each tranche are calculated as:

- the *maximum of*:
  - o the Tranche Stress Factor *divided by* the Collateral Stress Factor and
  - o one
- *multiplied by* the Collateral Default Probability.

To guard against "#N/A", where the rating is "NR", for not rated, the solution will be zero.

To illustrate, for Tranche 1 in cell C42, M_Tranche_Def_Prob, the formula is "=IF(M_Tranche_1_Rating="NR",0,MAX(M_Stress_Factor_Tranche_1/M_Stress _Factor_Coll,1)*M_Def_Prob_Coll)".

The range starting "M_Tranche_Rec_Rate", contains the recovery rates for each of the tranches. These are taken from the *Standard Warehouse Model*.

The Moody's Recovery Rate Toolkit is used for EMEA CLOs, or CLOs with more than 25% non-US assets. Based on the Diversity Score, the types of assets and their geographic

---

[14] See "Moody's Approach to Rating Collateralized Loan Obligations", Moody's Investors Service, 12 August 2009, page 9.

[15] See "Moody's Approach to Rating Collateralized Loan Obligations", Moody's Investors Service, 12 August 2009, Appendix 2, page 34.

	B	C	
290			
291	**Default Rate Stress Factors**		
292	Aaa	1.5	
293	Aa1	1.45	
294	Aa2	1.4	
295	Aa3	1.37	
296	A1	1.34	
297	A2	1.31	
298	A3	1.28	
299	Baa1	1.26	
300	Baa2	1.23	
301	Baa3	1.2	
302	Ba1	1.18	
303	Ba2	1.15	
304	Ba3	1.1	
305	B1	1	
306	B2	1	
307	B3	1	
308	Caa1	1	
309	Caa2	1	
310	Caa3	1	
311	Ca,NR,W	1	
312			

Figure 9.23 Default rate stress factors, © Moody's Investors Service, Inc. and/or its affiliates. Reprinted with permission. All Rights Reserved.

distributions, Moody's Toolkit will create a recovery rate distribution for each default scenario. Moody's Toolkit has divided the EMEA countries into eight tiers and applies different recovery distributions to each tier of country and each instrument type. For each geographical jurisdiction, Moody's has assessed the predictability of the length and outcome of the legal processes and the extent to which competing creditors' interests and other parties' interests are addressed under the laws of the jurisdiction.[16]

The Rate This? input is read in the VBA code and analysis is performed where "Y" is the cell value. The reader will see that "M_Tranche_Rate" is referred to in the VBA code below.

Again, Output Range? is used as "M_Output_Range" in the VBA script to determine where results from the scenario runs will be displayed in the **Moody's Sheet**.

The Loss for each of the tranches is referenced from Block_EL_1, Block_EL_2, to Block_EL_7 in the Moody's Result section, respectively.

Similarly, the Weighted Average Life is read from the WAL determined in the relevant Block_WAL_1, Block_WAL_2, to Block_WAL_7 in the Moody's Result section, respectively.

The Expected Loss Threshold is a lookup of the tranche rating and WAL in the Moody's Idealized Cumulative Expected Loss Rates table in the **Rating Agency Reference Sheet**, while also guarding against "#N/A". For example, for the Tranche 1 Expected Loss in cell C47 the formula is `"=IF(M_Tranche_1_Rating="NR",0,TREND(OFFSET`

---

[16] See "Moody's Approach to Rating Collateralized Loan Obligations", Moody's Investors Service, 12 August 2009, pages 7–8.

	Class A	Class B	Class C	Class D	Class E	Class F	Combo Note
Interest Rate Curves							
USD_Libor_Fwd	1	1	1	1	1	1	1
Forward 1σ UP	1	1	1	1	1	1	0
Forward 2σ UP	1	1	1	1	1	1	0
Forward 1σ DOWN	1	1	1	1	1	1	0
Forward 2σ DOWN	1	1	1	1	1	1	0

Figure 9.24   Interest rate curves

	Class A	Class B	Class C	Class D	Class E	Class F	Combo Note
Default Rate Curves							
YR1_50/10/10/10/10	1	1	1	1	1	1	1
YR1_10/50/10/10/10	1	1	1	1	1	1	1
YR1_10/10/50/10/10	1	1	1	1	1	1	1
YR1_10/10/10/50/10	1	1	1	1	1	1	1
YR1_10/10/10/10/50/10	1	1	1	1	1	1	1
YR1_10/10/10/10/10/50	1	1	1	1	1	1	1

Figure 9.25   Default rate curves

```
('Rating Agency Reference'!$B$203,MATCH(M_Tranche_1_Rating,'Rating
Agency Reference'!$B$204:$B$222,0),INT(M_Tranche_1_WAL),1,2),OFFSET
('Rating Agency Reference'!$B$203,0,INT(M_Tranche_1_WAL),1,2),
M_Tranche_1_WAL))".
```

The Result is determined by whether the Loss on the tranche is less than the Expected Loss. If it is less, the tranche will pass, if not it will fail. For example in cell C48 there is the formula `"=IF(M_Tranche_1_Par_Loss_Pct<C47,"PASS","FAIL")"`.

9.4.3 Interest rate curves and default rate curves

Figures 9.24 and 9.25 contain descriptions of the various vectors used and are described further below. The boxes are essentially "on/off" switches for each of the vectors where "1" is on and "0" is off. The columns of the box follow through from the tranche names above in the same columns in the Rated CDO Tranches Box.

9.4.4 Moody's Results

In the Moody's Results section there are Expected Loss Results for Blocks 1 to 7 in Rows 110 to 117. Block 1 Expected Loss Results can be used to illustrate the calculations.

The final Block 1 Expected Loss (Figure 9.26) is calculated in cell B108 by summing the individual expected loss results by the Moody's Expected Loss Result Weights in the **Rating Agency Reference Sheet**. For example, the calculation in cell B108 is `"=SUMPRODUCT(C112:G117,M_EL_Results_Weights)"`.

Similarly, the final Block 1A Weighted Average in cell B121 is determined by summing the average life results in Block 1A WAL by the Moody's Expected Loss Result Weights in the **Rating Agency Reference Sheet** (Figure 9.27). Therefore, the formula is `"=SUMPRODUCT(C125:G130,M_EL_Results_Weights)"`.

Figure 9.28 shows the individual Expected Loss and WAL results which are determined from the scenario runs using the VBA macro as described later in this chapter.

In the Block Curves there are vectors for the Probability of Default, the Percent Loss and the WAL (Figure 9.29).

The Number of Defaults is calculated by starting at zero and continuing until the Moody's Diversity End Input. For example, in cell B136, there is the formula `"=IF(B135<>"
",IF(B135+1<=M_Diversity_End,B135+1," ")," ")"`.

	A	B	C	D	E	F	G
106							
107		Block 1 Expected Loss					
108		0.0000%					
109							
110				Block 1 Loss			
111			USD_Libor_Fwd	Forward 1σ UP	Forward 2σ UP	Forward 1σ DOWN	Forward 2σ DOWN
112	YR1_50/10/10/10/10/10		-0.000000119%	-0.000000308%	-0.000000964%	-0.000000043%	-0.000000029%
113	YR1_10/50/10/10/10/10		-0.000000470%	-0.000001405%	-0.000005166%	-0.000000171%	-0.000000103%
114	YR1_10/10/50/10/10/10		-0.000000240%	-0.000000806%	-0.000003629%	-0.000000105%	-0.000000040%
115	YR1_10/10/10/50/10/10		-0.000000118%	-0.000000472%	-0.000002452%	-0.000000033%	-0.000000018%
116	YR1_10/10/10/10/50/10		-0.000000026%	-0.000000111%	-0.000000571%	-0.000000008%	-0.000000005%
117	YR1_10/10/10/10/10/50		-0.000000006%	-0.000000021%	-0.000000096%	-0.000000003%	-0.000000001%
118							

Figure 9.26   Block 1 expected loss

	F	G	H	I	J	K	L
267							
268			Moody's Expected Loss Results Weights				
269				Interest Rate Scenarios			
270	Year of Default Spike	Forward	Forward 1σ UP	Forward 2σ UP	Forward 1σ DOWN	Forward 2σ DOWN	Total
271	YR1_50/10/10/10/10/10	10.0%	4.0%	1.0%	4.0%	1.0%	20.0%
272	YR1_10/50/10/10/10/10	10.0%	4.0%	1.0%	4.0%	1.0%	20.0%
273	YR1_10/10/50/10/10/10	10.0%	4.0%	1.0%	4.0%	1.0%	20.0%
274	YR1_10/10/10/50/10/10	10.0%	4.0%	1.0%	4.0%	1.0%	20.0%
275	YR1_10/10/10/10/50/10	5.0%	2.0%	0.5%	2.0%	0.5%	10.0%
276	YR1_10/10/10/10/10/50	5.0%	2.0%	0.5%	2.0%	0.5%	10.0%
277	Total	50.0%	20.0%	5.0%	20.0%	5.0%	100.0%
278							

Figure 9.27   Moody's expected loss results weights

	A	B	C	D	E	F	G
119							
120		Block 1A Weighted Average Life					
121		5.57					
122							
123				Block 1A WAL			
124			Forward	Forward 1σ UP	Forward 2σ UP	Forward 1σ DOWN	Forward 2σ DOWN
125	YR1_50/10/10/10/10/10		5.28909976	5.288286018	5.287245313	5.289076878	5.289597949
126	YR1_10/50/10/10/10/10		5.401951938	5.399196886	5.396514801	5.403682841	5.404303888
127	YR1_10/10/50/10/10/10		5.560954584	5.55635081	5.54894156	5.56419787	5.566022188
128	YR1_10/10/10/50/10/10		5.712507181	5.709530415	5.70572362	5.715027072	5.715773104
129	YR1_10/10/10/10/50/10		5.847818211	5.846233785	5.843616236	5.848752373	5.849248886
130	YR1_10/10/10/10/10/50		5.919564448	5.919434664	5.918817732	5.919634235	5.919698987
131							

Figure 9.28   Individual expected loss and WAL results

	A	B	C	D	E
132					
133			Block 1 Curves		
134		Number of Defaults	Probability of Default	Percent Loss	WAL
135		0	0.00%	0.00%	6.103027496
136		1	0.00%	0.00%	6.110088014
137		2	0.00%	0.00%	6.117148533
138		3	0.00%	0.00%	6.124209051

Figure 9.29   Block 1 curves

The Probability of Default for each number of defaults is based on the formula described in Step Five above. Recall that the probability of "x" defaults in the portfolio is calculated as:

$$P_x = \frac{D!}{x!(D-x)!}p^x(1-p)^{D-x}$$

where:

- D is the diversity score
- x is number of default events
- D! is factorial D (i.e., the product of all the numbers from 1 to D).
- p denotes the probability of an event occurring and 1 − p is the probability of an event not occurring.

For example, for the probability of 1 default in the diversity portfolio, cell C136 contains the following formula: `"=BINOMDIST(B136,M_Diversity_Score,M_Tranche_1_Def_Prob,FALSE)"`.

9.5 DEFAULT PROFILES

Moody's uses a basic profile of applying defaults over 6 years, with 50% of the defaults occurring in one year and the remaining 50% spread out at 10% per annum over the remaining 5 years. The 50% default peak is advanced from the first year to year six and is intended to mimic the agglomeration of defaults often experienced in a recession. This is typical for transactions with reinvestment periods of 5 years or less and a 7–8 year average life. These patterns of default are applied to determine the sensitivity of the structure to the timing of defaults and Moody's typically reserves the right to add additional stresses or default patterns.[17]

Defaults are typically applied at each payment period, although it may be reasonable to apply the first year defaults at the year end. This removes the impact of any ramp-up in assets during the first year when calculating the losses. The Moody's default profiles for a quarterly paid loan deal appear on the **Vectors Sheet** in the *Cash Flow Model* in cells G502 to L584 and are labelled accordingly:

- YR1_50/10/10/10/10/10
- YR1_10/50/10/10/10/10
- YR1_10/10/50/10/10/10
- YR1_10/10/10/50/10/10
- YR1_10/10/10/10/50/10
- YR1_10/10/10/10/10/50

These are then referenced in the **Moody's Sheet** at "M_Default_Curves".

It should be noted that Moody's may be expected extend or truncate the default timing profiles where there are particularly long or short WALs. Moody's may also consider "back-end" default scenarios where collateral managers have displayed a tendency to delay realization of defaults.[18]

---

[17] See "Moody's Approach to Rating Collateralized Loan Obligations", Moody's Investors Service, 12 August 2009, section 2.3.3.5 page 12.

[18] See "Moody's Approach to Rating Collateralized Loan Obligations", Moody's Investors Service, 12 August 2009, page 13.

9.6 INTEREST RATE PROFILES

The Moody's methodology applies the following volatility stresses to the forward-forward curve, to stress the interest rates and to create the following curves:

- forward curve;
- forward curve, one sigma (σ) up;
- forward curve, two sigma (σ) up;
- forward curve, one sigma (σ) down; and
- forward curve, two sigma (σ) down

where sigma is the standard deviation or volatility of the rates.

Did you know? Standard deviation is a measure of variation in the expected value of a random variable. It is calculated as the square root of:

- The sum of:
  - (the difference between the value and the expected value) squared
  - multiplied by the probability of the value

In other words:

$$\sigma = \sqrt{\sum_{i=1}^{M} (x_i - \mu)^2 \, p_i}$$

where x_i is the value, μ is the expected value and p_i is the probability of the value i.

Using a volatility which is currently set at 18%,[19] the forward curve is calculated by:

$$r_s \quad r_z e^{n\sqrt{t}}$$

where:

- n is the stress factor (taking values $-1, -2, 1, 2$) and is used to generate the short-term forward-forward rate, and
- t is the time from the settlement date.

An additional input is therefore required on the **Moody's Sheet** for the Moody's Volatility at cell C20 named "M_Volatility".

The stressed curves (as listed above) are created on the **Vectors Sheet** in cells L302 to O384 and are referenced on the **Moody's Sheet** in the cells named "M_Interest_Curves".

The Period 1, Forward 1 σ up interest curve is calculated in cell L305 using "=$E305 *EXP(1*M_Volatility*SQRT($B305/Pay_Freq)".

Similarly, the Period 1 Forward 2 σ up interest curve is calculated in cell M305 as "=$E305 *EXP(2*M_Volatility*SQRT($B305/Pay_Freq)".

---

[19] See "Moody's Approach to Rating Collateralized Loan Obligations", Moody's Investors Service, 12 August 2009, pages 12–13.

The Period 1 Forward 1 σ down interest curve calculation in cell N305 is `"=$E305`
`*EXP(-1*M_Volatility*SQRT($B305/Pay_Freq)"` and the Period 1, Forward 2 σ down
interest curve calculation in cell O305 is `"=$E305`
`*EXP(-2*M_Volatility*SQRT($B305/Pay_Freq)"`.

9.7 RUNNING THE ANALYSIS

In general, the expected rating is determined by calculating the expected loss for each tranche
and comparing it with the benchmark expected loss.

Using a simple example to illustrate, suppose a US CLO with average rating of B1, a
minimum WARF of 2220, an 8-year covenanted weighted average life (taking into account
a 5-year reinvestment period) and a diversity score of 54. The following scenarios would be
required for the Aaa tranche:

- from 0 to 54 defaults
- 6 default vectors (for timing of the defaults):
  o YR1_50/10/10/10/10/10
  o YR1_10/50/10/10/10/10
  o YR1_10/10/50/10/10/10
  o YR1_10/10/10/50/10/10
  o YR1_10/10/10/10/50/10
  o YR1_10/10/10/10/10/50
- 5 interest rate vectors:
  o forward curve;
  o forward curve, one sigma (σ) up;
  o forward curve, two sigma (σ) up;
  o forward curve, one sigma (σ) down; and
  o forward curve, two sigma (σ) down

The 55 × 30 expected loss results would then have the weights[20] shown as in Figure 9.30
applied to each of the 55 defaults of 30 scenarios. After applying these weights to all of
the scenario results, the weight average expected loss would be compared to the benchmark
expected loss.

Moody's Expected Loss Results Weights						
Year of Default Spike	Forward	Forward 1 σ UP	Forward 2 σ UP	Forward 1 σ DOWN	Forward 2 σ DOWN	Total
YR1_50/10/10/10/10/10	10.0%	4.0%	1.0%	4.0%	1.0%	20.0%
YR1_10/50/10/10/10/10	10.0%	4.0%	1.0%	4.0%	1.0%	20.0%
YR1_10/10/50/10/10/10	10.0%	4.0%	1.0%	4.0%	1.0%	20.0%
YR1_10/10/10/50/10/10	10.0%	4.0%	1.0%	4.0%	1.0%	20.0%
YR1_10/10/10/10/50/10	5.0%	2.0%	0.5%	2.0%	0.5%	10.0%
YR1_10/10/10/10/10/50	5.0%	2.0%	0.5%	2.0%	0.5%	10.0%
Total	50.0%	20.0%	5.0%	20.0%	5.0%	100.0%

Figure 9.30 Expected loss results

[20] See "Moody's Approach to Rating Collateralized Loan Obligations", Moody's Investors Service, 12 August
2009, Appendix 10, page 48

The benchmark expected loss would be determined by looking up the WARF of the desired Aaa rating (1) and the 8-year covenanted weighted average life in the Moody's Idealized Loss tables and locating the idealized expected loss rate of 0.0036%.

If the weighted average expected loss of the scenarios is less than 0.0036%, then a modeller could expect a rating of Aaa for the tranche (based on modelling alone). Where the weighted average expected loss of the scenarios is greater than 0.0036% but less than the Aa1 idealized expected loss rate of 0.0369%, the modeller could expect a rating of Aa1 for the tranche (again, based on modelling alone). The highest rating a tranche will receive is the lowest benchmark threshold for which the weighted average expected loss for the tranche is less.

9.7.1 Other assumptions

When determining the modelling assumptions for rating-managed CDOs, the covenanted limits in the indenture (or trust deed) are used. For example, the minimum weighted average spread, minimum weighted average coupon (if applicable), minimum WARR, maximum WARF, maximum WAL and minimum Diversity Score are used. These assumptions are employed instead of the actual portfolio values because the collateral manger is able to trade the portfolio and thus the "worse case" covenanted assumptions are used.

Moody's will also assume bucket allowances where there is a mixture of floating and fixed pay assets. In the authors' experience, Moody's will usually not stress the minimum and maximum values for these buckets if the maximum fixed (or floating) bucket in a primarily floating (or fixed) CDO is five per cent or less.

Over-collateralization and Interest Coverage tests may be satisfied first from either interest proceeds or principal proceeds. See Chapter 7 for a discussion on the proceeds first used to cure breaches of coverage tests.

9.7.2 Saving time using the CRITBINOM() function

Is it necessary to generate all the probabilities of a binomial distribution when calculating a tranche-expected loss? No, as the contribution beyond probabilities of, say, less than 1e-5 will be minimal to the expected loss (when loss is expressed as a percentage). Therefore a total loss of 100% will contribute less than 1e-5 to the expected loss. As expected, loss is usually calculated to two significant figures; once the probability assigned to a given default level is less than 1e-5 then it is probably safe to ignore it.

Excel provides a function called CRITBINOM() to assist in calculating this critical point in the distribution, beyond which the probabilities are no longer significant to the calculation. This can significantly speed up the time needed to perform all of the Moody's analysis by ignoring those calculations that are not contributing to the expected loss.

Generating the binomial probabilities from 0 to the critical binomial point is a matter of defaulting the collateral with the appropriate timing and recovery, and then measuring the loss. As discussed, Moody's usually uses a single "tower" pattern, and stresses the interest rate curve up and down 1 and 2 standard deviations over the life. Thirty runs, comprising the five interest rate scenarios multiplied by the six default patterns, are therefore typically required for the analysis of one tranche of a CLO.

A major challenge in evaluating a tranche's expected loss is the total number of required "runs" that need to be performed. For a typical CLO with a diversity score of perhaps, 54 and 5 years reinvestment (and without considering the critical point of the distribution), would require $55 \times 5 \times 6$, or 1650, scenario runs to be performed. By calculating the cumulative default probabilities to the critical binomial point, up to 40% to 50% of the calculation time may be saved.

By way of an example, assume a CLO with average rating of B1, and a WARF of 2220, with a 7-year weighted average life, the default probability for a B1 (WARF 2220) is 19.13% from the Moody's Idealized Default Table in the **Rating Agency Reference Sheet**. Using the CRITBINOM() function, CRITBINOM(55, 0.1913, 0.9999999), gives a result of 27. Therefore it is only necessary to calculate up to 27 defaults rather than the full 55 to cover more than 99.99999% of the distribution, reducing the total number of calculations to 810, saving over 50% of the calculations.

9.7.3 Saving time through VBA

Even when CRITBINOM() is used to reduce the volume of scenario runs, there are still far too many calculations to be manually input and calculated by the modeller with any degree of reliability. Some degree of automation is both desirable and required in order to reduce the workload and the likelihood of human error. Excel has a built-in scenario generator called TABLE, which can take a number of inputs and generate summaries of the scenarios. One weakness of this approach is that the amount of time needed to calculate these summaries may be significant and a major drag on the performance of the model. Even with the TABLE function selectively disabled, the recalculation time can be prohibitive. It is therefore more common to use VBA to automate and summarize the expected loss calculation.

The following VBA code is used to run the various stress patterns outlined above and is found in "ModMoodys" in the *Cash Flow Model*:

```
Sub Run_M_Bet()
Dim r1 As Range 'input Range
Dim r2 As Range 'default output range

Dim rLoss As Range
Dim rWAL As Range
Dim rSummary As Range
Dim sSummary As String
Dim rSummaryA As Range
Dim sRange As String
Dim rAssumptions As Range

Dim c As Range 'found cell
Dim nRows As Integer
Dim nCols As Integer
Dim nFnd As Integer
Dim nTranches As Integer
Dim i As Integer
Dim nTranche As Integer
Dim maxTranche As Integer
Dim nCrv As Integer
Dim nDefCrv As Integer
Dim maxCrv As Integer
Dim maxDefCrv As Integer
```

```
Dim c_offset As Integer 'cell offset for input
Dim default_prob As Double
Dim dloss As Double
Dim dWAL As Double

Dim Calc_mode As XlCalculation
Dim out_range As String
Dim tstring As String

'inputs
Dim m_div As Double
Dim m_div_start As Double
Dim m_div_end As Double
Dim m_Init_sprd As Double
Dim m_Reinv_sprd As Double
Dim tranche As String
Dim WAL As String

'tranche inputs

Calc_mode = Application.Calculation

'read assumptions

Set rAssumptions = Range("Moodys_Assumptions")

For i = 1 To rAssumptions.Rows.count
 Range(rAssumptions.Cells(i, 3).Value) = rAssumptions.
 Cells(i, 2).Value
Next i

'set up variable

Set r2 = Range("Cum_Default_Rate")

m_div = Range("M_Diversity_Score").Value
m_div_start = Range("M_Diversity_Start").Value
m_div_end = Range("M_Diversity_End").Value
maxTranche = 6
maxCrv = 6
maxDefCrv = 6

For nTranche = 1 To maxTranche

 If Range("M_Tranche_Rate").Offset(0, nTranche).Value = "N" Then GoTo
 nextTranche
     tstring = "M_Tranche_" & nTranche & "_Rec_Rate"
     Range("Anticipated_Recovery_Rate").Value = Range(tstring).Value
     Range("Recovery_Rate").Value = Range(tstring).Value
```

```
sRange = Range("M_Output_Range").Offset(0, nTranche).Value
out_range = sRange & "_Curves"
Set r1 = Range(out_range)

Set rSummary = Range(sRange)
sSummary = Trim(sRange) & "A"
Set rSummaryA = Range(sSummary)

For nCrv = 1 To maxCrv
 If Range("M_Interest_Curves").Cells(nCrv, nTranche + 1).Value = 1
 Then
   Range("Interest_Vector").Value = Range("M_Interest_Curves").Cells
 (nCrv, 1).Value
 Else
  GoTo nextCrv
End If

  For nDefCrv = 1 To maxDefCrv
    If Range("M_Default_Curves").Cells(nDefCrv, nTranche + 1).
    Value = 1 Then
    Range("Default_Vector").Value = Range("M_Default_Curves").Cells
    (nDefCrv, 1).Value
    Else
     GoTo nextDefCrv
    End If

        tranche = "Tranche_" & nTranche & "_Par_Loss_Pct"
        Set rLoss = Worksheets("Outputs").Range(tranche)
        WAL = "Tranche_" & nTranche & "_WAL"
        Set rWAL = Worksheets("Outputs").Range(WAL)

        For i = m_div_start To m_div_end
          '
          default_prob = i / m_div
          r2.Value = default_prob
          '
          If Calc_mode = xlCalculationManual Then
            Application.Calculate
          End If
          r1.Cells(i + 2, 3).Value = rLoss.Value
          r1.Cells(i + 2, 4).Value = rWAL.Value

        Next i
        dloss = Application.WorksheetFunction.SumProduct(Range(r1.
Cells(2,2), r1.Cells(2 + m_div_end, 2)), Range(r1.Cells(2, 3),
 r1.Cells(2 + m_div_end, 3)))
        dWAL = Application.WorksheetFunction.SumProduct(Range(r1.
Cells(2,2),r1.Cells(2 + m_div_end, 2)), Range(r1.Cells(2, 4),
 r1.Cells(2 + m_div_end, 4)))
        rSummary.Cells(nDefCrv + 1, nCrv + 1).Value = dloss
        rSummaryA.Cells(nDefCrv + 1, nCrv + 1).Value = dWAL
```

```
nextDefCrv:
    Next nDefCrv

nextCrv:
    Next nCrv

nextTranche:
    Next nTranche

leave:

End Sub
```

9.7.4 Achieving targeted ratings

A modeller will typically adjust the attachment levels (or credit enhancement levels) to achieve targeted ratings for the tranche. Modellers would be wise to resist the desire to structure too "tightly", i.e., by providing very little cushion between the expected loss and output losses. Although tight structuring often provides for greater equity returns, some excess margin provides for a more stable rating, by allowing for some default events and down-grades in the collateral without necessarily impacting the rating. The authors know first-hand that restructuring affected or potentially affected CDOs after they have been issued is a time-consuming and often extremely frustrating process for all concerned: investors, analysts, modellers and salespeople to name just a few. Although it is not always possible to avoid restructuring, allowing reasonable margins should help avoid an otherwise unnecessary exercise.

Finally, it must be remembered that the modelled expected rating is just that – an expectation on the originator's part. Moody's will consider not only the modelled results of its methodology but will also assess various other aspects of the CDO, and ultimately ratings will be assigned based on the determinations of a rating committee.[21]

9.8 VARIATIONS ON THE BET

Moody's have used and continue to use several variations on the BET theme to analyse CDOs, including:

- Double BET technique;
- Moody's Alternative BET calculation;
- Correlated BET technique.

The Double BET technique[22] was introduced to deal with non-homogeneous collateral pools, i.e., pools barbelled with respect to credit quality, with a considerable high grade portion, a considerable low grade portion and not much in between these two extremes.

---

[21] See "Moody's Approach to Rating Collateralized Loan Obligations", Moody's Investors Service, 12 August 2009, section 2.3.5.5 page 15.

[22] See "The Double Binomial Method and Its Applications to a Special Case of CBO Structures", Moody's Investors Service, 20 March 1998.

These pools would have bi- or multi-modal expected losses. In order to deal with these types of transactions, Moody's split the pools into two independent pools and default them in a two-dimensional process.

The application of Multiple BET analysis dissuaded using barbelled portfolios to distort the credit quality or other characteristics of a portfolio. It is now more often used also when there are two or more markedly uncorrelated or disparate asset groups. It uses a more sophisticated alternative diversity calculation which takes into account different probabilities of default and differing correlation assumptions per asset class to calculate weighted average probability of default, correlation and, hence, diversity. In the authors' experience, typically a single diversity score would first be calculated. Then the pools would be split and the calculation for each pool performed. However, the diversity scores for these sub-pools would be chosen to match the overall diversity of the single pool. That is, it would not be possible to increase the overall diversity if one of the pools had small concentrations. This can be extended to more than two dimensions, i.e., triple binominals. By defaulting the riskier assets first and separately, there is less likelihood of the result being skewed by a higher average rating factor.

Moody's Alternative BET calculation[23] is based on relaxing the concept of using a diversity spreadsheet model. It relaxes the constraints of the standard BET calculation, namely, the constant correlation between obligors within an industry and zero correlation between obligors in different industries. It was initially used for structured finance CDOs, but was extended to other types of more correlated portfolios including commercial real-estate and trust preferred CDOs.

This was supplanted in 2005[24] by adding the asset classes and correlation assumptions to Moody's CDOROM model. CDOROM is a multi-period Monte Carlo Excel-based model originally used to calculate expected loss and projected ratings for synthetic CDOs. Diversity Score was effectively retired for low-diversity, multi-sector, real-estate, trust-preferred and emerging market CDOs and replaced with Moody's Asset Correlation number (or MAC score). This was effectively the weighted average correlation number as a percentage correlation. This output was then utilized in the Correlated BET model.[25] The correlated binomial expansion effectively relaxes the independence assumption implied by the simple diversity concept, resulting in a fatter tail for the default distribution, which compares favourably for kurtosis with a multivariate normal distribution, correlated via a Gaussian copula.

To use the Correlated BET approach the following steps are required:

1. Input the required data into the latest CDOROM model (at the time of writing, version 2.4) and run it.
2. Take the MAC output from the results sheet, along with the WARF and the number of obligors.
3. Run the CBET model to generate the binomial probabilities (see code below).
4. Run as before for a simple BET and calculate the expected loss.

---

[23] See "Moody's Approach to Rating Multisector CDOs", Moody's Investors Service, 15 September 2000, pages 3–6, Appendix II.

[24] See "Moody's Approach to Rating Structured Finance Cash Flow CDO Transactions", Moody's Investors Services, 26 September 2005.

[25] See "Moody's Correlated Binomial Distribution", Moody's Investor Services, 10 August 2004

Currently the Correlated BET is being largely applied to low diversity CDOs including structured finance, REIT and real-estate related,[26] trust preferred[27] and emerging market CDOs.[28]

That said, Moody's has on several occasions indicated that it intends to move to correlated binomial method for cash CDO transactions in the near future.

9.8.1 Alternatives to BET analysis

On occasion, Moody's can apply other forms of analysis, including:

- loss distribution from CDOROM^{TM};
- individual default runs from CDOROM^{TM};
- full simulation by using CDOROM^{TM} output.

Loss Distribution Data is produced on the OutputData Sheet and provides losses bucket by 0.1% intervals.

In addition, CDOROM^{TM} can produce (by selecting from the Print Data menu on the Input Sheet), a Stats file with one of the following options:

- Stats/Loss per Sim (.txt);
- Stats/Loss + default dates per Sim;
- Stats/ Full Data. (txt).

These produce varying degrees of information: Stats/Loss per Sim (.txt) produces only loss numbers for each simulation run; Stats/Loss + default dates per Sim produces default dates per simulation but no information on the obligor; whereas Stats/ Full Data. (txt) produces default dates and asset number defaults per simulation.

From the authors' experience and the direction given in Moody's recent publications, there seems to be a trend, at least within Europe, to move to a fully simulated rating approach, particularly in simpler structures such as balance sheet trades.

9.9 2009 METHODOLOGY UPDATE

On 4 February 2009,[29] Moody's announced a major methodology change for rating CLOs which involved:

- stressing the portfolio probability of default used in the BET calculation by a factor of 30%; and
- increasing the correlation (or decreasing the diversity) in transactions by altering the industry classifications used in the diversity calculator.

The announcement went on to say that Moody's would conduct a review of outstanding European and US CLOs by applying the new criteria. This was completed in the third quarter

---

[26] See "Moody's Approach to Rating U.S. REIT CDOs", Moody's Investor Services, 4 April 2004.

[27] "Moody's Approach to Rating U.S. Bank Trust Preferred Security CDOs", Moody's Investor Services, 14 April 2004.

[28] See "Moody's Revises Its Methodology For Emerging Market CDOs", Moody's Investor Services, 11 April 2007.

[29] See "Announcement: Moody's updates key assumptions for rating CLOs", Moody's Investor Services, 4 February 2009.

2009 for US CLOs. A paper released in August 2009 confirmed the new approach and provided an update on the whole methodology.[30]

Moody's explained that the portfolio stress of 30% was to accommodate the unprecented anticipated rise in defaults and the anticipated expected duration of at least two years for the credit markets to experience above-average defaults. As explained above, the authors believe that the idealized portfolio probability of default, once estimated from the interpolation of idealized default rate using the portfolio WARF and covenanted maturity from the idealized default table, needs then to be multiplied by 130%.

Moody's changes to the industry categories reflect their opinion on changes in the credit markets caused by "globalization, and increasing complexity and interdependence". The main points can be summarized below:

- reducing the total number of industries by 1 from 33 to 32;
- combining banking, insurance, real estate and finance into one industry;
- splitting the Utilities industry into three (local industries);
- reducing the number of local industries from 15 to 5 and subsequently increasing global industries from 3 to 12;
- splitting several categories allowing for increased diversification in utilities and media;
- introducing new categories to reflect a more modern view of the economy.

The effect of all these changes is to reduce diversity, potentially dramatically, within a . transaction and hence the tail of the default distribution will be longer and more pronounced.

---

[30] See "Moody's Approach to Rating Collateralized Loan Obligations", Moody's Investors Service, 12 August 2009.

10

Standard & Poor's Rating Methodology

10.1 THE S&P APPROACH

Standard and Poor's (S&P) ratings for cash CDOs currently range from "AAA" to "D". What do these ratings mean?

> **Did you know?** An "AAA" rated tranche is the highest rating that can be assigned by S&P. From there, lower degrees of rating can be assigned, down to a lowest rating, "D". A "D" rating is used when is in payment default and payments on the note are not made on the date due, even if the applicable grace period has not expired, unless S&P believes that payment will be made during the grace period. A "D" rating is also assigned upon the filing for bankruptcy or similar actions if the payments are an risk of not being made. Where "NR" is used, either no rating has been requested, there is not adequate information for which a rating can be established, or that S&P has a policy of not rating a particular obligation. See *"Standard & Poor's Ratings Definitions"* at www.standardandpoors.com.

When issuing a rating for a CDO tranche, S&P assess the likelihood of payment in full of interest and principal immediately when due (called "timely payment") or by the maturity of the note (commonly referred to as "ultimate repayment"). Unlike a Moody's rating which is based on the expectation of loss, an S&P rating addresses the probability of the first dollar of loss to the tranche.[1]

CDO tranches rated "AAA" to "AA" (and in some cases to "A") are commonly rated to timely payment of interest and ultimate payment of principal. It must be demonstrated through cash flow modelling of the tranches that the payments of interest and principal are made when due, and the likelihood of deferral of interest is low, at least with regard to portfolio default rates that are to be expected for the applicable rating. For "A-" ratings, interest can be deferred for no more than three consecutive years. It is the authors' experience that it is possible for tranches as highly rated as AAA to technically PIK as this may be acceptable to the rating analyst and committee if the likelihood of not paying current exceeds the probability of default for the portfolio. In other words, the failure to pay interest timely for a subordinate tranche may be permitted in the legal terms of the documents (i.e., it is not an event of default under the tranche documents); however, it may be extremely unlikely and only occur at cumulative default rates in excess of the scenario default rate (or "SDR") prescribed for the target rating.

For "BBB+" and lower rated notes, interest can be deferred to the legal final maturity, by which point both deferred and current interest must be paid in full.[2] That said, in the authors'

---

[1] See S&P "Global Cash Flow and Synthetic CDO Criteria", 21 March 2002, page 13.
[2] See S&P paper, "CDO Spotlight: General Cash Flow Analytics for CDO Securitizations", 25 August 2004, page 6.

experience, deferral for more than a year is likely to result in a rating review and the tranche is likely to be treated as defaulted in repackagings of CDOs (i.e., CDO squared transactions).

Where a tranche allows for deferral of interest without an event of default being called and where the possibility of this occurring is not sufficiently remote, S&P require that the legal description of the note specifically contains the words "deferred interest" or "deferrable" in the title.[3] In this case, the prospectus will often spell out that the ratings on these deferred interest notes address the ultimate repayment of interest and ultimate repayment of principal.

The S&P approach for rating CDO notes involves accessing the default probabilities of the portfolio, and generating times to default (each a single period Monte Carlo simulation), using hazard rate functions derived from cumulative default statistics per rating class and assessing the correlation assumptions between them.

> **Did you know?**   Hazard rate functions are functions that describe the probability of default as a function of another variable, usually time to default.

The S&P methodology uses Monte Carlo simulation in its CDO Evaluator™ to estimate the probability distribution of defaults for the portfolio. Usually at least 500,000 independent trials are required to be simulated and a vector is generated of random numbers equal in length to the number of assets in the portfolio. In each trial, each asset is either defaulted or not, depending on the value of its assigned random number and in a manner calibrated to be consistent with the probability of default associated with each asset's rating. The total principal amount of each defaulted asset is determined as a percentage of the total portfolio and this constitutes the default rate for each trial. Where 500,000 trials are performed, this number of observed default rates is then transitioned into a probability distribution of the default rates.[4]

> **Did you know?**   Monte Carlo simulation is a numerical integration technique which estimates the area of a function or distribution, in this case a cumulative probability distribution, by sampling the area under a distribution curve until the sampling error is statistically not significant.

The probability distribution for the default rates is used to create the scenario default rates or SDRs. The SDRs for each tranche of the CDO are calculated by determining the portfolio default rate at which the probability of defaults in the portfolio exceeding that rate is no greater than the probability of default of a corporate bond with that rating. The rate is then multiplied by an adjustment factor specifically designed for the particular CDO tranche rating.[5]

---

[3] See S&P paper, "CDO Spotlight: General Cash Flow Analytics for CDO Securitizations", 25 August 2004, page 6.

[4] See S&P paper, "CDO Spotlight: General Cash Flow Analytics for CDO Securitizations", 25 August 2004, page 43.

[5] See P&P paper, "CDO Evaluator Applies Correlation and Monte Carlo Simulation to the Art of Determining Portfolio Quality", 21 November 2001, page 2.

10.2 EVALUATING THE COLLATERAL

In Chapter 6, the *Simple Warehouse Model* was discussed. In Chapter 9, this model was extended in order to create the *Standard Warehouse Model*. The *Standard Warehouse Model* development is continued in this section in order to incorporate the S&P requirements.

As mentioned previously, a warehouse model at its most basic level will usually contain the following worksheets:

- an Inputs and Portfolio Sheet that describes the characteristics of the individual assets;
- a Summary Sheet to record the portfolio characteristics as a whole;
- a Reference Sheet with the relevant rating agency tables and other reference material.

10.2.1 The portfolio sheet

Looking at the *Standard Warehouse Model*, the **Inputs and Portfolio Sheet** has fields for each of the assets fields from the index ordinal (in cell B100) to the bullet/amortizing indicator (in cell W100). Additional fields have been added for S&P attributes:

- S&P Rating (cell AA100)
- Country (cell AB100)
- S&P Country Rating (cell AD100)
- S&P Industry (cell AG100)
- S&P Industry No. (cell AH100)
- Bond or Loan? (cell BD100)
- Country Group (cell BE100)
- Asset Type (cell BF100)
- If Specific, Asset Recovery Rating? (cell BG100)
- If Specific, Asset Specific Rating (cell BH100)
- If Specific Method and If Asset Specific Rating Not Known, Senior Secured or Subordinate Rating (cell BI100)
- Recovery Rate Lookup (cell BJ100)
- S&P AAA Recovery Rate (cell BK100)
- S&P AA Recovery Rate (cell BL100)
- S&P A Recovery Rate (cell BM100)
- S&P BBB Recovery Rate (cell BN100)
- S&P BB Recovery Rate (cell BO100)
- S&P B Recovery Rate (cell BP100)
- S&P Seniority (cell BQ100)
- S&P Country Code (cell BR100)

Did you know? S&P Country Codes are based on international dialing codes. For example, the USA has the S&P Country Code "1" and the united Kingdom has the S&P: Country Code "44".

Cells BD100 (Bond or Loan?) to BP100 (S&P B Recovery Rate) are discussed in the Modelling Recovery Rates section later in this chapter.

10.2.2 Summary Sheet

The **Summary Sheet** provides a summary of the key characteristics of the portfolio. A simple sheet has been provided in the *Standard Warehouse Model*. Most modellers create a summary of the porfolio that includes the constraints, or maximum/minimum bucket limits, for the collateral, and it will typically highlight breaches of any of these constraints.

The General Characteristics (in cells B3 to E18 and B25 to E25) are explained in Chapters 6 and 9.

Below the Moody's Rating Concentrations (discussed in Chapter 9) are the S&P Ratings Concentrations, in cells B49 to C66, which are determined by summing the notional amounts of the assets grouped by the desired rating by the total amount of the notional assets. For example, the S&P rating concentration for AAA-rated assets in the portfolio is calculated in cell C51 by the formula `"=SUMIF('Inputs and Portfolio'!AA$101:AA$399,Summary!B51, 'Inputs and Portfolio'!I$101:I$399)/SUM('Inputs and Portfolio' !I$101:I$399)"`.

In the final row of the S&P Rating concentrations section is a Total (Check). As stated in Chapter 9, it is strongly recommended that checks are built in as a way to protect against errors. The calculation in cell C67 is simply the sum of the concentrations above in cells C51 to C66.

To the right of the S&P Rating Concentrations section is a section for the S&P Major Ratings Concentrations (cells E49 to F67) (Figures 10.1 and 10.2). This table is simply a summary of each of the S&P Ratings Concentrations. For example, the A concentration in cell F53 is simply the sum of the A+, A and A- concentrations in cells C55 to C57.

The Country Concentrations (in cells B70 to E100), Basis Concentrations (in cells B103 to E107), Currency Concentrations (in cells B110 to E115) and Asset Concentrations (in cells B118 to E123) are discussed in Chapter 6.

	A	B	C
48			
49		**S&P Rating Concentrations**	
50		Rating	Portfolio Level
51		AAA	0.00%
52		AA+	0.00%
53		AA	0.00%
54		AA-	0.00%
55		A+	0.00%
56		A	0.00%
57		A-	0.00%
58		BBB+	0.00%
59		BBB	0.87%
60		BBB-	2.69%
61		BB+	4.31%
62		BB	13.31%
63		BB-	14.46%
64		B+	24.31%
65		B	27.38%
66		B-	12.67%
67		Total (Check)	100.00%
68			

Figure 10.1   S&P rating concentrations

	E	F	G	H
48				
49		**S&P Major Ratings Concentrations**		
50	Rating	Portfolio Level	Constraint/Covenant	Pass/Fail?
51	AAA	0.00%	100%	PASS
52	AA	0.00%	100%	PASS
53	A	0.00%	100%	PASS
54	BBB	3.56%	100%	PASS
55	BB	32.08%	100%	PASS
56	B	64.36%	80%	PASS
57	Total (Check)	100.00%		
58				

Figure 10.2   S&P major ratings concentrations

10.2.3 Asset Class (industry) Concentrations

To the right of the Moody's Largest Asset Class Concentrations (discussed in Chapter 9) are the S&P Largest Asset Class Concentrations (Figure 10.3). These are ascertained using the LARGE() function. For example, the largest S&P industry is established in cell H128 using the formula "=LARGE($H$136:$H$179,1)". Similarly, the second largest S&P Industry in cell H129 is determined with the formula "=LARGE($H$136:$H$179,2)". The concentrations in this section are referring to the S&P Asset Class Concentrations in cells H136 to H179 (Figure 10.4).

The S&P Asset Class Concentrations (cells H136 to H179) are calculated by summing the notional amounts of the assets of each of the industries present in the portfolio by the total amount of the notional assets. For example, the Zero Default Risk calculation in cell H136 is reading the S&P Industry Codes (cells AG101 to AG399) from the **Inputs and Portfolio Sheet** in the formula "=SUMIF('Inputs and Portfolio'!$AG$101:$AG$399,Summary !G136,'Inputs and Portfolio'!$I$101:$I$399)/SUM('Inputs and Portfolio'!$I$101:$I$399)".

Finally, the reader will notice that there is a Total (Check) calculation in cell I80 to ensure that all assets have been accounted for.

On the **Inputs and Portfolio Sheet**, the S&P Industry column (starting in cell AG100) uses a lookup of the S&P Industry Code (starting in cell AH100) provided by the user of the model. The S&P Industry Code is referenced from the **Reference Sheet** in the S&P Asset Classifications table (cells B402 to C590, named "SP_Asset_Class").

Therefore, the S&P Industry in cell AG101 of the **Inputs and Portfolio Sheet** is determined by the formula "=VLOOKUP(AH101,SP_Asset_Class,2)".

	G	H	I	J
125				
126		**S&P Largest Asset Class (Industry) Concentrations**		
127	Industry	Portfolio Level	Constraint/Covenant	Pass/Fail?
128	Largest Industry	7.23%	15.00%	PASS
129	Second Largest Industry	5.51%	11.00%	PASS
130	Third Largest Industry	5.05%	6.00%	PASS
131	Fourth Largest Industry	5.00%	6.00%	PASS
132	Fifth Largest Industry	4.62%	6.00%	PASS
133				

Figure 10.3   S&P largest asset class (industry) concentrations

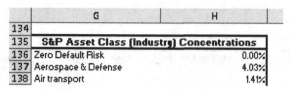

Figure 10.4   S&P asset class (industry) concentrations

	B	C
401		
402	**CDO Evaluator Asset Classifications**	
403	**Asset Code**	**Asset Description**
404	**Corporate Obligations**	
405	0	Zero Default Risk
406	1	Aerospace & Defense
407	2	Air transport

Figure 10.5   CDO evaluator asset classifications

In Chapter 9 the authors described using SIC Codes to make estimates for the industries to which an asset might apply. S&P have some solutions which might assist in determining these, including the subscription services www.ratingsdirect.com and their CDS Accelerator and other S&P CDO Suite models and tools.

10.3 MODELLING RECOVERY RATES

S&P have developed standard recovery ratings representative of its estimate of the likely recovery in the event of a payment default.[6] These recovery rates are first analysed in the *Standard Warehouse Model* and then certain characteristics are used in the *Cash Flow Model*.

At the time of writing, for corporate obligations S&P offered the option of using either:

- asset-specific corporate recovery rates; or
- general tiered asset-class recovery rates.

Both methods apply various recovery rate assumptions depending on the type of assets contained in the portfolio, their seniority in their respective capital structures, and the targeted rating of the respective CDO tranche.

If the choice is made to use asset-specific recovery ratings, then these rates must be used for all assets in the portfolio for which asset-specific ratings are available. Only when an asset-specific rating is not available may the general tiered asset-class recovery rates be used.

In contrast, if general tiered asset-class recovery rates are chosen to be used, then these must be used for all assets in the portfolio, irrespective of whether any asset-specific recoveries are available.[7]

A different recovery rate is applied depending on the targeted rating of the tranche and the seniority of the asset in the obligor's capital structure. This may seem strange, as ultimately

---

[6] See S&P paper, "CDO Spotlight: Using Standard & Poor's Recovery Ratings In Cash Flow CDOs", 17 October 2006, page 15.

[7] See S&P paper, "CDO Spotlight: Using Standard & Poor's Recovery Ratings In Cash Flow CDOs", 17 October 2006, pages 4–5.

US and Canada Tiered Corporate Loan Asset Recovery Rate Assumptions							
	CDO Tranche Rating						
	AAA	AA	A	BBB	BB	B	CCC
Senior Secured	56%	60%	64%	67%	70%	70%	70%
Senior Secured Cov-Lite	51%	54%	57%	60%	63%	63%	63%
Second Lien/Senior Unsecured	40%	42%	44%	46%	48%	48%	48%
Subordinated	22%	22%	22%	22%	22%	22%	22%

US and Canada Tiered Corporate Bond Asset Recovery Rate Assumptions							
	CDO Tranche Rating						
	AAA	AA	A	BBB	BB	B	CCC
Senior Secured	48%	49%	50%	51%	52%	52%	52%
Senior Unsecured	38%	41%	42%	44%	45%	45%	45%
Subordinated	19%	19%	19%	19%	19%	19%	19%

Figure 10.6 US and Canada tiered corporate loan asset recovery rate assumptions, © Standard and Poors

an asset's recovery level will be one rate. However, this can be viewed as an application of confidence intervals to mitigate the risk of variance in recovery (or the often-quoted contrary of "loss given default"). For example, senior secured leveraged loans typically recover very highly (80%), but with some variance. By allowing for additional or unexpected loss, the likelihood of incurring a loss on a higher-rated tranche is reduced.

The various recovery rates which S&P usually apply are largely reproduced in the **Reference Sheet** in the *Standard Warehouse Model*. Firstly, the different categories will be discussed, and then the application of these various recovery rates in the *Standard Warehouse Model* is reviewed.

10.3.1 General tiered asset-class recovery rates

The US and Canada Tiered Corporate Loan and Bond Asset Recovery Rate Assumptions[8] are shown in Figure 10.6.

To be considered "senior secured", an obligation should have first-priority security interest and cannot be subordinated to any other obligations. It follows that "unsecured" obligations should only be subordinated to senior secured debt and "subordinated" includes everything that is not "senior secured" or "unsecured".[9]

It should be noted that for US Loan Assets, where there are more than 15% second lien loans comprising the portfolio, only the first 15% will be deemed to be senior unsecured loans and the remainder will be considered subordinated loans.[10]

---

[8] See S&P "Updated Global Recovery Rates For Use In Cash Flow CDOs", 23 July 2007, page 6.

[9] See S&P, "CDO Spotlight: Using Standard & Poor's Recovery Ratings In Cash Flow CDOs", 17 October 2006, page 6, and see S&P "Updated Global Recovery Rates For Use In Cash Flow CDOs", 23 July 2007, page 6.

[10] See S&P "Update to General Cash Flow Analytics Criteria for CDO Securitizations", 17 October 2006, page 12 and S&P "Updated Global Recovery Rates For Use In Cash Flow CDOs", 23 July 2007, page 6.

European and Asian Loan Asset Recovery Rate Assumptions								
		CDO Tranche Rating						
		AAA	AA	A	BBB	BB	B	CCC
Senior Secured	A1	68%	73%	78%	81%	85%	85%	85%
Senior Secured	A2	56%	60%	64%	67%	70%	70%	70%
Senior Secured	B	48%	51%	55%	57%	60%	60%	60%
Senior Secured Cov-Lite	A1	61%	66%	70%	73%	77%	77%	77%
Senior Secured Cov-Lite	A2	50%	54%	58%	60%	63%	63%	63%
Senior Secured Cov-Lite	B	43%	46%	49%	52%	54%	54%	54%
Mezzanine/Second Lien/Senior Unsecured	A1	45%	47%	50%	52%	54%	54%	54%
Mezzanine/Second Lien/Senior Unsecured	A2	40%	42%	44%	46%	48%	48%	48%
Mezzanine/Second Lien/Senior Unsecured	B	35%	37%	39%	40%	42%	42%	42%
Subordinated	A1	20%	20%	20%	20%	20%	20%	20%
Subordinated	A2	17%	17%	17%	17%	17%	17%	17%
Subordinated	B	17%	17%	17%	17%	17%	17%	17%

European and Asian Bond Asset Recovery Rate Assumptions								
		CDO Tranche Rating						
		AAA	AA	A	BBB	BB	B	CCC
Senior Secured	A1	60%	61%	62%	63%	64%	64%	64%
Senior Secured	A2	48%	49%	50%	51%	52%	52%	52%
Senior Secured	B	43%	44%	45%	46%	47%	47%	47%
Senior Unsecured	A1	40%	42%	44%	46%	48%	48%	48%
Senior Unsecured	A2	38%	41%	42%	44%	45%	45%	45%
Senior Unsecured	B	32%	35%	36%	38%	39%	40%	40%
Subordinated	A1	18%	18%	18%	18%	18%	18%	18%
Subordinated	A2	18%	18%	18%	18%	18%	18%	18%
Subordinated	B	15%	15%	15%	15%	15%	15%	15%

Figure 10.7 European and Asian loan and bond asset recovery rate assumptions, © Standard and Poor's

European and Asian corporate recovery rate assumptions are categorized according to domicile groupings where each comprises:

- **Group A1**: UK, Ireland, Finland, Denmark, The Netherlands, South Africa, Australia and New Zealand.
- **Group A2**: Belgium, Germany, Austria, Spain, Portugal, Luxembourg, Switzerland, Sweden, Norway, Hong Kong and Singapore.
- **Group B**: France, Italy, Greece, Japan, Korea and Taiwan.[11]

The European and Asian Loan and Bond Asset Recovery Rate Assumptions[12] are reproduced in Figure 10.7.

It is assumed that the upper recovery rate for senior loans is higher than that for senior bonds because bank loans usually:

- rank higher in order of priority;
- have mandatory workout provisions between the lender and the obligors;
- are subject to stricter covenants;
- are subject to increased scrutiny by lenders; and
- are easier to restructure.

---

[11] See S&P "Updated Global Recovery Rates For Use In Cash Flow CDOs", 23 July 2007, page 4–5.
[12] See S&P "Updated Global Recovery Rates For Use In Cash Flow CDOs", 23 July 2007, page 6.

Emerging Market Recovery Rate Assumptions							
	AAA	AA	A	BBB	BB	B	CCC
Sovereign Debt	37	38	40	47	49	50	50
Corporate Debt	22	24	32	33	35	37	37

Figure 10.8 Emerging market recovery rate assumptions

Recovery Rates and Ranges		
Rating	Description	Recovery Range (%)
1+	Highest expectation, full recovery	100
1	Very high recovery	90–100
2	Substantial recovery	70–90
3	Meaningful recovery	50–70
4	Average recovery	30–50
5	Modest recovery	10–30
6	Negligible recovery	0–10

Figure 10.9 Recovery rates and ranges

Lenders are often restricted payments to bond holders if covenants on their loans are not being met. This in turn usually triggers default provisions under the bond terms and conditions.

Although not reproduced in the *Standard Warehouse Model*, for emerging market countries (where the sovereign foreign currency rating is lower than "AA-" and is not assigned to groups A1, A2 or B above), the corporate recoveries apply[13] as shown in Figure 10.8.

10.3.2 Asset-specific corporate recovery rates

Most of the following asset-specific recovery rates[14] for corporate obligors are also reproduced in the **Reference Sheet** in the *Standard Warehouse Model*.

The rating scales of 1+ to 6 represent an indicative recovery benchmarked to S&P's LossStats® database which, at the time of writing, provides recovery data on over 3500 defaulted and emerged debt instruments.

Figure 10.9 provides a description of what these Recovery Ratings mean. It should be noted that the Recovery Rate refers to the principal and accrued but unpaid interest at the time of default.[15]

Figures 10.10 to 10.12 show the asset-specific corporate recovery rates used in cash flow CDO modelling. Where an asset has a specific recovery rate, the following "Recovery Rates For Assets With Recovery Ratings" will apply.[16]

---

[13] See S&P "Updated Global Recovery Rates For Use In Cash Flow CDOs", 23 July 2007, page 7.

[14] Current recovery rates can be found on S&P's website www.bankloanrating.standardandpoors.com.

[15] See S&P paper, "CDO Spotlight: Update Global Recovery Rates For Use In Cash Flow CDOs", 23 July 2008, page 3.

[16] See S&P paper, "CDO Spotlight: Using Standard & Poor's Recovery Ratings In Cash Flow CDOs", 17 October 2006, pages 9–10.

Recovery Rates For Assets With Recovery Ratings							
	CDO Tranche Rating						
	AAA	AA	A	BBB	BB	B	CCC
1+	100%	100%	100%	100%	100%	100%	100%
1	92%	94%	96%	98%	100%	100%	100%
2	78%	81%	84%	87%	90%	90%	90%
3	58%	61%	64%	67%	70%	70%	70%
4	38%	41%	44%	47%	50%	50%	50%
5	16%	20%	24%	27%	30%	30%	30%
6	6%	7%	8%	9%	10%	10%	10%

Figure 10.10   Asset-specific corporate recovery rates (1)

US and Canada Recovery Rates On Senior Unsecured Debt If Senior Secured Has a Recovery Rating							
	CDO Tranche Rating						
	AAA	AA	A	BBB	BB	B	CCC
Senior Secured Asset Recovery Rating							
1+	53%	55%	57%	59%	61%	61%	61%
1	48%	50%	52%	54%	56%	56%	56%
2	43%	45%	47%	49%	51%	51%	51%
3	39%	41%	43%	45%	47%	47%	47%
4	22%	24%	26%	28%	30%	30%	30%
5	8%	10%	12%	14%	15%	15%	15%
6	4%	4%	4%	4%	4%	4%	4%

US and Canada Recovery Rates On Subordinated Debt If Senior Secured Has a Recovery Rating							
	CDO Tranche Rating						
	AAA	AA	A	BBB	BB	B	CCC
Senior Secured Asset Recovery Rating							
1+	25%	25%	25%	25%	25%	25%	25%
1	22%	22%	22%	22%	22%	22%	22%
2	20%	20%	20%	20%	20%	20%	20%
3	20%	20%	20%	20%	20%	20%	20%
4	10%	10%	10%	10%	10%	10%	10%
5	5%	5%	5%	5%	5%	5%	5%
6	2%	2%	2%	2%	2%	2%	2%

Figure 10.11   Asset-specific corporate recovery rates (2)

Where an asset does not have an asset-specific recovery rating, S&P will typically attempt to establish whether the obligor has other debt which has an asset-specific recovery rate assigned. If an obligor has more-senior debt with an asset-specific rating but does not have an assigned senior unsecured debt and subordinate debt recovery rates, this can be determined from Figure 10.10.[17]

For the US and Canada, Figure 10.11 shows "Recovery Rates On Senior Unsecured and Subordinated Debt If Senior Secured Has a Rating".[18] Figure 10.12 shows the "Europe and Asia Recovery Rates On Senior Unsecured and Subordinated Debt If Senior Secured Has a Rating".[19]

---

[17] See S&P paper, "CDO Spotlight: Update Global Recovery Rates For Use In Cash Flow CDOs", 23 July 2008, page 9.

[18] See S&P paper, "CDO Spotlight: Update Global Recovery Rates For Use In Cash Flow CDOs", 23 July 2008, pages 9–10.

[19] See S&P paper, "CDO Spotlight: Update Global Recovery Rates For Use In Cash Flow CDOs", 23 July 2008, pages 9–11.

Europe and Asia Recovery Rates On Senior Unsecured Debt If Senior Secured Has a Recovery Rating								
		CDO Tranche Rating						
		AAA	AA	A	BBB	BB	B	CCC
Senior Secured Asset Recovery Rating								
A1	1+	65%	68%	71%	73%	76%	76%	76%
A1	1	57%	60%	63%	65%	68%	68%	68%
A1	2	50%	53%	55%	57%	59%	59%	59%
A1	3	42%	45%	47%	49%	51%	51%	51%
A1	4	18%	18%	18%	18%	18%	18%	18%
A1	5	8%	8%	8%	8%	8%	8%	8%
A1	6	4%	4%	4%	4%	4%	4%	4%
A2	1+	53%	55%	57%	59%	61%	61%	61%
A2	1	48%	50%	52%	54%	56%	56%	56%
A2	2	43%	45%	47%	49%	51%	51%	51%
A2	3	39%	41%	43%	45%	47%	47%	47%
A2	4	18%	18%	18%	18%	18%	18%	18%
A2	5	8%	8%	8%	8%	8%	8%	8%
A2	6	4%	4%	4%	4%	4%	4%	4%
B	1+	45%	46%	48%	49%	51%	51%	51%
B	1	41%	43%	44%	46%	47%	48%	48%
B	2	37%	39%	41%	42%	44%	44%	44%
B	3	33%	39%	37%	39%	40%	41%	41%
B	4	16%	16%	16%	16%	16%	16%	16%
B	5	6%	6%	6%	6%	6%	6%	6%
B	6	3%	3%	3%	3%	3%	3%	3%

Europe and Asia Recovery Rates On Subordinate Debt If Senior Secured Has a Recovery Rating								
		CDO Tranche Rating						
		AAA	AA	A	BBB	BB	B	CCC
Senior Secured Asset Recovery Rating								
A1	1+	22%	22%	22%	22%	22%	22%	22%
A1	1	20%	20%	20%	20%	20%	20%	20%
A1	2	18%	18%	18%	18%	18%	18%	18%
A1	3	18%	18%	18%	18%	18%	18%	18%
A1	4	9%	9%	9%	9%	9%	9%	9%
A1	5	4%	4%	4%	4%	4%	4%	4%
A1	6	2%	2%	2%	2%	2%	2%	2%
A2	1+	22%	22%	22%	22%	22%	22%	22%
A2	1	20%	20%	20%	20%	20%	20%	20%
A2	2	18%	18%	18%	18%	18%	18%	18%
A2	3	18%	18%	18%	18%	18%	18%	18%
A2	4	9%	9%	9%	9%	9%	9%	9%
A2	5	4%	4%	4%	4%	4%	4%	4%
A2	6	2%	2%	2%	2%	2%	2%	2%
B	1+	20%	20%	20%	20%	20%	20%	20%
B	1	17%	17%	17%	17%	17%	17%	17%
B	2	15%	15%	15%	15%	15%	15%	15%
B	3	15%	15%	15%	15%	15%	15%	15%
B	4	8%	8%	8%	8%	8%	8%	8%
B	5	3%	3%	3%	3%	3%	3%	3%
B	6	1%	1%	1%	1%	1%	1%	1%

Figure 10.12   Asset-specific corporate recovery rate (3), © Standard and Poor's

These various recovery rates are tied into the analysis of the collateral in the **Inputs and Portfolio Sheet** of the *Standard Warehouse Model* in the following cells:

- S&P Rating (cell AA100)
- Country (cell AB100)
- S&P Country Rating (cell AD100)
- S&P Industry (cell AG100)
- S&P Industry No. (cell AH100)
- Bond or Loan? (cell BD100)
- Country Group (cell BE100)
- Asset Type (cell BF100)
- If Specific, Asset Recovery Rating? (cell BG100)
- If Specific, Asset Specific Rating (cell BH100)
- If Specific Method and If Asset Specific Rating Not Known, Senior Secured or Subordinate Rating (cell BI100)
- Recovery Rate Lookup (cell BJ100)
- S&P AAA Recovery Rate (cell BK100)
- S&P AA Recovery Rate (cell BL100)
- S&P A Recovery Rate (cell BM100)
- S&P BBB Recovery Rate (cell BN100)
- S&P BB Recovery Rate (cell BO100)
- S&P B Recovery Rate (cell BP100)

In cell BE10 there is a switch for the S&P Recovery Rate Method. The cell is named "SP_RR_Method" and the drop-down list provides two choices:

- "General" for applying general tiered asset-class recovery rates; or
- "Specific" for applying asset-specific corporate recovery rates.

The Bond or Loan? column (BD100) is a simple user input to specify the asset's type of debt. This input is used to determine recovery rates from the general tier asset recovery rates. It is not used if asset-specific recovery rates are employed, as no distinction in the type of debt is required for these.

The Country Group (starting cell BE100) is read from the Country column starting in AB100. There are two lookups: one to convert Canada to the US (apologies to any Canadian readers); and the other to convert countries into their S&P country group. In cell BE101 is the formula `"=IF(AB101="",0,IF(OR(AB101="US",AB101="Canada"),"US",VLOOKUP(AB101,SP_Groups,2)))"`, where "SP Groups" refers to the cells O402 to P427 in the S&P section of the **Reference Sheet** (Figure 10.13).

The Asset Type (starting in cell BF100) in the *Standard Warehouse Model* includes the following choices and is used when applying general tier recovery rates:

- Senior Secured
- Senior Secured Cov-Lite
- Second Lien/Senior Unsecured
- Mezzanine/Second Lien/Senior Unsecured
- Subordinated

Where asset-specific corporate recovery rate method is chosen, "If Specific, Asset Recovery Rating?" in cell BG100 provides a drop-down list allowing for the following choices:

- "With RR" refers to assets with asset-specific corporate recovery rates;

	O	P
401		
402	**S&P Country Groups**	
403	UK	A1
404	Ireland	A1
405	Finland	A1
406	Denmark	A1
407	The Netherl;	A1
408	South Afric;	A1
409	Australia	A1
410	New Zealanc	A1
411	Belgium	A2
412	Germany	A2
413	Austria	A2
414	Spain	A2
415	Portugal	A2
416	Luxembourg	A2
417	Switzerland	A2
418	Sweden	A2
419	Norway	A2
420	Hong Kong	A2
421	Singapore	A2
422	France	B
423	Italy	B
424	Greece	B
425	Japan	B
426	Korea	B
427	Taiwan	B
428		

Figure 10.13   S&P country groups, © Standard and Poor's

- "With Sen Unsec RR" refers to assets with asset-specific senior unsecured debt ratings;
- "With Sub RR" refers to assets with asset-specific subordinated debt ratings;
- "Without RR" refers to assets for which there is no asset-specific rating, no senior unsecured debt rating and no subordinated debt rating.

Reading across to column BH, which is labelled, "If Specific, Asset Specific Rating" in cell BH100. This column is where the rating is input for the asset, if it is known. When it is not known or there is no asset specific available, rating the input is 0.

The column labelled "If Applicable, If Asset RR Group Number Not Known, Asset RR Group Number for Senior Secured" (cell BI100) is where the rating for the senior unsecured or subordinate rating is input. If an asset specific rating is available, the input here should be 0. Additionally, if there are no specific ratings at all for the obligor, the input should also be 0.

The formula in the column labelled "Recovery Rate Lookup" (commencing in cell BJ100) combines both the general and specific method data in order to determine the various recovery rates in columns BK to BP. The formula used accomplishes the following steps:

Step 1: If the "General" option for the general tiered method is chosen (in cell BE10), the following inputs are combined:
- Bond or Loan?, (column BD)
- Country Group (column BE)
- Asset Type (column BF); or

Step 2: If the "Specific" option for the asset-apecific method is chosen (in cell BE10), the "If Specific, Asset Recovery Rating?" in column BG is assessed:

Step 2a: If "Without RR" is input, the general tiered recovery rating description is applied such that the following inputs are combined in the formula in the "Recovery Rate Lookup" column BJ:

- o Bond or Loan?
- o Country Group
- o Asset Type; or if

Step 2b: If "With RR" is chosen, the following inputs are combined in the formula in the "Recovery Rate Lookup" column BJ:

- SP RR Method? Input in cell BE10, which will be "Specific"
- If Specific, Asset Recovery Rating (column BG)
- IF Specific, Asset Specific Rating (column BH)

Step 2c: If any other input is chosen, the following inputs will be combined in the "Recovery Rate Lookup":

- SP_RR_Method? Input
- If Specific, Asset Recovery Rating
- Country Group
- IF Specific Method and if Asset Specific Rating Not Known, Senior Secured or Subordinate Rating

The final formula can be seen to cell BJ101, `"=IF(SP RR Method?="General",SP RR Method?&" "&BD101&" "&BE101&" "&BF101,IF(BG101="Without RR","General "&BD101&" "&BE101&" "&BF101,IF(BG101="With RR",SP RR Method?&" "&BG101&" "&BH101,SP RR Method?&" "&BG101&" "&BE101&" "&BI101)))"`.

This is then used by the formulas in cells BK101:BP184 to lookup the applicable recovery rate from the reference tables.

The recovery rates that are determined for each of the assets in the portfolio are given in the following:

- S&P AAA Recovery Rate (cell BK100)
- S&P AA Recovery Rate (cell BL100)
- S&P A Recovery Rate (cell BM100)
- S&P BBB Recovery Rate (cell BN100)
- S&P BB Recovery Rate (cell BO100)
- S&P B Recovery Rate (cell BP100)

For each of these, the Recovery Rate Lookup value in column BJ is matched to the S&P Recovery Rate table in the **Reference Sheet**. For example, in cell BK101 there is the formula `"=VLOOKUP($BJ101,SP_RR,MATCH(BK$100,Reference!$F$404:$M$404,0),0)"`.

The S&P Recovery Rate Assumptions table in cells E402 to M545 of the **Reference Sheet** is a composite of the recovery rate tables explained earlier (Figure 10.14).

10.3.3 Covenant-lite loan recoveries

Covenant-lite or "Cov-lite" loans reached the height of their popularity in 2006 and 2007 when competition to lend was high and lender underwriting standards were relaxed. These are loans which only have incurrence tests and lack traditional maintenance tests and financial triggers.

	E	F	G	H	I	J	K	L	M
401									
402		S&P Recovery Rate Assumptions							
403					CDO Tranche Rating				
404	Description	Asset Type & RR Group	AAA	AA	A	BBB	BB	B	CCC
405	General Tiered US or Canada Senior Secured Loan	General Loan US Senior Secured	56%	60%	64%	67%	70%	70%	70%
406	General Tiered US or Canada Senior Secured Loan	General Loan US Senior Secured Cov-Lite	51%	54%	57%	60%	63%	63%	63%
407	General Tiered US or Canada Second Lien/Senior Unsecured Loan	General Loan US Second Lien/Senior Unsecured	40%	42%	44%	46%	48%	48%	48%
408	General Tiered US or Canada Subordinated Loan	General Loan US Subordinated	22%	22%	22%	22%	22%	22%	22%
409	General Tiered Country Group A1 Senior Secured Loan	General Loan A1 Senior Secured	68%	73%	78%	81%	85%	85%	85%
410	General Tiered Country Group A1 Senior Secured Loan	General Loan A1 Senior Secured Cov-Lite	61%	66%	70%	73%	77%	77%	77%
411	General Tiered Country Group A1 Mezzanine/Second Lien/Senior Unsecured Loan	General Loan A1 Mezzanine/Second Lien/Senior Unsecured	45%	47%	50%	52%	54%	54%	54%
412	General Tiered Country Group A1 Subordinated Loan	General Loan A1 Subordinated	20%	20%	20%	20%	20%	20%	20%

Figure 10.14 S&P recovery rate assumptions

	A	B	C	D	E
19		Weighted Average S&P AAA Recovery Rate	67.98%	65%	PASS
20		Weighted Average S&P AA Recovery Rate	70.75%	68%	PASS
21		Weighted Average S&P A Recovery Rate	73.52%	70%	PASS
22		Weighted Average S&P BBB Recovery Rate	77.03%	73%	PASS
23		Weighted Average S&P BB Recovery Rate	80.29%	76%	PASS
24		Weighted Average S&P B Recovery Rate	80.54%	78%	PASS

Figure 10.15 Weighted average recovery rates

Incurrence tests mean that the borrower is not required to maintain tests or pass them at all times, but rather is only required to not take any action which might cause the tests to fail.

These loans can potentially lead to lower recoveries as the absence of maintenance tests may prevent a lender from repricing credit risk, thus reducing its ability to restructure the loans in order to mitigate its potential losses. Accordingly, S&P allows the following three options when structuring a CLO containing cov-lites:

- use asset-specific corporate recovery rates; or
- prohibit the investing in "cov-lite" loans in the CLO; or
- reduce the general tiered corporate recovery rates by 10%, i.e., "haircut", for any "cov-lite" loans.[20]

As at the time of writing, cov-lite loans have fallen out of favour. Although they are provided under the asset types in the *Standard Warehouse Mode*, recovery rates and haircuts have not been provided for. Nevertheless, it would be quite easy to add a column in the **Inputs and Portfolio Sheet** for a "switch", whereby if an asset was a cov-lite loan, a 10% reduction would apply in the general tier.

10.3.4 Applying the recovery rates

Once recovery rates are assigned to each asset in the CDO, the weighted average recovery rate for each tranche is calculated (Figure 10.15). This is done on the **Summary Sheet** in cells B19 to E24.

For the purposes of cash flow modelling, in order to determine the initial ratings of the CDO notes, S&P will seek to have the maximum covenanted allocations possible in those asset classes with the lowest recoveries. Hence, the usual practice is to use the weighted average recovery rates achieved for each tranche in the portfolio and add a reasonable cushion between these and the minimum recovery rates. The minimum recovery rates generated from the *Standard Warehouse Model* are applied to the *Cash Flow Model*.

It is worth noting at this point that the remainder of this chapter will concentrate on the S&P criteria as they apply to the *Cash Flow Model*.

---

[20] See S&P paper, "CDO Spotlight: The Covenant-Lite Juggernaut Is Raising CLO Risks – And Standard & Poor's Is Responding", 12 June 2007, page 2.

	B	C	D	E	F	G	H	I
24								
25				Rated CDO Tranches				
26	Tranche Number	1	2	3	4	5	6	7
27	Run RateTranche?	Y	Y	Y	Y	Y	Y	Y
28	CDO Class Name	Class A	Class B	Class C	Class D	Class E	Class F	Combo Note
29	Amount	278,000,000	34,000,000	20,000,000	16,000,000	22,000,000	30,000,000	21,000,000
30	S&P Desired Rating	AAA	AA	A	BBB	BB	NR	B
31	S&P SDR	43.07%	39.36%	37.11%	32.14%	26.04%	#N/A	21.61%
32	S&P Break-Even Percentile	5%	10%	35%	50%	60%	#N/A	70%
33	S&P Break-Even Rate	64.09%	59.70%	53.53%	45.47%	34.88%	#N/A	#NUMI
34	S&P Break-Even Result	PASS	PASS	PASS	PASS	PASS	#N/A	#NUMI
35	S&P	55%	59.00%	62.00%	65%	68%	NA	45%
36	Net Present Value	0.00%	0.00%	0.0%	0.0%	0.0%	0.0%	-
37	Weighted Average Life	5.59	6.66	7.00	7.27	7.79	9.27	5.01
38	Output Block	SP_Block_1	SP_Block_2	SP_Block_3	SP_Block_4	SP_Block_5	SP_Block_6	SP_Block_7
39								

Figure 10.16   Rated CDO Tranches

In cells B35 to I35 of the **Input Sheet** of the *Cash Flow Model* are inputs for the S&P covenanted minimum weighted average recovery rates.

The timing of recovery rates in the *Cash Flow Model* will depend on the asset class and the intention of the asset manager or workout agent. If workouts are not foreseen, then it is assumed that recoveries will occur in the same payment period as the default. That said, it is assumed that interest on any defaulted assets does not accrue during that period (i.e., the default is modelled to have occurred at the beginning of the period) and recoveries occur at the end of the payment period. Interest on these proceeds will not be modelled to occur until the first day of the following payment period if the recoveries are reinvested.[21] Thus, in the *Cash Flow Model*, the Recovery Lag in this instance is 0.

10.4 CDO EVALUATOR

As described briefly at the beginning of this chapter, the CDO Evaluator™ is S&P's proprietary implementation of a Monte Carlo model that is used for assessing the credit quality of a portfolio and establishing the default level of the portfolio at each rating level. The main use of the CDO Evaluator™ is to determine the portfolio Scenario Default Rates (commonly abbreviated to "SDRs").

The SDRs are the levels of default that the collateral needs to be able to sustain without the tranche that is being rated, experiencing a loss. The scenario default rate levels have a corresponding rating.

For corporate assets, the primary factors in ascertaining the SDRs are the credit rating of the obligors, and the concentration of obligors in a number of predefined industry categories and domiciles. The primary elements in determining the recovery rates of defaulted obligors are:

- the seniority of the instrument (senior, mezzanine, subordinated);
- security (secured, first or second lien, fixed or floating charge);
- domicile of the obligation; and
- the rating of the target CDO liability tranche.[22]

The general inputs for a typical cash CDO in the CDO Evaluator[23] are:

- obligor ID;
- asset type;
- S&P rating;

---

[21] See S&P "Update to General Cash Flow Analytics Criteria for CDO Securitizations", 17 October 2006, pages 11–12.

[22] See S&P "Global Cash Flow and Synthetic CDO Criteria", 21 March 2002, pages 15–16.

[23] See S&P CDO Evaluator 4.1, available at www.sp.cdointerface.com.

- maturity date;
- current balance;
- country code.

These inputs are then used to determine to the following:

- the sector correlation coefficients;
- the table of default probabilities for the assets;
- the table of default probabilities for the CDO rating tranches.

Additional outputs are also available from the CDO Evaluator, including:

- collateral default correlation;
- asset distribution;
- asset distribution by rating;
- asset distribution by rating/country;
- asset distribution by maturity/rating;
- benchmark sensitivity analysis;
- portfolio default distribution;
- S&P default measure, S&P variability measure, S&P correlation measure and weighted average rating.

S&P usually require a minimum of 500,000 Monte Carlo simulation runs. However, the sampling error is examined and if not sufficiently low and convergent, more runs may be required.

The outputs from the SDR Sheet are then taken from the CDO Evaluator and entered as Inputs on the **S&P Sheet** in cells B104 to C124 of the *Cash Flow Model* (Figure 10.17).

Scenario Default Rates	
Rating	SDR
AAA	43.07%
AA+	41.54%
AA	39.36%
AA-	38.69%
A+	37.82%
A	37.11%
A-	35.90%
BBB+	34.01%
BBB	32.14%
BBB-	28.96%
BB+	27.81%
BB	26.04%
BB-	24.35%
B+	23.12%
B	21.61%
B-	19.72%
CCC+	15.80%
CCC	13.32%
CCC-	10.19%

Figure 10.17 Scenario default rates

10.5 DEFAULT RATES

10.5.1 Standard default patterns

S&P typically prescribes a standard set of default timing patterns to the cash flows in the CDO during analysis for a rating. The first three listed below are spread over 5 years and the fourth is spread over 4 years:[24]

- 15/30/30/15/10
- 40/20/20/10/10
- 20/20/20/20/20
- 25/25/25/25

To be clear: for the first default pattern 15% of the original portfolio would be defaulted in year 1, 30% in year 2, 30% in year 3, 15% in year 4 and 10% in year 5.

Typically, S&P will require these patterns to be shifted from the beginning of the transaction until the end of the reinvestment period. That is to say, for a transaction with a typical 5-year reinvestment period, The first pattern would be run five times with the first default (i.e., 15%) occurring in each of years 1, 2, 3, 4 and 5 respectively. This is explained further below.

S&P believes that timing patterns which place greater default levels during the beginning of a transaction have the effect of stressing a CDO's dependence on excess spread, whereas evenly applied defaults stress the later years of a transaction. When a transaction is highly stressed with default early in its life, this leads to fewer interest-generating assets which usually results in coverage test failures and hence excess funds being used to pay down liabilities.[25]

The patterns are only extended fully to the end of the reinvestment period for AAA and AA-rated tranches. It is the authors' experience that the extension can be one year less than the end of the reinvestment period for single A tranches, two years less for BBB tranches and three years less than the end of the reinvestment period for BB tranches.

10.5.2 Saw tooth default patterns

In addition to the above patterns, S&P often also applies "saw tooth" default patterns to stress CDOs where principal is used to pay deferred interest on subordinate tranches before it is used to amortize the senior classes. For tranches rated "BBB-" and higher:[26]

- Saw tooth pattern 1: Defaults are applied evenly every other year, starting in year 1 and ending in the last year of the covenanted WAL at the end of the reinvestment period. Defaults are not spread out over the year, but rather lumped at the end of each applicable year.
- Saw tooth pattern 2: Defaults are applied evenly every third year, starting in year 1 and finishing in the last year of the covenanted WAL at the end of the reinvestment period. Defaults are applied at the end of the year.

---

[24] See S&P "Global Cash Flow and Synthetic CDO Criteria", 21 March 2002, page 79.

[25] See S&P "Global Cash Flow and Synthetic CDO Criteria", 21 March 2002, pages 79–80.

[26] See S&P paper, "CDO Spotlight: General Cash Flow Analytics for CDO Securitizations", 25 August 2004, page 9.

For tranches rated "BB+" and lower:[27]

- Saw tooth pattern 3: Defaults are applied evenly every other year starting in year 1 and ending in year 7. Defaults are applied as a lump at the end of the year.

Consequently, if a CDO has a reinvestment period of 4 years and a covenanted maximum WAL for the collateral of 5 years, at the end of the reinvestment period the saw tooth patterns will be:

- Saw tooth pattern 1: 20/0/20/0/20/0/20/0/20
- Saw tooth pattern 2: 25/0/0/25/0/0/25/0/0/25
- Saw tooth pattern 3: 25/0/25/0/25/0/25

In other words, for saw tooth pattern 1 the following defaults would apply at the end of each year:

Year 1: 20%
Year 2: 0%
Year 3: 20%
Year 4: 0%
Year 5: 20%
Year 6: 0%
Year 7: 20%
Year 8: 0%
Year 9: 20%

Saw tooth patterns may result in the coverage tests failing, funds being used to pay down liabilities, the coverage tests then going into compliance again and then being triggered again, etc. Saw tooth patterns have the effect of measuring the sensitivity of the transaction to intermittent defaults. The idea behind the saw tooth patterns is that by repeatedly applying defaults which result in interest deferring, an analysis is performed on the CDO's ability to pay out all of the principal due on the rated tranches after principal has been diverted to pay interest.[28]

10.5.3 Potential additional default patterns

It should be noted that rating agencies will always reserve the right to apply additional stresses to CDOs where they believe the circumstances warrant. Where portfolios have very low credit quality, there is a very short legal final maturity for the CDO and where there are interest rate mismatches, S&P will apply additional default patterns stresses.[29]

For example, for transactions which may be back-ended, i.e., having collateral that is deeply discounted, in the authors' experience, S&P has reserved the right to run back-ended

[27] See S&P paper, "CDO Spotlight: General Cash Flow Analytics for CDO Securitizations", 25 August 2004, page 9.
[28] See S&P paper, "CDO Spotlight: General Cash Flow Analytics for CDO Securitizations", 25 August 2004, page 9.
[29] See S&P paper, "CDO Spotlight: General Cash Flow Analytics for CDO Securitizations", 25 August 2004, pages 10–12.

default timings where the peak default occurs towards the end of the transaction rather than the beginning.

10.5.4 Timing of defaults based on WAL

The default patterns start to be applied in year 1. The start year is then shifted to year 2, and so on until the final default in the pattern occurs in the same year that the last of the collateral is expected to mature. This expected maturity is based on the term of the reinvestment period and the WAL of the collateral. The maximum WAL at the end of the reinvestment period is usually the correct assumption for the WAL as it is at this point that the CDO becomes static.[30]

An example provides clarity as to how this works. Assume that a CDO has a reinvestment period of 4 years and a covenanted maximum WAL for the collateral of 5 years at the end of the reinvestment period. As the balance of the portfolio will mature in year 9, the latest default patterns will start in year 5 so that they will be applied to the end of the maximum WAL covenanted.

It should be noted that for static CDOs (where there is no reinvestment period), the default patterns are reduced to being based only on the collateral's weighted dollar average maturity.[31]

10.5.5 Timing of defaults based on rating

In addition to the WAL, the rating of the tranche will have an effect on how late the default pattern starts, as higher-rated tranches are expected to withstand more strenuous defaults over longer time periods.[32] Accordingly AAA and AA rated tranche default vectors will start the latest in the transaction. Starting with A rated tranches, the latest starting year will be reduced by one year per rating category.[33] Where the WAL is not an integer, it will be rounded up at the half-year mark.[34]

Therefore, following the previous example of a CDO with a reinvestment period of 4 years and a covenanted maximum WAL for the collateral of 5 years from the end of the reinvestment period, the latest default patterns for A rated tranches will start in year 4; for the BBB-rated tranches, year 3; for the BB-rated tranches, year 2; and for the B-rated tranches only year 1.[35]

10.5.6 Smoothing of defaults patterns

S&P assumes that defaults occur at the end of the period, but with no interest being paid on such defaulted asset in that period or thereafter.[36] S&P will allow for the standard annual default patterns to be applied as often as quarterly for CDOs where a minimum of 80% of the

---

[30] See S&P paper, "CDO Spotlight: General Cash Flow Analytics for CDO Securitizations", 25 August 2004, page 7.

[31] See S&P "Global Cash Flow and Synthetic CDO Criteria", 21 March 2002, page 81.

[32] See S&P "Global Cash Flow and Synthetic CDO Criteria", 21 March 2002, page 80.

[33] See S&P "Global Cash Flow and Synthetic CDO Criteria", 21 March 2002, page 81.

[34] See S&P paper, "CDO Spotlight: Update to General Cash Flow Analytics Criteria for CDO Securitizations", 17 October 2006, page 8.

[35] See S&P paper, "CDO Spotlight: General Cash Flow Analytics for CDO Securitizations", 25 August 2004, page 8.

[36] See S&P "Global Cash Flow and Synthetic CDO Criteria", 21 March 2002, page 81.

	Class A	Class B	Class C	Class D	Class E	Class F	Combo Note
			Default Curves				
YR1_15/30/30/15/10	1	1	1	1	1	0	1
YR1_40/20/20/10/10	1	1	1	1	1	0	1
YR1_20/20/20/20/20	1	1	1	1	1	0	1
YR1_25/25/25/25	1	1	1	1	1	0	1
YR2_15/30/30/15/10	1	1	1	1	1	0	1
YR2_40/20/20/10/10	1	1	1	1	1	0	1
YR2_20/20/20/20/20	1	1	1	1	1	0	1
YR2_25/25/25/25	1	1	1	1	1	0	1
YR3_15/30/30/15/10	1	1	1	1	0	0	0
YR3_40/20/20/10/10	1	1	1	1	0	0	0
YR3_20/20/20/20/20	1	1	1	1	0	0	0
YR3_25/25/25/25	1	1	1	1	0	0	0
YR4_15/30/30/15/10	1	1	1	0	0	0	0
YR4_40/20/20/10/10	1	1	1	0	0	0	0
YR4_20/20/20/20/20	1	1	1	0	0	0	0
YR4_25/25/25/25	1	1	1	0	0	0	0
YR5_15/30/30/15/10	1	1	1	0	0	0	0
YR5_40/20/20/10/10	1	1	1	0	0	0	0
YR5_20/20/20/20/20	1	1	1	0	0	0	0
YR5_25/25/25/25	1	1	1	0	0	0	0
COMBO_YR1_50/25/25	0	0	0	0	0	0	1
COMBO_YR1_60/20/10/10	0	0	0	0	0	0	1
COMBO_YR1_70/10/10/10	0	0	0	0	0	0	1
COMBO_YR2_50/25/25	0	0	0	0	0	0	1
COMBO_YR2_60/20/10/10	0	0	0	0	0	0	1
COMBO_YR2_70/10/10/10	0	0	0	0	0	0	1

Figure 10.18 Default curves

collateral is at least quarterly paying. That said, for the first year of the transaction, defaults should be applied in a lump at the end of the year.[37]

For example, if we take a semi-annual paying transaction with the 40/20/20/10/10 default pattern starting in year 1, the following profile of defaults would be modelled:

Period 1: 0%
Period 2: 40%
Period 3: 10%
Period 4: 10%
Period 5: 10%
Period 6: 10%
Period 7: 5%
Period 8: 5%
Period 9: 5%
Period 10: 5%
Period 11: 0%

and the remainder of the periods having 0% defaults.

As defaults are applied to the original par balance of the collateral portfolio (*not* the outstanding collateral balance), if the original par balance is $100, the dollar defaults will be as follows: Period 1– $0; Period 2 – $40; Period 3 – $10; Period 4 – $10; and so on. This may seem very obvious, but if the outstanding collateral amount is defaulted instead, more favourable results will be achieved but they will not be accepted.

It should be noted, however, that defaults occurring in total at the end of each year can be accepted;[38] however, this would not be optimal for achieving the best possible ratings as collateral tests, and particularly the over-collateralization tests may be periodically breached.

In the **S&P Sheet** the Default Curves in cells B74 to H101 are represented as in Figure 10.18.

This then corresponds to the **Vectors Sheet** where these default curves are set out in cells N502 to AG584 (Figure 10.19).

---

[37] See S&P paper, "CDO Spotlight: General Cash Flow Analytics for CDO Securitizations", 25 August 2004, page 10.

[38] See S&P "Global Cash Flow and Synthetic CDO Criteria", 21 March 2002, page 81.

	N	O	P	Q	R	S	T	U	V
501									
502									
503	YR1_15/30/30/15/10	YR1_40/20/20/10/10	YR1_20/20/20/20/20	YR1_25/25/25/25	YR2_15/30/30/15/10	YR2_40/20/20/10/10	YR2_20/20/20/20/20	YR2_25/25/25/25	YR3_15/30/30/15/10
504	0.00%	0.00%	0.00%	0.00%	0.00%	0.00%	0.00%	0.00%	0.00%
505	0.00%	0.00%	0.00%	0.00%	0.00%	0.00%	0.00%	0.00%	0.00%
506	0.00%	0.00%	0.00%	0.00%	0.00%	0.00%	0.00%	0.00%	0.00%
507	0.00%	0.00%	0.00%	0.00%	0.00%	0.00%	0.00%	0.00%	0.00%
508	15.00%	40.00%	20.00%	25.00%	0.00%	0.00%	0.00%	0.00%	0.00%
509	7.50%	5.00%	5.00%	6.25%	3.75%	10.00%	5.00%	6.25%	0.00%
510	7.50%	5.00%	5.00%	6.25%	3.75%	10.00%	5.00%	6.25%	0.00%
511	7.50%	5.00%	5.00%	6.25%	3.75%	10.00%	5.00%	6.25%	0.00%
512	7.50%	5.00%	5.00%	6.25%	3.75%	10.00%	5.00%	6.25%	0.00%
513	7.50%	5.00%	5.00%	6.25%	7.50%	5.00%	5.00%	6.25%	3.75%
514	7.50%	5.00%	5.00%	6.25%	7.50%	5.00%	5.00%	6.25%	3.75%
515	7.50%	5.00%	5.00%	6.25%	7.50%	5.00%	5.00%	6.25%	3.75%
516	7.50%	5.00%	5.00%	6.25%	7.50%	5.00%	5.00%	6.25%	3.75%
517	3.75%	2.50%	5.00%	6.25%	7.50%	5.00%	5.00%	6.25%	7.50%
518	3.75%	2.50%	5.00%	6.25%	7.50%	5.00%	5.00%	6.25%	7.50%
519	3.75%	2.50%	5.00%	6.25%	7.50%	5.00%	5.00%	6.25%	7.50%
520	3.75%	2.50%	5.00%	6.25%	7.50%	5.00%	5.00%	6.25%	7.50%
521	2.50%	2.50%	5.00%	0.00%	3.75%	2.50%	5.00%	6.25%	7.50%
522	2.50%	2.50%	5.00%	0.00%	3.75%	2.50%	5.00%	6.25%	7.50%
523	2.50%	2.50%	5.00%	0.00%	3.75%	2.50%	5.00%	6.25%	7.50%
524	2.50%	2.50%	5.00%	0.00%	3.75%	2.50%	5.00%	6.25%	7.50%
525	0.00%	0.00%	0.00%	0.00%	2.50%	2.50%	5.00%	0.00%	3.75%
526	0.00%	0.00%	0.00%	0.00%	2.50%	2.50%	5.00%	0.00%	3.75%
527	0.00%	0.00%	0.00%	0.00%	2.50%	2.50%	5.00%	0.00%	3.75%
528	0.00%	0.00%	0.00%	0.00%	2.50%	2.50%	5.00%	0.00%	3.75%

Figure 10.19   Default curves

10.6 INTEREST RATE STRESSES

In its methodology S&P specifies at least five general interest rate stress categories to be used:

- Index Forward
- Index Up
- Index Down
- Index Up/Down
- Index Down/Up[39]

Additionally "At Swap" and "At Cap" stresses can be used where interest rate hedges form part of the transaction, applying a flat curve at the average swap/cap rate over the life of the transaction.

There is an Excel model that S&P often makes available to modellers in order to calculate the above mentioned interest rate stresses.[40] On the **S&P Sheet** the following Interest Rate Stress Vectors are referred to:

Forward

For the AAA-rated Notes:

AAA_UP
AAA_DOWN
AAA_DOWN/UP
AAA_UP/DOWN

For the AA-rated tranches:

AA_UP
AA_DOWN
AA_DOWN/UP
AA_UP/DOWN

---

[39] See S&P "Global Cash Flow and Synthetic CDO Criteria", 21 March 2002, page 82.
[40] The reader should contact an S&P analyst for further information.

	B	C	D	E	F	G	H
40							
41				Interest Curves			
42		Class A	Class B	Class C	Class D	Class E	Class F
43	USD_Libor_Fwd	1	1	1	1	1	0
44	AAA_UP	1	0	0	0	0	0
45	AA_UP	0	1	0	0	0	0
46	A_UP	0	0	1	0	0	0
47	BBB_UP	0	0	0	1	0	0
48	BB_UP	0	0	0	0	1	0
49	B_UP	0	0	0	0	1	0
50	CCC_UP	0	0	0	0	0	0
51	AAA_DOWN	1	0	0	0	0	0
52	AA_DOWN	0	1	0	0	0	0
53	A_DOWN	0	0	1	0	0	0
54	BBB_DOWN	0	0	0	1	0	0
55	BB_DOWN	0	0	0	0	1	0
56	B_DOWN	0	0	0	0	0	0
57	CCC_DOWN	0	0	0	0	0	0
58	AAA_DOWN/UP	1	0	0	0	0	0
59	AA_DOWN/UP	0	1	0	0	0	0
60	A_DOWN/UP	0	0	1	0	0	0
61	BBB_DOWN/UP	0	0	0	1	0	0
62	BB_DOWN/UP	0	0	0	0	1	0
63	B_DOWN/UP	0	0	0	0	0	0
64	CCC_DOWN/UP	0	0	0	0	0	0
65	AAA_UP/DOWN	1	0	0	0	0	0
66	AA_UP/DOWN	0	1	0	0	0	0
67	A_UP/DOWN	0	0	1	0	0	0
68	BBB_UP/DOWN	0	0	0	1	0	0
69	BB_UP/DOWN	0	0	0	0	1	0
70	B_UP/DOWN	0	0	0	0	0	0
71	CCC_UP/DOWN	0	0	0	0	0	0
72							

Figure 10.20 Interest curves

	Q	R	S	T	U	V	W	X	Y
303	AAA_UP	AA_UP	A_UP	BBB_UP	BB_UP	B_UP	CCC_UP	AAA_DOWN	AA_DOWN
304									
305	4.92%	4.73%	4.60%	4.50%	4.42%	4.34%	4.27%	3.21%	3.40%
306	6.01%	5.59%	5.31%	5.09%	4.91%	4.75%	4.60%	2.65%	2.97%
307	6.76%	6.18%	5.80%	5.51%	5.26%	5.05%	4.85%	2.40%	2.78%
308	7.35%	6.65%	6.19%	5.84%	5.55%	5.29%	5.06%	2.25%	2.67%
309	7.86%	7.04%	6.53%	6.13%	5.80%	5.50%	5.24%	2.17%	2.61%
310	8.31%	7.40%	6.82%	6.38%	6.02%	5.69%	5.40%	2.11%	2.58%

Figure 10.21 Interest rate curves

These patterns are repeated for each of the relevant tranches according to their desired rating and decline in number in accordance with the target rating as previously discussed. Therefore the applicable interest rate curves can be summarized in cells B41 to H71 on the **S&P Sheet** as in Figure 10.20.

Figure 10.20 is then read by the applicable VBA code direct to the appropriate curve in the Interest Rate Curves area in cells Q302 to AR384 on the **Vectors Sheet** (Figure 10.21).

10.7 AMORTIZATION

The amortization schedule for S&P is calculated on an asset-by-asset basis. For each asset that matures before the end of the reinvestment period is added the time equal to the covenanted WAL of the collateral at the end of the reinvestment period. If this does not result in the maturity occurring after the end of the reinvestment period, then the WAL is added again until this is achieved.[41]

For example, if a CDO has a reinvestment period of *five* years and a covenanted maximum WAL for the collateral of *three* years at the end of the reinvestment period:

- If an asset matures at the end of year 1, six years are then added to this asset.
- If an asset matures at the end of year 3, three years are then added to this asset.
- If an asset matures at the end of year 5, three years are added to this asset.
- If an asset matures at the end of year 6, this maturity date is used.
- If an asset matures at the end of year 10, this maturity date is used.

---

[41] See S&P paper, "CDO Spotlight: Update to General Cash Flow Analytics Criteria for CDO Securitizations", 17 October 2006, pages 5–6.

The new maturity dates for the collateral are then used in the CDO Evaluator and for the amortization curve used in the scenario stress runs.

S&P currently make an amortization calculator freely available for download from www2.standardandpoors.com. The authors strongly recommend that this is obtained, as it is a way to save time and will also ensure that the BDRs (Breakeven Default Rates) are in line with those that S&P will achieve when they are modelling the relevant CDO.

10.8 ADDITIONAL S&P MODELLING CRITERIA

10.8.1 Fixed/floating rate asset mix

Usually where there is a mixture of types fixed and floating collateral interest rates, S&P will require a collateral quality covenant to restrict the minimum and maximum collateral types. They will then usually require the modeller to run the model at the extremes of these covenants. In the reinvestment criteria, where at least 95% of the collateral is covenanted to be floating rate, or 95% of the collateral must be fixed rate, the following can be modelled at the option of the modeller:

- 95% floating rate, or fixed rate, is modelled at 100% of same; or
- the collateral is modelled at a maximum percentage of each.

If there is less than 95% collateral as floating (or fixed) rate, S&P will require that the maximum concentrations for these assets be modelled.[42] Hence, if there is a minimum of 80% and a maximum of 100% floating assets covenanted and a minimum of 0% and maximum of 20% fixed rate assets required, each of (i) 80% floating and 20% fixed and (ii) 100% floating will usually need to be run as additional stress scenarios.

Where a mixture of floating rate and fixed rate assets is required to be modelled, the most efficient way is to create another collateral pool on the **Collateral Sheet**. The reader will note that as the **Collateral Sheet** is set up to allow for more than one collateral pool, it is convenient (but not without some time commitment) to model this.

10.8.2 Biased asset default

Where S&P has concerns about particular assets, they may require additional stresses to be performed. For example, if a portion of comparatively low-rated assets pay a higher than usual spread or coupon, a default in these assets might result in a significant dent in the interest available. In this case, a bias of defaults towards these assets might be required.[43] Again, the most logical way of modelling this would be to create a separate collateral pool on the **Collateral Sheet** for these assets.

10.8.3 Payment in kind assets

Where more than 5% of a portfolio might be invested in PIK assets, S&P will usually apply an additional stress to take this into account.[44]

---

[42] See S&P paper, "CDO Spotlight: General Cash Flow Analytics for CDO Securitizations", 25 August 2004, page 14.

[43] See S&P paper, "CDO Spotlight: General Cash Flow Analytics for CDO Securitizations", 25 August 2004, pages 20–21.

[44] See S&P paper, "CDO Spotlight: General Cash Flow Analytics for CDO Securitizations", 25 August 2004, page 18.

10.8.4 Long-dated corporate assets

Where the portfolio is permitted to contain more than 5% of assets that have a final legal maturity date beyond that of the CDO transaction, S&P will apply a stress which reduces the par credit for each long-dated asset by a present value of 10% per year to each principal payment due on the asset beyond the final legal maturity of the CDO. This is to reflect the potential effect of a forced sale in a potentially weak market.[45]

10.8.5 Interest on assets

In general, the weighted average spread and weighted average coupon that must be used when performing S&P stress runs are the covenanted minimum WAS and WAC. S&P may apply exceptions and apply not as stringent WAS assumptions where:

- a CDO is static and hence the collateral acquired at issuance cannot change and substitution by a collateral manager is not possible;
- a CDO only allows for substitution of assets where a new asset has the same interest cash flows as the asset being replaced;
- a CDO is very close to being fully ramped-up at the issuance date and the WAS and/or the WAC is substantially in excess of the minimums.[46]

If a portfolio is fully ramped-up at closing and reinvestment is provided for, credit can be given to the WAS or WAC at the issuance date. S&P will allow for the WAS or WAC applied to migrate downward on a straight line basis to the covenanted minimum WAS or WAC over the first two years of the transaction.[47] Thus, if the WAS at issuance is 250 bps and the minimum WAS covenanted is 230 bps and the CDO is semi-annual pay, for the first four periods the WAS may be modelled as: Period 0 – 250 bps; Period 1 – 244 bps; Period 2 – 240 bps; Period 3 – 235 bps; and Period 4 and thereafter – 230 bps.

10.8.6 Interest on interest

Funds collected during the payment periods are assumed to be invested in eligible investments and that such interest is earned for only half of the payment period. It should also be noted that interest is not deemed to be earned on recovery proceeds invested in eligible investments during the period in which they are recovered. Interest earned on eligible investment is modelled at a spread of –100bps.[48]

10.8.7 Administration, trustee and collateral management fees

Where an administrator, trustee or collateral manager has agreed to perform services in relation to a CDO for senior fees that may be considered below market, S&P has been known to require

---

[45] See S&P paper, "CDO Spotlight: General Cash Flow Analytics for CDO Securitizations", 25 August 2004, page 18.

[46] See S&P "Global Cash Flow and Synthetic CDO Criteria", 21 March 2002, page 84.

[47] See S&P paper, "CDO Spotlight: General Cash Flow Analytics for CDO Securitizations", 25 August 2004, page 17.

[48] See S&P "Global Cash Flow and Synthetic CDO Criteria", 21 March 2002, page 81; and S&P paper, "CDO Spotlight: General Cash Flow Analytics for CDO Securitizations", 25 August 2004, page 18.

higher fees to be modelled when stress runs are performed. The reasoning for this is to ensure that, should a replacement collateral manager or servicer be necessary, the rated CDO notes can withstand higher senior fees.

S&P will look to have modelled the lower of the agreed collateral management fee and 15 bps for corporate CLOs and CBOs and for ABS CDOs. That said, consideration will be given to the role of the manager and the size of the CDO. For example, where the size of the CDO is 1 billion dollars or euros, a senior fee of 10 bps may be an acceptable minimum stress. In addition, where a CDO is static, lower fees might also be used.[49] Moreover, lower fees or no fee may also be acceptable if, when a manager has resigned and no replacement can be found, the transaction becomes static (i.e., not managed and the reinvestment period ends).

10.9 BUILDING THE S&P SHEET AND RELATED REFERENCES

The **S&P Sheet** is added at this stage of the *Cash Flow Model*. In addition, reference tables are added to the **Rating Agency Reference Sheet** and various vectors are added to the **Vectors Sheet**.

The **S&P Sheet** is divided into two sections and further subsections:

1. S&P Inputs:
   - S&P Inputs
   - Rated CDO Tranches
   - Interest Rate Curves
   - Default Rate Curves
   - Scenario Default Rates
2. Break-even Results
   - Blocks 1 to 7

Below is an examination of each of the subsections.

10.9.1 S&P Inputs

The S&P Inputs box is named "SP_Inputs" (Figure 10.22). It is located in cells B10 to C22 and contains the following inputs:

- **Running Senior Management Fee** (named "SP_Sr_Mgt_Fee"): this is usually set at a level at which S&P believes a typical replacement manager would perform services.
- **Running Junior Management Fee** (named "SP_Jr_Mgt_Fee"): assuming that this fee is paid below the notes for which an S&P rating is sought, in the authors' experience this amount will usually be taken as it is in the legal documentation.
- **Initial Weighted Average Spread** ("SP_Initial_WAS" found in cell C13): this is the minimum covenanted weighted average spread (expressed in bps) at the beginning of the deal as set out the in legal documentation.
- **Reinvestment Weighted Average Spread** (named "SP_Reinvest_WAS): this should be input at the minimum covenanted weight average reinvestment spread as set out in the legal documentation for the deal. This is usually the same as the Initial Weighted Average Spread.

---

[49] See S&P paper, "CDO Spotlight: General Cash Flow Analytics for CDO Securitizations", 25 August 2004, page 21.

	B	C	D	
9				
10	**S&P Inputs**		**Target Range**	
11	Running Senior Management Fee (bps)	10	Sr_Mgt_Fee	
12	Running Junior Management Fee (bps)	40	Jr_Mgt_Fee	
13	Initial Weighted Average Spread (bps)	275	Initial_WAS	
14	Reinvestment Weighted Average Spread (bps)	275	Reinvest_WAS	
15	Mandatory Liquidation of Collateral Period End	80	Coll_Liquidation	
16	Interest on Interest Proceeds (bps)	-100	Int_On_Int_Spread	
17	Constant Default Rate Used? (1=Yes)	0	Constant_Default_Rate_Used	
18	Default Original (1) Or Outstanding Balance (0)	1	Default_Original_or_Outstanding	
19	Default Reinvestment (1=Yes)	-	Default_Reinvestment	
20	Recovery Lag Periods	4	Recovery_Lag	
21	Amortization Curve	Base	Amort_Vector	
22	Cohorts? (1=Yes)	1	Cohorts?	
23				

Figure 10.22   S&P inputs

- **Mandatory Liquidation of Collateral Period End** ("SP_Coll_Liquidation"): this should be set to the legal final end of the deal when running S&P analysis.
- **Interest on Interest Proceeds** (see the current setting in "SP_Int_On_Int_Spread"): this is usually set at –100 bps for S&P purposes.
- **Constant Default Rate Used**? (named SP_Constant_Default_Rate_Used): this should be switched to 0 so that a constant default rate is not used.
- **Default Original Or Outstanding Balance** ("SP_Default_Original_or_Outstanding"): this will be switched to the original beginning collateral balance to be defaulted for S&P analysis.
- **Default Reinvestment** ("SP_Default_Reinvestment" in cell C19): this will always be switched on for the purposes of S&P analysis.
- **Recovery Lag Periods** (cell C20 or "SP_Recovery_Lag"): these can be set at 0 for the purposes of S&P analysis.
- **Amortization Curve** ("SP_Amort_Curve"): this is the amortization curve agreed with S&P.
- **Cohorts**?: this is the switch for determining whether cohorts in the **Collateral Sheet** will be used.

Unlike Moody's, S&P do not place much emphasis on WAL covenants and tend to model the transaction to maturity based upon expected average life of the underlying assets. In this instance, it is more likely that the modeller will have to model each reinvestment as a separate cohort in order to put realistic assumptions on the reinvestment and to generate an overall weighted average life. When modelling cohort redemption profiles, the modeller has three choices:

1. use the current amortization profile but normalize it for any prior payments;
2. shift the amortization profile to start in the period of the reinvestment;
3. shift the amortization profile and normalize it so that it finishes at the maturity date of the transaction.

In (1), the modeller takes the remaining outstanding amortization and divides through by the percentage already amortized at that date. In situation (2), the modeller shifts the start of the amortization profile to commence in the period after reinvestment. Without normalizing the amortization profile, the average life of the transaction will extend. The final option, (3), is

	B	C	D	E	F	G	H
24							
25				Rated CDO Tranches			
26	Tranche Number	1	2	3	4	5	6
27	Run RateTranche?	Y	Y	Y	Y	Y	Y
28	CDO Class Name	Class A	Class B	Class C	Class D	Class E	Class F
29	Amount	278,000,000	34,000,000	20,000,000	16,000,000	22,000,000	30,000,000
30	S&P Desired Rating	AAA	AA	A	BBB	BB	NR
31	S&P SDR	43.07%	39.36%	37.11%	32.14%	26.04%	#N/A
32	S&P Break-Even Percentile	5%	10%	35%	50%	60%	#N/A
33	S&P Break-Even Rate	64.09%	59.70%	53.53%	45.47%	34.88%	#N/A
34	S&P Break-Even Result	PASS	PASS	PASS	PASS	PASS	PASS
35	S&P	55%	59.00%	62.00%	65%	68%	NA
36	Net Present Value	0.00%	0.00%	0.0%	0.0%	0.0%	0.0%
37	Weighted Average Life	5.59	6.66	7.00	7.27	7.79	9.27
38	Output Block	SP_Block_1	SP_Block_2	SP_Block_3	SP_Block_4	SP_Block_5	SP_Block_6
39							

Figure 10.23   Rated CDO tranches

typically normalized for prior amortizations, with all cohorts terminating on the final payment date. When should each be used? Option (1) is typically used for simple models and (2) is typically used to model loans as their amortizations are typically front ended. The final option, (3), is typically used to model bullet maturity instruments such as bonds.

10.9.2 Rated CDO Tranches

The Rated CDO Tranches box is located in cells B25 to I38 (Figure 10.23) and contains the following:

- Tranche Number is taken from the Inputs Sheet.
- Run Rate Tranche? (named "SP_Tranche_Rate") allows for an input of "Y" or "N" depending on whether the stress scenarios for the tranche are desired to be run.
- CDO Class Name and Amount and S&P Desired Rating are also each taken from the Inputs Sheet.
- S&P SDR is a lookup function taking from the SDRs box depending on the S&P Desired Rating. Thus for Tranche Number 1, the formula in cell C31 is "=VLOOKUP(C30,SP_SDRs,2,0)".
- S&P Break-Even Percentile is also a lookup function. It takes from the Break-even Percentile table depending on the S&P Desired Rating. Thus for Tranche Number 1 in cell C30, "=VLOOKUP(C30,SP_BE_Percentiles,2,0)".
- S&P Break-Even Rate will profile the specified percentile value from the break-even results. For example, cell C33 contains the formula "=PERCENTILE(G133:G299,C32)".
- S&P Break-Even Result is determined to be a "PASS" if the S&P Break-Even Rate is less than the S&P SDR. Otherwise the result is "FAIL". Hence in cell C34 the reader will see "=IF(C33>C31,"PASS","FAIL")".
- Covenanted Minimum Recovery Rate references the minimum covenanted recovery rate as input on the Inputs Sheet. Referencing it again on the S&P Sheet allows easy manipulation of this input.
- Net Present Value is referenced from the Outputs Sheet NPV. For example, for the Class A NPV in cell C36, the formula is expressed as "=Outputs!Tranche_1_Par_Loss_Pct".
- Weighted Average Life is also referenced from the Outputs Sheet WAL. Therefore, for the Class A WAL in cell C37, the formula is "=Outputs!Tranche_1_WALt".
- Output Block, for which cell B38 is named "SP_Output_Range", is the block in which the VBA automation will read as the area to report the results of the scenario runs.

	B	C	D	E	F	G	H
40							
41				Interest Curves			
42		Class A	Class B	Class C	Class D	Class E	Class F
43	USD_Libor_Fwd	1	1	1	1	1	0
44	AAA_UP	1	0	0	0	0	0
45	AA_UP	0	1	0	0	0	0
46	A_UP	0	0	1	0	0	0
47	BBB_UP	0	0	0	1	0	0
48	BB_UP	0	0	0	0	1	0
49	B_UP	0	0	0	0	0	0
50	CCC_UP	0	0	0	0	0	0
51	AAA_DOWN	1	0	0	0	0	0
52	AA_DOWN	0	1	0	0	0	0
53	A_DOWN	0	0	1	0	0	0
54	BBB_DOWN	0	0	0	1	0	0
55	BB_DOWN	0	0	0	0	1	0
56	B_DOWN	0	0	0	0	0	0
57	CCC_DOWN	0	0	0	0	0	0
58	AAA_DOWN/UP	1	0	0	0	0	0
59	AA_DOWN/UP	0	1	0	0	0	0
60	A_DOWN/UP	0	0	1	0	0	0
61	BBB_DOWN/UP	0	0	0	1	0	0
62	BB_DOWN/UP	0	0	0	0	1	0
63	B_DOWN/UP	0	0	0	0	0	0
64	CCC_DOWN/UP	0	0	0	0	0	0
65	AAA_UP/DOWN	1	0	0	0	0	0
66	AA_UP/DOWN	0	1	0	0	0	0
67	A_UP/DOWN	0	0	1	0	0	0
68	BBB_UP/DOWN	0	0	0	1	0	0
69	BB_UP/DOWN	0	0	0	0	1	0
70	B_UP/DOWN	0	0	0	0	0	0
71	CCC_UP/DOWN	0	0	0	0	0	0
72							

Figure 10.24 Interest curves

10.9.3 Interest curves

There are five standard pattern interest rate stresses run per major rating category, as described above. These are found in the Interest Rate Curves box located at "SP_Interest_Curves" or cells B41 to G71 (Figure 10.24).

The box is structured such that the interest curves are set out in column B and the switch for whether each is on or off is in the relevant column with a "1" for On and a "0" for Off.

10.9.4 Default Curves

As previously discussed, there are four standard pattern default rate stresses. They are each run for each relevant start year and are located in the Default Rate Curves box found at "SP_Default_Curves" or cells B74 to G95 (Figure 10.25).

As with the Interest Rate Curves box, the Default Rate Curves box is structured such that the various default rate curves are set out in column B and the switch for whether each are on or off is in the relevant column with a "1" for On and a "0" for Off.

	B	C	D	E	F	G	H
73							
74				Default Curves			
75		Class A	Class B	Class C	Class D	Class E	Class F
76	YR1_15/30/15/10	1	1	1	1	1	0
77	YR1_40/20/20/10/10	1	1	1	1	1	0
78	YR1_20/20/20/20	1	1	1	1	1	0
79	YR1_25/25/25/25	1	1	1	1	1	0
80	YR2_15/30/15/10	1	1	1	1	1	0
81	YR2_40/20/20/10/10	1	1	1	1	1	0
82	YR2_20/20/20/20	1	1	1	1	1	0
83	YR2_25/25/25/25	1	1	1	1	1	0
84	YR3_15/30/15/10	1	1	1	1	0	0
85	YR3_40/20/20/10/10	1	1	1	1	0	0
86	YR3_20/20/20/20	1	1	1	1	0	0
87	YR3_25/25/25/25	1	1	1	1	0	0
88	YR4_15/30/15/10	1	1	1	0	0	0
89	YR4_40/20/20/10/10	1	1	1	0	0	0
90	YR4_20/20/20/20	1	1	1	0	0	0
91	YR4_25/25/25/25	1	1	1	0	0	0
92	YR5_15/30/15/10	1	1	1	0	0	0
93	YR5_40/20/20/10/10	1	1	1	0	0	0
94	YR5_20/20/20/20	1	1	1	0	0	0
95	YR5_25/25/25/25	1	1	1	0	0	0
96	COMBO_YR1_50/25/25	0	0	0	0	0	0
97	COMBO_YR1_60/20/10/10	0	0	0	0	0	0
98	COMBO_YR1_70/10/10/10	0	0	0	0	0	0
99	COMBO_YR2_50/25/25	0	0	0	0	0	0
100	COMBO_YR2_60/20/10/10	0	0	0	0	0	0
101	COMBO_YR2_70/10/10/10	0	0	0	0	0	0
102							

Figure 10.25 Default curves

Scenario Default Rates	
Rating	**SDR**
AAA	37.67%
AA+	36.44%
AA	34.49%
AA-	33.76%
A+	32.97%
A	32.34%
A-	31.08%
BBB+	29.30%
BBB	27.55%
BBB-	24.57%
BB+	23.51%
BB	21.83%
BB-	20.30%
B+	19.15%
B	17.72%
B-	16.01%
CCC+	12.53%
CCC	10.35%
CCC-	7.67%

Figure 10.26   Scenario default rates

	B	C	D	E	F	G
130						
131	SP_Block_1					
132	Tranche	Amortization Curves		Interest Curves	Default Curves	Break-Even Rate
133	Class A			USD_Libor_Fwd	YR1_15/30/30/15/10	68.9321%
134	Class A			USD_Libor_Fwd	YR1_40/20/20/10/10	68.2828%
135	Class A			USD_Libor_Fwd	YR1_20/20/20/20/20	70.5764%

Figure 10.27   Break-even results

10.9.5 Scenario Default Rates

The Scenarios Default Rates as taken from the S&P CDO Evaluator are found in "SP_SDRs" in cells B96 to C116 (Figure 10.26).

10.9.6 Break-even Results

The Break-even Results which start in row 131 are generated as a result of the VBA code described below (Figure 10.27).

10.10 RUNNING THE STRESS SCENARIOS

The Break-even Default Rate (BDR) is computed for each scenario run. The BDR represents that portfolio default rate at which the first dollar of loss is experienced (for PIK-able tranches) and/or the rate at which the promised cash flows cannot be made in accordance with the tranche terms and conditions (for non PIK-able tranches) when the stress scenario is applied.[50]

---

[50] See S&P paper, "CDO Spotlight: General Cash Flow Analytics for CDO Securitizations", 25 August 2004, page 5.

Break-even Percentiles	
Rating	**Percentile**
AAA	5%
AA	10%
A	35%
BBB	50%
BB	60%
B and lower	70%

Figure 10.28   Break-even percentiles

10.10.1 Break-even default rate percentiles

In the past, S&P's stated criteria was that the minimum BDR had to be greater than the applicable SDR produced by the CDO Evaluator[51] with exceptions negotiated on a case-by-case basis. However, in an effort to implicitly imply confidence by rating levels instead of absolute minimums, S&P now generally applies a percentile approach. The BDR percentiles in Figure 10.28 are applied to each rating category and can be found at "SP_BE_Percentiles" in cells B102 to C121 of the **Rating Agency Reference Sheet**.[52]

The percentile is the number or percentage below which the number of observations falls. In order to manually calculate a percentile, the number of break-evens must be ranked highest to lowest. A 5% percentile will then be the lowest 5% of the observations. To use a very simple example, assume the following break-even results from stress runs on an AAA-rated tranche: 47%, 46%, 45%, 41%, 40%, 37%, 34%, 33%, 31%, and 29%. The BDR for this tranche will then be 29.90% (the 5th percentile of this range of results).

Excel provides a PERCENTILE() and the PERCENTRANK() function which obviates the modeller from having to manually do any of the above. PERCENTILE() can be used directly on the generated BDR numbers to check that the number at the targeted percentile is above the SDR for each targeted rating. Alternatively, PERCENTRANK() returns the percentile of the SDR in the BDR returns. However, it will return #N/A! if it is not in the range.

Thus, using the PERCENTILE(Array,K) function with the example above, the percentile of the array {47,46,45,41,40,37,34,33,31,29} with "K" as the percentile of 0.05, the function will return the result of 29.90%.

10.10.2 Automating the stress scenario runs

Performing each of the various combinations of stress run scenarios manually is a *very* time consuming process. For example, assume a CLO with four rated classes of notes at AAA, AA, A and BBB with a reinvestment period of 4 years and a covenanted maximum WAL for the collateral of 5 years at the end of the reinvestment period. Also assuming that the collateral

---

[51] See S&P paper, "CDO Spotlight: General Cash Flow Analytics for CDO Securitizations", 25 August 2004, page 5.

[52] See S&P paper, "CDO Spotlight: Update to General Cash Flow Analytics Criteria For CDO Securitizations", 17 October 2006, page 3.

exhibits a bullet amortization curve, then generally, as a bare minimum, a modeller would have 380 scenario runs to calculate:

- For the AAA-rated notes, typically a minimum of 110 scenario runs (22 default patterns multiplied by 5 interest rate stresses):
  - 4 standard default patterns starting in each of years 1, 2, 3, 4 and 5, respectively and saw tooth patterns 1 and 2;
  - 5 Interest Rate Stresses of Forward, AAA Up, AAA Down, AAA Down/Up and AAA Up/Down.
- For the AA-rated notes, a total of 110 scenario runs (22 default patterns multiplied by 5 interest rate stresses):
  - 4 standard default patterns starting in each of years 1, 2, 3, 4 and 5, respectively and saw tooth patterns 1 and 2;
  - 5 Interest Rate Stresses of Forward, AA Up, AA Down, AA Down/Up and AA Up/Down.
- For the A-rated notes, a total of 90 scenario runs (18 default patterns multiplied by 5 interest rate stresses):
  - 4 standard default patterns starting in each of years 1, 2, 3 and 4, respectively and saw tooth patterns 1 and 2;
  - 5 Interest rate Stresses of Forward, A Up, A Down, A Down/Up and A Up/Down.
- For the BBB rated notes, a total of 70 scenario runs (14 default patterns multiplied by 5 interest rate stresses):
  - 4 standard default patterns starting in each of years 1, 2, and 3, respectively, and saw tooth patterns 1 and 2;
  - 5 Interest Rate Stresses of Forward, BBB Up, BBB Down, BBB Down/Up and BBB Up/Down.

Instead of performing each of these manually, VBA code can be used to automate this process. Below is the VBA code which the authors have used in the *Cash Flow Model* in **ModStandardandPoors**.

The code uses a simple bisection algorithm to try to resolve to the first dollar of loss. In order for a bisection algorthim to work, the start and end points of the section need to bracket the zero or crossing point of the function; in this case the function is the loss on the tranche. The code makes a first guess between zero and the subordination divided by the recovery rate. This is generally too low, and a fixed multiplier (in this case 20%) is applied to shift the high point up or the low point down. The authors have used other functions and approaches in order to resolve the BDRs, including secant methods and Newton-Raphson. One issue in solving the function is that it is one sided, in that when the default is too low there are no losses. This makes root solving slower as when the default rate is too low there is no feedback to improve an algorithm. One approach which the authors have used but not demonstrated here is a double bisection or secant approach. In this approach, cashflows due to the tranches below the target tranche are used as the other half of the function, and the algorthim attempts to minimize payments to the lower tranches in addition to minimizing losses on the target tranche, in order to find the highest BDR before the target tranche experiences a loss or "breaks".

```
Sub Run_SandP()
Dim r1 As Range 'input Range
Dim r2 As Range 'Default output range
```

```
Dim rLoss As Range
Dim rWAL As Range
Dim rSummary As Range
Dim sSummary As String
Dim rAssumptions As Range

Dim c As Range 'found cell
Dim nRows As Integer
Dim nCols As Integer
Dim nFnd As Integer
Dim nTranches As Integer
Dim i As Integer
Dim nTranche As Integer
Dim maxTranche As Integer
Dim nCrv As Integer
Dim nDefCrv As Integer
Dim maxCrv As Integer
Dim maxDefCrv As Integer

Dim dBEven As Double
Dim iCnt As Integer


Dim c_offset As Integer 'cell offset for input
Dim default_prob As Double
Dim dloss As Double
Dim dWAL As Double
Dim spCurve As String
Dim spDefCurve As String
Dim spTranche As String

Dim Calc_mode As XlCalculation
Dim out_range As String

'inputs

Dim m_Init_sprd As Double
Dim m_Reinv_sprd As Double
Dim tranche As String
Dim WAL As String


'tranche inputs

Calc_mode = Application.Calculation

'read assumptions

  Set rAssumptions = Worksheets("S&P").Range("B11:D22")

  For i = 1 To rAssumptions.Rows.count
```

```
  Range(rAssumptions.Cells(i, 3).Value) = rAssumptions.Cells(i, 2).
  Value
 Next i

'set up variable

Set r2 = Range("Cum_Default_Rate")

maxTranche = 6
maxCrv = 18
maxDefCrv = 20
'
'
For nTranche = 1 To maxTranche
 i = 1
 If Range("SP_Tranche_Rate").Offset(0, nTranche).Value = "N" Then GoTo
 nextTranche
 spTranche = Range("SP_Class_Name").Offset(0, nTranche).Value
 Range("Anticipated_Recovery_Rate").Value = Range("SP_Tranche_Rec_
 Rates").Offset(0, nTranche + 1).Value

 out_range = Range("SP_Output_Range").Offset(0, nTranche).Value
 Set r1 = Range(out_range)

  For nCrv = 1 To maxCrv
   If Range("SP_Interest_Curves").Cells(nCrv, nTranche + 1).Value = 1
   Then
      Range("Interest_Vector").Value = Range("SP_Interest_Curves").
      Cells(nCrv, 1).Value
      spCurve = Range("SP_Interest_Curves").Cells(nCrv, 1).Value
   Else
    GoTo nextCrv
   End If

    For nDefCrv = 1 To maxDefCrv
        If Range("SP_Default_Curves").Cells(nDefCrv, nTranche + 1).
        Value = 1 Then
          Range("Default_Vector").Value = Range("SP_Default_Curves").
          Cells(nDefCrv, 1).Value
          spDefCurve = Range("SP_Default_Curves").Cells(nDefCrv, 1).
          Value
        Else
         GoTo nextDefCrv
        End If


          tranche = "Tranche_" & nTranche & "_Par_Loss"
          Set rLoss = Worksheets("Outputs").Range(tranche)
'
          Call Bisection(rLoss, r2, 0.000001, dBEven, iCnt)
```

```
            r1.Offset(i, 0).Value = spTranche
            r1.Offset(i, 3).Value = spCurve
            r1.Offset(i, 4).Value = spDefCurve
            If iCnt < 200 Then
                r1.Offset(i, 5).Value = dBEven
            Else
              r1.Offset(i, 5).Value = "Not Resolved"
            End If


            i = i + 1
            'dloss = Application.WorksheetFunction.SumProduct
            (Range(r1.Cells(2, 2), r1.Cells(2 + m_div_end, 2)),
Range(r1.Cells(2, 3), r1.Cells(2 + m_div_end, 3)))
'           dWAL = Application.WorksheetFunction.SumProduct
            (Range(r1.Cells(2, 2), r1.Cells(2 + m_div_end, 2)),
Range(r1.Cells(2, 4), r1.Cells(2 + m_div_end, 4)))
            'rSummary.Cells(nDefCrv + 1, nCrv + 1).Value = dloss

nextDefCrv:
    Next nDefCrv

nextCrv:
    Next nCrv

nextTranche:
    Next nTranche

leave:

End Sub

Sub Bisection(ByRef loss As Range, ByRef rate As Range, ByVal
precision As Double, ByRef Breakeven As Double, ByRef count As
Integer)

Dim dX1 As Double
Dim dX2 As Double
Dim dX3 As Double

Dim dLoss1 As Double
Dim dLoss2 As Double
Dim dloss3 As Double
Dim i As Integer
Dim myCalcMode As XlCalculation

 myCalcMode = Application.Calculation

 i = 0
 dX1 = rate.Value
 dLoss1 = -loss.Value
```

```
Do
 dX3 = dX2 + (dX1 - dX2) / 2#
  rate.Value = dX1
  If myCalcMode = xlCalculationManual Then Application.Calculate

  dLoss1 = -loss.Value
  If dLoss1 <= 1 And dLoss1 > precision Then
    Breakeven = dX1
    GoTo found
  End If

  rate.Value = dX2
   If myCalcMode = xlCalculationManual Then Application.Calculate
  dLoss2 = -loss.Value
  If dLoss2 <= 1 And dLoss2 > precision Then
   Breakeven = dX2
   GoTo found
  End If

   rate.Value = dX3

  If myCalcMode = xlCalculationManual Then Application.Calculate
   dloss3 = -loss.Value
   If dloss3 <= 1 And dloss3 > precision Then
   Breakeven = dX3
   GoTo found
   End If
 If dLoss1 > 1 And dloss3 > 1 Then
   dX1 = dX3
 ElseIf dLoss1 > 1 And dloss3 = 0 Then
   dX2 = dX3
 ElseIf dLoss2 > 1 Then
   dX1 = dX2
   dX2 = 0.8 * dX1
 Else   ' both zero
   dX2 = dX1
   dX1 = 1.2 * dX1
 End If

 i = i + 1

Loop While loss.Value > 1 Or loss.Value <= precision Or i = 200
found:
count = i

End Sub
```

10.10.3 Achieving targeted ratings

As with obtaining a rating with Moody's, a modeller is wise to resist the desire to structure too "tightly", i.e., by allowing for too little margin between the BDRs and the SDRs. Although

Obligor Rating	Target CDO Liability Rating						
	AAA	AA	A	BBB	BB	B	CCC
'AAA' to 'CCC-'	2	1	-	-	-	-	-
'AA' to 'CCC-'	3	2	1	-	-	-	-
'A' to 'CCC-'	4	3	2	1	-	-	-
'BBB' to 'CCC-'	6	4	3	2	1	-	-
'BB' to 'CCC-'	8	6	4	3	2	1	-
'B' to 'CCC-'	10	8	6	4	3	2	1
'CCC' to 'CCC-'	12	10	8	6	4	3	2

Figure 10.29   Target CDO liability rating

tight structuring often provides for greater equity returns, some excess margin provides for a more stable rating, by allowing for some potential default and/or downgrades in the portfolio without necessarily impacting the ratings of the notes.

10.10.4 Recent changes in methodolgy

As a result of an RFC ("request for comment"), published in March 2009, S&P released its latest criteria as of writing for Corporate CDOs on 17 September 2009.[53] The changes, in summary, included:

(a) recalibration of default rates for corporate borrowers;
(b) adjustment of correlation assumptions;
(c) adjustment of recovery assumptions;
(d) the introduction of out of model concentration tests.

   The first three of these changes were incorporated in a new version of CDOEvaluator, 5.0, which was released contemporaneously. CDOEvaluator 5.0 is only applicable to corporate credit transactions. The changes involved looking at credit crises since the early 1980s and calibrating models. The view expressed in the paper is that these peaks were commensurate with a BBB stress for corporate CDOs. Hence stresses for higher ratings needed to stress these figures.
   Finally, the "out of model" concentration tests screen for various obligor concentrations, and industry concentrations are discussed. The obligor concentration tests depend on the rating of the target tranche and the rating of the underlying obligors. For each rating category of the liability, the largest number of obligors in the appropriate bucket is defaulted with a fixed recovery rate of 5% (Figure 10.29).

---

[53] "Update to Global Methodolgies and Assumptions For Corporate Cash Flow and Synthetic CDOs", Standard and Poors, 17 September 2009.

	Target CDO Tranche Rating	
Obligor Rating	AAA	AA
'AAA' to 'CCC-'	4	2
'AA' to 'CCC-'	6	4
'A' to 'CCC-'	8	6
'BBB' to 'CCC-'	12	8
'BB' to 'CCC-'	16	12
'B' to 'CCC-'	20	16
'CCC' to 'CCC-'	24	20

Figure 10.30   Alternative industry test

The test is performed "outside of the model" as cash flows are not considered. An adjusted overcollateralization calculation is performed, where the numerator is the *sum of*:

- par balance of the performing asset pool; *plus*
- cash balances in transaction accounts; *less*
- the highest of the losses from the largest obligor test; *less*
- the balances of any performing obligors rated below CCC– (i.e., assumed defaulted); *plus*
- the expected recoveries on assets that are currently in default and still in the pool.

The denominator is the amount of liabilites which have target ratings senior or pari passu to the liability being tested.

In order to meet these tests the resultant quotient needs to be greater than 1.

The largest industry default test involves defaulting the largest industry category (by notional) and the second largest industy category, with a fixed recovery of 17%. This test applies for any tranche with a target rating of AA– or higher. The modified overcollaterization mechanics used in the largest obligor test are applied to the largest industry test also.

If the tranche fails the largest industry test it still might reach its target rating if it passes an alternative industry test (Figure 10.30). The alternative industry test is a sort of hybrid between the two, in which a number of the largest obligors in each industry are defaulted with a 5% recovery rate, rather than the whole industry's recovery rate. To be clear, in the above instances the tests are mutually exclusive and not cumulative.

The impact of these changes resulted in a large number of downgrades of existing transactions in 2009 and will reduce the leverage in new transactions going forward.

11

Advanced Waterfall Modelling

11.1 HEDGE AGREEMENTS

There are various instances in cash flow modelling when a hedge agreement (also called a "swap" or interest rate derivative) will be required to tailor cash flows between the assets and liabilities. This most often occurs when there are assets which pay on both a fixed and floating interest rate basis in the collateral pool. This situation can be dealt with in three ways:

1. issue liabilities which initially match the ratio of fixed and floating rate assets in the collateral;
2. enter into swaps such that the fixed rate assets are effectively converted to floating rates (i.e., an asset swap), or enter into a macro or average rate hedge, perhaps with options, on the entire pool;
3. do nothing and have the structure run the basis risk.

In this section the modelling of interest rate swaps is examined.

11.1.1 Why are interest rate swaps necessary?

A very simplified example will help explain why interest rate swaps are necessary in CDOs. Suppose the collateral in a CDO consists of $300 million and the CDO issuance is comprised of Class A, B, and Equity Notes, totalling $300 million. There are no expenses other than promised sequential interest payments to the Class A and Class B Notes. The Equity Notes receive residual cash flows only. There is generally a much larger investor appetite for floating rate liabilities than for fixed rate liabilities, as the fixed rate liabilities have additional risks other than pure credit risk (i.e., interest rate risk and redemption issues).

Assume the collateral has the following characteristics:

- 60% of the collateral pays based on a floating interest rate (LIBOR) and the weighted average spread is 2.00%; and
- 40% of the collateral is fixed rate with a weighted average coupon of 6.00%.

If LIBOR is assumed to be 4.00%, the weighted average interest rate on the collateral is 6.00% (calculated very obviously as $[(2.00\% + 4.00\%) * 60\%)] + [6.00\% * 40\%] = 6.00\%$). Assume the following about the liabilities:

- The Class A Notes consist of 70% of the issuance and have a promised interest rate of LIBOR + 1.00%.
- The Class B Notes consist of a further 20% of the issuance and have a promised interest rate of LIBOR + 1.50%.
- The Equity Notes consist of a final 10% of the issuance and are entitled to the remaining interest cash flows after the Class A and Class B Notes have been paid.

As LIBOR is assumed to be 4.00%, the weighted average cost of capital of the Class A and Class B Notes is 4.60% (calculated as [(1.00% + 4.00%) * 70%)] + [(1.50% + 4.00%) * 20%] = 4.60%).

Given this, a simplified "back of the envelope" estimation for the return to the equity is 14.00% (very basically calculated as the weighted average interest rate on the collateral less the weighted average cost of the Class A and B Notes, divided by the size of the Equity issuance ((6.00% − 4.60%) / 10% = 14.00%).

Now, *assume that LIBOR increases to 8.66%*. What is the effect on the equity returns?

- For the collateral, the weighted average interest rate increases to 8.796% (calculated as [(2.00% + 8.66%) * 60%)] + [6.00% * 40%] = 8.796%).
- On the liabilities side, the weighted average cost of the Class A and Class B Notes increases to 8.794% (calculated as [(1.00% + 8.66%) * 70%)] + [(1.50% + 8.66%) * 20%] = 8.794%).
- The simplified estimation for the return to the Equity Notes decreases to 0.02% (determined by (8.796% – 8.794%) / 10% = 0.02%).

It is worth noting that, once LIBOR increases to 8.67% and above, not only will the Equity Notes fail to receive interest payments but also the Class B Notes will not receive promised interest due (and possibly the Class A Notes, depending on how high LIBOR goes).

Finally, *assume that LIBOR stays at 8.66%; however the collateral consists of 100% floating rate pay assets* and the weighted average spread is 2.00%.

- For the collateral, the weighted average interest rate increase is 10.66% (calculated as 2.00% + 8.66% = 10.66%).
- On the liabilities side, the weighted average cost of the Class A and Class B Notes remains the same at 8.794%.
- Now, the return to the Equity Notes increases to 18.66% (determined by (10.66% – 8.794%) / 10% = 18.66%).

This very simplified example helps to illustrate the interest rate risk a CDO (particularly note holders lower in the capital structure) assumes when there is a disparity between the basis on which assets and liabilities are paid.

11.1.2 What is an interest rate swap?

A fixed-floating interest rate swap is a bilateral contract, i.e., between two parties, where one party agrees to make fixed rate payments and another party agrees to make floating rate payments. Figure 11.1 illustrates this relationship.

The fixed rate payments will be typically known and or set at the beginning of the contract, and are usually set on the day the swap is traded. However, the actual floating rate payments (other than perhaps the first period) will be unknown at the outset, as they will depend on the

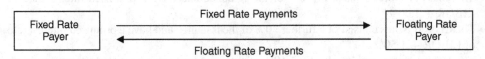

Figure 11.1 Interest rate swap

future rates of the index to which they are referenced which are set by the market. There is typically no exchange of principal in a fixed-floating interest rate swap.

The date on which the terms of a swap are agreed upon is known as the "Trade Date". The "Effective Date" is when the first fixed and floating payments begin to accrue. The last payment date is known as the "Termination Date".

In interest rate swaps a concept known as "netting of payment", or set off, is often elected (where previously agreed by the counterparties), whereby the fixed leg payment and the floating leg payment are subtracted from each other, and only the positive net difference is paid by the respective party.

11.1.3 Modelling interest rate swaps

Payments to counterparties under the hedges are typically paid senior in the Interest Waterfall and Principal Waterfall. Termination Payments are typically not modelled for two reasons:

1. Termination payments are not known or are not permitted for the SPE (unless they can be terminated for a known or zero cost, i.e., the SPE purchases swaptions).
2. Termination payments arising from so-called "affected party" events (i.e., where the swap counterparty has defaulted) are made at a subordinate level in the waterfall, typically just above the equity.

Figure 11.2 illustrates the hedges' usual positions in the Interest Waterfall where hedge payments occur and Figure 11.3 illustrates the position of hedge payments in the Principal Waterfall.

11.1.4 Hedges Sheet

The Hedges Inputs are as follows (Figure 11.4):

- **Swap Hedge Amount** is the notional amount of the swap.
- **Swap Fixed Rate** is the price of the hedge.
- **Floating Rate Spread** is the spread to be received on the floating leg of the swap.
- **Swap Cap** is the cap on the LIBOR or index rate paid on the floating leg.
- **Swap LIBOR Curve** is the applicable curve to be applied from the **Vectors Sheet**.
- **Swap Default Curve** is the default curve (if any) to be applied from the **Vectors Sheet**.
- **Day Count** is Act/360 for the floating leg, and can either be annual Act/360 or semi-annual 30/360 for the fixed leg in US swaps.

The following vectors (Figure 11.5) are taken from the **Vectors Sheet** and are:

- Period
- Dates
- LIBOR Rate
- Fixed Rate
- Amortization
- Default

For Period 0, the **Balance** in cell I104 is the Swap Amount in cell C4 After this, it is simply the New Balance from the previous period. For example, in cell I105 the reader will see the formula "=L104".

1)	Taxes
2)	Fees and Expenses of the Trustee and Administrators up to a cap
3)	Senior Collateral Management Fee
4)	Scheduled payments or termination payments under any Hedge Agreements
5)	Class A Interest
6)	Class B Interest

17)	Class E Interest
18)	Class E Deferred Interest
19)	Any unpaid Fees and Expenses, to the extent not paid in (2) above
20)	Cost of entry into Hedge Agreements and Termination Payments under any Hedge Agreements
21)	Junior Collateral Management Fee
22)	Class F Notes payment until the Class F Notes have received a minimum IRR
23)	a) Incentive Management Fee and b) Remaining Interest Proceeds to the Class F Note holders

Figure 11.2   Hedges' positions in the interest waterfall

| 1) | Amounts in paragraphs (1) to (9) and (11) of the Interest Waterfall to the extent not paid from Interest Proceeds |
| 2) | During the Reinvestment Period, to acquire Additional Portfolio Assets |

| 15) | After the end of the Reinvestment Period, (a) Incentive Management Fee and (b) Remaining Principal Proceeds to the Class F Note holders |

Figure 11.3   Hedge payments in the principal waterfall

	A	B	C
2			
3		**Inputs**	
4		Swap Hedge Amount	20,000,000
5		Swap Fixed Rate	Swap_Fixed_1
6		Floating Rate Spread	3.00%
7		Swap Cap	5.00%
8		Swap LIBOR Curve	Forward
9		Swap Amortization Curve	Swap_4
10		Swap Default Curve	YR2_25/25/25/25
11		Day Count	Act/360
12			

Figure 11.4 Hedges inputs

	A	B	C	D	E	F	G
101							
102				**Vectors**			
103		Period	Dates	LIBOR Rate	Fixed Rate	Amortization	Default
104		0	03/09/2009	0.00%	6.50%	0.00%	0.00%
105		1	03/12/2009	0.11%	6.50%	0.00%	0.00%
106		2	03/03/2010	0.28%	6.50%	0.00%	0.00%

Figure 11.5 Vectors sheet

The **Amortization** and **Defaults** are calculated based on the vectors for these provided on the Vectors Section of the sheet beginning in cells F103 and G103. Hence for Periods 1, the amortization in cell J105 is `"=I105*F105"` and the defaults in cell K105 are `"=G105*I105"`.

The **New Balance** is then:

- Balance
- *less* Amortization
- *less* Defaults (Figure 11.6).

The formula found in cell L105 is `"=I105-J105-K105"`.

The **Fixed Rate Amount** is determined by:

- New Balance
- *multiplied by* the Swap Fixed Rate
- *multiplied by* the days in the period *divided by* 360. Day count conventions will vary and for USD there are two main conventions, annual Act/360 and semi-annual bond basis, 30/360.

For example, the period 1 Fixed Rate Amount in cell N105 is `"=L105*(E105*(C105-C104)/360)"`.

The **Floating Rate Amount** is calculated as:

- New Balance
- *multiplied by*:
  - the *minimum of* LIBOR for the period and the Swap Cap rate
  - *plus* the Floating Spread for the Swap
- *multiplied by* the days in the period divided by 360.

	I	J	K	L	
101					
102		**Hedge Balance**			
103	**Balance**	**Amortization**	**Defaults**	**New Balance**	
104	20,000,000			20,000,000	
105	20,000,000	-	-	20,000,000	
106	20,000,000	-	-	20,000,000	

Figure 11.6   Hedge balance

	N	O	P	
101				
102		**Hedge Payments**		
103	**Fixed Rate Amount**	**Floating Rate Amount**	**Net Difference**	
104				
105	328,611	157,022	171,589	
106	325,000	163,853	161,147	

Figure 11.7   Hedge payments

For example, for Period 1, cell O105 contains the formula `"=L105*((MIN(D105,Swap_Cap)+Swap_Float_Spread)*(C105-C104)/360)"`.

The Net Difference is simply:

- Fixed Rate Amount
- *less* Floating Rate Amount.

In cell P105 there is the formula `"=N105-O105"`.

Payments from Hedge Counterparty are the values when the Net Difference is negative. For example, the value in cell R105 from the formula `"=IF(P105<0,-P105,0)"` is then fed through to the **Collateral Sheet** to form part of the Interest Proceeds.

Payments to Hedge Counterparty are the values when the Net Difference is positive. To illustrate, the value from the formula `"=IF(P105>0,P105,0)"` in cell S105 is then taken through to the **Waterfall Sheet** to be paid out as a liability (Figure 11.8).

11.1.5 Inputs Sheet

On the **Inputs Sheet** there is an on/off switch for the Hedges named "Hedges (Swaps) (1 = On, 0 = Off)" in cell C74". This can be useful for either debugging the model or for measuring the impact of the hedge.

11.1.6 Collateral Sheet

The Payments from the Hedge Counterparty starting in cell R103 are added to the **Collateral Sheet**. The Collateral Summary section of the **Collateral Sheet** area is added in cells starting at AN100.

	R	S
101		
102	**Payments To and From CDO**	
103	**Payments from Hedge Counterparty**	**Payments to Hedge Counterparty**
104		
105	-	171,589
106	-	161,147

Figure 11.8 Payments to and from hedge counterparty

The **Hedges Counterparty Payments** (Figure 11.9) is taken directly from the **Hedges Sheet** and multiplied by the Hedges Switch from the **Inputs Sheet**. For Period 1, cell AN105 has the formula `"=Hedges!R105*Swaps?"`

To the **Interest Proceeds Aggregate Interest Collections** is added the Total Collections Due to Hedges. To illustrate, cell AP105 now has the formula `"=W105+AM105+AK105"`.

11.1.7 Waterfall Sheet

To include the Payments to Hedge Counterparty in the waterfall, a column is added before (or to the left of) the Senior Management Fee from the 300s to 800s.

The Hedge Payment in the Interest Waterfall is the *median of*:

- the Hedge Payment Due;
- the funds available after the payment of the Trustee/Admin Fees;
- zero.

For example, the period 1 Hedge Payment in cell J305 is "MEDIAN(I405,J505,0)".
The Interest Waterfall Available Funds After Payment is the:

- funds available after payment of the Trustee/Admin Fees
- *less* the Hedge Payment in the Interest Waterfall

Thus, in cell J405 the formula is `"=I405-J305"`.

	AM
101	
102	**Hedges**
103	**Hedges Counterparty Payments**
104	-
105	-
106	-

Figure 11.9 Hedges counterparty

The Interest Waterfall Calculation of the Hedge Payment (for period 1, cell J505) is taken directly from the Payments to the Hedge Counterparty in the **Hedges Sheet** and multiplied by the Hedges Switch (for period 1, `"=Hedges!S105*Swaps?"`).

The Hedge Payment in the Principal Waterfall is the *median of*:

- the Hedge Payment Due
- the funds available after the payment of the Trustee/Admin Fees
- zero

The period 1 Hedge Payment in cell J605 is `"=MEDIAN(I705,J805,0)"`.

The Principal Waterfall Available Funds After Payment is the:

- funds available after payment of the Trustee/Admin Fees in the Principal Waterfall Available Funds after Payment
- *less* the Hedge Payment in the Principal Waterfall

Thus, in cell "J705", there is the formula `"=I705-J605"`.

The Principal Waterfall Calculation of the Hedge Payment is the maximum of:

- Interest Waterfall Calculation for the Hedge Payment *less* the Hedge Payment Paid in the Interest Waterfall
- zero

For cell J805, the formula is `"=MAX(J505-J305,0)"`.

11.1.8 Payment under Hedge Agreements

The various accounts of the CDO are discussed in Chapter 6. Where the CDO is structured to include Hedge Agreements, the various payments will usually be treated as follows:

- Where collateral posted by a Hedge Counterparty has been released to the Issuer under the Hedge Agreement it will commonly be paid into the Principal Collection Account.
- Interest Payments that are made by Hedge Counterparties to the Issuer are usually paid into the Interest Collection Account.
- Amounts payable to a Hedge Counterparty (other than termination payments due to a Hedge Counterparty), are usually paid on payment dates in accordance with the waterfall) and are paid *from* the Interest Collection Account.
- Amounts payable upon entry into a replacement Hedge Agreement up to an amount equal to any termination payments received upon termination of the Hedge Agreement which is being replaced are paid *from* the Interest Collection Account

11.1.9 Uses and misuses of interest rate derivatives

The shape of the Swap Amortization Curve will have an effect on the equity IRR returns. On the **Vectors Sheet** in the *Cash Flow Model* the reader will notice that four Swap Amortization Vectors are provided. If they are graphed, they look as in Figure 11.10.

As each of these curves is applied to the interest rate swap, from Swap_1 to Swap_4, the reader will notice that the equity IRRs increase if each curve is replaced with those taking the amortization to a longer date. Depending on the leverage in the CDO, this can have a significant effect on projected equity returns.

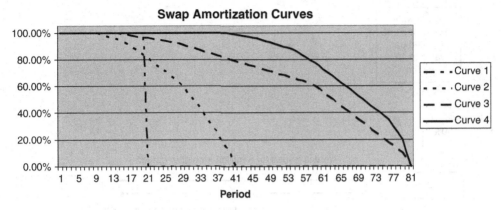

Figure 11.10 Swap amortization curves

Similarly, on the **Vectors Sheet** in the *Cash Flow Model* the reader will notice that four Swap Fixed Rate Vectors are provided. Graphed, they look as in Figure 11.11.

As each of these curves is applied to the interest rate swap, from Swap_Fixed_1 to Swap_Fixed_4, the reader will notice that the equity IRRs increase (at an even greater rate than with the different amortization curves provided) if each curve is replaced with those taking the fixed rate lower as time goes on in the CDO.

Equity returns can also be boosted by "shaping" the interest rate schedules over the life of the transaction – for example, by paying a below par rate early on in the transaction and an above par rate towards the end of the transaction, as opposed to a flat rate throughout, with the difference accruing as additional income to the equity holders.

Swaps can also be used for creative problem solving in CDOs. For example, if an asset is available at discount but the par spread is too low for the collateral manager to purchase it or the manager is prevented from purchasing assets that are discounted below a certain level, a swap can be entered into using a simple SPE structure. The asset can be purchased by an SPE at the discount price and sold on to the CDO at a new higher par spread and a new higher amount. The SPE is thus in effect acting as a swap counterparty by repacking the asset and selling it on a repacked note using swap technology. This is effectively converting principal

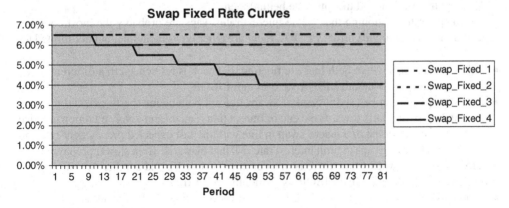

Figure 11.11 Swap fixed rate curves

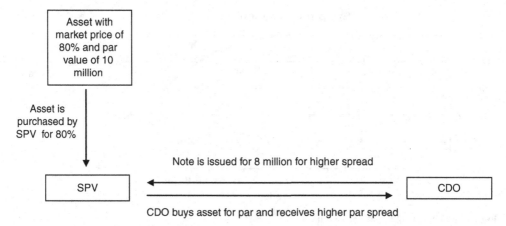

Figure 11.12   Creative problem solving in CDOs

to income, by converting the discounted principal implied by a discount margin into a current margin by way of an asset swap (Figure 11.12).

For example, an asset has a notional value of 10 million, a market value of 80% and pays a par spread of 2.50%. An SPE can purchase the asset for 80% and issue a note with a nominal value of 10 million to the CDO at a purchase price of 100% – an greatly enhanced par spread. This can be approximately calculated as an increase in spread by dividing the difference between par and the purchase price by the swap duration. If the swap duration was, for example, 5 years, the increase in spread by paying the 20% would be approximately 4%.

In the past managers have also performed the reverse transaction; that is, to convert income to principal by asset swapping a high coupon (usually fixed rate) asset to a lower spread that was suggested by a par-par asset swap, i.e., effectively discounting at a lower yield and generating an above par price. This above par amount is paid upfront by the swap counterparty and has been used for varying purposes in transactions, including to pay fees (to the manager and/or arranger) or to reinvest in new assets to restore principal proceeds.

Each of these practices effectively transfers some value away from the note holders, particularly the senior note holders. Therefore, as a note holder it is important to understand the hedges in a transaction, and the rationale behind them.

It is also worth mentioning that, while interest rate swaps are probably the most common type of derivative in single currency CDOs, there are other types including, but not limited to:

- basis swaps: swaps where both legs are floating, but each is referenced to a different index or index tenor, e.g., 3-month LIBOR vs. 6-month LIBOR;
- interest rate caps can be used instead of swaps to limit both counterparty risk and notional mismatches, particularly towards the end of transaction (i.e., it is relatively common practice to amortize the notional of a macro swap in line with the fast expected prepayment rate and have forward starting caps to limit interest rate risk that may arise from slower prepayments);
- currency swaps: swaps where there is one currency on one leg and another currency on the other leg, e.g., 3-month GBP LIBOR vs. 3-month USD LIBOR;
- combinations of interest rate, basis, currency and various other creative swaps to hedge risks in the CDO.

11.2 FIXED NOTES

It is possible to create a CDO or tranches of a CDO that pay interest to note-holders on a fixed basis. There are various reasons why this might be done:

- if all or a portion of the collateral is fixed pay;
- at the request of an investor who wants a fixed paying tranche within the CDO.

Where all of the collateral is payable on a fixed basis, there are two ways that this can be achieved in the *Cash Flow Model*:

- the calculations throughout the *Cash Flow Model* can be altered to remove reference to LIBOR and the "spreads" in the model can be used at the fixed coupon rates;
- LIBOR can be reduced to zero and the "spreads" can again be treated as the fixed coupon rates.

If only a portion of the collateral is payable on a fixed basis and an issuance of fixed notes in the same proportion is desired, another pool of collateral should be created which is modelled as fixed (i.e., without reference to LIBOR) and the relevant tranche can be de-linked from LIBOR. It should be noted that as amortization, prepayments and potential defaults may differ from the fixed payment assets as compared to the floating pay assets, it may have negative consequences for the equity notes to have any potential imbalance in the amount of fixed pay asset versus fixed pay liabilities.

If a fixed pay tranche is being created at the request of an investor and the assets are all floating pay, the most efficient way to structure this is to use an interest rate swap on the liability side.

11.3 VARIABLE FUNDING NOTES

Thus far, consideration has only been given to CDO notes that are issued in full on the date of issuance. Variable funding notes and delayed draw notes ("VFNs" and "DDNs" respectively) are notes which are created on the issuance date but may not be fully "drawn" or "funded" at that time. Variable funding notes provide the CDO with an ability to more closely match its liability levels (during the life of the VFN) with its asset levels. The main difference between a VFN and DDN is that a VFN is typically a revolver – that is, the balance may vary both higher and lower over the life of the transaction. A DDN, once fully drawn, will only amortize thereafter.

VFNs are commonly used in CLOs when:

- there are revolving or delayed draw notes in the collateral;
- the manager wants some flexibility on timing for reinvestments in order to avoid (a) negative carry (caused by holding large amounts of cash) or (b) being "forced" to purchase unsuitable assets, by temporarily paying down the senior tranche and then drawing it when a suitable reinvestment opportunity arises.

For example, suppose a CDO's target portfolio collateral is $300 million and the maximum CDO issuance, of Class A, B, and Equity Notes, totals $300 million. There are no expenses other than promised sequential interest payments to the Class A and Class B Notes. The Equity Notes receive residual cash flows only. Any uninvested cash is earning only interest rates which will be much lower than the weighted average cost of capital, causing a drag on the income from the collateral pool.

Further assume that 100% of the target portfolio is invested in loans paying LIBOR plus 2.50%.

If LIBOR is assumed to be 4.00%, the weighted average interest rate on the collateral is 6.50% (calculated as 2.50% + 4.00% = 6.50%).

Assume the following about the liabilities:

- The Class A Notes comprise 70% of the capital structure and are fully issued (non-variable) having a promised interest rate of LIBOR + 0.50%.
- The Class B Notes consist of a further 20% of the issuance and have a promised interest rate of LIBOR + 1.00%.
- The Equity Notes consist of a final 10% of the issuance and are entitled to the remaining interest cash flows after the Class A and Class B Notes have been paid.

As LIBOR is assumed to be 4.00%, the weighted average cost of the Class A and Class B Notes is 4.15% (calculated as [(0.50% + 4.00%) * 70%)] + [(1.00% + 4.00%) * 20%] = 4.15%).

Given this, a simplified estimation for the return to the equity is 23.50% (very basically calculated as the weighted average interest rate on the collateral less the weighted average cost of the Class A and B notes, divided by the size of the Equity Notes ((6.50% − 4.15%) / 10% = 23.50%).

Now, *assume that only 80% of the target portfolio is fully invested.* (The remaining 20% will be in cash earning LIBOR less 100 perhaps.) What is the effect on the equity returns?

- For the collateral, the weighted average interest rate decreases to 5.80% (calculated as (2.50% + 4.00%) * 80% + (−1.00% + 4.00%) * 20% = 5.80%).
- On the liabilities side, the weighted average cost of the Class A and Class B Notes remains at 4.15%.

The simplified estimation for the return to the equity decreases to 10.50% (determined by (5.80% − 4.15%) / 10% = 16.50%).

Finally, *assume that 80% of the target portfolio is fully invested; however, the Class A Note is a VFN whereby the undrawn commitment fee is 0.25% and hence only 71.43% of the VFN is funded.*

- For the collateral, the weighted average interest rate stays at 5.20%.
- On the liabilities side, the interest rate on the funded portion of the VFN is LIBOR + 0.50% and the fee on the unfunded portion of the VFN is 0.25%.
- Therefore, the weighted average cost of the liabilities (the VFN and Class B Notes) decreases to 3.30% (calculated as [(0.50% + 4.00%) * 50%)] + [0.25% * 20%] + [(1.00% + 4.00%) * 20%] = 3.30%).
- Because the cost of the liabilities has decreased, the simple return to the equity increases to 19.00% (determined by (5.20% − 3.30%) / 10% = 19.00%).

This very simplified example helps to illustrate the substantial benefits to the equity returns when levels of liabilities are matched with those of assets. It is also worth noting that, in general, the more leveraged a CDO, the more damaging the effect of not matching the underlying fluctuating collateral asset with mirrored liabilities.

Rating agencies usually require that the VFN be run at fully funded and fully unfunded for each scenario analysis performed.

11.4 LIQUIDITY FACILITIES

Often CDOs are structured with a liquidity facility (sometimes called a liquidity swap) in place. The primary reason for including a liquidity facility is to temporarily overcome any shortage of required funds to meet a specified level of liability amounts due to technical issues around ramp-up, reinvestment or timing differences between collections and payments.

There is often a difference between the first period collateral cash flows and the actual cash flows received in the first period. This is because, when modelling, it is assumed that 100% of the interest on the collateral is received at the beginning of each period.

In reality, interest collections occur throughout the period. Where there are assets which do not pay in the first period, there may be a shortfall in the funds available to pay the liabilities.

To a large extent the size of a liquidity facility depends on the estimate of any potential shortfall in the interest collections in the first few periods of the CDO. As the facility is usually provided by the bank structuring the CDO, its size and terms will also depend on the internal procedures and policies in place.

As will be explained further in Chapter 13, the CDO will usually pay upfront for the accrued interest on the assets purchased and a modeller will usually use this modelling to also project at least the first and second period cash flows.

A liquidity facility will usually have the following basic terms:

- Maximum amount
- Term
- Undrawn cost
- Drawn cost

Sometimes liquidity facilities are used to make interest payments to all of the notes, including the Equity Notes. In other instances, facilities are restricted to being used only to pay interest due on the rated notes, or sometimes only to a certain level of rated note (for example, only down to the A/A-rated notes).

It can be modelled as a swap where liability payments are made each period, depending on what amount of the facility has been drawn, and funds are received depending on how much of the facility is used each period.

Liquidity facility payments to the liquidity facility provider are usually set out quite senior in the waterfall, usually in sequence above the Class A, or most senior tranche of notes.

11.5 INTEREST RESERVE ACCOUNTS

Interest reserve accounts generally can refer to one of two things:

1. an account in which upfront funds from the issuance of the CDO notes are held for distribution as Interest Proceeds on the first or first few payment dates;
2. an account in the liability structure in which funds are "trapped" for use, most commonly if there are losses in the portfolio and/or if a coverage test is breached.

Accounts described in definition (1) above are utilized when shortfalls in the Interest Proceeds available for distributions are expected in the first or first few periods (this will be discussed in more detail in Chapter 13).

Although the mechanics of interest reserve accounts described in (2) above can be structured in various ways, one possible way is as an account that sits at some point above the Equity

Notes in the Interest Waterfall and collects a certain amount of funds each payment period for use only where there are insufficient funds to pay interest on some or all of the rated notes.

Interest reserve accounts are usually most popular with those note holders whose notes sit senior in priority to the interest reserve account, as the collection of funds into the account will have a diminishing effect on the Interest Proceeds available to those classes of notes below the interest reserve account. The existence of an interest reserve account can also be expected to have a negative effect on equity IRRs.

Where an interest reserve account can be most useful is when the modeller is running rating agency default scenarios which are back-ended. If defaults are concentrated towards the end of the deal, the build-up of a cash value in the CDO can provide additional protection.

A special form of interest reserve account is a so-called "smoothing account". A smoothing account is used to reserve a portion of interest from an asset (not subject to a swap) paying less frequently than the liabilities, to pay in a later liability payment period. For example, if the transaction normally pays quarterly, but has a small percentage (typically 5% or less) of unhedged semi-annually paying assets, then half interest paid on those semi-annual paying assets can be paid in one quarter and the other half in the succeeding quarter. The smoothing account holds the reserved half of the coupon until required.

11.6 OTHER STRUCTURAL FEATURES

11.6.1 Pro-rata payment of CDO liabilities

Most CLO structures are sequential payment structures for principal, that is to say, the notes are paid principally in the order of seniority. In some CDOs, particularly those using structured finance assets, there is usually a period after the reinvestment period, if the deal is performing in line with its covenants, when the principal is paid in proportion to the initial amounts outstanding, at least for the rated notes. This is usually done in an effort to maintain equity returns, as sequential pay down of principal has the effect of de-leveraging the transaction, whereas pro rata pay down preserves this. Standard and Poors have criteria dealing with pro-rata payment structures, where the payment priority must revert to sequential when the outstanding asset balance drops below 50% of the effective date par requirement.[1]

11.6.2 Turbos

It is generally accepted that the more subordinate a tranche, the higher the return. As transactions de-lever, either post the reinvestment period or as a result of covenant breaches, the cost of the capital structure typically increases as it is usual that the most senior and hence most inexpensive (from a spread perspective) tranche is paid off first. If the transaction is projected to extend to maturity, then it may be possible that the future cost of the capital structure will exceed the return on the assets. A turbo feature is a principal pay down acceleration mechanism, usually on the junior notes in a transaction, utilizing the interest in excess of that required to pay the senior fees and liabilities. It is in effect the equity reducing its leverage by buying in part of the principal junior mezzanine, i.e., the equity is reinvesting some of its dividends back into the CDO to potentially extend the time it will receive payments.

---

[1] See "CDO Spotlight: Pro Rata Payment of Liabilities in Global CDOs Introduce Certain Risks", 19 October 2005.

Some senior investors have been disquieted in the past by having junior notes receiving principal before them; however, for them there is no change in their subordination; it is effectively a reallocation of principal between the mezzanine and the equity. Turbo features usually appear very low down in the capital structure, usually between the lowest rated note and the equity, or sometimes additionally between the lowest two notes. For example, if there is a junior BB/Ba-rated note and a junior BBB/Baa rated note, there may be turbos between both the BB/Ba-rated note and equity, and the BBB/Baa and BB/Ba rated note. The turbo is usually a fixed payment and may commence almost immediately and terminate at or shortly after the end of the reinvestment period.

11.6.3 Reverse turbos

A more unusual feature is the so-called "reverse turbo" feature. As discussed previously, on a covenant breach it is normal to pay down the most senior notes first, no matter at what level in the transaction the breach occurs. For example, it is normal to pay down the A notes even if the D note over-collateralization test or interest coverage test is breached. With a reverse turbo feature, interest proceeds may be used to pay down in reverse order for junior covenant breaches. These "reverse turbo" features typically only apply to the most junior tranches, and only in the Interest Waterfall. This feature makes economic sense particularly for interest coverage breaches as, when applied, the cure will reduce the cost of capital and give it more "bang for buck" to gain a bigger cure.

11.6.4 Revolver facilities

Revolvers are notes or loans that can be drawn and then repaid and drawn again. They are increasingly more common in loan transactions, hybrid transactions and multicurrency transactions.

In loan transactions, the action of the revolver is to manage ramp-up and reinvestment risk. That is to say, during the ramp-up, the assets match the liabilities; at the end of the ramp-up, both the liabilities should be fully drawn and the assets fully invested to the "target amount". During the reinvestment period, rather than being forced to purchase perhaps undesirable (from a credit perspective) collateral, the manager has the additional option of temporarily repaying the revolver and redrawing later when a more suitable investment arises.

Revolvers can also feature in hybrid transactions, i.e., transactions that combine credit default swaps (CDS or, colloquially, "synthetics") and cash securities. The revolver can be used in these transactions to switch between cash and synthetic positions, or to fund physical deliveries of "defaulted" CDS transactions (as CDS transactions typically provide for cash settlement or physical settlement). In a synthetic transaction the senior most tranche is typically also a portfolio credit default swap. Hence there may not be the cash to pay for physical settlement, effectively converting part of the senior CDS tranche to a pro-rata funded revolving facility.

In transactions that invest in assets denominated in more than one currency, one strategy used to match the currencies of the assets and liabilities is to issue multi-currency liabilities. Where a manager is allowed to reinvest principal proceeds, unless he is restricted to buying same currency for same currency (i.e., buying only dollar assets with dollar proceeds), cross investment will introduce imbalances. One strategy to mitigate these potential imbalances is to allow the manager to repay the currency and draw the currency of the proposed investment.

A revolving tranche introduces the credit risk of the revolving note holder(s) as counter-parties, and consequently for AAA/Aaa and AA/Aa rated transactions, only the highest rated counterparties can participate. Typically a revolving note holder is required to be rated at least A-1/P-1 on a short-term basis to be eligible. If the note holder is downgraded below that or even placed on watch for a downgrade, then the note holder usually is required to either allow the manager to fully draw the revolver or be replaced as the counterparty within a relatively short period, usually in the order of 30 days.

11.6.5 Enforcement waterfalls

Increasingly, transactions have included a different priority of payments: if the transaction is accelerated because of an event of default, a so-called "enforcement waterfall" occurs. A typical enforcement waterfall changes the priorities of payments such that all proceeds are directed in order of payment, both interest and principal, until that tranche has been repaid in full, upon which all the remaining interest and principal are redirected to the next most senior tranche, and so on until all tranches are repaid.

11.7 COMBINATION NOTES

There are two main types of combination (combo) note: simple ratio notes or repacks; and specifically tailored notes. Simple ratio notes do not change the waterfall, and simply combine the existing cash flows from the selected tranches and rate them at a usually different promise. Tailored combo notes have provision for different types of cashflows in the waterfall, and may include, for example, zero coupon type accrual notes high in the waterfall (which can be rated separately), combined with other cash flows. These bespoke or tailored notes are referenced directly in the transaction documents, whereas the repacks typically are not.

Commonly, although not always, combination note investors are seeking to combine exposure to a rated tranche with exposure to equity. In this instance, the promised coupon will not be the same as the paid coupon as residual cash flows from the equity portion of the note will also be received by the combo note holder.

11.7.1 Modelling combination notes

A repackaging combination note has been modelled on the **Outputs Sheet** of the *Cash Flow Model*. As there may be various combination notes that are part of a CDO, additional combo notes can be modelled by building on what is currently provided in the model.

The authors wish to draw to the readers' attention that combo notes which are "repacks" are not modelled on the **Waterfall Sheet** as the creation of this type of combination note does not affect the waterfall.

In the example provided (Figure 11.13), a combo note has been created using 50% of the Class E tranche and a third of the Class F (equity) tranche.

The first step in modelling this is to aggregate the cash flows according to the portions of each tranche. Therefore, beginning in cells BU103 to BW103 the portion of the Class E tranche is determined (Figure 11.14):

- **Class E Portion of Combo Note Interest Paid**: the Interest Paid from the **Waterfall Sheet** multiplied by the Percent Portion of the Class E tranche in the Combo Note.

	BV	BW	BX	
4				
5	**Combo Note Break Down**			
6		Amount	Percent of Tranche	
7	Class E	11,000,000	50.00%	
8	Class F	10,000,000	33.33%	
9	Total Note Amount	21,000,000.00		
10				

Figure 11.13   Creating a combo note

	BU	BV	BW	BX	BY	BZ	
101							
102		**Class E Portion of Combo Note**		**Class F Portion of Combo Note**			
103		Class E Portion of Combo Note Interest Paid	Class E Portion of Combo Note Principal Paid	Class E Portion of Combo Note: Total Paid	Class F Portion of Combo Note: Interest Paid	Class F Portion of Combo Note: Principal Paid	Class F Portion of Combo Note: Total Paid	
104			(11,000,000)	(11,000,000)		(10,000,000)	(10,000,000)	
105		169,779	-	169,779	396,856	-	396,856	
106		172,619	-	172,619	396,203	-	396,203	

Figure 11.14   Aggregating cash flows

- **Class E Portion of Combo Note Principal Paid**: the Principal Paid from the **Waterfall Sheet** multiplied by the Percent Portion of the Class E tranche in the Combo Note.
- **Class E Portion of Combo Note Total Paid**: The sum of the Combo Note portion of the Interest Paid and Principal Paid on the Class E Notes.

The same is done for the Class F Notes starting in cells BX103 o BZ103.

Starting in cell CA103, the aggregate of the Class E and Class F cash flows is determined in the Combo Note Total Paid column. This will be compared with the results in column CJ, Combo Note Total Paid, and compared as a check in column CK.

The Combo Note Promised calculations are done in CB103 to CD103 as:

- **Combo Note Promised Rate** (cell CB103): this is the rate of interest that is promised on the Combo Note. This is not necessarily the rate of interest that ends up being paid as interest proceeds may be paid in excess of this rate.
- **Beginning of Period Principal** (cell CC103): this is the promised principal.
- **Combo Note Promised Interest Due** (cell CD103): the promised interest due is based on the promised principal outstanding at the beginning of each period.
- **Combo Note Interest Paid** (cell CE103): median of the Interest Paid, the Interest due and zero.
- **Combo Note Deferred Interest** (cell CF103): this is the maximum of the Interest Due less the Interest Paid, and zero.
- **Combo Note Principal Paid** (cell CG103): is determined by the median of:
  o the Combo Note Total Paid less the Combo Note Interest Paid
  o the beginning of Period Principal, Combo Note Total Paid
  o zero
- **Combo Note End of Principal** (cell CH103) is the sum of the Beginning of Period Principal, the Combo Note Deferred Interest and minus the Combo Note Principal Paid.

- **Excess Interest** (cell CI103) is determined by the Combo Note total Paid less the Combo Note Interest Paid less the Combo Note Principal Paid.
- **Combo Note Total Paid** is the sum of the Combo Note Interest Paid, the Combo Note Principal Paid and the Excess Interest.

The General Calculations for IRR and WAL and the various calculations at Par Spread and Discount Margin are calculated as they have been described in Chapter 8 for the other tranches of the CDO.

11.7.2 Moody's approach to rating combo notes

Moody's ratings for combo notes address the expected loss with regard to the present value of the promised payments on the combo note. Moody's use a five-step process to rate combo notes.

Step 1: Generate the cash flows for the combo note by aggregating each portion of the combo note using the recovery rates and stresses relevant to the target rating.

Step 2: Determine the promised cash flows and discount the cash flows paid and the cash flows promised by the index rates used in Step 1.

Step 3: Calculate the expected loss and duration of the rated promised note.

Step 4: Compare the expected loss of the combo note from Step 4 with the relevant benchmark bonds to determine the combo note rating.[2]

11.7.2.1 Step 1: Generate the cash flows for the combo note

This step is done as described above.

11.7.2.2 Step 2: Determine the promised cash flows and discount the cash flows paid and the cash flows promised

When a note is non-PIKable, non-puttable, non-callable and non-prepayable, the promise of the note is the discounted rated interest when due plus the discounted principal from the final legal maturity. Thus the discount rate is calculated as it has been done for regular floating rate coupon pay tranches of the notes. The promise is either greater than or less than par, depending on whether the coupon rate is greater or less than the discount rate. Once this is determined, all the cash flow scenarios are compared against this single value and losses are recorded for any scenario in which the present value of the scenario cash flows is less than the promised present value.[3]

With a combo note, it is possible for principal to be prepaid at any time and interest can be deferred (as long as interest on interest is paid) until the legal final maturity date without this being recognized as a loss. Thus the present value of the promise on a combo note will vary depending on the path which the cash flows take. The various possible promises will depend on the cash flows which are realized.

---

[2] See Moody's paper "Using the Structured Note Methodology to Rate CDO Combo-Notes", 26 February 2004, page 2.

[3] See Moody's paper "Using the Structured Note Methodology to Rate CDO Combo-Notes", 26 February 2004, pages 4–5.

For a PIKable combo note, the loss is the present value of all amounts which are unpaid at the final legal maturity date. The promise is the sum of the present value of all payments received and the loss. PIKable combo notes can be described as "path dependent" because interest and principal can be paid at any time, in any amount, and as long as all of the principal and deferred interest (and interest on interest) due is paid by the legal maturity of the bond, there will be no losses.

In the **Outputs Sheet**, the Promise is calculated in cell CC7 as "=SUMPRODUCT(CD105: CD184,CL105:CL184)+SUMPRODUCT(CL105:CL184,CG105:CG184)+NPV(CL184, CH184)".

11.7.2.3   Step 3: Calculate the expected loss and duration of the rated promised note

The expected loss and durations are calculated in the same manner as for the other notes on the **Outputs Sheet**. See Chapter 8 for a review of this.

11.7.2.4   Step 4: Compare the expected loss of the combo note from step 4 with the relevant benchmark bonds to determine the combo note rating

On the **Rating Agency Reference Sheet** the Combo Note Benchmark analysis is determined.

The Combo Notes Expected Loss Benchmarks are set out in cells B314 to G635. Column B is an index ordinal. Columns C and D are the Duration and Expected Loss respectively, as taken from the calculations further below in the sheet according the Ratings in column E. The Integer duration is simply the integer of the Duration in column C (for example in cell F316 the formula is "=ROUND(C316,0)". The Index is the combination of the Integer Duration (column F) and the Rating (column E). This table is referenced on the **Moody's Sheet**, as explained further below.

The Combo Notes Benchmark Calculations are found in cells B638 to R1006.

The Aaa tranche (from cells B638 to R661) will be used as an example to describe the process of creating the benchmarks. First, the Years from 1 to 20 are listed, starting in column B.

The Promised Rate in cell C642 is based on the same free-risk LIBOR rates used to generate the combo note cash flows and discount the combo note cash flows, with the caveat that the benchmarks are based on yearly rates. Hence the Promised Rates is calculated on the **Vector Sheet** starting in cells G103 to K103.

On the **Vector Sheet** in cells G103 to G184 the 3 month LIBOR In Use is as lookup from the Interest Rate Vector in the cell named "Interest_Vector" on the **Inputs Sheet**. Hence for period 1 in cell G105 there is the formula "=HLOOKUP(Interest_Vector,Interest_Rate_Vectors,$B105+2,FALSE)".

The 3 month LIBOR Contribution starting the cell H103 is the period contribution of the 3 month LIBOR in use determined by:

- one
- *plus* the day count *multiplied by* the LIBOR in Use

In cell H105 there is the formula "=(1+E105*G105)".
The Years are provided for reference in cells I103 to I124.
The Geometric Mean of 3-month LIBOR is determined by:

- the *product* of each of the relevant 3-month LIBOR contributions for the relevant period which comprises the year *minus* one

- *multiplied by* the day count of 360 divided by 365.

For cell J105 the formula is `"=(PRODUCT(H105:H107)-1)*360/365"`.
The Effective 1 Year LIBOR is determined by the equation:

$$r_n = n[(1 + r_m/m)^{m/n} - 1]$$

where:

r_n is the effective rate for n compounding periods per year (in this case, 1); and
r_m is the rate for m compounding periods per year (in this case, 4).

For cell K105 the formula to determine the effective 1-year LIBOR is `"=1*((1+J105/4)^`
`(4/1)-1)"`. This is shortened to `"=(1+J105/4)^4-1"`.

The Effective 1-year LIBOR Year is then summed with the promised combination note spread to form the Promised rates in cells C343 to C362 on the **Rating Agency Reference Sheet**.

The Discount Factors on the **Rating Agency Reference Sheet** are determined as calculated throughout the model and the Promised Rate Duration is taken as:

- the current discount factor
- *multiplied by* the numbers of days
- *multiplied by* the current year.

Hence the calculation in cell E642 is `"=D642*365/360*B642"`.

The Idealized Cumulative Survival Rates are looked up in the Idealized Cumulative Survival Rates table in cells B247 to AF266, based on the targeted rating of the combo note. For example, cell F642 contains the formula `"=VLOOKUP($B639,$B$247:$AF$266,B642+1,0)"`.

The Individual Yearly (Non-Cumulative) Marginal Default Rates are, after the first year:

- one
- *minus* the cumulative survival rates
- *minus* the *sum of* the previous yearly marginal default rates.

Hence in cell G643 there is the equation `"=1-F643--SUM(G$642:G642)"`.

The Probability of No Default Prior to Current Period and Default in Current Period is determined by:

- the current period Individual Yearly (Non-Cumulative) Marginal Default Rates
- *multiplied by* the previous periods Idealized Cumulative Survival Rate.

For example, in cell H643, the calculation is `"=G643*F642"`.

The Surviving Promised Rate is determined as:

- the Promised Rate
- *multiplied by* the Discount Factor
- *multiplied by* the Idealized Cumulative Survival Rate.

For example, cell I643 holds the formula `"=C643*D643*F643"`.

The Surviving Principal is calculated as the Idealized Cumulative Default Rate multiplied by the discount factor.

The Recovery is:

- the Moody's Recovery Rate for the collateral (45%)
- *multiplied by* the Discount Factor
- *multiplied by* Probability of No Default Prior to Current Period and Default in Current Period.

Cell K643 holds the formula `"=0.45*D643*H643"`.
The Difference, in the second year, is determined by:

- one
- *minus*
  - the Cumulative Surviving Promised Rate to current year
  - *plus* the Surviving Principal
  - *plus* the Cumulative Recovery.

Therefore, cell L643 contains the formula `"=1-(SUM($I$642:$I643)+J643+SUM($K$642:K643))"`.
The Discounted Cumulative Survival Rates, starting in cell M643, are determined as:

- the Discount Factor
- *multiplied by* the Idealized Cumulative Survival Rate

such that `"=D643*F643"`.
The Default Implied Credit Spread is then calculated as:

- the Difference
- *divided by the sum* of the Discounted Cumulative Survival Rates.

Hence, cell N643 contains the formula `"=L643/SUM($M$643:M643)"`.
The Default Implied Coupon is determined by:

- the Promised Rate *plus* the Spread
- *multiplied by* the day count (365/360)
- *multiplied by* the Idealized Cumulative Default Rate
- *multiplied by* the Discount Factor.

Cell O643 contains the formula `"=(C643+N643)*365/360*F643*D643"`.
MaxPV is determined by:

- the sum of:
  - each period's Promised Rate multiplied by each Discount Rate to the current period
  - multiplied by the day count (365/360)
- plus the sum of:
  - each period's Default Implied Credit Spread multiplied by each Discount Rate to the current period
  - multiplied by the day count (365/360)
- plus the current period Discount Factor.

For year 2, the MaxPV in cell P643 is calculated as

```
"=SUMPRODUCT(OFFSET($C$642,0,0,B643,1),OFFSET($D$642,0,0,B643,1))*
365/360+SUMPRODUCT(OFFSET($N$642,0,0,B643,1),OFFSET($D$642,0,0,
B643,1))*365/360+D643".
```

	B	C	D	E	F	G	H	I
35								
36			Rated CDO Tranches					
37	Tranche Number	1	2	3	4	5	6	7
38	CDO Class Name	Class A	Class B	Class C	Class D	Class E	Class F	Combo Note
39	Amount	278,000,000	34,000,000	20,000,000	16,000,000	22,000,000	30,000,000	21,000,000
40	Moody's Desired Rating	Aaa	Aa2	A2	Baa2	Ba2	NR	B2
41	Moody's Stress Factor	1.5	1.4	1.31	1.23	1.16	0	1
42	Moody's Default Probability	30.57%	28.53%	26.69%	25.08%	23.434240%	0.00%	20.38%
43	Covenanted Minimum Recovery Rate	45.37%	45.09%	49.12%	53.18%	57.24%	NA	58.69%
44	Rate This?	N	N	N	N	Y	N	Y
45	Output Range?	M_Block_1	M_Block_2	M_Block_3	M_Block_4	M_Block_5	M_Block_6	M_Block_7
46	Loss	0.00%	0.00%	0.01%	0.08%	3.53%	0.00%	8.41%
47	WAL (Duration for Combo Note Tranche 7)	5.569	7.220	7.728	7.979	8.593		6.873
48	Expected Loss Threshold	0.0019%	0.0640%	0.4382%	1.5624%	6.7358%	0.0000%	
49	Result	PASS	PASS	PASS	PASS	PASS	FAIL	
50								

Figure 11.15   Rated CDO Tranches

The Expected Loss is equal to:

- the MaxPV *minus* one
- *divided by* the MaxPV.

Thus, for year 2, in cell Q643, the expected loss is calculated as `"=(P643-1)/P643"`. The Expected Duration is determined by:

- *(the sum of:*
  - ○ each of the Promised Rates multiplied by each corresponding Promised Rate Duration
  - ○ plus the current period Promised Rate Duration
  - ○ plus the sum of the Promised Rate durations to date
- *multiplied* by current period Default Implies Credit Spread)
- *divided* by the MaxPV.

Hence, the year 2 Duration, in cell R643, is `"=(SUMPRODUCT($C$642:C643,$E$642: E643)+E643+SUM($E$642:E643)*N643)/P643"`.

On the **Moody's Sheet** additional columns are created for the combo note. These columns naturally follow along with those already described in Chapter 9.

In addition, another Block of results is added, starting in cells AK103 to cells AP103.

	B	C	D	E	F	G
106						
107	**Block 1 Expected Loss**					
108	**0.0000%**					
109						
110			Block 1 Loss			
111		USD_Libor_Fwd	Forward 1σ UP	Forward 2σ UP	Forward 1σ DOWN	Forward 2σ DOWN
112	YR1_50/10/10/10/10/10	-0.000000119%	-0.000000308%	-0.000000364%	-0.000000043%	-0.000000029%
113	YR1_10/50/10/10/10/10	-0.000000470%	-0.000001405%	-0.000005166%	-0.000000171%	-0.000000103%
114	YR1_10/10/50/10/10/10	-0.0000000240%	-0.000000806%	-0.000003629%	-0.000000105%	-0.000000040%
115	YR1_10/10/10/50/10/10	-0.000000118%	-0.000000472%	-0.000002452%	-0.000000033%	-0.000000018%
116	YR1_10/10/10/10/50/10	-0.000000026%	-0.000000111%	-0.00000057b%	-0.000000008%	-0.000000005%
117	YR1_10/10/10/10/10/50	-0.000000006%	-0.000000021%	-0.000000096%	-0.000000003%	-0.000000001%
118						
119						
120	**Block 1A Weighted Average Life**					
121	**5.57**					
122						
123			Block 1A WAL			
124		Forward	Forward 1σ UP	Forward 2σ UP	Forward 1σ DOWN	Forward 2σ DOWN
125	YR1_50/10/10/10/10/10	5.289099976	5.288286018	5.287245313	5.289076878	5.289597949
126	YR1_10/50/10/10/10/10	5.401951938	5.399196886	5.396514801	5.403682841	5.404303888
127	YR1_10/10/50/10/10/10	5.560954584	5.55635081	5.54894156	5.56419787	5.566022188
128	YR1_10/10/10/50/10/10	5.712507181	5.709530415	5.70572362	5.715027072	5.715773104
129	YR1_10/10/10/10/50/10	5.847818211	5.846233785	5.843616236	5.848752373	5.849248896
130	YR1_10/10/10/10/10/50	5.919564448	5.919434664	5.918817732	5.919634235	5.919698987
131						

Figure 11.16   Moody's block results

	C	D	E	F	G	H	I
			Rated CDO Tranches				
Tranche Number	1	2	3	4	5	6	7
Run RateTranche?	Y	Y	Y	Y	Y	Y	Y
CDO Class Name	Class A	Class B	Class C	Class D	Class E	Class F	Combo Note
Amount	278,000,000	34,000,000	20,000,000	16,000,000	22,000,000	30,000,000	21,000,000
S&P Desired Rating	AAA	AA	A	BBB	BB	NR	B
S&P SDR	43.07%	39.36%	37.11%	32.14%	26.04%	#N/A	21.61%
S&P Break-Even Percentile	5%	10%	35%	50%	60%	#N/A	70%
S&P Break-Even Rate	64.09%	59.70%	53.53%	45.47%	34.88%	#N/A	#NUM!
S&P Break-Even Result	PASS	PASS	PASS	PASS	PASS	PASS	PASS
S&P	55%	59.00%	62.00%	65%	68%	NA	45%
Net Present Value	0.00%	0.00%	0.0%	0.0%	0.0%	0.0%	-
Weighted Average Life	5.59	6.66	7.00	7.27	7.79	9.27	5.01
Output Block	SP_Block_1	SP_Block_2	SP_Block_3	SP_Block_4	SP_Block_5	SP_Block_6	SP_Block_7

Figure 11.17   Rated CDO Tranches

The Combo Note Analysis is in cells AY105 to BE138 of the **Moody's Sheet**. The first Integer Duration in cell AY107 is referenced from cell I46, the duration for the combo note tranche. The Ratings for each of the two integer durations nearest the duration in cell I46 are listed in column AZ.

The Ordinal Index in column BA is a lookup of the index number in the Combo Notes Expected Loss. Benchmarks are set out in cells B314 to G635 of the **Reference Sheet**. Cell BA107 contains the formula `"=MATCH(AY107&AZ107,'Rating Agency Reference'!$G$316:$G$635,0)"`.

The Expected Loss and Duration values in columns BB and BC are also lookups of the values in the Combo Notes Expected Loss Benchmarks are set out in cells B314 to G635 of the **Reference Sheet**. Cell BB107 holds the formula `"=INDEX('Rating Agency Reference'!$C$316:$D$635,$BA107,2)"` and cell BC107 has `"=INDEX('Rating Agency Reference'!$C$316:$D$635,$BA107,1)"`.

The Expected Loss for each rating is then interpolated in column BD. Cell BD108 has `"=TREND(BB107:BB108,BC107:BC108,$I$46)"`.

Finally, the result of the interpolation is assessed in column BE. Cell BE108 uses the basic formula of `"=IF(BD108>M_Tranche_7_Par_Loss_Pct,"PASS","FAIL")"`.

11.7.3 S&P approach to rating combo notes

When rating equity notes or combination notes which contain equity notes, S&P will first assume that the junior administrative expenses which were not paid senior in the waterfall are equal to the cap at the senior level.[4]

There are also three additional default patterns that are applied to the scenario runs:

Default Pattern for Equity 1: 50/25/25
Default Pattern for Equity 2: 60/20/10/10
Default Pattern for Equity 3: 70/10/10/10[5]

On the **S&P Sheet**, additional columns are created for the Combo Note. These columns naturally follow along with those already described in Chapter 10.

The additional default curves are added to the Default Curves box in the **S&P Sheet**.

---

[4] See S&P's paper "CDO Spotlight: general Cash Flow Analytics for CDO Securitizations", 25 August 2004, page 21.

[5] See S&P's paper "CDO Spotlight: general Cash Flow Analytics for CDO Securitizations", 25 August 2004, page 21.

	Class A	Class B	Class C	Class D	Class E	Class F	Combo Note
			Default Curves				
YR1_15/30/30/15/10	1	1	1	1	1	0	1
YR1_40/20/20/10/10	1	1	1	1	1	0	1
YR1_20/20/20/20/20	1	1	1	1	1	0	1
YR1_25/25/25/25	1	1	1	1	1	0	1
YR2_15/30/30/15/10	1	1	1	1	1	0	1
YR2_40/20/20/10/10	1	1	1	1	1	0	1
YR2_20/20/20/20/20	1	1	1	1	1	0	1
YR2_25/25/25/25	1	1	1	1	1	0	1
YR3_15/30/30/15/10	1	1	1	1	0	0	0
YR3_40/20/20/10/10	1	1	1	1	0	0	0
YR3_20/20/20/20/20	1	1	1	1	0	0	0
YR3_25/25/25/25	1	1	1	1	0	0	0
YR4_15/30/30/15/10	1	1	1	0	0	0	0
YR4_40/20/20/10/10	1	1	1	0	0	0	0
YR4_20/20/20/20/20	1	1	1	0	0	0	0
YR4_25/25/25/25	1	1	1	0	0	0	0
YR5_15/30/30/15/10	1	1	1	0	0	0	0
YR5_40/20/20/10/10	1	1	1	0	0	0	0
YR5_20/20/20/20/20	1	1	1	0	0	0	0
YR5_25/25/25/25	1	1	1	0	0	0	0
COMBO_YR1_50/25/25	0	0	0	0	0	0	1
COMBO_YR1_60/20/10/10	0	0	0	0	0	0	1
COMBO_YR1_70/10/10/10	0	0	0	0	0	0	1
COMBO_YR2_50/25/25	0	0	0	0	0	0	1
COMBO_YR2_60/20/10/10	0	0	0	0	0	0	1
COMBO_YR2_70/10/10/10	0	0	0	0	0	0	1

Figure 11.18   Default curves

Finally, on the **Vectors Sheet**, the corresponding Default Curves (Figure 11.18) are added in the Defaults Section in Rows 500 to 600.

11.8 COLLATERAL MANAGER EQUITY ANALYSIS

Often Collateral Managers will also invest in the equity tranche of the CDO. When this happens it can prove useful to examine the cash flows to the collateral manager. The **Equity Analysis Sheet** (Figure 11.19) is a useful tool that allows the modeller to examine the combined return profile of management fees and the management investment in the equity piece.

On this sheet, the management fees (senior, junior and incentive) are combined with the equity returns on the manager's investment in the equity (if any) to determine the total return to the management company.

The amounts for **Senior Management Fee Paid** (starting in E9) and the **Junior Management Fee Paid** (starting in F9) are both referenced from the **Fees and Expenses Cash Flows** in the **Waterfall Sheet**. For Period 1, "E11" contains the formula "=Waterfall!M205" and cell "F11" contains the formula "=Waterfall!O205"

The **Incentive Fees Paid** is taken from two places in the **Waterfall Sheet**: the **Interest Waterfall** section and the **Principal Waterfall** section. Cell "G11" has the Period 1 calculation "=Waterfall!AB305+Waterfall!AE605".

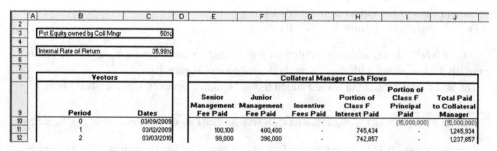

	Vectors		Collateral Manager Cash Flows					
			Senior Management Fee Paid	Junior Management Fee Paid	Incentive Fees Paid	Portion of Class F Interest Paid	Portion of Class F Principal Paid	Total Paid to Collateral Manager
Period	Dates							
0	03/09/2009		-	-	-		(15,000,000)	(15,000,000)
1	03/12/2009		100,100	400,400	-	745,434	-	1,245,934
2	03/03/2010		99,000	396,000	-	742,857	-	1,237,857

Pct Equity owned by Coll Mngr   50%

Internal Rate of Return   35.99%

Figure 11.19   Equity analysis sheet

The **Portion of Class F Interest Paid** and **Portion of Class F Principal Paid** (beginning in cells H9 and I9, respectively) are also referenced from the **Waterfall Sheet**, but are multiplied by the **Percentage of Equity owned by the Collateral Manager** in cell C3. For Period 1, the Portion of Class F Interest Paid in cell H11 has the formula `"=Waterfall!AW105*$C$3"` and the Portion of Class F Principal Paid contains the formula `"=Waterfall!AX105*$C$3"`.

All of the cash flows to the collateral manager are then summed in the **Total Paid to Collateral Manager** calculations where for Period 1 in cell J11 there is the formula `"=SUM(E11:I11)"`.

Finally, in cell C5, the **Internal Rate of Return** is calculated (as explained previously in Chapters 4 and 8) as `"=XIRR(J10:J90,C10:C90)"`.

12

Maintaining the Cash Flow Model

12.1 ADAPTING YOUR MODEL FOR DIFFERENT CAPITAL STRUCTURES

Building a cash flow model for one transaction or even one type of transaction is one thing; maintaining it for various different transactions is another thing entirely. Change should be considered inevitable. Many software theorists believe that software systems have "entropy". Entropy is a concept arising from the second law of thermodynamics which states that in a closed system, entropy – or "disorder" – will increase over time. When applied to software systems, it can be interpreted that, over time, software will deteriorate, particularly where it is not regularly updated or bugs and errors are allowed to continue to exist.

The same principle can be applied to Excel-based models: over time, using – and particularly changing – a model to suit new requirements will effectively degrade the initial structure of the model, i.e., it starts to deteriorate, in a similar way to a refined metal, oxidizing back to its base or chaotic state. The theory, as applied to software, holds that not only is this likely to happen, but it is inevitable. Model deterioration can be forestalled by regularly "shining" the model. Often, usually from the need to be expedient, changes and new features are added quickly without considering the best way to incorporate them. By taking time out to regularly "tidy" these expedient changes and either delete them or incorporate them more expeditiously, many errors can be avoided.

However, the modeller should recognize that change is likely to happen and plan for it. For this reason, the authors have structured their models on a modular spreadsheet basis in order to make it relatively easy to supplement or supplant the various main elements of the model, i.e.:

- Inputs Sheet
- Collateral Sheet
- Waterfall Sheet
- Outputs Sheet

These are the four core sheets of the model on which all other parts rely. The authors over the years have replaced Waterfall Sheets and Collateral Sheets as they have become too chaotic or even too specific. Adding new features such as multiple currencies or hybrid features (i.e., synthetic assets and liabilities) which were not originally planned can typically be the catalyst for either redesigning or replacing the Waterfall Sheet or the Collateral Sheet.

12.1.1 Manually changing the model

Manually changing the waterfall requires creating vertical strips of cells:

- for the Interest Waterfall: from rows 300 through 599; and
- for the Principal Waterfall: from rows 600 to 899.

To add a tranche or calculation, the calculation is entered in the rows from 500 onwards by referencing the appropriate calculation, then adjusting the available cash, by copying the formula from the previous cells. For example, to add a payment in the Interest Waterfall to the right of the current Class B Interest, first highlight the cells from N501 to N599 and, using the Insert->Cells menu, shift them right. Next, for each period, enter the calculation or the reference to the calculation in cells N503: N590, starting with the name of the payment. The available cash then needs to be adjusted to take into account the new draw from it, as cells O405 to O489 will refer to cells M405 to M489 as they were previously adjacent. By copying cells M305 to N305 and O305, and copying O305 and N305 down to the last period, the new payments are taken care of. Moving up the inserted column of cells, to cells N305, again simply copying M305 to N305 and copying down should in most instances incorporate the new cash flow in the Interest Waterfall. Finally, the new cash needs to be allocated to the tranche or fee by referencing that payment. Other additional steps may include duplicating the payment in the Principal Waterfall and, most definitely, including it in the **Audit Sheet** (as described below). After this, it is important to create the appropriate tranche on the **Outputs Sheet**.

Inclusion in the **Audit Sheet** is relatively simple and can be described simply by the following steps:

1. Extend the referenced Interest Waterfall by inserting a group of cells in the appropriate place (i.e., after the same payment reference in the **Waterfall Sheet**) and copying from the previous cell to the left to pick up the appropriate reference.
2. Allocate the payment to the appropriate tranche on the **Audit Sheet** and compare outputs to those made on the **Output Sheet**

12.1.2 Manually removing tranches or steps

Removing waterfall steps manually is slightly more tedious and can be fraught with the danger of introducing #REF errors, arising from referencing the deleted cells. The steps for removing a cash flow or tranche are summarized below:

1. SAVE THE MODEL! Save the model under a new name or version before removing the tranche. This will insure against introducing significant errors if the removal was not completed correctly.
2. Highlight the first cell in the waterfall payment area (typically rows 300–399 for interest payments. Examine the formula, ideally through the audit tool bar (dependents button) to find dependent cells. Click on the arrow drawn by the audit tool to transit to the dependent cell. Remove the reference in the dependent cell. It may also be wise at this point to remove the reference in the dependent cell area for all other periods.
3. Use F5 to return to the original cell. Repeat step 2 until there are no dependent cells. Remember to remove any **Audit Sheet** references.
4. Move down the available cash area and remove the links between the payment above and the available balance in the cells to the immediate left. That is, as described above about removing column N, delete the link between N305 and N405, and reference M405 in the available cash cell O405. Repeat this in the range N405 to N499 until there are no further links in this region.
5. Finally remove calculations in the cell range 505 through 599. It should be possible to delete column of cells for that part of the waterfall.

6. At this point recalculate the sheet. Ideally there should be no #REF errors. If that is the case, save the file and continue. Otherwise it may be wise to reload the previous version and TRY AGAIN!

As the reader can appreciate, there is quite a lot of effort involved in adding and even more in removing steps to the waterfall. It is therefore not surprising that many modellers create generic models which can be adapted by switches rather than having to insert and delete steps in the waterfall. Generally, one approach to avoiding the issue of change is to build most of the anticipated flexibility into the model. As will be seen below, there is potential for adding a large degree of complexity to the model in order to address divergent requirements and structural features.

12.1.3 Dynamic cell linking

More dynamic cell linking formulas can be utilized but at some cost to execution speed. Dynamic linking can be achieved through the use of such functions as

- SUM(), SUMIF()
- OFFSET()
- MATCH()
- INDEX()
- VLOOKUP(),HLOOKUP()

Dynamic cell linking can be performed to varying degrees. A simple strategy of dynamic linking can, for example, be added in the available funds sections of the waterfall. Rather than hard linking the cash from the cell immediately to the left, by using an OFFSET() function the cell to the immediate left can be referenced dynamically or indirectly. For example, in the Interest Waterfall replacing M405 as `"=L405-M305"`, as `"=OFFSET(M405,0,-1)-M305"`, would allow for the deletion of that cell without the need to re-link the adjacent cells (i.e., L405 and the current N405).

This can be extended to a fully dynamically linked Waterfall Sheet by using a "tagging" scheme. A tagging scheme is a systematic "naming" scheme used in indexing functions to select targeted cells from large ranges. This is not to be confused with named ranges.

The advantages of tagging are:

- it allows for general adding of tranches by adding, deleting and changing the order of the tags;
- there is a reduction in the likelihood of creating circular references;
- Waterfalls can be potentially built from short descriptions.

The disadvantages of a fully dynamically linked structure are mostly related to performance issues. It can be easy to link the wrong tranches if the wrong tags are used. In addition, the use of a dynamically linked structure does not mitigate the need for auditing.

Rather than fully describe the sheet as before, the following description will concentrate on the basic techniques in a fully dynamically linked structure as the "business" related calculations are the same, only the waterfall logic equations are different.

12.1.4 Dynamically linked structures

Dynamically linked structures, as described above, use tags to index into a range to extract the value of interest. A tag is just a string but usually a structured string. The naming scheme in this example is based on: {tranche/fee/test}, {calculation}, {due/paid}, {waterfall}.

All calculations are made initially in the relevant summary block, tags with the {due} tag go into the calculation block, and the formula in the calculation block is an index into the relevant fee or tranche or test block.

For example, place the following tags over the tranche 1 calculation block for just interest only A-CI-D-I (A current interest (CI) due (D) Interest Waterfall (I)), in cell I101. Adjacent to that is the interest actually paid current, that is tagged with A-CI-P-I (A1 current interest (CI) paid (P) Interest Waterfall (I)), which is the tag placed in the waterfall region to "pick-up" the result. Naming H101 as "wf_liab_start", and the range say H101:BA101 as "wf_liabilities", the formula in L505, currently `"=I505"`, can be replaced with: `"=OFFSET(wf_liab_start, $B505+3,MATCH(I$501,wf_liabilities,0)-1)"`.

Copying that down from K505 to K589 dynamically links the required calculation to the calculation column. To dynamically link the result can be achieved by placing a paid tag in cell J301 and replacing the formula in J105 of `"= K305+J605"`, with `"=SUMIF($D301: $Q$301,J$101,$D305:$Q305)+K605"` to pick up the interest paid in the Interest Waterfall. In using the tagging approach, it makes sense to perform all the calculations in the tranche, fee or test block. To that purpose it makes sense to split up the calculations in order to make dynamic linking work.

By replacing all "hard" links with dynamic links as mentioned above, it is relatively easy to insert, delete and change items in the waterfall by simply changing or creating new tags in the appropriate order. Also it makes sense to create an interim cure account as a placeholder for calculated cures already paid a "cure account", in order to avoid hard linking the cure logic, i.e., being able to account for previously paid cures higher in the waterfall or in a different waterfall.

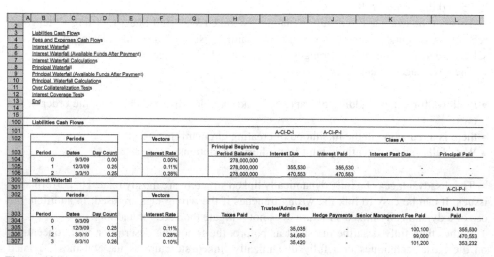

Figure 12.1   Dynamic linking

As mentioned above, it would not be too difficult to generate a simple macro to create the waterfalls from a description, at least the initial cut of the waterfall. Hopefully the reader has an appreciation of how to create a dynamically linked model.

12.2 AUDIT SHEET

How can a modeller be confident that a model is correct, particularly after making changes? An overall audit summary sheet is definitely one answer. By effectively replicating the logic of the model in reverse and checking that the allocations match the waterfall, most common errors can be avoided, particularly those of omission and duplication.

Additionally, the **Audit Sheet** makes a good summary page for distribution to third parties as it is effectively a summary of the whole model.

There are three key levels of the **Audit Sheet**. These are:

- cash counting;
- cash allocation;
- comparison.

Cash counting basically counts cash and collateral balances in and out of the model. This makes sure that there is nothing missing with regard to cash flows in and out.

On the **Audit Sheet** the first check is on the collateral and cash generated from it:

- rows 100–199 hold the collateral summary (including both original and reinvestment pools) and the tranche allocation summary;
- rows 200–299 hold the Interest Waterfall summary and checks;
- rows 300-399 hold the Principal Waterfall summary and checks.

12.2.1 Audit summary

Column E contains the combined initial starting balance from the **Collateral Sheet** (Figure 12.2), i.e., cell E105 contains `"=Collateral!L105+Collateral!Z105"`, which is the sum of the initial collateral pool balance and the reinvestment pool balance.

Column F contains the ramp-up purchases and reinvestment amounts for the **Collateral Sheet**, i.e., cell F105 contains `"=Collateral!M105+Collateral!AA105"`.

Defaults in both the original and reinvestment pools are summarized in column G, i.e., G105 contains `"=Collateral!N105+Collateral!AB105"`.

Recoveries from defaults in the original and reinvestment pools are collated in column H, as in cell H105, `"=Collateral!P105+Collateral!AD105"`.

Collateral Sheet consolidated interest payments are in column I, i.e., I105 contains `"=Collateral!AP105"`.

	E	F	G	H	I	J	K	L	M	N
101										
102					Collateral					
103	Balance	Purchased and Reinvested Amounts	Default	Recovery	Interest	Amortizations	Prepayments	Sales	Closing Balance	Check
104	396,000,000	-	-	-	-	-	-	-	396,000,000.00	TRUE
105	396,000,000	-	-	-	2,958,889	-	-	-	396,000,000	TRUE
106	396,000,000	-	-	-	3,095,889	-	-	-	396,000,000	TRUE

Figure 12.2   Collateral

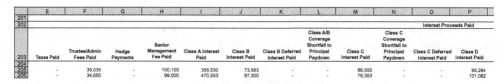

	E	F	G	H	I	J	K	L	M	N	O	P
201												
202												Interest Proceeds Paid
203	Taxes Paid	Trustee/Admin Fees Paid	Hedge Payments	Senior Management Fee Paid	Class A Interest Paid	Class B Interest Paid	Class B Deferred Interest Paid	Class A/B Coverage Shortfall to Principal Paydown	Class C Interest Paid	Class C Coverage Shortfall to Principal Paydown	Class C Deferred Interest Paid	Class D Interest Paid
204												
205	-	35,035	-	100,100	355,530	73,563	-	-	68,550	-	-	95,284
206	-	34,650	-	99,000	470,553	87,300	-	-	76,353	-	-	101,082

Figure 12.3   Interest proceeds paid

Next, in column J, is the consolidated amortization payments from original and reinvestment pools, i.e., the formula in J105 is `"=Collateral!Q105+Collateral!AE105"`.

Prepayments of the collateral principal are covered in column K. Cell K105 has the formula `"=Collateral!R105+Collateral!AF105"`.

Column L contains the sales proceeds from an early termination of the CDO if there is a call by the equity note holders, and references the sales proceeds from the original and reinvestment pools. Cell L105 for example contains `"=Collateral!S105+Collateral!AG105"`.

Column M contains the end of period balance for the collateral. For example, cell M105 contains the formula `"=Collateral!T105+Collateral!AH105"`, the end of period balances for the original and reinvestment pools.

Column N is the check column and compares the final balance with the original balance less the amortizations, defaults and sales with the final balance, if they are the same then the check is true. For example, N105 has the formula `"=(E105-SUM(G105,J105,K105, L105,M105))<0.000001"`.

12.2.2 Interest Waterfall

Cells in columns E through Y, rows 205 to 299, contain the payments made from the **Waterfall Sheet**. For example, E205 contains `"=Waterfall!H305"`, which is the taxes paid cell from the waterfall.

The checks for the Interest Waterfall are in columns AB and AC. Column AB contains the sum of the payments from each period from column E to Column Z. This is then compared with total interest proceeds available, which appears in Column AC, and the test result is in column AD and is given by, for example, AD205 which contains `"=AB205-AC205"`. If relative totals match, then the difference between them will be zero. This result is formatted

	AB	AC	AD
201			
202	**Interest Sources and Uses**		
203	**Sum of Uses**	**Sum of Sources**	**Net**
204			
205	2,958,889	2,958,889	-
206	3,095,889	3,095,889	-

Figure 12.4   Interest sources and uses

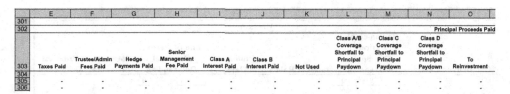

	E	F	G	H	I	J	K	L	M	N	O
301											
302											Principal Proceeds Paid
303	Taxes Paid	Trustee/Admin Fees Paid	Hedge Payments Paid	Senior Management Fee Paid	Class A Interest Paid	Class B Interest Paid	Not Used	Class A/B Coverage Shortfall to Principal Paydown	Class C Coverage Shortfall to Principal Paydown	Class D Coverage Shortfall to Principal Paydown	To Reinvestment
304											
305	-	-	-	-	-	-	-	-	-	-	-
306	-	-	-	-	-	-	-	-	-	-	-

Figure 12.5   Principal proceeds paid

to show "-", using conditional formatting. However, if there is a difference, the conditional formatting will highlight in red.

Maintaining the Waterfall and the **Audit Sheet** will assure the modeller that all cash flows are allocated. Any missing or double counted cash flows will show up as a positive or negative balance in column AD.

12.2.3 Principal Waterfall

The Principal Waterfall audit is handled similarly and appears in columns E through AJ in rows 305 to 399. The cells refer solely to the Principal Waterfall on the **Waterfall Sheet**. Summary and check cells appear in columns AL (the sum of the Principal Waterfall payments), AM (the available cash) and AN (the difference). Again, if all cash is allocated and there has been no duplication, then the balance in AN will be zero. However, as before, a negative balance (implying more cash is available that has not been allocated), will appear in red and in brackets. If more cash was "spent" in the Principal Waterfall than available then a positive red number will appear (without brackets).

12.2.4 Allocation

The final part of the audit is to check the allocation of cash flows to the appropriate tranches.

The first step is to aggregate the cures paid from both the Interest and Principal Waterfalls (Figure 12.6). The interest cures are aggregated in column AF, rows 205 through 299, as the sum of all the cures, i.e., AF205 contains the formula "=L205+N205+Q205+T205".

The principal cures are aggregated in column AP, rows 305 to 399, as the sum of all the principal cures paid from the Principal Waterfall. This is calculated as the sum of the cures in the Interest Waterfall.

	AE
301	
302	**Cures**
303	**Coverage Test Principal Shortfall Payments**
304	
305	-
306	-

Figure 12.6   Cures

	X	Y	Z	AA	AB	AC	AD
102				Class A			
103	Unused Cures	Beginning of Period Principal Outstanding	Interest Paid	Principal Paid	End of Period Principal Outstanding	Interest Difference	Principal Difference
104		278,000,000			278,000,000		
105	·	278,000,000	355,530	·	278,000,000	·	·
106	·	278000000	470,553	·	278,000,000	·	·

Figure 12.7   Class A tranche allocation checks

Finally, each tranche is checked for correct allocation of cash; this includes interest from both the Interest Waterfall and Principal Waterfall, principal from the Principal Waterfall and cure allocations from the combined cures. The interest and principal payments are then compared to the **Outputs Sheet** to see if there are any discrepancies between the model outputs and the calculations. The allocation check will help identify allocation errors, such as missing interest or principal, as although the basic cash-in/cash-out checks test for money not being lost or double counted, they do not check for money effectively disappearing into a "black-hole", i.e., used in the waterfall but not allocated to the correct tranche, fee or account.

Checks for each tranche are broadly the same. Thus, only one will be explained in detail and then the differences will be explained for the remaining tranches.

Columns X through AD, rows 105 through 199, hold the allocation checks for the first tranche, Class A1 (Figure 12.7). Column X contains the available cures from the Principal and Interest Waterfalls, e.g., cell X105 contains the formula `"=AF205+AP305"`.

Column Y contains the beginning of the period balance. It is initially set to the Tranche_1_Amount.

The beginning of period balance in column Y, for periods subsequent to period 1, is just the end of period balance from the previous period, i.e., column AB. For example in period 2, cell Y107 references cell AB106.

Subsequent periods it is the previous periods end balance, i.e. column AB, i.e. cell Y107 references the formula `"=AB106"`.

Next, in column Z, is the interest paid, referencing the **Audit Sheet** Interest and Principal Waterfall payments. Cell Z105 contains the following formula, `"=I205+I105"`, which are the interest payments in the Interest and Principal Waterfall respectively.

Principal payments are collated in column AA. However, rather than just containing the aggregate principal payments from the Principal Waterfall, the formulas in column AA incorporate the cure payments aggregated in column X. The formula, for example in cell AA107, is `"=MIN(X107, Y107-V307)+V307"`, where V307 is the principal payment, X107 is the available cure payment, and Y107 is the beginning of the period balance. The total payment is the principal payment from the Principal Waterfall, plus the lesser of the principal balance adjusted for the payment from the Principal Waterfall, i.e., the remaining balance and the available cure.

The end of period balance is summarized in column AB, as the beginning of period balance less the principal paid in that period, i.e., AB107 contains the formula, `"=Y107-AA107"`.

Principal and interest checks are made in columns AC and AD, by comparing the payments calculated in columns Z and AA to the payments for Tranche_1 on the **Output Sheet**. For example, cell AC105 compares the payment in cell Z105 to the payment in cell I105 on the **Outputs Sheet**, i.e., the formula is `"=Z105-Outputs!I105"`.

As before with the cash-in/cash-out checks, the result is conditionally formatted to highlight differences in red. A positive red payment, i.e., not bracketed, would mean that more cash is allocated on the **Audit Sheet** than on the **Outputs Sheet**. A negative balance would imply that some cash is missing on the **Audit Sheet** that is present on the **Outputs Sheet**.

The principal checks are performed in a similar fashion. The principal check performed in AD105 compares the principal paid in the **Audit Sheet** to that on the **Outputs Sheet**, with the formula, `"=AA105-Outputs!J105"`.

Each subsequent tranche is checked and compared in a similar way, with the exception that available cures are reduced by those paid to the prior tranches. For example, see cell AE105, the available cures for Tranche_2, which has the formula `"=X105-MIN(Y105-V305,X105)"`. In addition, more subordinate tranches may have additional interest rate payments for tranches which can PIK.

12.3 DEBUGGING

12.3.1 Back of the envelope equity IRR calculations

There may be times when things seem too good to be true (or too bad to be right) to the modeller (particularly when assessing equity returns). The **Audit Sheet** provides a lot of information to assist the modeller in tracking down logic errors, particularly after substantial changes have been made to the model.

A systematic approach is to first simplify the input assumptions so that discrepancies become more obvious. The authors suggest the following steps to simplify the model:

1. Run the model to call/bullet maturity.
2. Use flat interest rate curves.
3. Set default rates initially to zero.
4. Turn off interest on interest calculation.
5. Turn off the hedges.

Doing the above gives a well defined model which makes it easy to spot potential anomalies.

With no defaults then the total amount of collateral paid down should be the initial amount and all notes should pay off, at least to the extent of the initial asset coverage. Simple "back of the envelope" checks can be performed with regards to the zero-default equity returns. An example helps to illustrate this.

Suppose we have a simple CLO with the tranches shown in Figure 12.8.

The weighted average cost of capital is 0.613% [(70%*0.50%) + (10%*0.75%) + (5%*1.25%) + (5%*2.50%)].

If all running fees and expenses for the CDO total 0.60% and the weighted average spread on the portfolio is 2.50%, the free flow to the equity tranche is 1.288%.

	Class A	Class B	Class C	Class D	Equity
% of Issuance	70%	10%	5%	5%	10%
Spread over LIBOR	0.50%	0.75%	1.25%	2.50%	NA

Figure 12.8 Simple CLO

The return to equity will therefore be the free spread multiplied by the leverage plus one multiple of the floating index to term. Assuming LIBOR to 5 years is 4%, then the return without defaults should be:

- 1.288% *multiplied* by the 10% of equity in the CDO
- *plus* 4% of LIBOR

which equals 16.875%.

12.3.2 Excel errors

Errors in the Excel can be a great source of frustration to the modeller and can most often include:

- Circular references
- #REF errors
- #NAME? errors
- #N/A errors

12.3.2.1 Circular references

Circular references are the bane of all Excel users. No matter how diligently one tries to avoid them it is usually only a matter of time before a modeller will have to deal with them.

The first and probably most effective strategy to avoid them is to use a layout strategy that minimizes the chances of a circular reference. Second, frequent (every few hours) saves of new versions under slightly different names, particularly when making frequent changes, can mean that a modeller might lose only a few hours if the "Gordian knot" of circular references is accidentally introduced into the model. Making up for this loss of a few hours work could be considerably shorter in terms of time expenditure than trying to "unpick" the error.

Nevertheless, if the modeller has sufficient time (and inclination) or has no choice, what strategies and techniques are useful for unpicking a circular reference?

Often the first indications of a circular reference are an inordinate amount of time for a calculation to return, a pop-up modal box indicating the detection of a circular reference, and the appearance of the circular reference toolbar which will potentially have a list of circular references. If the circular reference is confined to the current sheet it may be relatively easy to resolve. Irrespective of how bad it may look, the first rule is not to panic. Second, it may be useful to turn on the "iteration" option in the "calculation" section of the "Options" from the "Tools" in the menu bar. To do this, select Tools, then Options, then Calculation. Click on the "Iteration" box and set the "Maximum Iterations" to 1. The advantages of compiling a layout from the top left corner and trying to keep the distance between cells as short as possible should now be evident. Select the first circular reference from the list which has the lowest column and row reference. Select the "Trace Precedents" on the circular reference toolbar. Selecting into the formula will also highlight the precedent cells. If the distance between the precedent cells and the formula cell is large, click on the trace arrow/line to take the cursor to the precedent cell. Re-clicking on the line (or pressing F5 on the keyboard) will return the cursor to the original cell. By examining the formula and seeing the impact of calculation when activating the F9 key it should be possible to determine errors in the reference.

> **Did you know?** The circular reference tool is a specialization of the audit tool bar and allows the Excel user to trace precedents and dependents of a cell in order to determine circular references.

In the *Cash Flow Model* a common, but not immediately obvious, introduction of circular references is a translation error by one cell. As discussed previously, each cell should reference those with lower number row references and lower alphabet column references. A potentially obvious error could be a cell with one higher reference. For example, if the cell formula referred largely to row 105, and one reference was to row 106, this could be the most likely candidate for the circular reference.

12.3.2.2   #REF! errors

#REF! errors can arise in several ways including:

• deleting a referenced sheet, row, column or cell; and
• incorrectly entering array formulas.

It is often a good idea to save the model as a new version prior to any major deletions in order to be able to revert to an earlier model if wholesale #REF! errors have been introduced.

A more subtle #REF! error arises when array formulas have been incorrectly entered, such as conditional SUM statements. Recall that array formulas require special keys, usually SHIFT-CNTL-ENTER, to be recognized as array formulas.

12.3.2.3   #NAME! errors

#NAME errors typically arise either when required add-ins have not been loaded or a named range or function has not been defined. A common #NAME error occurs when the ATP has not been loaded and the ATP function has been referenced in the spreadsheet.

12.3.2.4   #N/A! Errors

#N/A errors typically occur when a lookup style function attempts to lookup using an undefined key. It should be noted that #N/A errors can be guarded for by using the IFNA() function.

13

Advanced Structuring Issues

13.1 PROJECTING ACCRUED INTEREST

Accrued interest is the compensation paid from the buyer (the CDO) to the seller (the warehouse provider) on the closing date to cover the interest which the seller would have earned on the next payment date had the asset not been sold. Where an asset is sold on its payment date, the accrued interest is zero. With each day that goes by, the accrued interest will increase until the next payment date, when it is again zero.

It is worth emphasizing the importance of projecting an accurate accrued interest amount to be purchased by the CDO on closing. If an error is made in estimating this amount the ramifications can persist throughout the life of the CDO. As this is an upfront payment made on closing and can be quite sizeable, a shortfall in estimating this can have potentially severe negative consequences on the cash flows to the equity. Paying for accrued interest transfers principal paid at the closing into the interest account. Unless the assets are purchased at a significant discount, then this money needs to be reclaimed. Most CDOs have a definition of principal proceeds that allows for the reclaiming of purchased accrued interest. However, this can be a significant drag on the equity returns as the cash required to be reclaimed is paid into the reinvestment account rather than the equity and the reinvested income will be delayed at least one payment period, if not longer. One important modelling decision to be made is the issuance date for the transaction, and modelling the accrued and selecting a date where this will be at a minimum can help reduce the drag on income.

While it is easy to perform a simple estimation of accrued interest, the authors do not recommend relying on simple estimations alone when in the final stages of a primary issuance of a CDO.

13.1.1 Simple estimation of accrued interest

An example might best explain how a simple estimation can be performed. Assume the following:

- issuance date for the CDO of 3 June 2010;
- collateral portfolio size on issuance of $300,000,000;
- all of the assets are floating rate and based on an average 1-month/3-month LIBOR of 4.00%;
- weighted average spread is 2.50%;
- 50% of the assets pay on a monthly basis and the weighted average last monthly payment date prior to issuance is 25 May 2010;
- 50% of the assets pay on a quarterly basis and the weighted average last quarterly payment date prior to issuance is 19 April 2010.

In this example, the monthly pay assets have 9 days of accrued interest and the quarterly pay assets have 45 days of accrued interest. It can then be estimated that the monthly pay assets accrued interest is:

$$(4.00\% + 2.50\%)^*(\$300,000,000)^*50\%^*9/360 = \$243,750$$

and the quarterly pay assets accrued interest is:

$$(4.00\% + 2.50\%)^*(\$300,000,000)^*50\%^*45/360 = \$1,228,750$$

The total estimated accrued interest due on closing is $1,462,500.

Simple estimations are most useful when warehousing has not yet begun on a transaction, and thus the actual roll dates of assets are unknown. This crude level of estimate should not be relied upon once actual assets are identified.

13.1.2 Estimating accrued interest

When a modeller knows both the coupon and the last payment date prior to closing, it is fairly straightforward to project the accrued interest on the issuance date. However, where a coupon rate has not yet been set because the date for determining LIBOR has not yet occurred, a modeller will need to estimate this.

The level of complexity modelled will depend on the level of accuracy desired for the projection of accrued interest. A structurer at a financial institution is always wise to check her accrued interest calculations with those of the trader monitoring the warehouse in an effort to avoid any unpleasant surprises.

In the *Standard Warehouse Model*, the **Accrued Interest Sheet** provides a more detailed way of modelling accrued interest. At the top of the **Accrued Interest Sheet** are the following inputs and outputs (Figure 13.1):

- CDO Issuance/Closing Date (cell C3)
- Current Date (cell C4): this cell is intended to contain the formula "=TODAY()"
- Assumed 1-month LIBOR (cell C5)
- Assumed 3-month LIBOR (cell C6)
- Assumed 6-month LIBOR (cell C7)
- Projected Accrued Interest on Closing (cell C9): this cell will be the sum of the Estimated Accrued Interest (in Column T)

Across the **Accrued Interest Sheet** in Row 100 are the following entries for the collateral:

- Identifier No. (Column B)
- Asset/Borrower Name (Column C)

	A	B	C
2			
3		CDO Issuance/Closing Date	03-Sep-09
4		Current Date	11-Jul-09
5		Assumed 1m LIBOR	0.28%
6		Assumed 3m LIBOR	0.50%
7		Assumed 6m LIBOR	0.97%
8			
9		Projected Accrued Interest on Closing	713,026.34
10			

Figure 13.1   Accrued interest sheet

- Tranche (Column D)
- Identifier (CUSIP, ISIN or Internal Identifier Code) (Column E)
- Original Balance (Column F)
- Current Factor (Column G)
- Current Balance (Column H): This is calculated as the Original Balance multiplied by the Current Factor
- Floating or Fixed? (Column I)
- Par Spread/Coupon (Column J)
- Payment Frequency (Payments Per Year) (Column K)
- Second Last Payment Date Prior to Closing (Column L)
- Last Payment Date Prior to Closing (Column M): these cells have conditional formatting applied such that where this date is later than the CDO Issuance/Closing Date the cell entry will be in red
- Coupon Known or Assumed? (Column N)
- Assumed Coupon (Column O)
- Known Coupon (Column P)
- Coupon Applied (Column Q): the value here depends on whether "Known" or "Assumed" is chosen in the "Coupon Known or Assumed" column. Where "Known" is chosen, the "Known Coupon" is applied; otherwise the "Assumed Coupon" is used
- Day Count (Column R): the calculations in this sheet are based on act/360. Where this is not the case for assets, the calculation for "Estimate Accrued Interest" should be changed accordingly
- Days of Accrued Interest (Column S): these values are calculated as the CDO Issuance/Closing Date less the asset's Last Payment Date Prior to Closing. Conditional formatting has been applied to these cells such that where the cell value is less than zero, it will appear in red
- Estimated Accrued Interest (Column T): This is determined by multiplying:
  - Current Balance
  - Coupon Applied
  - Days of Accrued Interest divided by 360.

Again, conditional formatting has been applied such that where a value in this cell is less than zero, it will appear in red.

As this sheet relies heavily on up-to-date information and inputs, some basic error checking sections have been added:

- Next Payment Date Prior to Closing Date? (Column V): where the Last Payment Date Prior to Closing (in column M) is greater than the CDO Issuance/Closing Date (in cell C3), "ERROR" will appear as the cell value; otherwise, the cell value will be 0
- Coupon Should be Known (Column W): if the Last Payment Date Prior to Closing (in column M) is less than Current Date (in cell C4) and if the Coupon Known or Assumed? (in column N) states "Assumed", "ERROR" will appear as the cell value; otherwise, the cell value will be 0
- Fixed Being Calculated As Floating (Column X): Where column I, Floating or Fixed?, contains "Fixed", if the Coupon Applied (in column Q) does not equal the Par Spread/Coupon in Column J, the cell value will be "ERROR"
- Negative Days of Accrued Interest (Column Y): If the Day of Accrued Interest (in column S) is less than zero, "ERROR" will be given

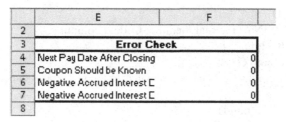

	E	F	
2			
3	**Error Check**		
4	Next Pay Date After Closing	0	
5	Coupon Should be Known	0	
6	Negative Accrued Interest C	0	
7	Negative Accrued Interest C	0	
8			

Figure 13.2   Error check

Any "ERROR" values that appear in these columns are summarized in the Error Check section (cells E3 to F7) where the "ERRORS" are counted in each of the relevant columns described above (Figure 13.2). Conditional formatting has been applied such that if any of the values in cells F4 to F7 are greater than zero, the value will appear in red. In this way, it is easier to ensure that the sheet is less likely to contain blatant errors.

13.2 COLLATING COLLATERAL CASH FLOWS

Collecting and organizing the cash flows of the collateral is an important way to build an amortization portfolio and can assist in projecting cash flows for the purposes of the first few payment periods of a CDO's life or for projecting payments to the CDO Notes, especially the CDO equity notes. The *Collateral Cash Collator Model* illustrates one way in which cash flows can be collected and organized. The model contains two examples:

1. Consolidation of quarterly pay assets for quarterly pay liabilities (**Qrtly Pay Assets CF Inputs Sheet** and **Qrtly Pay Asset Collated Sheet**, both with pink tabs).
2. Consolidation of months' and quarterly pay assets for quarterly pay liabilities (**Mixed Pay Assets CF Inputs Sheet**, **Mixed Pay Asset Collated Sheet** and **Mixed Pay Assets VBA Collated**, all with blue tabs).

The first step in using this model is to collect the asset cash flows on either of the Inputs Sheets. Each of the Inputs Sheets provides for the following inputs for each asset:

- Date
- Opening Balance
- Coupon Rate
- Interest
- Principal Payment
- Closing Balance

Once all the individual asset cash flows have been input they need to be collated for each payment period. This can be performed by using Excel formulae or using VBA.

Each of the **Qrtly Pay Asset Collated Sheet** and the **Mixed Pay Asset Collated Sheet** show the collection of payments into single streams.

Using Excel formulae requires the generation of the collation dates. The choice of these dates will depend on the accuracy of the model. A simple model may choose the payment dates of the CDO liabilities as the payment dates. Technically, however, this is not correct as most cash CDOs have what is called a "Determination Date".

What is the Determination Date? It usually occurs between two and five business days prior to the payment of the liabilities. It is the day the trustee determines the amount of interest and principal receipts in the due period and calculates the waterfall, and determines the payments owed to the CDO liabilities. It may also correspond to the registration or record date for registered bonds. This is the day that the owner of the CDO note is determined and the account that will be credited on the payment date.

Using the date generation routines, as previously described, the collection dates are generated, then using the OFFSET() function indexes by the number of rows or columns per asset, and lastly the MATCH() function is used to find the asset payment date which is less than the determination date. That is to say, an index ordinal is used for each asset, and that is multiplied by the number of columns for each modelled asset. For example, if there are six columns for each asset, the offset required between each asset is a multiple of six. First use MATCH() to find the payment period during which an asset payment will be made. If MATCH() does not find a result it will return #N/A, so the formula must guard for that.

This will work as long as the payment frequency on the assets is less than or equal to the payment frequency of the determination date. Otherwise there will be more than one correct value from the match. How should assets paying more frequently than the transaction payment frequency be dealt with? One approach is to generate intermediate payment days, collecting monthly and quarterly again for the actual determination dates. For example, if there is one monthly paying asset and two quarterly paying assets the transaction pays quarterly and is determined on the first of the month. Using the previous example, the formula would miss the intermediate payments. By generating monthly dates and collection for those dates, summing them as before and then collecting for each quarter, the intermediate payments are also collected.

Alternatively, a more detailed collation can be built using VBA to find and accumulate the intermediate dates. This is shown on the **Mixed Pay Asset VBA Collated Sheet**.

```
Sub VBA_Collection()
Dim r1 As Range
Dim r2 As Range

Dim d1 As Date
Dim pd1 As Date
Dim pd2 As Date

Dim interest As Double
Dim principal As Double
Dim i As Integer
Dim j As Integer
Dim k As Integer

Set r1 = Range("MixedAssetsStart")
Set r2 = Range("CD_Start")

i = 1
j = 2
k = 0

While r2.Offset(j, 0).Value <> "" And j < 9
```

```
pd2 = r2.Offset(j, 0).Value
pd1 = r2.Offset(j - 1, 0).Value
For k = 0 To 2   ' k is no of assets
  On Error GoTo nextAsset
  Do
    d1 = r1.Offset(i, k * 6).Value
    If d1 > pd1 And d1 < pd2 Then
       pymt = pymt + r1.Offset(i, k * 6 + 3).Value
    End If
    i = i + 1
  Loop While d1 < pd2

  i = 1
nextAsset:
 Next k
 r2.Offset(j, 1) = pymt
 pymt = 0
 j = j + 1
Wend


End Sub
```

14

Sourcing and Integrating Data From
External Systems

14.1 DATA REQUIREMENTS

As may be apparent from previous chapters, data requirements for cash flow CDOs can be extensive. Information required for obligors will usually include:

- date and times (issuance date, payment dates, call dates, maturity dates);
- interest payments (payment dates, coupon basis, coupon type, payment frequency);
- amortization schedules (potentially several different scenarios and prepayments rates);
- industry;
- key agents;
- guarantors;
- ratings.

There are several readily available sources for finding this information, such as trustee reports and Bloomberg.

14.2 TRUSTEE REPORTS

One of the best potential sources of data for previously issued transactions are the trustee reports that are produced on a regular (often monthly or quarterly) basis for each CDO. Most trustees provide reports in an Adobe PDF format, and it can can be tedious to extract the information from them. However, trustees are increasingly willing to provide the data in Excel or CSV (comma separated variable format) which can be readily imported into data bases or Excel.

Investors in CDOs should receive monthly reports and payment date reports at the relevant payment frequency. A monthly report typically details the collateral, collateral quality tests, trading activity and any events of default. It may also detail monthly collections on the principal and interest collection accounts. The payment date report basically extends this reporting to cover the covenant tests and details the waterfall sources and uses, i.e., official collection for the accrual period and the payments to the appropriate tranches.[1]

Commonly the following will be provided in monthly reports:

- information relating to the collateral assets, including:
  - the principal balance outstanding, interest rate, stated maturity, obligor, industry and rating of each asset;
  - the principal balance outstanding of any defaulting assets, and the details of any asset sold or acquired since the last monthly report;

---

[1] A sample trustee report can be found at http://archives1.sifma.org/market/CDO_Trustee_Template.pdf. In addition, further information can be found at http://www.sifma.org/services/stdforms/RevisedTemplateCDOTrusteeReport.html.

o each of the rating agency industry classifications and country of issuer for each asset;
o the percentage, by country, of the aggregate principal balances outstanding of the assets;
o typically, the three or five highest concentrations of assets in each of the rating agency industry classification groups;
o often, the three or five highest concentrations of assets in each obligor;
o the weighted average price of acquisition of each asset.
• information relating to the accounts: the amount standing to the credit of each of the accounts (which will generally include the Principal Collection Account, the Interest Collection Account, the Payment Account, the Expense Reimbursement Account, the Unused Proceeds Account and other potential accounts depending on the assets in the CDO. Various typical accounts are discussed in Chapter 6);
• information concerning the coverage tests, collateral quality tests and concentration limits:
o the over-collateralization ratios and whether each of the over-collateralization tests is satisfied;
o the interest coverage ratios and whether each of the interest coverage tests is satisfied;
o the Moody's diversity score or Moody's Asset Correlation test and whether the test is satisfied;
o the weighted average life of the assets and whether the maximum weighted average life test is satisfied;
o for each of the applicable rating agencies, the minimum weighted average recovery rates and whether the minimum weighted average recovery rate tests are satisfied;
o the weighted average spread (and weighted average fixed rate coupon, if applicable) and whether the minimum spread test (and, if applicable, the minimum coupon test) is satisfied;
o the Moody's (and/or Fitch, if applicable) weighted average rating factor and whether the rating factor test is satisfied;
o the percentage of the maximum amount concentration limits allowed for each asset characteristic (commonly referred to as "buckets") itemized against each aggregate amount invested in each bucket and whether each concentration limitation is satisfied.

A payment date report (or "note valuation report" or "distribution date report") is usually delivered a few days prior to each payment date to various parties related to the CDO, including the note holders. The payment date reports generally contain most or all of the information in the monthly reports described above, usually in addition to the following information.

• Information regarding the CDO notes:
o the aggregate principal amount outstanding for each class of CDO notes;
o the percentage of the current amount outstanding to the initial amount issued on closing, for each class of notes;
o the amount of principal payments to be made on each class of notes on the applicable payment date;
o the percentage of the current amount outstanding to the initial amount issued on closing for each class of notes, after the payment of any principal on the applicable payment date
o the interest payable for each class of notes on the applicable payment date.
• Details of the waterfall payments: an itemized account of the amounts to be distributed under the interest and the Principal Waterfall (priority of payments).
• Information about the accounts: the amounts standing to the credit of each of the Accounts as of the determination date and immediately after all payments are made on the payment date.

- Information regarding the coverage tests:
  - the over-collateralization ratios and the interest coverage ratios, both as of the determination date and immediately after all payments are made on the payment date and whether each of the coverage tests is satisfied in each instance.

While these reports were traditionally sent by post, Trustees have readily adopted new technologies to provide the information on demand. These days, most operate subscriber-based websites to enable interest parties to download the appropriate information. The majority are subscription-fee free, but users may have to show either some economic interest in the subscribed transactions, or get permission from either the underwriter or the manager to gain access.

As discussed, parsing trustee reports should be a thing of the past. However, if no other source of information is available, cut and paste from the PDF file to a spreadsheet and convert it to cells by using either Excel's text-to-data functions or commercially available software. If in paper format, it may be possible to use OCR (Optical Character Recognition) software to convert to text and use VBA to parse the information as required.

14.3 BLOOMBERG

For those readers privileged to have access to Bloomberg, the Bloomberg system (with the appropriate licensing of course), can provide a wealth of information for CDO modelling. This includes readily downloadable information such as:

- ratings;
- payment details (payment frequency, payment dates, amortization profiles);
- past payments;
- industry information;
- pricing information;
- agents;
- historical information;
- indices.

Bloomberg provides for an interface through several methods including dynamic data exchange (often referred to as DDE) for static and real-time quotes, somewhat supplanted by real-time data (often referred by its acronym, RTD), page-based information and historical and bulk data. The information required will depend on the type of the underlying collateral. Bloomberg provides information on the following types of securities:

- public corporate bonds in some detail (and attendant CDS);
- sovereign bonds (including emerging market sovereigns in some detail);
- structured finance bonds (including RMBS, ABS, some CMBS, CDO/CLO);
- limited syndicated loan data.

The following information can be sourced for public corporate bonds and the attendant CDS (particularly if the reference obligation is known):

- ratings;
- dates (issue date, maturity date, payment dates, payment frequency, first and last and next coupon dates);

- coupons (particularly for floating rate corporate debt, index reference, margin over the index);
- cash flows;
- prior payments;
- equity information including SIC codes and industry information for correlation inputs.

Bloomberg presents the information via several interfaces. It has an application programming interface (API), in C/C++ and VBA. Bloomberg can "publish" real-time information via a real-time interface for most static and pricing information. That is to say, the client – in this case the Excel spreadsheet – subscribes to the data via a function call (either through the historic DDE BLP() function interface or the newer BDP() function). As the data changes in Bloomberg, information will update in the spreadsheet. The data available in this format is effectively formatted fields from the Bloomberg databases. Fields can be subscribed in bulk or individually. Additionally, Bloomberg allows for overrides to utilize Bloomberg calculations in the spreadsheet. This can be useful for pricing bonds via asset swaps or discount margin functions.

Historical data, particularly for rates and prices, can be downloaded via the Historic Data tool. This formats a number of fields and makes a bulk submission to the Bloomberg system and retrieves it. This is not a real-time subscription for the data but effectively a "snapshot" of data.

Bloomberg also allows for bulk data downloads for vector type information such as payment schedules, cashflows, and amortization. This can be accessed via a VBA interface to automate downloads of significant amounts of data.

Finally, it is possible to subscribe and parse whole Bloomberg pages for information that is not available by real-time subscription or bulk download fields. This can include payment histories, prior payments, etc. Bloomberg representatives can be helpful in demonstrating how to extract ratings, payment dates, payment frequency, coupons, payment type and general bond information, such as accrued interest.

14.4 LOAN LEVEL INFORMATION SOURCES

Loans such as senior secured loans, senior unsecured loans and subordinated loans are typically private corporate loans. They are negotiated by one or several commercial banks and syndicated among a group of institutional investors and banks. Therefore, loan information is typically extracted from a bank's loan systems. However, there are a number of third party loan management systems in use, including:

- ACBS LoanTrak is a secondary loan trading system and a popular portfolio management tool. It is part of the ACBA Loan systems Suite offered by Fidelity National Information Services, Inc.[2]
- Through their Wall Street Office suite, Markit Group Limited offers a selections of solutions aimed at the management of portfolio and structured deals.[3]
- LA Pro is a loan software system offered by Misys plc.[4]

---

[2] For more information see: http://www.fidelityinfoservices.com/FNFIS/Markets/FinancialIndustries/ACBS/LoanTrak/.

[3] More information can be found at: http://www.fcsoft.com/n.x/Public/Home/Solutions/Wall%20Street%20Office.

[4] See http://www.laproiq.com/product/productdetails.htm for more information.

15

Regulatory Applications of CDO Technology

15.1 THE BASEL ACCORDS

Regulators have long required that banks maintain minimum amounts of capital. This has been done to try and prevent the serious economic consequences which would arise from relatively large financial losses or declines in values of assets, and to preserve solvency in the banking industry in the face of such an event. The Basel Accords came about as a result of regulators' desire to have a set of international minimum capitalization requirements for banks.

The Basel Accords are agreements among representatives of the member states of the Group of Ten (G-10) countries and Spain. The first Basel Accord concluded in 1988 (Basel I) and was further revised in agreed format in 2006 (Basel II) at the Bank of International Settlements (BIS) in Basel, Switzerland.

> **Did you know?** The G-10 countries are Belgium, Canada, France, Germany, Italy, Japan, the Netherlands, Sweden, Switzerland, the United Kingdom and the United States of America.

15.1.1 Basel I

Basel I contains four main pillars:

1. Pillar 1 sets out the components of capital.
2. Pillar 2 addresses risk weighting.
3. Pillar 3 deals with the target standard ratio.
4. Pillar 4 deals with transitional and implementing agreements.

Pillar 1 of Basel I describes two types of capital reserves which a bank can hold:

- Tier 1 capital consists of disclosed cash reserves, and capital paid for by the sale of bank equity (such as shares).
- Tier 2 capital encompasses:
  - reserves created to cover potential loan losses;
  - hybrid debt-equity holders;
  - subordinate debt holding; and
  - possible gains from the sale of assets purchased through the sale of bank stock.

Pillar 2 describes the risk weights applied to a bank's assets. These range from 0% weighting for riskless assets held by a bank (such as cash, sovereign debt held and funded in a domestic currency, all OECD[1] debt and other claims on OECD central governments), to 100% weighting for high-risk assets (such as claims on the private sector, non-OECD bank debt with a maturity in excess of one year, claims on non-OECD dollar-denominated debt or Eurobonds, equity assets held by a bank and all other assets) and up to 1250% for bank capital instruments.

> **Did you know?** OECD is the Organisation for Economic Co-operation and Development and consists of 30 member countries: Australia, Austria, Belgium, Canada, Czech Republic, Denmark, Finland, France, Germany, Greece, Hungary, Iceland, Ireland, Italy, Japan, Korea, Luxembourg, Mexico, The Netherlands, New Zealand, Norway, Poland, Portugal, Slovak Republic, Spain, Sweden, Switzerland, Turkey, United Kingdom, and the United States of America.

Pillar 3 requires that a minimum of 8% of a bank's risk-weighted assets must be covered by Tier 1 and Tier 2 capital reserves. Four percent of a bank's risk-weighted assets must be covered by Tier 1 capital.

Pillar 4 deals with transitional and implementing agreements for the Basel Accords.

One of the main aims of Basel I was to cap the leverage levels of banks. However, several loopholes drove the creation of such things as balance sheet CLOs and the creation of SIVs.

As there is no concept of credit ratings in Basel I, there was a major discrepancy between the amount of capital required to hold investment grade-rated loans on balance sheet or securitize them in the form of a CLO. Equity/mezzanine sizes in CLOs were typically half or less of the Tier 1 and Tier 2 amounts required under Basel I. This difference grew dramatically the more highly-rated the pool of loans became, and gave rise to the synthetic CLO technology employed in transactions such as BISTRO (Broad Index Secured Trust Offering 1997-1, 1998-1,1998-2, etc.), Eisberg Finance Ltd., and SBC Glacier Finance Ltd. This tended to skew the residual credit risk of the bank by way of the "negative selection" problem. That is, the residual portfolio was on average worse from a credit rating perspective; however, there was no penalty envisaged under Basel I for holding lower-rated/higher risk corporate debt.

Additionally, the relatively high penalties for holding subordinated bank debt and highly-rated asset backed securities created the SIV market, allowing banks effectively to invest off balance sheet from a regulatory perspective and provide support via undrawn short-term liquidity lines (typically zero weighted under Basel I). Both techniques allowed banks to increase their leverage through off balance sheet vehicles.

15.1.2 Basel II

As a result of many criticisms and perceived shortcomings in Basel I, in 1999 the Basel Committee decided to propose a new revised capital adequacy accord known as Basel II.[2] Basel II compromises three main pillars:

---

[1] For more information see www.oecd.org.

[2] This is formally known as "A Revised Framework on International Convergence of Capital Measurement and Capital Standards".

1. Pillar 1 deals with minimum capital requirements.
2. Pillar 2 tackles the supervisory review process.
3. Pillar 3 contains guidelines for market discipline

15.1.2.1   Pillar 1

Pillar 1 provides minimum capital requirement rules for three types of risk: credit risk; operational risk; and market risk.

For credit risk, the Pillar 1 provides two methods to assess the credit riskiness of a bank's assets:

- Standardized Approach: using external rating agency credit ratings to determine risk weightings;
- Internal Ratings-based Approach: using the bank's internal credit ratings to determine the risk weightings, as long as the regulators approve of the bank doing so.

Pillar 1 also introduces three methods for determining reserves to guard against operational risk:

- the Basic Indicator Approach, which recommends that a bank hold 15% (or such amount the regulators may require) of the average gross income it has earned over the past three years;
- the Standardized Approach divides a bank into business lines to determine the amount of reserves required to protect against operation risk. Each line is weighted by its relative size within the bank to create the percentage of reserve assets the bank must hold such as, for example, 15% for commercial banking and 12% for asset management.
- the Advanced Measurement Approach permits banks to develop their own reserve calculations or operational risks which must be approved by regulators.

Finally, Pillar 1 determines reserves required to be held to counter market risk. In assessing this, a distinction is drawn between fixed income and other products such as commodity, exchanges and equity. A distinction is also made between two principal market risks: interest rate risk and volatility risk.

A risk measurement called "value at risk" (VaR) is used by banks to develop their own calculations to determine the reserves needed to protect against interest rate and volatility risk for fixed income assets on a position-by-position basis.

Banks which do not use the VaR model for assessing capital reserves for fixed income assets have a choice of two methodologies:

- For interest rate risk, the reserve recommendations are tied to the maturity of the asset. For example, maturities of one month or less have a risk weighting of 0%, whereas maturities of over 20 years have 12.5%.
- For volatility risk, the recommended reserves are tied to the rating agency credit risk ratings given to the assets. Thus, AAA to AA- have a risk weighting of 0%; assets rated below B- have 12%.

For the final calculation of the total amount of reserves needed to protect against market risk for fixed income assets, the value of each asset is multiplied by the interest rate risk weighting and the volatility risk weighting and all are summed.

The risk weighting for all other assets are based on three main types of rating methodologies:

- The Simplified Approach relies on dividing assets by type, maturity, volatility and origin and assign risk weights from 2.25% to 100%.
- The Scenario Analysis assigns risk weights based on possible scenarios assets could face in each country's markets.

The Internal Model Approach allows banks to develop their own models.

Once a bank has calculated the reserves required to protect against operational and market risk and has adjusted its asset base according to credit risk, it can calculate the on-hand capital reserves it requires to achieve "capital adequacy" under Basel II.

Under Basel II, Tier 2 capital reserves are limited to 100% of Tier 1 capital reserves, and 8% is the minimum level of required reserve. It follows that a bank's reserves will be calculated as:

- 8% *multiplied by* risk weighted asset
- *plus* operation risk reserves
- *plus* market risk reserves

15.1.2.2 Pillar 2

The second pillar of Basel II deals with regulators' interactions with the banks.

15.1.2.3 Pillar 3

The third pillar of Basel II recommends the quarterly public release of the Tier 1 and Tier 2 capital, the risk weighted capital adequacy ratio, reserve requirements for credit, market and operational risk and a description of the bank's risk migration approaches. Essentially, it deals with market disclosure issues.

This chapter discusses the credit risk portion of Pillar 1, insofar as it applies to originating banks and investors in cash CDOs. Also included is a simple regulatory capital model to illustrate how the Basel securitization framework can apply to CDO exposures. It should be noted that the formal Basel II provisions should be referred to when the reader is seeking to make definitive calculations. It should also be noted that, although the June 2006 CRD provisions of Basel II provide guidelines for global regulators, these guidelines are open to a significant degree of interpretation at a national supervisory level. Each regulator employs its own interpretation and application of the basic framework and there can be significant variations across regions.

15.2 REGULATORY CAPITAL REQUIREMENTS FOR CDO NOTES

Where a bank has exposure to a cash CDO, the Securitization Framework must be applied.[3] This is because a cash CDO falls into the definition of "traditional securitization" under the Securitization Framework.[4]

---

[3] *International Convergence of Capital Measurement and Capital Standards: A Revised Framework*, Basel Committee on Banking Supervision, paragraph 538, page 120.

[4] A "traditional securitization" is generally defined as a structure where cash flows from a pool of assets are used to service at least two different tranches, reflecting different degrees of credit risk and where payments to the tranche holders depend upon the performance of the underlying collateral pool. Underlying assets securitized can include loans, commitments, asset-backed and mortgage-backed securities, corporate bonds, equity securities, and

For an originating bank[5] of a cash CDO, all the following conditions must be met in order to exclude underlying collateral from the calculation of risk weighted assets and for the bank to only hold regulatory capital against CDO exposures they retain:[6]

- there must be a "significant credit risk" transferred to third parties;
- the transferor cannot maintain effective control over the transferred exposures;[7]
- the investors who purchase the securities can only have a claim against the underlying pool of assets;[8] the assets must be transferred to a special purpose entity (SPE[9]) and the holders of the beneficial interests in the SPE must have the right to pledge or exchange those interests without restriction;
- if the CDO includes a clean-up call,[10] (i) the exercise of the clean-up call must not be mandatory, but must be at the discretion of the originating bank; (ii) it must not be structured to avoid allocating losses to credit enhancements or positions held by investors or otherwise structured to provide credit enhancement;[11] and (iii) it must only be exercisable when 10% or less of the original underlying collateral portfolio remain (or for synthetic CDOs when 10% or less of the original reference portfolio value remains);[12]
- the CDO cannot contain provisions which: (i) require the originating bank to alter the underlying exposures such that the pool's weighted average credit quality is improved, unless this is achieved by selling assets to independent and unaffiliated third parties at market prices; (ii) permit increases in a retained first loss position or credit enhancement provided by the originating bank after the inception of the CDO; or (iii) increase the yield payable to third parties in response to a deterioration in the credit quality of the underlying pool.

Banks must hold regulatory capital against their securitization exposures, including where they have provided "credit risk mitigants", investments in CDOs, and extensions of liquidity facilities or credit enhancements.[13]

---

private equity investments. See *International Convergence of Capital Measurement and Capital Standards: A Revised Framework*, Basel Committee on Banking Supervision, paragraphs 539 and 542, page 120.

[5] A bank is an originator if it originates, directly or indirectly, underlying exposures included in the securitization. *International Convergence of Capital Measurement and Capital Standards: A Revised Framework*, Basel Committee on Banking Supervision, paragraph 543, pages 120–121.

[6] *International Convergence of Capital Measurement and Capital Standards: A Revised Framework*, Basel Committee on Banking Supervision, paragraph 554, pages 122–123.

[7] The assets must be legally separate from the originating bank such that they are beyond the reach of the originating bank or its creditors. This must be supported by a legal opinion. A transferor will be deemed to have maintained control over transferred assets if it is able to repurchase them from the transferee in order to realize their benefits or it is obligated to retain the risk of the transferred assets. It should be noted that maintaining servicing rights to the exposures does not necessarily constitute indirect control of the assets.

[8] The securities issued cannot result in an obligation of the originating bank.

[9] "SPE" is defined in *International Convergence of Capital Measurement and Capital Standards: A Revised Framework*, Basel Committee on Banking Supervision, paragraph 552, page 122.

[10] "Clean-up Call" is defined in *International Convergence of Capital Measurement and Capital Standards: A Revised Framework*, Basel Committee on Banking Supervision, paragraph 545, page 121.

[11] Credit enhancements are defined as contractual arrangements in which banks assume a securitization exposure and provide some degree of added protection to other parties to the transaction. *International Convergence of Capital Measurement and Capital Standards: A Revised Framework*, Basel Committee on Banking Supervision, paragraph 546, page 121.

[12] *International Convergence of Capital Measurement and Capital Standards: A Revised Framework*, Basel Committee on Banking Supervision, paragraph 557, page 124.

[13] *International Convergence of Capital Measurement and Capital Standards: A Revised Framework*, Basel Committee on Banking Supervision, paragraph 560, page 125.

In general, a bank is required to deduct a CDO exposure from regulatory capital equally from Tier 1 and Tier 2.[14]

When a bank provides implicit support to a CDO, it must, at the minimum, hold capital against all of the exposures associated with the securitization as if they have not been used as collateral in the CDO.[15] Implicit support is where a bank provides support to a CDO in excess of its contractual obligation.[16]

Where a bank has exposure to a cash CDO, the treatment of this holding can be more complicated than it seems in the first instance. Clearly, where a bank holds an unhedged position in a cash CDO, this will generally be seen as an exposure by the bank to the CDO. Providing liquidity facilities, credit enhancement and implicit support (through mechanisms such as certain types of mandatory clean-up calls) can be interpreted as creating exposures for a bank. In general, there must be a significant transfer to third parties of credit risk in a securitized exposure for it not to be considered an exposure of a bank.

Where a bank meets the requirements set out above, it must choose between two method-ologies for determining its capital *requirements*:

• the Standardized Approach;
• the Internal Ratings Based Approach.

The Standardized Approach allows for external credit assessments (effectively, rating agency credit ratings) to be used for assigning risk weights. The higher the rating, the lower the probability of default, and hence the lower the assigned risk weight can be.

The Internal Ratings-based (IRB) Approach permits banks, where they have the explicit approval of the regulators, to establish their own models and self-assess the risks related to the assets they hold. Capital adequacy is then determined as a result of these self-determined risk weightings.

Where a bank uses the Standardized Approach to determine risk weightings for the type of underlying assets securitized, it must also use the Standardized Approach for its exposure to the CDO Notes. Similarly, if a bank uses the IRB Approach for the type of underlying assets for part of the CDO, then they must use this same approach when evaluating CDO exposures.

The IRB approach allows two methods for calculating capital:

• the Ratings Based Approach (RBA);
• the Supervisory Formula (SF).

For both the Standardized and IRB approaches there are criteria that apply for the use of external credit assessments. For the purposes of this chapter, it is assumed that the Moody's, S&P and or Fitch ratings meet these criteria.[17]

---

[14] *International Convergence of Capital Measurement and Capital Standards: A Revised Framework*, Basel Com-mittee on Banking Supervision, paragraph 561, page 125.

[15] *International Convergence of Capital Measurement and Capital Standards: A Revised Framework*, Basel Com-mittee on Banking Supervision, paragraph 564, page 125.

[16] *International Convergence of Capital Measurement and Capital Standards: A Revised Framework*, Basel Com-mittee on Banking Supervision, paragraph 551, page 122.

[17] For more information see *International Convergence of Capital Measurement and Capital Standards: A Revised Framework*, Basel Committee on Banking Supervision, paragraph 565.

Where two rating agencies have rated the same tranche differently, the lower rating (higher risk weight) will apply. Where three or more rating agencies have rated the same tranche differently, the higher of the two lowest ratings must be used.[18]

15.3 THE STANDARDIZED APPROACH FOR CDOs

Where a bank uses the Standardized Approach for the type of assets which are securitized, it must also then use the Standardized Approach under the Securitization Framework for the CDO.[19]

The risk-weighted asset amount of a securitization exposure is determined by multiplying the amount of the position by the relevant risk weight.[20]

For off-balance sheet exposures, banks are generally required to apply a Credit Conversion Factor (CCF) and then the relevant risk weight. If an exposure is rated, a CCF of 100% must be applied.[21]

In general,[22] when a bank is required to deduct a securitization exposure from regulatory capital, the deduction must be taken 50% from Tier 1 and 50% from Tier 2 capital. Credit enhancing I/Os are generally deducted equally from both Tier 1 and Tier 2.[23]

Where a bank provides implicit support to a CDO, it must hold capital against all of the exposures associated with the securitization transaction as if they had not been securitized.[24]

While originating banks are required to deduct from capital all retained CDO exposures rated BB+ and lower,[25] third-party investors may recognize external credit assessments that are equivalent to BB+ to BB− for risk weighting purposes. An unrated cash CDO exposure must be deducted unless it is (i) the most senior exposure in a securitization or (ii) eligible liquidity facilities.[26]

If the most senior exposure in a securitization is unrated, a bank that holds or guarantees it may determine the risk weight by applying the "look-through" treatment, provided the composition of the underlying pool is known at all times. In the look-through treatment, the unrated most senior position receives the average risk weight of the underlying exposures.

---

[18] See *International Convergence of Capital Measurement and Capital Standards: A Revised Framework*, Basel Committee on Banking Supervision, paragraphs 97 and 98.

[19] *International Convergence of Capital Measurement and Capital Standards: A Revised Framework*, Basel Committee on Banking Supervision, paragraph 566.

[20] For more information see *International Convergence of Capital Measurement and Capital Standards: A Revised Framework*, Basel Committee on Banking Supervision, paragraph 567.

[21] For more information see *International Convergence of Capital Measurement and Capital Standards: A Revised Framework*, Basel Committee on Banking Supervision, paragraph 567.

[22] The exception to this being where there is a "gain-on-sale" as described in *International Convergence of Capital Measurement and Capital Standards: A Revised Framework*, Basel Committee on Banking Supervision, paragraph 562.

[23] *International Convergence of Capital Measurement and Capital Standards: A Revised Framework*, Basel Committee on Banking Supervision, paragraph 561.

[24] *International Convergence of Capital Measurement and Capital Standards: A Revised Framework*, Basel Committee on Banking Supervision, paragraph 564.

[25] *International Convergence of Capital Measurement and Capital Standards: A Revised Framework*, Basel Committee on Banking Supervision, paragraph 570.

[26] *International Convergence of Capital Measurement and Capital Standards: A Revised Framework*, Basel Committee on Banking Supervision, paragraphs 569 and 571.

Table 15.1   Long-term rating category

External credit assessment	Long-term rating category				
	AAA to AA−	A+ to A−	BBB+ to BBB−	BB+ to BB−	B+ and below or unrated
Risk weight	20%	50%	100%	350%	1250%

However, if a bank is unable to determine the risk weights assigned to the underlying credit risk exposures, the unrated position must be deducted.[27]

15.3.1 Liquidity facilities

Where there is a liquidity facility in the CDO, depending on the circumstances under which it may be drawn, differing capital factors will be applied. A liquidity facility will be considered to be an "eligible liquidity facility" if the following criteria are satisfied:[28]

* The ability to draw under the facility:
  o must be limited to the amount that is likely to be repaid fully from the liquidation of the underlying collateral exposures and any seller-provided credit enhancements;
  o must not cover any losses incurred in the underlying pool of exposures prior to a draw; and
  o must not allow for predetermined regular or continuous draws.
* The facility must be subject to an asset quality test that precludes draws to cover credit risk from defaulted exposures.[29]
* Where the exposures are externally rated securities, the facility can only be used to fund securities that are externally rated investment grade.
* The facility must no longer allow for draws after all applicable credit enhancements from which it benefits have been exhausted.
* Repayment of draws on the facility cannot be subordinate to any note holder interests or subject to deferral or waiver.

Where an obligation meets the requirements of an eligible liquidity facility, the following CCFs may be applied:

* 0% CCF to the amount of the facility if it is available only in the event of general market disruption;
* 20% CCF if it has an original maturity 1 year of less;
* 50% CCF if it has an original maturity more than 1 year.[30]

---

[27] For more information see *International Convergence of Capital Measurement and Capital Standards: A Revised Framework*, Basel Committee on Banking Supervision, paragraphs 572 and 573.

[28] *International Convergence of Capital Measurement and Capital Standards: A Revised Framework*, Basel Committee on Banking Supervision, paragraph 578.

[29] This is further defined in *International Convergence of Capital Measurement and Capital Standards: A Revised Framework*, Basel Committee on Banking Supervision, paragraphs 452 to 459.

[30] *International Convergence of Capital Measurement and Capital Standards: A Revised Framework*, Basel Committee on Banking Supervision, paragraphs 579 and 580.

Liquidity facilities that are not eligible receive a 100% CCF to the amount of the facility. In addition, where an external rating of the facility is used for risk weighting purposes, a 100% CCF must be used.[31]

Where servicer cash advances are contractually provided for, and are unconditionally cancellable without notice, the servicer is entitled to full reimbursement and this right is senior to all other claims on cash flows, a 0% CCF may be possible, otherwise a 100% CCF will apply.[32]

Where an eligible liquidity facility does not meet the conditions above, the risk weight applied to the exposure's credit equivalent amount will be equal to the highest risk weight assigned to any of the underlying individual exposures covered by the facility.[33]

Thus, where an off-balance sheet securitization exposure does not meet the criteria outlined above, as an eligible liquidity facility or an eligible servicer cash advance facility, a 100% CCF will apply.[34]

Where overlapping facilities are provided by the same bank, the bank does not need to hold additional capital for the overlap. Thus, for example, if a bank has provided a multicurrency facility where a draw in one currency precludes all or part of a draw on the facility in another currency, the overlap will not cause additional capital to be held. However, if the overlapping parts of the facilities are subject to different conversion factors, the bank must attribute the overlapping part to the facility with the highest conversion factor. Notwithstanding this, if overlapping facilities are provided by different banks, each bank is required to hold capital for the maximum facility amount.[35]

15.3.2 Early amortization

If a CDO allows for early amortization and the underlying pool contains revolving assets or exposures, the originating bank is required to hold additional capital against an investor's interest in the securitization. This is because there is a risk that the levels of credit risk to which the bank is exposed may increase once early amortization begins. The capital charge is calculated by multiplying:

- the portion of the underlying pool containing revolving exposures;
- the notional of the investors' and the banks' interest;
- the capital factor; and
- the appropriate credit conversion factor (CCF).

An originating bank is required to hold capital against all or a portion of an investor's interest in a revolving CDO note (including both the drawn and undrawn balances) when the

---

[31] *International Convergence of Capital Measurement and Capital Standards: A Revised Framework*, Basel Committee on Banking Supervision, paragraphs 577 and 579.

[32] *International Convergence of Capital Measurement and Capital Standards: A Revised Framework*, Basel Committee on Banking Supervision, paragraph 582.

[33] *International Convergence of Capital Measurement and Capital Standards: A Revised Framework*, Basel Committee on Banking Supervision, paragraph 576.

[34] *International Convergence of Capital Measurement and Capital Standards: A Revised Framework*, Basel Committee on Banking Supervision, paragraph 577.

[35] *International Convergence of Capital Measurement and Capital Standards: A Revised Framework*, Basel Committee on Banking Supervision, paragraph 595

structure contains an early amortization feature. This early amortization treatment must be applied to that portion of the underlying pool containing revolving exposures.[36]

An early amortization feature allows investors to be paid out prior to the legal final maturity of the CDO notes issued. For Basel purposes, early amortization features are considered either controlled or noncontrolled. A controlled early amortization feature will meet all of the following criteria:[37]

(a) a bank must have an appropriate plan to ensure that it has sufficient capital and liquidity available in the event of early amortization;
(b) throughout the duration of the CDO, there must be a pro rata sharing of interest, principal, expenses, losses and recoveries based on the bank's and investors' relative shares of the receivables outstanding at the beginning of each month;
(c) a bank must set a period for amortization that would be sufficient for a minimum of 90% of the total debt outstanding at the beginning of the early amortization period to have been repaid or deemed to be in default; and
(d) the pace of repayment should not be more rapid than would be allowed by straight-line amortization over the period in (c) above.

Where an early amortization feature does not meet all of the conditions for a controlled early amortization provision, it will be treated as a noncontrolled early amortization provision.[38]

Where the following conditions are met, banks will not be required to calculate a capital requirement for early amortizations:

- the underlying exposures do not revolve and the early amortization ends the ability of the bank to add new exposures;
- CDOs with revolving assets contain early amortization features that mimic term structures; in other words, where the risk on the underlying facilities does not return to the originating bank;
- a bank securitizes one or more credit lines and investors remain fully exposed to future draws by borrowers even after an early amortization event has occurred; and
- the early amortization feature is solely triggered by events not related to the performance of the securitized assets or the selling bank (for example, material changes in tax laws or regulations).[39]

For a bank subject to the early amortization treatment, the total capital charge for all of its positions will be subject to a maximum capital requirement equal to the *maximum of*:

- the amount required for retained securitization exposures;
- the capital requirement that would apply had the exposures not been securitized.[40]

An originating bank's capital charge for the investors' interest is determined as the *product of*:

---

[36] *International Convergence of Capital Measurement and Capital Standards: A Revised Framework*, Basel Committee on Banking Supervision, paragraphs 590 and 592.

[37] *International Convergence of Capital Measurement and Capital Standards: A Revised Framework*, Basel Committee on Banking Supervision, paragraph 548.

[38] *International Convergence of Capital Measurement and Capital Standards: A Revised Framework*, Basel Committee on Banking Supervision, paragraph 549.

[39] *International Convergence of Capital Measurement and Capital Standards: A Revised Framework*, Basel Committee on Banking Supervision, paragraph 593.

[40] *International Convergence of Capital Measurement and Capital Standards: A Revised Framework*, Basel Committee on Banking Supervision, paragraph 594.

- the investors' interest;
- the appropriate CCF; and
- the risk weight appropriate to the underlying exposure type, as if the exposures had not been securitized.[41]

Assuming the CDO does not comprise retail revolving credit exposures (i.e., credit card receivables), controlled early amortization features will be subject to a 90% CCF against the off-balance sheet exposures and non-controlled early amortization features will be subject to a 100% CCF against the off-balance sheet exposures.[42]

15.3.3 Credit risk mitigation

When a bank other than the originating bank(s) provides credit protection to a CDO exposure, it must calculate a capital requirement on the covered exposure as if it were an investor in that securitization. If a bank provides protection to an unrated credit enhancement, it must treat the credit protection provided as if it were directly holding the unrated credit enhancement.[43]

Did you know? The concept of "credit protection" includes various credit risk mitigants including guarantees, credit derivatives such as credit default swaps, and on-balance sheet netting.

Credit protection provided by the following entities will be recognized:

- sovereign entities, public sector entities, banks and securities firms with a lower risk weight than the counterparty;
- other entities rated A- or better, including credit protection provided by parent, subsidiary and affiliate companies when they have a lower risk weight than the obligor.[44]

SPEs are not recognized as eligible guarantors.

Where guarantees or credit derivatives fulfil certain criteria,[45] banks can take account of the credit protection in calculating capital requirements for securitization exposures.[46] The protected portion of the CDO exposure will be assigned the risk weight of the protection provider whereas the uncovered portion of the exposure will be assigned the risk weight of the underlying counterparty.[47] Where there are materiality thresholds below which protection payments are not made in the event of loss, this will be seen as equivalent to retained first loss positions and must be deducted in full from the capital of the bank purchasing the credit

---

[41] *International Convergence of Capital Measurement and Capital Standards: A Revised Framework*, Basel Committee on Banking Supervision, paragraph 595.

[42] For more information see *International Convergence of Capital Measurement and Capital Standards: A Revised Framework*, Basel Committee on Banking Supervision, paragraphs 597 to 605.

[43] *Convergence of Capital Measurement and Capital Standards: A Revised Framework*, Basel Committee on Banking Supervision, paragraph 584.

[44] *International Convergence of Capital Measurement and Capital Standards: A Revised Framework*, Basel Committee on Banking Supervision, paragraphs 195 and 586.

[45] For more information see *International Convergence of Capital Measurement and Capital Standards: A Revised Framework*, Basel Committee on Banking Supervision, paragraph 189 to 194.

[46] *International Convergence of Capital Measurement and Capital Standards: A Revised Framework*, Basel Committee on Banking Supervision, paragraph 587.

[47] *International Convergence of Capital Measurement and Capital Standards: A Revised Framework*, Basel Committee on Banking Supervision, paragraph 196.

protection.[48] If the amount guaranteed, or against which credit protection is held, is less than the amount of the exposure, and guaranteed and non-guaranteed portions are at the same subordination level, capital relief will be afforded on a proportional basis.[49] When credit protection is denominated in a different currency from the exposure, a haircut will be applied to the amount of the exposure deemed to be protected.[50] Finally, if the exposures being hedged have different maturities, the longest maturity must be used.[51]

15.4 THE INTERNAL RATINGS-BASED APPROACH FOR CDOs

Where a bank has received approval to use the IRB approach for the type of assets which are securitized, it must also then use the IRB approach under the Securitization Framework for the CDO exposures it holds. It logically follows that if a bank is using the IRB approach for some types of exposures and the Standardized Approach for other types of exposures, it should generally use the approach which corresponds to the majority of exposures in the underlying pool.[52] There are generally two approaches available within the IRB approach: the Ratings-based Approach (RBA) and the Supervisory Formula (SF).

The RBA must be applied to securitization exposures that are rated, or where a rating can be inferred. The SF must be applied only where an external or an inferred rating is not available. Securitization exposures to which none of these approaches are applicable will attract a capital deduction.

If the underlying asset types have no specific IRB treatment, originating banks are approved to use the IRB approach. They must calculate capital charges on their securitization exposures using the Standardized Approach in the securitization framework, and investing banks with approval to use the IRB approach must apply the RBA.[53]

Where a securitization exposure is rated or where a rating can be inferred, the RBA must be applied. However, where an external or an inferred rating is not available, the SF must be applied.[54]

Where a bank is using the IRB approach, in general, the maximum capital requirement for the securitization exposures it holds is equal to the IRB capital requirement that would have been assessed against the underlying exposures had they not been securitized.[55]

---

[48] *International Convergence of Capital Measurement and Capital Standards: A Revised Framework*, Basel Committee on Banking Supervision, paragraph 197.

[49] *International Convergence of Capital Measurement and Capital Standards: A Revised Framework*, Basel Committee on Banking Supervision, paragraph 198.

[50] For more information see *International Convergence of Capital Measurement and Capital Standards: A Revised Framework*, Basel Committee on Banking Supervision, paragraph 200.

[51] *International Convergence of Capital Measurement and Capital Standards: A Revised Framework*, Basel Committee on Banking Supervision, paragraph 589.

[52] For more information see *International Convergence of Capital Measurement and Capital Standards: A Revised Framework*, Basel Committee on Banking Supervision, paragraphs 606 and 607.

[53] *International Convergence of Capital Measurement and Capital Standards: A Revised Framework*, Basel Committee on Banking Supervision, paragraph 608.

[54] *International Convergence of Capital Measurement and Capital Standards: A Revised Framework*, Basel Committee on Banking Supervision, paragraph 609

[55] In the *International Convergence of Capital Measurement and Capital Standards: A Revised Framework*, Basel Committee on Banking Supervision, paragraph 610 also allows that banks must deduct the entire amount of any gain-on-sale and credit enhancing I/Os arising from the securitization transaction.

15.5 THE INTERNAL RATINGS-BASED APPROACH FOR CDOs: THE RATINGS-BASED APPROACH

Under the Ratings Based Approach (RBA), the risk-weighted assets are determined by *multiplying* the amount of the exposure by the appropriate risk weight.[56] The risk weights that will apply will depend on various factors:

- the external credit rating or an available inferred rating;
- whether the credit rating (external or inferred) represents a long-term or a short-term credit rating;
- the granularity of the underlying pool; and
- the seniority of the position.[57]

As CDO tranches are traditionally only given long-term credit ratings, short-term credit ratings are not examined in this chapter.

A securitization exposure under the RBA will be treated as a senior tranche if it is effectively secured by a first claim on the entire assets in the underlying collateral pool. Thus, "Risk Weights for senior positions" are applied where the effective number of underlying exposures (N) is six or more and the position is senior. Where the position is not senior but the number of underlying exposures (N) is six or more, the "Base Risk Weights" are applicable. Finally, in all other cases, the "Risk Weights for tranches backed by non-granular pools" is applied (Table 15.2).[58]

N, the effective number of exposures, is calculated as:

$$N = \frac{\left(\sum_i EAD_i \right)^2}{\sum_i (EAD_i)^2}$$

where EAD_i is the exposure for the i-th instrument in the underlying pool.

To use an inferred rating, the following must be satisfied:[59]

- the reference-rated exposures must be subordinate in all respects to the unrated securitization exposure;
- the maturity of the reference-rated exposure must be equal to or longer than that of the unrated exposure;
- on an ongoing basis, any inferred rating must be updated continuously to reflect any changes in the external rating of the reference-rated exposure.

---

[56] *International Convergence of Capital Measurement and Capital Standards: A Revised Framework*, Basel Committee on Banking Supervision, paragraph 611.

[57] *International Convergence of Capital Measurement and Capital Standards: A Revised Framework*, Basel Committee on Banking Supervision, paragraph 612.

[58] *International Convergence of Capital Measurement and Capital Standards: A Revised Framework*, Basel Committee on Banking Supervision, paragraphs 613 and 615.

[59] *International Convergence of Capital Measurement and Capital Standards: A Revised Framework*, Basel Committee on Banking Supervision, paragraphs 617–618.

Table 15.2

Long-term external rating	Risk weights for senior positions	Base risk weights	Risk weights for tranches backed by non-granular pools
AAA	7%	12%	20%
AA	8%	15%	25%
A+	10%	18%	35%
A	12%	20%	35%
A−	20%	35%	35%
BBB+	35%	50%	50%
BBB	60%	75%	75%
BBB−	100%	100%	100%
BB+	250%	250%	250%
BB	425%	425%	425%
BB−	650%	650%	650%
Below BB− and unrated	1250%	1250%	1250%

15.6 THE INTERNAL RATINGS-BASED APPROACH FOR CDOs: THE SUPERVISORY FORMULA APPROACH

Under the Supervisory Formula, the risk-weighted assets (RWA) are determined by *multiplying the capital charge by 12.5.*

Under the Supervisory Formula, the capital charge for a CDO tranche depends on five factors:

- the IRB capital charge had the underlying exposures not been securitized (K_{IRB});
- the tranche's credit enhancement level (L);
- the tranche's thickness (T);
- the pool's effective number of exposures (N);
- the pool's exposure weighted average loss-given-default (LGD).

A tranche's IRB capital charge is calculated as the amount of exposures that have been securitized *multiplied by the maximum of*:

- $0.0056 \times T$
- $(S[L+T] - S[L])$

Where a bank holds only part of a tranche, the capital charge will equal the bank's pro-rated share of the capital charge for the entire tranche.[60] The Supervisory Formula is expressed as:[61]

> When $x <= K_{IRB}$,
> $S[x] = x$
> When $x > K_{IRB}$
> $S[x] = K_{IRB} + K[x] - K[K_{IRB}] + (d * K_{IRB}/\omega)(1 - e^{\omega*(K_{IRB}-x)}/K_{IRB})$

---

[60] *International Convergence of Capital Measurement and Capital Standards: A Revised Framework*, Basel Committee on Banking Supervision, paragraph 623.

[61] *International Convergence of Capital Measurement and Capital Standards: A Revised Framework*, Basel Committee on Banking Supervision, paragraph 624.

where:[62]

$h = (1 - K_{IRB} / LGD)^N$

$c = K_{IRB} / (1 - h)$

$v = [(LGD - K_{IRB}) * K_{IRB} + 0.25 * (1 - LGD) * K_{IRB}] / N$

$f = [(v + K_{IRB}^2) / (1 - h)] - c^2 + [(1 - K_{IRB}) * K_{IRB} - v] / (1 - h) * \tau$

$g = [(1 - c) * c] / f - 1$

$a = g * c$

$b = g * (1 - c)$

$d = 1 - (1 - h) * (Beta[K_{IRB}; a, b])$

$K[x] = (1 - h) * ((1 - Beta[x; a, b]) * x + Beta[x; a+1, b] * c)$, where $Beta[x; a, b]$ is the cumulative beta distribution with parameters a and b evaluated at x.[63]

$\tau = 1000$

$\omega = 20$

K_{IRB} is calculated as:

- the IRB capital requirement including the EL portion for the underlying exposures in the pool (calculated in accordance with the applicable minimum IRB standards as if the exposures in the pool were held directly by the bank) *divided by*
- the exposure amount of the pool.[64]

The credit enhancement level (L) is determined by *dividing* the nominal amount of tranches subordinate to the relevant tranche by the amount of exposures in the pool.[65]

Where there is a reserve account funded by accumulated cash flows from the underlying exposures that is subordinate to the relevant tranche, it can be included in the calculation of L. However, unfunded reserve accounts may not be included if they will be funded from future receipts from the underlying exposures.[66]

The thickness of the exposure (T) is generally determined by *dividing* the nominal size of the tranche of interest by the notional amount of exposures in the pool.[67]

N, the effective number of exposures, is calculated as:

$$N = \frac{\left(\sum_i EAD_i\right)^2}{\sum_i (EAD_i)^2}$$

where EAD_i is the exposure-at-default for the i-th instrument in the pool.

---

[62] For securitizations involving retail exposures, subject to supervisory review, "h" and "v" may be set equal to zero. See *International Convergence of Capital Measurement and Capital Standards: A Revised Framework*, Basel Committee on Banking Supervision, paragraph 635.

[63] *International Convergence of Capital Measurement and Capital Standards: A Revised Framework*, Basel Committee on Banking Supervision, paragraph 625.

[64] *International Convergence of Capital Measurement and Capital Standards: A Revised Framework*, Basel Committee on Banking Supervision, paragraph 627.

[65] *International Convergence of Capital Measurement and Capital Standards: A Revised Framework*, Basel Committee on Banking Supervision, paragraph 630.

[66] *International Convergence of Capital Measurement and Capital Standards: A Revised Framework*, Basel Committee on Banking Supervision, paragraph 631.

[67] *International Convergence of Capital Measurement and Capital Standards: A Revised Framework*, Basel Committee on Banking Supervision, paragraph 632.

Multiple exposures in the same obligor must be consolidated. For CDOs of ABS and other securitization-of-securitization exposures, N applies to the number of securitization exposures in the pool (not the number of underlying exposures in the original pools). If the portfolio share associated with the largest exposure, C_1, is available, the bank may compute N as $1/C_1$.[68]

The formula to determine the exposure-weighted average LGD is:

$$LGD = \frac{\sum_i EAD_i LGD_i}{\sum_i EAD_i}$$

where LGD_i is the average LGD associated with all exposures to the i-th obligor.[69]

In the case of re-securitization, an LGD of 100% applies for the underlying securitized exposures.[70]

If the largest exposure in the underlying pool, C_1, is no more than 3% of the underlying pool, then for purposes of the Supervisory Formula:

- LGD can be set at 0.50;
- N may be determined by:
  - $N = \{C_1 * C_m + [(C_m - C_1)/(m - 1)] * max(1 - m * C_1, 0)\}^{-1}$, or
  - $N = 1/C_1$.

where, C_m is the share of the pool corresponding to the sum of the largest "m" exposures and the level of "m" is set by each bank.[71]

15.7 THE INTERNAL RATINGS-BASED APPROACH: LIQUIDITY FACILITIES, OVERLAPPING EXPOSURES, CREDIT RISK MITIGATION AND EARLY AMORTIZATION FEATURES

15.7.1 Liquidity facilities and overlapping exposures

Liquidity facilities are treated like any other securitization exposure and receive a CCF of 100% unless otherwise specified below. If the facility is externally rated, a bank may rely on the external rating under the RBA. If the facility is not rated and an inferred rating is not available, the bank must apply the SF.[72]

An eligible liquidity facility that can only be drawn in the event of a general market disruption is assigned a 20% CCF under the Supervisory Formula. Therefore, an IRB bank must recognize a 20% CCF, unless the eligible facility is externally rated in which case the

---

[68] *International Convergence of Capital Measurement and Capital Standards: A Revised Framework*, Basel Committee on Banking Supervision, paragraph 633.

[69] *International Convergence of Capital Measurement and Capital Standards: A Revised Framework*, Basel Committee on Banking Supervision, paragraph 634.

[70] *International Convergence of Capital Measurement and Capital Standards: A Revised Framework*, Basel Committee on Banking Supervision, paragraph 634.

[71] *International Convergence of Capital Measurement and Capital Standards: A Revised Framework*, Basel Committee on Banking Supervision, paragraph 636.

[72] *International Convergence of Capital Measurement and Capital Standards: A Revised Framework*, Basel Committee on Banking Supervision, paragraph 637.

bank may rely on the external rating under the RBA provided it assigns a 100% CCF rather than a 20% CCF to the facility.[73]

On an exceptional basis and only when regulatory consent is obtained, if it is not practical for a bank to use either the bottom-up or the top-down approach for calculating K_{IRB}, it might be allowed temporarily to apply the following method. If the liquidity facility qualifies as an "eligible liquidity facility" (as described above under the Standardized Approach), the highest risk weight assigned under the Standardized Approach to any of the underlying individual exposures covered by the liquidity facility can be applied. In addition, where it is an "eligible liquidity facility" the following CCFs must be applied:

- 50% CCF for a facility with an original maturity of one year or less;
- 100% CCF if the facility has an original maturity of more than one year;
- 20% CCF if the facility is only available in the event of a general market disruption.[74]

Overlapping facility exposures will be treated as described above under the Standardized Approach. In addition, eligible servicer cash advances will also be treated as described above under the Standardized Approach.[75]

15.7.2 Credit risk mitigation

A bank may reduce the capital charge proportionally when a credit risk mitigant covers first losses or losses on a proportional basis. Otherwise, a bank must assume that the credit risk mitigant covers the most senior portion of the securitization exposure.[76]

15.7.3 Early amortization features

An originating bank must use the criteria set out above under the Standardized Approach for determining if any capital must be held against the investors' interest. For banks using the IRB approach, investors' interest is defined as investors' drawn balances related to securitization exposures and EAD associated with investors' undrawn lines related to securitization exposures. For determining the EAD, the undrawn balances of securitized exposures would be allocated between the seller's and investors' interests on a pro rata basis. The capital charge attributed to the investors' interest is determined by the product of:

- the investors' interest;
- the applicable CCF, and
- K_{IRB}.[77]

---

[73] *International Convergence of Capital Measurement and Capital Standards: A Revised Framework*, Basel Committee on Banking Supervision, paragraph 638.

[74] *International Convergence of Capital Measurement and Capital Standards: A Revised Framework*, Basel Committee on Banking Supervision, paragraph 639.

[75] *International Convergence of Capital Measurement and Capital Standards: A Revised Framework*, Basel Committee on Banking Supervision, paragraphs 640 and 641.

[76] *International Convergence of Capital Measurement and Capital Standards: A Revised Framework*, Basel Committee on Banking Supervision, paragraph 642

[77] *International Convergence of Capital Measurement and Capital Standards: A Revised Framework*, Basel Committee on Banking Supervision, paragraph 643.

15.8 SUPERVISORY PROVISIONS

The Basel regulations can also make use of "Pillar 2 Supervisory Provisions" such that the regulators can require a bank to hold on to capital in excess of what its own risk model might suggest. Therefore, although a simple regulatory capital model has been included to illustrate how the Basel securitization framework calculations may apply to a CDO, the Basel II provisions and applicable regulatory handbooks, guidances and advice should be consulted before final conclusions are drawn.

It is likely that banks will utilize CDO/CLO technology and the supervisory formula in the coming years to reduce risk weighted assets and facilitate higher return on capital.

Additionally, CLO/CDO technology can facilitate the creation of "bad bank" solutions by transferring toxic assets off-balance sheet and separately capitalizing them, thus preserving the "good bank" from being contaminated. Real risk reduction, however, can only come from either the sale of the junior tranches to unrelated third parties or via CDS/financial guaranties from third parties.

15.9 UPDATES TO BASEL II

In January 2009, the BIS released a number of proposals designed to enhance the Basel II capital framework. While at the time of writing these proposals were subject to comment, intended final comment periods were relatively short and extensive discussions has already taken place with the larger banks. Hence, there is a general expectation that the final implementation will broadly represent these proposals. The new proposals are designed to significantly increase the level of capital held in comparison to existing requirements for securitizations, and eliminate any internal arbitrage between holding these securities on the trading book versus the banking book. The following is a brief summary of the proposals as related to securitizations, CDOs and conduits:[78]

1. **Trading book positions**: The capital charge for securitization positions will be consistent across the trading book and banking book, and the current trading book VaR model will be effectively replaced by a banking book risk-weight asset approach. Other trading book positions will be subject to an Incremental Risk Capital charge over and above the existing VaR model charges, to take into account default risk and migration risk. In addition, a "stressed" VaR calculation will be introduced. The intended Implementation date for this change is to be no later than 31 December 2010.
2. **Banking book positions (Securitizations)**: A new securitization sub-category for CDOs of ABS – "Re-securitizations" – will be introduced. Banks will be required to apply higher risk weights to these exposures (e.g., IRB risk weight for AAA re-securitization will increase from 7% to 20%, A- will increase from 20% to 60%).
3. **Use of ratings subject to self-guarantee**: For example, where a bank owns AAA CP issued by a conduit, but the external rating is due to a liquidity facility or other support provided by the same bank, the external rating must be ignored when determining capital charge for the CP held by the bank.
4. **Credit analysis to support external ratings**: Banks will no longer be able to rely solely on an external/internal rating without further internal review, including a comprehensive

---

[78] For more information regarding changes to other matters see http://www.bis.org/publ/bcbs/basel2enh0901.htm.

understanding of risks as well as detailed information on underlying pools and their ongoing performance.

5. **Liquidity facilities**: The CCF under the Standardized Approach will be amended to 50% for all maturities (i.e., no longer any benefit of a rolling 364-day facility). There will be an elimination of the favourable treatment for liquidity facilities; it will be restricted to drawing under general market disruption events.

Additional internal review (Pillar 2) and external disclosure (Pillar 3) requirements are under review and the proposed implementation date is no later than 31 December 2009.

16
CDO Valuation

16.1 INTRODUCTION

What is value? As can be seen from previous chapters, although at first glance cash flow CDOs may be considered quite simple, in fact they contain a large degree of complexity and valuing them is not trivial.

In a CSO (collateralized synthetic obligation, i.e., a credit default swap tranche), the main risks to be evaluated are typically limited to the following:

- default risk (severity and timing);
- correlation risk;
- recovery risk;
- charged asset risk (credit risk and payment variability);
- perhaps CSO^2 and higher risks.

Evaluation is typically limited to assessing the above as the underlying contracts tend to be homogenous with regard to maturity, payment dates and payment terms.

Additional risks to consider might include counterparty issues and "cheapest to deliver" options for recovery.

Managed CSO transactions might require additional consideration in the following areas:

- replacement risk, i.e., allowing the manager to substitute credits;
- manager expertise and experience, i.e., whether they have sufficient experience and expertise.

In comparison, the following factors should be considered when evaluating a cash flow CDO:

- default risk (severity and timing);
- default correlation risk;
- LGD or recovery risk;
- interest rate risk;
- basis risk, i.e., mismatches between liabilities and assets;
- currency risk;
- replacement/reinvestment risk;
- prepayment;
- termination: optional and in the event of default;
- CDO^2 and structured finance issues;
- manager expertise and experience.

A brief discussion of each of these risks follows.

16.1.1 Default risk

The severity and timing of defaults has the biggest impact on the CDO value. Given the nature of the leveraged investment, a loss experienced of more than the expected loss can seriously affect the value of the equity and subordinated debt tranches. Further stress to the loss rate and payments to the senior tranches can also be affected. Given the path dependence of cash flows to the debt, largely caused by of the presence of cash diversion triggers, the timing of defaults is also very important. For example, a loss to the equity holder of 10% at the end of the transaction, after experiencing several years of double digit returns is less damaging, than a loss in year one, with the additional prospect of being "triggered out" of payments for the immediate future.

16.1.2 Default correlation risk

High correlation between obligors tends to favour the equity at the expense of the senior notes, as high correlation usually means either an extremely good result with fewer defaults or an extremely poor result with significantly higher defaults. The impact of correlation on the mezzanine tranches is not so clear cut, as their performance is liable to take on characteristics of both the equity and the senior tranches depending on the performance of the pool. Correlation is not constant and estimating correlation for infrequently traded collateral (bonds, loans) is difficult. Unlike the synthetic markets, where correlation is traded every day, observed correlation between obligors in a cash CDO, unless they are obligations of companies that are publicly listed and traded on an equity exchange, is virtually non-existent. It generally requires the use of proxy company risk and a lot of guesswork. This problem is further exacerbated in the structured finance space. It does not necessarily make a lot of sense to estimate a gross correlation between different issuers of mortgage backed securities. Actual correlation will depend on both (a) the macro economic effects and the micro economy for the underlying mortgages and (b) the relative position in the capital structure. These issues are further clouded for CDOs where the CDO holds other CDO tranches which in turn may contain a number of the same credits as the holding CDO's portfolio. Correlation in these instances depends not only on the default correlation of the obligors, but also on the position of the tranche in the capital structure, i.e., if the held tranche is senior and an obligor common to the CDO and the held tranche defaults, then a loss will definitely be experienced in the holding CDO portfolio, whereas in the tranche held, no loss may be experienced.

16.1.3 Loss given default/recovery risk

Agency analysis (other than Moody's non-US CLO analysis) tends to use fixed recovery rates. Recovery rates usually vary by the legal domicile of the obligor, as the legal process and protection for lenders is different in each country. Additionally, recovery rates have been shown to alter inversely to the level of the default rate.[1] A high default rate tends to lead to lower recoveries and vice versa. This makes some sense as there is a somewhat limited universe of purchasers able to buy distressed companies and their assets. As default rates rise, the opportunities open to these potential purchasers outweigh their capacity to buy, hence the "opportunity cost" of utilizing a rare resource will tend to drive yields up and therefore prices

---

[1] See Altman, Edward I., "Default Recovery Rates and LGD in Credit Risk Modeling and Practice: An Updated Review of the Literature and Empirical Evidence" November 2006; "The Relationship Between Default Rates and Recovery", Standard and Poors, 24 January 2007; Altman, Edward I. with Karlin, Brenda J., "Special Report on Defaults and Returns in the High-Yield Bond Market: The Year 2007 in Review and Outlook", 7 February 2008.

down. In addition, recoveries for defaulted structured finance assets assigned by the rating agencies in the past have been shown to be too optimistic and have been revised lower as of the date of writing.

16.1.4 Interest rate risk

Rating agencies tend to prefer static hedging strategies which can be terminated at little or no cost, as their models generally cannot size the potential mark to market cost of terminating interest rate derivatives early. However, unless expensive "quanto" or default contingent asset specific hedges are used, there will be differences in notional schedules arising between the fixed rate coupon assets and their associated hedges as a result of prepayments, defaults and potential trading by the portfolio manager. In addition, termination costs arising from either voluntary termination (i.e., equity call options) or forced termination related to events of default (or "EOD") can be considerable. And while mismatched hedging can add value to the equity tranche, particularly in the early years, other tranches generally suffer an increase in expected loss so, for them, mismatched hedges are generally subtractive from value.

16.1.5 Basis risk

A related issue to interest rate risk is basis risk. Basis risk refers to the differences in the payment "basis" between the assets and liabilities arising through different index resets, payment frequencies, payment dates, and indices. Basis swaps, "timing" swaps, and smoothing accounts can help to minimize basis risks.

16.1.6 Currency risk

For multi-currency deals, i.e., transactions with assets and potential liabilities denominated in different currencies, currency rate volatility, particularly in concert with defaults or pre-payments, can add to or amplify losses. Additionally, cross-currency basis interest rate risk presents another area of potential loss or at least underperformance; interest rates in different currencies can be markedly different and hedging mismatches will show up as interest shortfalls or excesses. Additionally, cross-currency defaults can result in significantly lower recoveries, as the recovery rate is converted to a different currency.

16.1.7 Replacement/reinvestment risk

Replacement or reinvestment is an option granted to a collateral manager to replace or replenish credits from the portfolio with the cash received from maturing debt or from the sales of assets. The benefits of this option largely accrue to the equity tranche holders and the portfolio manager; by keeping the assets under management high, the management fee is maximized, and by maintaining leverage, the return to equity is maximized. However, in the authors' opinion, it is highly likely that, going forward, this option will come under review and may not be granted by the debt holders so freely in the future. This has come about because, in many earlier unaffected vintage transactions, particularly structured finance CDOs, returns were damaged and greater losses were experienced than initially expected by reinvestment in issues of the 2006/2007 vintage that have experienced extraordinarily high levels of loss. Additionally, portfolio managers have often been forced to reach for yield in order to maintain weighted average spread and/or coupon covenants when reinvesting. Agencies typically deal with the lack of certainty over the portfolio by requiring limits with regard to credit quality and concentrations.

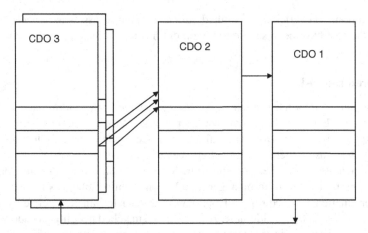

Figure 16.1 Potential CDO overlap

16.1.8 Prepayment

Prepayment itself is not an additional risk; however, the variation in prepayment rates tends to amplify the other previously-mentioned risks, particularly the hedging and basis issues. Over-collateralization haircuts used in calculating the principal balance can also accelerate prepayment on the liability side, further increasing the likelihood of mismatch.

16.1.9 Termination: optional and event of default (EOD)

The prevalence of CDOs issued with EOD-linked collateral balance tests, incorporating haircuts for lower rated assets, means that many CDOs were not rated to ultimate loss or default but instead to a contingent market value and downgrade. The chance that these CDOs will trigger an EOD is consequently much higher than if the EOD was purely related to defaults on the underlying assets. Therefore the value of these CDOs is not purely default and loss related, but should also reflect the potential mark to market of the credit instruments and associated hedges in liquidation once the EOD has been triggered (see discussion in Section 16.6 on transition matrices).

16.1.10 CDO^2 and structured finance issues

As of writing this book, correlation, recovery and default risk in CDOs of CDOs and ABS are in the process of being recalibrated by the agencies and market participants. The capability of CDOs to invest in other CDOs, which in turn may have invested in other CDOs, highlights a potential problem of circularity. The fact that some of these may be invested at different parts of the capital structure also highlights the potential complexity issues that may arise. Suppose, for example, a transaction called ABC CDO Ltd, a high grade ABS deal. It may have a bucket to purchase CDO AAA/Aaa rated tranches whose underlying assets are predominately mezzanine tranches. It buys a senior Aaa/AAA-rated tranche of a transaction called DEF CDO Ltd, a mezzanine structured finance deal which is able to purchase the tranches of other mezzanine CDOs. Suppose a third transaction where GHI CDO Ltd is purchased by DEF CDO Ltd, and GHI CDO in turn may have already purchased, or may in future purchase, a mezzanine tranche issued by ABC CDO. Consequently, the original ABC CDO now indirectly references itself through the DEF CDO.

Hence there is a potential blind spot that can only be addressed by performing a complete "bottom-up" analysis to assess the overlap and correlation risks. Currently, to the authors' knowledge, there are no systems generally available to provide the required information. Recovery rates for structured finance assets have also proved difficult to estimate, particularly for CDOs where realized recoveries are significantly lower than those estimated at the time of rating. Recovery rates could be relatively high for a CDO that suffers a "technical" default, i.e., defaults related to legal or tax reasons. However, for EODs related to performance or ability to pay, recovery may ultimately be determined from a fire sale of the assets or a final payout on the last day of the transaction. As many structured finance deals have original tenors of 30 years or more, the recovery of tranches from distressed transactions is likely to be very low, and this is reflected in the often single digit bids for these assets in the secondary market.

16.1.11 Manager expertise and experience

While difficult to measure quantitatively with respect to an individual transaction, collateral manager expertise has been shown to make a difference with regard to overall performance.[2] Managers who actively monitor credit situations, have a long track record in preserving capital rather than generating excess returns, have a strong sell discipline for troubled credits, and have resources sufficient to perform frequent and timely credit analysis, tend to outperform their peers.

Of these 11 factors described above, the following three factors tend to dominate the determination of value: (1) default risk (severity and timing); (2) default correlation risk; and (3) LGD or recovery risk. Accordingly, they should be considered the general driving factors for analysis.

To more fully evaluate a cash CDO, the following would ideally be required: a model to generate correlated defaults; a recovery model (preferably linked to level of default); a LIBOR market model or similar full-term structure model to evaluate interest rate basis risk; and derivative exposure and associated termination costs. Given the systems and data requirements, it is hardly surprising that this approach has not been widely adopted and instead investors have tended to focus more on a sensitivity analysis approach.

16.1.12 Prerequisites

What data is required in order to begin assigning value to a CDO tranche? The following information should be considered the bare minimum:

- portfolio (ideally with current prices);
- documents (trust deed and agency agreements/indenture);
- offering memorandum;
- swap agreements;
- other agreements (portfolio management, collateral administrator, if not covered in the indenture);
- trustee reports (for secondary positions);
- rating agency reports (new issue and surveillance if available).

It may also be useful to have the marketing material when analysing a new issue.

In addition to the above, in order to fully evaluate the risks in CDOs some processes/evaluation vectors are required for:

---

[2] "CDO Manager Quality: A Critical Consideration", Standard and Poors, 2 October 1981.

- defaults (severity and timing);
- loss given default (or the complementary recovery);
- interest rates;
- currencies (if applicable);
- prepayments;
- termination collateral values.

16.2 BASIC VALUATION APPROACHES

There are at least four currently-used approaches to CDO valuation:

1. traditional underwriter view point;
2. fundamental cash flow analysis;
3. market value;
4. accounting value.

16.2.1 Traditional underwriter viewpoint

Given the complexities outlined above, it is not surprising that most investors and underwriters prefer a much simpler form of sensitivity analysis. The traditional analysis and presentation of value concentrates on sensitivity to small changes to key values in the model, such as default rates, loss severity and income.

16.2.2 Fundamental cash flow analysis

In the past fundamental cash flow analysis has typically used "buy and hold" investors, such as banking book investors, other CDOs and CDO funds, and insurance companies.

This approach generates cash flows typically probability weighed by some measure(s) and discounts them at an appropriate level, i.e., the assessment addresses the likelihood of being repaid over the life of the investment.

16.2.3 Market value

Market value is more appropriate for investors who have purchased CDOs on to the trading book, have a mark to market fund, or have leveraged their position in the repo market.

The lack of a readily tradable market means that approximations have often been used to attribute market value to a CDO tranche.

One simple approach is to create yield curves for CDOs and mark them to market using the curves. As there is often no readily available information other than generic research levels published by some of the investment banks, some counterparts have taken to using new issue levels plus some bid offer to mark to market. While this is a reasonable approach for performing CDOs, it becomes more difficult for off-the-run CDOs (i.e., older issues with some impairment). This approach can be supplemented by re-tranching the transaction and equating the new tranches to the performing market (with some adjustment for the impairment). While these will not be actual trading values, it would at least be the beginning point of a negotiated sale.

16.2.4 Accounting value

Given the difficulty of obtaining market prices from underwriters and the lack of an agreed fundamental approach, a final view of the CDO could be to take an accounting view of the balance sheet of the SPE. This would tend to ignore the waterfall, unless adjustments are made for the occurrence of any triggers (over-collateralization or interest coverage) and any leakage of principal for interest. Consequently, it would be more applicable to the senior tranches of a transaction and may be useful for evaluating impaired tranches (i.e., other than retranching/mark to curve). A typical approach would be to mark to market all the underlying assets and derivatives. Values for the tranches are then determined by assigning the aggregate mark to market value from the top down to each tranche in turn, with the lower tranches taking the loss first. For example, suppose there is a simple two-tranche structure where the senior tranche is 90% and the junior tranche is 10%. If the value of the portfolio is 92%, it would be reasonable to assign a value of par to the senior note and a value of 20% to the junior note.

16.3 TRADITIONAL UNDERWRITER ANALYSIS

Rather than present a value for a CDO tranche, a series of sensitivity analyses is typically presented for each tranche. Usually the underwriter presents the scenarios for the analysis and assumptions are required to be made with regard to:

- ramp-up of the portfolio (speed and spread);
- initial spread/coupon;
- timing of the occurrence of the first default;
- fees and expenses;
- amortization;
- reinvestment spread;
- recovery upon default (both timing and degree).

The analysis usually uses a constant annual default rate which is typically applied to the outstanding balance rather than the maximum anticipated notional. Recoveries are usually assumed to be instantaneous, i.e., within the same period as the default occurred. A series of cases for the rated notes and the equity is then presented which varies some of the above parameters while holding the others fixed, i.e., a sensitivity analysis.

For rated notes, the analysis typically involves finding the maximum constant annual default rate that a note can withstand at a particular recovery rate. Then the rated yield (i.e., first dollar of loss at the coupon spread/initial sales price) and the "return of principal" (i.e., the constant default rate which the implied yield is zero or slightly negative) are broken and the investor receives only their principal (or less) back. The analysis is typically presented as a family of curves of yield versus default rate with various assumed recovery rates. Usually an "expected default case" is also presented based upon the long term average annual defaults for the portfolio. Alternatively, as shown below, it is possible to calculate the discount margin at various default rates.

Key assumptions for rated note analysis include the following.

- **Ramp-up considerations** (i.e., portfolio at close and ramp-up time): This may present structuring issues such as return on excess cash awaiting investment if liabilities are fully drawn or modelling delayed draw or revolving lines of credit. However, usually a ramp-profile assumption is presented. Ramp-up issues can be less of an issue for rated notes as usually default timings are selected to start some time after the end of the ramp-up period. Often the main consideration for rated notes is having enough cash to pay the first coupon.

- **Weighed average spread on the portfolio**: This usually exceeds the covenanted minimum weighted average spread and assumptions are usually presented for both initial pool and the reinvestments.
- **Recovery rate**, i.e., degree and timing: These are usually fixed and may be subject to some sensitivity analysis.
- **Defaults**: Timing and severity of defaults are usually presented as a constant rate applied to the outstanding balance (not original balance) of both the original and reinvestment pool. Whether reinvestments are also subject to default can vary from scenario to scenario. Usually defaults are chosen not to apply for the first period (i.e., before the end of the ramp-up). However, underwriters have been known to delay the onset of defaults for as long as 18 months to two years in their analysis.
- **Other assumptions**: These can include weighted average life for the initial pool and reinvestments, reinvestment amortization profiles, prepayment rates on the loans/bonds, weighted average lives, and fees and expenses both upfront and ongoing.

Equity analysis will typically show various IRR returns based upon constant annual default rates and assumed recoveries. Often these will be shown to the first call date of the CDO but may also be shown to the legal final maturity. Often the analysis will also be shown as a family of curves with various assumed recovery rates. Additionally, a price yield table might be shown.

Often these presented cases will stimulate requests for further analysis from an investor. Analysis from more seasoned investors may include:

- cumulative default rate analysis with default timing vectors similar to those used by rating agencies;
- step changes in the constant annual default rate; for example, assume defaults are doubled for two years and then return to expected average rates;
- interest rate stresses, particularly if a hedge is involved;
- pre-payment and investment rate stresses in line with investor expectation and/or experience.

16.3.1 Modelling requirements

When presenting a traditional analysis, there are potentially hundreds of scenarios which are required to be run for the traditional analysis alone, but this can also be multiplied by the number of potential investors that request additional analysis. It can therefore be very tedious and potentially very error-prone to perform these calculations by varying the inputs manually. Most models, as in the rating agency analysis, will provide a mechanism for varying the parameters of the model automatically. Additionally, the parameters will vary from the rating agency parameters and may even vary by potential investor. Consequently, even if models are saved for each case, maintaining multiple models can be very difficult and prone to errors as well. By having the ability to store the parameters for these scenarios, it should be possible to reproduce the results at a later stage without having to remember all the changes to the inputs and assumptions, or having to maintain separate models.

The **Scenario Analysis Sheet** in the *Cash Flow Model with Simulation Controls* provides such a mechanism to run multiple cases and automatically drive the model. To create a scenario case, three named ranges are required to be created:

- an assumptions range;

- an inputs range; and
- an outputs range.

The relevant case is selected in cell C3 via a combo box, and the macro "Run_Scenario" is run when the "Run Scenario" button is activated. The macro loads the contents of the assumptions range once, at the beginning of the scenario, in order to set up the model to a known initial state which conforms to the base assumptions for the scenario. For example, cells B6 to C14 on the **Scenario Analysis Sheet** carry the assumptions range for the named Equity case, and have a list of named ranges. The first, in cell C8, is the collateral liquidation period, "Coll_Liquidation". Cell C8 holds the value that this input will set for each combination of inputs in the scenario. In this case the Coll_Liquidation is set to 80 or the last period of the transaction. The purpose of this scenario is to generate equity IRR until maturity. However, it should be self evident that if the modeller wishes to run the equity IRR to call date, it would be a simple matter of changing this input to 20, if the first call period of the transaction is, say, five years.

The other cells in the "Equity_Assumptions" range hold the Liquidation Price (cell C9), the Interest Rate Vector (cell C10), and the default types (cells C13 and C14). The macro as described above will load each variable via the named range at the start of the macro.

The inputs range for the "Equity Scenario", in cells B16 to D24, holds the inputs that will vary during this analysis. In this case, the equity price, the recovery rate and the constant default rate will change. The logic employed in the macro varies the inputs from right to left. Hence, in this example the first iteration will set the CDR named range to 0%, the Recovery_Rate named range to 80%, and the Tranche_6_Price named range to 80%. It will then vary the CDR from 0% to 5%, before changing the "Recovery_Rate" to 70%. Similarly, after holding the price and recovery at 80% and 70%, it will iterate through the CDR again. It will continue to do this until it exhausts the "Recovery_Rate" range. It will then iterate the price by setting it to 85%, and begin again. This continues until all combinations of the inputs are exhausted.

The Equity Outputs range is in cells B26 to C29. The active range is in cells A25 to B26, with column A holding the named range, and column B holding label text to describe the output. In this case, the scenario will record the dollar duration and the annualized (XIRR) IRR equity return. There is one additional named range for each scenario, which may be empty if no additional processing is required. The Equity Routine named range in cells D28 to D29. This is a one cell range that refers to a VBA subroutine that will run during each iteration of the "Run_Scenario" macro. This is mainly used to solve for break-evens either in losses or yields/discount margins.

Adding to the ranges is relatively straightforward. A row in the table can be selected, and another assumption processed by highlighting cells prior to the end of the assumptions range. Similarly, to add another input, cells can be inserted before the CDR column and the values input. To remove an input or assumption the range can be cleared, with the following caveat: the macro will stop at the first empty cell in a range, i.e., it will not skip over an empty cell to an occupied cell. In addition, running the inputs with more than three to four variables will mean both a large running time and potentially a large output to deal with. It is additionally constrained by the size of the worksheet. Changing the layout of the results is simply a matter of changing the order of the inputs.

Varying the number of outputs is as simple as inserting a row in the output range, and putting in the appropriately named range and text field. Ordering and removal of output parameters can be treated similarly as for the assumptions and inputs, with the same caveat about empty cells. The macro is shown below.

```
Sub Run_Scenario()

' get scenario from case cell
' setup assumptions
' Read input cases
' set input case
' calculate
' write output
'
' Dimension variables
'
Dim r1, r2 As Range
Dim r4 As Range
Dim r3() As Range
Dim vcount() As Integer
Dim itranches() As Integer

Dim case_name, range_name, case_string As String
Dim a, b, c, d As Integer
Dim i, j, k, l, m, n As Integer
Dim scenario_value As Variant
Dim ws1, ws2, ws5, ws6 As Worksheet
Dim outrange() As Range
Dim varcnt, scencnt, outcnt As Integer
Dim xoffset, yoffset As Integer
Dim scenecnt() As Integer
Dim totalscenes As Integer
Dim aux_subroutine As String
Dim doAuxillaryProcessing As Boolean
Dim solved As Boolean


Worksheets("Scenario Analysis").Range("F10:cB500").ClearContents
'
' find out which scenario to run
'
case_name = [Case]
Set ws1 = Worksheets("Collateral")
Set ws2 = Worksheets("Outputs")

Set ws5 = Worksheets("Inputs")
Set ws6 = Worksheets("Scenario Analysis")

range_name = case_name & "_Routine"
If Range(range_name).Value <> "" Then
    doAuxillaryProcessing = True
    aux_subroutine = Range(range_name).Value
Else

    doAuxillaryProcessing = False
End If
```

```
solved = False

range_name = case_name & "_assumptions"
Set r1 = Range(range_name)
n = r1.Rows.count

'
' set assumptions
'
For i = 1 To n
 range_name = r1.Cells(i, 1)
 scenario_value = r1.Cells(i, 2)
 If range_name <> "" Or Len(range_name) > 0 Then
    Set r2 = Range(range_name)
    r2.Cells(1, 1) = scenario_value
 End If
Next i

'
' outputs
'
range_name = case_name & "_outputs"
Set r1 = Range(range_name)
outcnt = r1.Rows.count
ReDim itranches(1 To outcnt)


ReDim outrange(1 To outcnt) As Range
For i = 1 To outcnt
 range_name = r1.Cells(i, 1)
 If range_name <> "" Then

    Set outrange(i) = ws2.Range(range_name)

    itranches(i) = CInt(Mid(range_name, 9, 1))
 Else
   outcnt = i - 1
   GoTo ToInputs
 End If
Next i
'
' drive scenarios
'
ToInputs:
range_name = case_name & "_inputs"

Set r1 = Range(range_name)
m = r1.Columns.count
n = r1.Rows.count
varcnt = m
scencnt = n
```

```
ReDim scenecnt(1 To varcnt) As Integer
'
' set up a counter to count the scenarios for each variable
'
For i = 1 To m
 scenecnt(i) = 0
 For j = 2 To n
  If r1.Cells(j, i) <> "" Then
    scenecnt(i) = scenecnt(i) + 1
  Else
    Exit For
  End If
  Next j
 Next i


'
' For each input find the range and store it
'
ReDim r3(1 To m) As Range
ReDim vcount(1 To m) As Integer
For j = 1 To varcnt ' no of variables
 range_name = r1.Cells(1, j)
 Set r3(j) = Range(range_name)
 vcount(j) = 1
Next j

k = 1

l = varcnt - 2 ' is the excess variables above 2

'write columns and rows
If l > 0 Then
While l > 0
  While vcount(l) <= scenecnt(l)

  For a = 1 To l
    case_string = r1.Cells(1, a) & " = " & r1.Cells(vcount(a) + 1, a)


    For b = 1 To outcnt
      [scen_out].Offset(k - 2, xoffset + 1) = Range(case_name &
"_outputs").Cells(b, 2)
      [scen_out].Offset(k - 1, xoffset) = case_string

    For i = 1 To scenecnt(m - 1) ' scenario count
      [scen_out].Offset(k, i + 1 + xoffset) = r1.Cells(i + 1,
m - 1)
    Next i
    For j = 1 To scenecnt(m) 'scenario count
      [scen_out].Offset(j + k, 1 + xoffset) = r1.Cells(j + 1, m)
    Next j
```

```
    xoffset = xoffset + scenecnt(m - 1) + 2
  Next b
  Next a

  xoffset = 0
  vcount(l) = vcount(l) + 1
  k = k + n + 2
  Wend
l = l - 1
Wend
Else
  For b = 1 To outcnt
  [scen_out].Offset(k - 2, xoffset + 1) = Range(case_name &
"_outputs").Cells(b, 2)
  [scen_out].Offset(k - 1, xoffset) = case_string
    For i = 1 To scenecnt(m)  'scenario count
      [scen_out].Offset(k, i + 1 + xoffset) = r1.Cells(i + 1, m - 1)
     Next i
    For j = 1 To scenecnt(m) 'scenario count
      [scen_out].Offset(j + k, 1 + xoffset) = r1.Cells(j + 1, m)
    Next j

    xoffset = xoffset + scenecnt(m - 1) + 2
  Next b
End If
'
' generate and calculate scenarios
'Reset counters
'
For i = 1 To varcnt
 vcount(i) = 1
 r3(i).Cells(1, 1) = r1.Cells(vcount(i) + 1, i)
Next i
'set initial values
xoffset = scenecnt(m - 1) + 2 ' scenario count
yoffset = 1
totalscenes = 1
For i = 1 To varcnt
 totalscenes = totalscenes * scenecnt(i)
Next i

k = 1

'
' calculate scenarios
'
While k <= totalscenes

'Application.Calculate
```

```
' write output
For j = 1 To outcnt

  If doAuxillaryProcessing Then

  If aux_subroutine = "Solve4DM" Then
   Solve4DM itranches(j)
  End If
  Else
  'Calculate scenarios
    If Application.Calculation = xlCalculationManual
And solved = False Then
      solved = True
      Application.Calculate
    End If
  End If

    [scen_out].Offset(yoffset + vcount(varcnt), (j - 1) * xoffset +
vcount(varcnt - 1) + 1) = outrange(j).Cells(1, 1)
  Next j
'
k = k + 1
solved = False
'


' set next variable
For i = varcnt To 1 Step -1
  vcount(i) = vcount(i) + 1

  If vcount(i) <= scenecnt(i) Then '
   r3(i).Cells(1, 1) = r1.Cells(vcount(i) + 1, i)
   If (i = varcnt - 2) Then
     yoffset = yoffset + scencnt + 2
    End If
    Exit For
  Else
  vcount(i) = 1
  r3(i).Cells(1, 1) = r1.Cells(vcount(i) + 1, i)
  If (i = varcnt - 2) Then
    yoffset = yoffset + scencnt * (m - 1) + 2
  End If
 End If
Next i
'set initial values
Wend
End Sub
```

Running the Equity Scenario produces two columns of two-dimensional results which can
then be presented either in a document or in graphical form (Table 16.1).

Table 16.1 Equity scenario

Duration Tranche_6_Price = 0.8	0.800	0.700	0.600	0.500	IRR Tranche_6_Price = 0.8	80.000%	70.000%	60.000%	50.000%
-	2.510	2.510	2.510	2.510	0.000%	24.650%	24.650%	24.650%	24.650%
0.010	2.491	2.474	2.456	2.435	1.000%	23.201%	22.459%	21.687%	20.878%
0.020	2.467	2.432	2.532	2.778	2.000%	21.716%	20.063%	17.576%	14.851%
0.030	2.439	2.623	3.114	3.798	3.000%	20.167%	16.447%	12.444%	7.926%
0.040	2.526	3.072	3.978	5.261	4.000%	17.948%	12.786%	6.929%	1.771%
0.050	2.712	3.628	5.078	6.728	5.000%	15.592%	8.746%	2.216%	-4.402%

Duration Tranche_6_Price = 0.85	0.800	0.700	0.600	0.500	IRR Tranche_6_Price = 0.85	80.000%	70.000%	60.000%	50.000%
-	2.787	2.787	2.787	2.787	0.000%	22.730%	22.730%	22.730%	22.730%
0.010	2.767	2.749	2.730	2.710	1.000%	21.299%	20.563%	19.797%	18.995%
0.020	2.741	2.707	2.850	3.148	2.000%	19.831%	18.195%	15.836%	13.329%
0.030	2.712	2.957	3.481	4.218	3.000%	18.298%	14.792%	10.825%	6.630%
0.040	2.832	3.432	4.403	5.751	4.000%	16.205%	11.153%	5.695%	0.860%
0.050	3.055	4.025	5.553	7.288	5.000%	14.017%	7.379%	1.270%	-5.085%

Duration Tranche_6_Price = 0.9	0.800	0.700	0.600	0.500	IRR Tranche_6_Price = 0.9	80.000%	70.000%	60.000%	50.000%
-	3.073	3.073	3.073	3.073	0.000%	21.023%	21.023%	21.023%	21.023%
0.010	3.053	3.036	3.019	3.001	1.000%	19.610%	18.881%	18.123%	17.338%
0.020	3.029	3.004	3.191	3.519	2.000%	18.158%	16.558%	14.321%	11.862%
0.030	3.006	3.316	3.858	4.646	3.000%	16.659%	13.360%	9.385%	5.467%
0.040	3.158	3.799	4.835	6.246	4.000%	14.651%	9.687%	4.584%	0.030%
0.050	3.423	4.430	6.032	7.849	5.000%	12.629%	6.152%	0.407%	-5.713%

Duration Tranche_6_Price = 0.95	0.800	0.700	0.600	0.500	IRR Tranche_6_Price = 0.95	80.000%	70.000%	60.000%	50.000%
-	3.373	3.373	3.373	3.373	0.000%	19.491%	19.491%	19.491%	19.491%
0.010	3.360	3.346	3.331	3.318	1.000%	18.116%	17.393%	16.643%	15.848%
0.020	3.340	3.327	3.560	3.882	2.000%	16.682%	15.080%	12.996%	10.427%
0.030	3.322	3.677	4.244	5.082	3.000%	15.179%	11.966%	8.093%	4.416%
0.040	3.509	4.176	5.273	6.744	4.000%	13.303%	8.370%	3.577%	-0.732%
0.050	3.763	4.841	6.515	8.411	5.000%	11.138%	5.043%	-0.383%	-6.294%

Duration Tranche_6_Price = 1	0.800	0.700	0.600	0.500	IRR Tranche_6_Price = 1	80.000%	70.000%	60.000%	50.000%
-	3.692	3.692	3.692	3.692	0.000%	18.129%	18.129%	18.129%	18.129%
0.010	3.679	3.665	3.660	3.657	1.000%	16.757%	16.026%	15.297%	14.529%
0.020	3.663	3.669	3.912	4.254	2.000%	15.335%	13.781%	11.628%	9.134%
0.030	3.658	4.026	4.639	5.523	3.000%	13.872%	10.585%	6.925%	3.459%
0.040	3.861	4.561	5.716	7.245	4.000%	11.974%	7.179%	2.657%	-1.435%
0.050	4.112	5.259	7.001	8.974	5.000%	9.791%	4.032%	-1.113%	-6.835%

The assumptions are

- run to maturity;
- vary recovery rate from 80% to 50%;
- initial weighted average spread of 285 bps;
- constant default rates from 0% to 5%.

The output recorded is the dollar duration and the equity IRR.

Another scenario provided is named Equity2, which varies the initial portfolio weighted average spread around 285 bps plus or minus approximately 10%, i.e. 255 and 315 bps.

The assumptions are

- run to maturity;
- vary the initial spread at the original covenant weighted average spread plus or minus 10%;

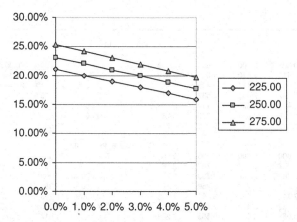

Figure 16.2   Results of modelled transaction

- recovery 80% and instantaneous;
- constant default rates from 0% to 5%.

   The results for the modelled transaction for "Equity scenario 2" are shown in Table 16.2 and Figure 16.2.

   Figure 16.1 shows the results for just the first block of data, i.e. with a price of 80%.

   The final scenario calculates the discount margin and yield of the senior tranche under constant default and recovery scenarios. The main difference here is that the scenario runs a routine to resolve for the discount margin under the applied default and recovery rate. As can be seen from the yield or IRR table, because of changes to the weighted average life the yield can change without a loss being incurred, which can give false information with regard to the sensitivity (Table 16.3).

16.3.2 Extending the number scenarios

The lookup combo bar has a dynamic range to populate the list in cell B1. The range is called "Scenario_Lookup" and, in this case, refers to cells AC1:AC100. It would be relatively easy to extend these by typing a different scenario name. The formula for the dynamic range is `"=OFFSET(AC1, 0,0,COUNT(AC1:AC100),1)"`, and is entered into the Insert->Name-> Define menu option, from the insert menu. After selecting the name, the assumptions, inputs and outputs range have to be created. This is done by copying a previous block and editing it. Finally, the ranges have to be named again using Insert->Name->Define menu, and should be consistently named, XXX-Assumptions, XXX-Inputs, XXX-Outputs, and XXX-Routine, where XXX is the scenario name. The supplied examples provide the ranges that need to be defined.

16.4 FUNDAMENTAL CASH FLOW ANALYSIS

Investors wishing to make their own analysis of a CDO should examine the default and recovery assumptions carefully. A fundamental analysis examines the losses and assigns a probability to each loss scenario. The following is a discussion on alternatives to using traditional scenario

Table 16.2   Results of modelled transaction

	F	G	H	I	J	K
13						
14			**IRR**			
15		**Tranche_6_Price = 0.8**				
16				255.000	285.000	315.000
17			-	0.202	0.245	0.293
18			0.010	0.163	0.207	0.257
19			0.020	0.104	0.147	0.195
20			0.030	0.040	0.078	0.123
21			0.040	(0.016)	0.017	0.053
22			0.050	(0.066)	(0.044)	(0.006)
23			**IRR**			
24		**Tranche_6_Price = 0.85**				
25				255.000	285.000	315.000
26			-	0.186	0.226	0.270
27			0.010	0.148	0.189	0.235
28			0.020	0.090	0.132	0.175
29			0.030	0.030	0.065	0.107
30			0.040	(0.024)	0.008	0.041
31			0.050	(0.072)	(0.051)	(0.014)
32			**IRR**			
33		**Tranche_6_Price = 0.9**				
34				255.000	285.000	315.000
35			-	0.172	0.209	0.250
36			0.010	0.135	0.172	0.214
37			0.020	0.077	0.117	0.158
38			0.030	0.021	0.054	0.092
39			0.040	(0.030)	(0.000)	0.031
40			0.050	(0.078)	(0.057)	(0.022)
41			**IRR**			
42		**Tranche_6_Price = 0.95**				
43				255.000	285.000	315.000
44			-	0.160	0.194	0.232
45			0.010	0.122	0.158	0.197
46			0.020	0.066	0.103	0.143
47			0.030	0.012	0.043	0.079
48			0.040	(0.036)	(0.008)	0.022
49			0.050	(0.083)	(0.063)	(0.029)
50			**IRR**			
51		**Tranche_6_Price = 1**				
52				255.000	285.000	315.000
53			-	0.149	0.180	0.216
54			0.010	0.110	0.144	0.181
55			0.020	0.055	0.090	0.130
56			0.030	0.005	0.034	0.067
57			0.040	(0.042)	(0.015)	0.013
58			0.050	(0.088)	(0.069)	(0.035)
59						

Table 16.3 Yield (IRR) table

A_DM

A_DM	80%	70%	60%	50%
0.0%	75.00	75.00	75.00	75.00
5.0%	75.00	75.00	75.00	75.00
10.0%	75.00	75.00	75.00	75.00
15.0%	75.00	75.00	75.00	75.00
20.0%	75.00	75.00	75.00	75.00
25.0%	75.00	75.00	75.00	75.00
30.0%	75.00	75.00	75.00	75.00
35.0%	75.00	75.00	75.00	(3.00)
40.0%	75.00	75.00	75.00	(131.86)
45.0%	75.00	75.00	47.06	(245.39)

A WAL

	80.00%	70.00%	60.00%	50.00%
0.00%	8.50	8.50	8.50	8.50
5.00%	8.58	8.59	8.54	8.45
10.00%	8.56	8.41	8.32	8.25
15.00%	8.48	8.35	8.30	7.60
20.00%	8.57	8.37	7.24	5.70
25.00%	8.26	7.35	5.56	4.80
30.00%	7.51	6.06	4.30	4.33
35.00%	7.04	5.26	3.89	4.63
40.00%	5.99	3.91	3.32	5.10
45.00%	4.26	2.70	3.43	5.62

A_IRR

	80.00%	70.00%	60.00%	50.00%
0.00%	5.24%	5.24%	5.24%	5.24%
5.00%	5.25%	5.25%	5.24%	5.24%
10.00%	5.25%	5.24%	5.23%	5.23%
15.00%	5.25%	5.24%	5.24%	5.19%
20.00%	5.25%	5.24%	5.17%	5.03%
25.00%	5.25%	5.20%	5.04%	4.96%
30.00%	5.22%	5.12%	4.90%	4.92%
35.00%	5.21%	5.06%	4.86%	4.08%
40.00%	5.16%	4.91%	4.79%	2.70%
45.00%	5.02%	4.65%	4.49%	1.51%

analysis. The alternatives are usually more demanding with regard to computation and analysis. The authors have regularly used some or all of the following techniques but the computational requirements currently exceed the capacity of a purely Excel-based model. However, this may not be the case in the future, so a discussion (with examples) is still merited.

In order to perform a fundamental cash flow analysis the following information is required:

- asset cash flows (or a proxy for them);
- rates (interest and currency (if required);
- timing and severity of defaults;
- analysis of haircuts (if applicable); and
- call analysis.

16.4.1 Cash flows

Cash flows can be generated from the *Complex Warehouse Model* using the initial portfolio. Dealing with reinvestment is also worth considering here.

16.4.2 Rates

Rates can be run on a forward basis, deterministically or simulated using single- or multi-factor models. The authors have currently only utilized single-factor Cox-Ingersoll-Ross (CIR) style models, and usually have only done so to determine period rates and prices for assets. A more thorough approach would adopt a multi-factor curve approach in order to determine the forward value of interest rate derivatives.

16.4.3 Default risk

The main assumptions required to perform a weighted average probability analysis are:

- default probability;
- correlation;
- loss given defaults.

16.4.3.1   Default probability

Default probability (PD) can be determined by:

- prices/spreads (if they are liquid);
- rating idealized losses/recoveries; or
- historical performance (internal ratings).

Credit risk is typically broken down into expected loss (EL) and unexpected loss. Expected loss is typically defined as PD × LGD (loss given default), or PD × (1-Recovery). Accordingly, PDs can be estimated from ELs by assuming an LGD. This is similar to the approach taken when performing a Moody's rating analysis. Additionally, if the portfolio is bar-belled with regard to credit quality it may make sense to break up the pools and analyse them separately.

16.4.3.2 Correlation

Correlation[3] can be estimated from a number of sources:

- corporate obligors can be estimated from equity price, i.e., implied asset correlation;
- CDS spread co-movement;
- rating movement particularly for ABS/structured finance assets;
- correlation in losses/delinquencies and prepayments, particularly for consumer finance assets;
- for CMBS correlations, corporate correlations of the underlying lessee could be applied.

16.4.3.3 Default timing

Default timing can be generated by:

- using deterministic patterns, such as the tower patterns used in the rating agency approaches;
- selectively defaulting the worst credits; this approach is quite often used by traders to quickly evaluate secondary positions;
- outputs from rating agency models such as CDOROM™ and CDOEvaluator™, can produce both default distributions and individual simulations runs as outputs that can be utilized by investors to analyse portfolios and may be used by the agencies as a supplementary form of analysis;
- simulation via transition matrixes; and
- simulation via time to default models.

16.4.3.4 Methods for determining default

Defaulting the portfolio with probability assumptions can be performed in several ways, including:

(a) a modified BET or correlated BET analysis;
(b) actuarial analysis;
(c) single period Monte Carlo simulations either from the aggregate loss distribution or individual runs;
(d) multi-period Monte Carlo simulations to simulate transition.

Approaches (a), (b) and (c) require a process for timing of loss as well. Approached (c) and (d) will generate times to default as well.

16.4.4 Cohorts/transition matrices

A further refinement on a single weighted average point estimate is to examine cohort transition performance. For example, each year Moody's publishes various studies with regard to credit performance (typically at least one for corporate obligors and another for structured finance issuers) which detail rating transition by year and type of issuer. That is, Moody's will bucket a particular set of issuers by type and year of issue and then track their performance

---

[3] See "Moody's Revisits Its Assumptions Regarding Corporate Default (and Asset) Correlations for CDOs", Moody's Investors Services, 30 November 2004.

until one of two events occur: maturity or default. Maturity is typically recorded as rating withdrawn, although it may also include corporate events such as merger or (less often) a rating withdrawn request. Moody's will then typically provide a long-term average of the cohorts' performance and sometimes also idealize them by excluding outlier technical defaults, such as the Texaco/Getty Oil defaults in the 1980s.

Before using the rating agency models it is wise to check the licensing arrangements.

16.5 USING RATING AGENCY MODELS

16.5.1 Using CDOROM™

CDOROM™ allows the user to override assumptions such as correlation, probability of default can be adjusted via notching or adjusting ratings, and recoveries can be either fixed or random with the random correlation parameter also adjustable. Although at the time of writing Moody's is not using CBET for corporate credit CDO (i.e. CLOs), it is being used in conjunction with the CBET for structured finance transactions.

It is possible to use CDOROM™ in several ways, including CBET analysis, loss distribution analysis and individual simulations.

It is also possible to have CDOROM™ produce an equivalent MAC (Moody's Asset Correlation) number and the associated default probabilities. The CDOROM™ xla has a function called CBETMAC() to generate default probabilities from a correlated binomial distribution. These probabilities can then be used to evaluate the expected loss over the life of the transaction. This could then be equated to a rating and used to infer a price from a CDO spread curve. When examining cash flows it is important to check the timeliness of the payment, such that the payment frequency and reliability is compatible with the rating (e. g., an Aa2 rating pays interest timely). Even if the losses are comparable to a rating of Aa2, if it is not paying timely it is likely to be downgraded. As CBET analysis does not have a timing assumption, typically tower patterns are selected.

The next level analysis is to select the "Stats/No Data", Output File option on the calculation sheet. This produces a probability loss distribution, graduated in 0.1% increments, from 0% to 100%. This can be used instead of a binomial analysis, by evaluating the default of the obligor amounts and comparing them to the probability of default. Timing is not provided so a timing assumption, as for CBET analysis, is required.

Finally by selecting the "Stats/Full Data.txt" option on the Calculation worksheet, the application will write the results of each simulation to a text file with the name and location as specified in cells C394, the "DataFile_Location.Refdata" named range on the RefData worksheet. Output for the full data will be rows of space separated data looking something like

$$\text{xx yy (z)z.zzzzz (a)a 0.bbbbbb}$$

where "xx" is the simulation number, "yy" is the antithetic variable (i.e., another simulation), the field described by the "zs" is the time to default as years and fractions of years, the "a" column is the asset number and the number described by "b" is the recovery rate. This default information can be fed into the *Complex Warehouse Model* to generate the coupon vector, default vector and recovery amounts which can be fed into the *Cash Flow Model with Simulation Controls*. The results can be averaged as a uniform distribution, i.e., one to the number of simulations. The reader should be warned that the file produced by this option can be rather large and the authors suggest reducing the number of simulations in the range of 25,000 to 50,000.

This approach can be used by Moody's, particularly in evaluating cross-currency transactions where the number of parameters that require sensitivity analysis can be quite large. For example, on a European CLO with three currencies, 50 diversity would require$186 \times 30 \times 50 \times 3 \times$ (number of tranches), different scenarios.

One issue to deal with in simulation of cash flow CDOs is that of reinvestment. How does the simulation deal with new, unknown obligors, with regard to default risk, correlation and recovery? S&P has chosen to overcome this by effectively extending the maturity of assets that mature before the end of the reinvestment period by the same initial time to maturity increment until the reinvestment period is exceeded. It may be simpler to explain by way of an example. Suppose a loan is scheduled to mature in 1.5 years into a 5-year reinvestment period, the S&P approach would assume the asset did not mature until year 6, i.e., effectively the manager has reinvested in the same asset four times, at inception, 1.5 years, 3 years and 4.5 years. Typically, even for cash flow CDOs that utilize CDOROM^{TM}, Moody's use parameters in a BET or CBET analysis that reflect the maximum covenanted maturity, spread and default probability related to covenanted maturity. The S&P approach may be adopted by Moody's if and when they ever use a CDOROM^{TM} approach to analyse CLOs.

16.5.2 Using S&P CDO Evaluator^{TM}

The S&P CDO Evaluator^{TM4} has similar capabilities to override the default rating agency analysis and for users to provide their own inputs for correlation, default and recovery. The correlation inputs are on the **Correlation Assumptions Sheet**. Although S&P's CDO Evaluator^{TM} can produce a cross correlation matrix, there is no ability to override correlations at the individual obligor, but at broad levels in both intra- and inter-industry sectors, and different values both national, regional and inter-regional for each of the major sectors: corporate, ABS, CDO, Muni (municipals) and SME (small and medium enterprise loans). There also exist overrides by industry codes. These are usually used to provide direct overrides for "troubled assets". If there is a requirement to analyse a particular obligor or small set of obligors, then by assigning an unused industry category it is possible to provide overrides at group or obligor level.

Default rate assumptions are input in the **Default Tables Sheet**, which allows the user to override by rating, sector, maturity, and the default probabilities for corporate obligors, CDOs, ABS, Munis and SMEs. There is no need to worry about changes to these inputs affecting future rating applications, as S&P have thoughtfully provided reset buttons for all inputs, as well as on a sector by sector approach. Recovery assumptions can either be fixed point estimates or simulated via a beta function. The probability assumptions are summarized by seniority in the capital structure, instrument type and region/country on the **Recovery Assumptions Sheet**. The assumptions provided are for corporate and sovereign obligor and are typically used in a beta function with probability and standard deviation inputs. ABS and CDO recoveries tend to be fixed estimates. To override the default or correlation assumptions, the "Custom" radio button must be selected with running the simulations, i.e., when SDR/SLR choice is selected from the main menu, the user has the opportunity to override the radio buttons.

The output of the S&P CDO Evaluator^{TM} can produce a wide range of statistics and the detail on the portfolio. There are two places to select the outputs that are produced: in the "Run SDR/SLR", under the "Scenario Loss Rates" menu and the "Simulation Options" menu. In the

---

[4] The authors are referencing Standard and Poor's CDO Evaluator version 5.0.

"Scenario Loss Rates", in the "Compute/Display" section, the user can select the "Collateral Default Correlation", "Asset Distribution", "Asset Distribution (by rating)", "Asset Distribution (by Rating/Country)", "Asset Distribution (by Rating/Maturity)", "Portfolio Default Distribution", and "DM, VM, CM and WA Rating", the default measure, volatility measure, correlation measure and weighted average rating, which create outputs within the Excel workbook. There are button options under the "Simulations Options" to produce text files in the CDOEvaluator[TM] program Output director, for time to default (option "Generate Time to Default Table"), which generates "Time to DefaultTable.txt". A loss table option ("Loss Table") produces "LossTable.txt"; a loss given default (LGD) option ("Generate Loss Given Default File") produces "LGDOutput.txt". Other options include:

- "Create Unsorted Default Distribution" which produces "DefaultVectorUnsorted.txt";
- "Create Sorted Default Distribution" which produces "DefaultVector.txt";
- "Create Default Distribution File" which creates "CDOTransaction_DefaultDistribution. csv"; and
- "Create a Default Histogram" option which produces "DefaultHistogram.txt".

In addition there are options to produce the correlation matrix and a simulation convergence file.

The most interesting files are the default distribution. This is the same information as presented on the "Default Distribution" tab in the Excel workbook, which shows the default distribution, cumulative default distribution and the inverse cumulative default distribution, in 2% increments. It also shows the time to default file which shows the default time per simulation for each obligor, as a column per obligor, and a time to default per simulation by rows. Default times longer than the transaction maturity are effectively not defaults.

It is possible to analyse the portfolio two ways: (a) by using the default distribution, with a suitable default time profile; or (b) by applying the default times from the default time file.

16.5.3 Recovery rate

There have been ongoing and extensive studies[5] on the relationship between default rates and recovery rates for corporate bond obligors. These studies have been replicated by the rating agencies for other asset types such as leverage loans.

What they tend to show is the inverse relationship between the annual default rate and the realized recovery rate. This is hardly surprising as there are a limited number of purchasers of companies or their assets in default (usually referred to as "vulture investors"). As default rates rise, the opportunity cost of deploying capital to purchase defaulted assets means that the premium (in the form of projected yield) rises, and hence the price falls. Most approaches to modelling stochastic recovery rates revolve around the use of inverse beta probability distributions. Altman *et al.*, Moody's and Standard and Poor's have published regression analysis linking the annual default rate to the recovery rate. However, what is less apparent is where and by how much the variance of recovery changes. It would seem likely that, as the average loss given default increases, the variance and dispersion would also increase.

---

[5] Ibid. Altman *et al.*

16.5.4 Modelling

The *Complex Warehouse Model* has been prepared to provide the following:

- templates for easy loading into CDO Evaluator™ and CDOROM™;
- additional lookups for support those sheets on the reference sheets;
- additional inputs on the portfolio sheet;
- a sheet to load default simulations from the agency tools;
- a sheet to produce cash flows from the assets including defaults from default times;
- an interface to the curve sheet to enable forwards to be readily produced; and
- a sheet which can drive the main *Cash Flow Model with Simulation Controls*.

16.5.5 CDO Evaluator™ Template

It is quite common for both modellers and managers to run versions of the CDO Evaluator™ on a regular basis. Therefore it is convenient to create a template to take information from the **Inputs and Portfolio Sheet** and format it in such a way that it can be easily copied and pasted to the **S&P Evaluator Template Sheet**.

The required inputs for the input sheet include:

- **Obligor ID** on the **S&P Evaluator Template Sheet** is linked directly to column B, row 101 onwards in the **Inputs and Portfolio Sheet**.
- **Asset Type** is the link to the industry/asset codes in cells AN101 to AN200, on the **Inputs and Portfolio Sheet**, linked via the **Reference Sheet** codes.
- **S&P Credit Rating** is linked to cells in column AG on the **Inputs and Portfolio Sheet**.
- **Maturity Date**: in line with S&P guidance, this should be extended in managed transactions to take into account the effect of reinvestment. There is a switch in cell C9 on the **Inputs and Portfolio Sheet** to enable the use of either the original maturities or the extended maturities to extend beyond the end of the reinvestment period. For example, if the original maturity of the asset is 3 years, and there is a 5-year reinvestment period, then S&P would have the asset modelled as a 6 year asset, i.e., it has been reinvested into 1 time at expiry. Cell C9 in the true state uses the original maturity date, and in the false state selects the extended maturity.
- **Current Balance** is linked to the balance in cells in column L on the **Inputs and Portfolio Sheet**.
- **Assumed Recovery** and **Assumed Recovery Standard Deviation** are overrides mainly used for non-corporate borrowers. The seniority is a lookup driven from the asset type in column F (i.e., Senior Secured Loan, Second Lien, Structured Finance Bond), which in turn determines via a lookup on the **Reference Sheet** the seniority (1 = "Senior Secured", 2 = "Senior Unsecured", 3 = "Subordinate").
- **Seniority**: this is, by way of the example in cell I4, a lookup using the formula `"=VLOOKUP('Inputs and Portfolio'!F101,SP_Sec_Type,2,FALSE)"`, which converts the asset class in the **Inputs and Portfolio Sheet** into a seniority level.
- **Country Code** and **Sovereign Foreign Currency Rating**: the Country Code is effectively the international dialling code (i.e., what you would need to dial to connect to a telephone subscriber in a particular country). For example, cell J4 contains the formula for a lookup from `"=VLOOKUP('Inputs and Portfolio'!AH101,Country_Codes,3,FALSE)"`, which converts the country name in column AH of the **Inputs and Portfolio Sheet** to the

appropriate country code. The Sovereign Foreign Currency Rating for the country is taken directly from the column AJ on the **Inputs and Portfolio Sheet**.

A copy/paste value operation can be used to transfer the values to the CDO Evaluator™ Assets Sheet.

16.5.6 CDOROM™ Template

While CDOROM™ is currently not used to analyse CLOs, Moody's have stated on numerous occasions that they ultimately may do so. The inputs required for CDOROM™ are:

- **ID** is a pure ordinal number from the portfolio sheet (column B).
- **Debt Number, CUSIP, ISIN, ID Type, Org Number/ID, Mother Entity Org Number** and **Parent Entity Name** are used in conjunction with Moody's reference database, or can be made to be consistent manually for obligors not in the database or for those not using it.
- Reference Entity is taken from the Asset/Borrower Name in column C of the **Inputs and Portfolio Sheet**.
- **Amount** is the exposure at default taken from column I in the **Inputs and Portfolio Sheet**.
- **SU Rating** is the senior unsecured rating of the obligor, not to be confused with the issue rating as it might be higher or lower depending on security or subordination issues, and is linked to column I on the portfolio sheet. However, the senior unsecured rating addresses the likelihood of default of the issuer. Notching allows for the increased default stress on the portfolio.
- **Notching** is used when assets do not have ratings from Moody's.
- **RO Seniority** is related to the seniority of the rated obligation and is linked through a lookup from the asset type via, for example, `"=VLOOKUP('Inputs and Portfolio'!F101,M_Types,2,FALSE)"`.
- **Industry/ABS Code** is linked to column AL on the **Inputs and Portfolio Sheet**.
- **ISO/Country** is the ISO two-letter code linked to column AH on the **Inputs and Portfolio Sheet**.
- **EDS Trigger, CDS Trigger** and **MIR Gap** are not relevant for a cash flow CDO.

The next fields relate only to CDO and ABS obligors including CLOs:

- **Transaction Name** is linked to column CM on the **Inputs and Portfolio Sheet**.
- **Issue Date** influences the correlation numbers as it affects the vintage issues for CDOs and ABS and is linked to column CL of the **Inputs and Portfolio Sheet**.
- **Guarantor/Wrapper** is not relevant to this portfolio but is useful for mono-line insured bonds.
- **Key Agent** is the servicer for ABS and the manager for managed CDOs. This is linked to column CO on the Inputs and Portfolio Sheet.
- **% Initial Deal** and **Initial Rating** determine the recovery rate applied for structured finance assets and are linked to columns CN and L on the **Inputs and Portfolio Sheet** respectively (as there have been no downgrades).
- **Weighed Average Life**: as with S&P can be determined as the original weighed average life or the average life taking into account reinvestment which can be selected using the following formula in cell Z3, `"=IF('Inputs and Portfolio'!$C$9,'Inputs and Portfolio'!CG101,'Inputs and Portfolio'!CK101)"`, from either the original average life or the adjusted average life.

The modeller can, as before, copy/paste values from a template sheet to the portfolio sheet of CDOROM™.

16.5.7 Detailed cash flow generation sheet

The **QF Pay Assets CF Sheet** generates the cash flows for each individual asset. A horizontal layout is chosen for each asset because 10 lines are required to generate the detail for each obligor. This limitation would typically restrict the number of generated line items to 25, because of Excel's shortcomings prior to the 2007 version.

The **QF Pay Assets CF Sheet** generates the cash flows for each obligor by taking information from the portfolio sheet. Taking the first obligor as an example, column B holds the information from the portfolio sheet, described by the labels in column A. Columns D onwards hold the per payment cash flow detail as described by the labels in Column C. The inputs required from the **Inputs and Portfolio Sheet** are:

- **Asset No** is a direct index on the **Inputs and Portfolio Sheet**.
- **Notional** is addressed as an offset onto the **Inputs and Portfolio Sheet** using the following formula. For example in C5, `"=OFFSET('Inputs and Portfolio'!$B$100,C4,10)"`, i.e., it indexes the 10th column on the **Inputs and Portfolio Sheet**. Care should be used in amending the **Inputs and Portfolio Sheet** when using OFFSET() formulas, as inserting rows can upset the indexing. It is often better to put any changes at the end of the range to avoid amending the indexing formulas.
- **Previous Coupon Date** and **Next Coupon Date** are indexed from the **Inputs and Portfolio Sheet** and are calculated using the COUPPCD() and COUPNCD() formulas from the Analysis ToolPak (ATP).
- **Current Coupon** takes the fixing from column P on the **Inputs and Portfolio Sheet**.
- **Maturity** also uses the OFFSET() formula to index the values from column V on the **Inputs and Portfolio Sheet**.
- **Periods** is calculated as the difference between the valuation date in cell A1 and the maturity date; for example, cell B19 contains the formula `"=ROUND((B18-$A$1)/365.25*4,0)"`.
- **Frequency** is better described as the months between payments and is calculated as 12 divided by the payment frequency indexed from column W on the **Inputs and Portfolio Sheet**.
- **Spread** is the margin over the flowing index, in this case LIBOR, taken from column P on the **Inputs and Portfolio Sheet**.
- **Bullet** is a true or false indication, and not really used as it is assumed all obligors have a single payment at maturity. However, if there are senior structured finance obligations in the **Inputs and Portfolio Sheet** then there is potentially significant pre-payment of the obligation before the legal final maturity. In that case, usually a separate amortization sheet is utilized with the amortization profiles on it, and the percentage payments are indexed by period to pay down the obligation in principal payment row.
- **Default** takes the default time (in years) for the asset from the **Inputs and Portfolio Sheet** and converts it to the associated payment period. This is illustrated in cell B12 as, `"=ROUND(OFFSET('Inputs and Portfolio'!$B$100,B2,79)*12/B9+MAX($A$1-B4,0)/365,0)"`.

The outputs per obligor are:

- **Period** is the payment period in question and is an ordinal going out to the last payment period of the transaction.
- **Payment Dates** and **Discount Factor** are generated using EDATE() as before. However, rather than continually recalculating what is essentially static information, a macro is utilized to calculate the payment dates and the discount factors.
- **Coupon** is taken as the difference in the discount factors and the spread added, for example as in cell F7, `"=IF(F4 = 1,$C8,(E6/F6-1)*360/(F5-E5)+$C12)"`.
- **Opening Balance**, **Interest**, **Default, Principal**, **Recovery** and **Closing Balance**: a running total of opening balance, interest, defaults, repayments and closing balance is created. The recovery row is not utilized in this example but could be linked to either a fixed recovery or simulated recovery function. Opening balance is initially taken from the cell in column C, but is later determined by the prior period closing balance, i.e., cell F8 contains the formula `"=C5"`, where as cell G8 has `"=F13"`. Interest is simply the opening balance less any defaults multiplied by the interest rate and the days in the period, i.e. `"=(F8-F10)*(F5-E5)/360*F7"`, for cell F9. This spreadsheet is currently purely for floating rate instruments but can be quickly adapted to accommodate fixed rate instruments also. The default amount in the next row is taken from the default period in column B, which in turn is taken from the **Inputs and Portfolio Sheet** and converted into the effective period number by, for example, the formula in cell C14, `"=ROUND(OFFSET('Inputs and Portfolio'!$B$100,C4,79)*12/C11+MAX($C$3-C6,0)/365,0)"`, which generates the default period. The formula for recording the actual default is to compare the default period to the current period; if there is a default then it effectively reduces the principal and interest to zero from that period onwards, i.e. `"=IF(F4 = $C14,F8,0)"`, for cell F10. Finally, the closing balance is simply the opening balance less redemptions or defaults, i.e., in cell F13 there is `"=F8-F11-F10"`.

A macro, Generate_Dates, is used to generate the dates and another macro called Generate_Rates is used to generate the discount factors; the code for each is reproduced below. The macros are linked to the corresponding buttons. While originally the rates and dates were generated by formulas in the appropriate cells, this was found to add significant recalculation burden with no benefit.

```
Sub Generate_Dates()
Dim dateRange As Range
Dim portfolioRange As Range
Dim fieldNames As Range
Dim pcdDate As Double
Dim ncdDate As Double
Dim MatDate As Double
Dim payDate As Double
Dim i As Integer
Dim j As Integer
Dim k As Integer
Dim dFreq As Double
Dim nextDate As Date
'
```

```
Dim pcdOffset As Integer
Dim ncdOffset As Integer
Dim rollOffset As Integer
Dim matOffset As Integer
Dim freqOffset As Integer

Set dateRange = Worksheets("QF Pay Assets CF").Range("D2")
Set portfolioRange = Worksheets("Inputs and Portfolio").
Range("B100")
Set fieldNames = Worksheets("Inputs and Portfolio").
Range("B100:CA100")

' find offset

pcdOffset = Application.WorksheetFunction.Match("Previous Payment
Date", fieldNames, 0) - 1
ncdOffset = Application.WorksheetFunction.Match("Next Payment
Date", fieldNames, 0) - 1
matOffset = Application.WorksheetFunction.Match("Final Legal
Maturity", fieldNames, 0) - 1
rollOffset = Application.WorksheetFunction.Match("Roll Day",
fieldNames, 0) - 1
freqOffset = Application.WorksheetFunction.Match("Payment
Frequency", fieldNames, 0) - 1
i = 1
k = 1
While portfolioRange.Offset(i, 0).Value <> ""
' process all credits until a blank line
 ' get pcdDate
 pcdDate = portfolioRange.Offset(i, pcdOffset).Value
 ' get next coupon date
 ncdDate = portfolioRange.Offset(i, ncdOffset).Value
 ' get roll date
 payDate = portfolioRange.Offset(i, rollOffset).Value
 ' get Maturity
 MatDate = portfolioRange.Offset(i, matOffset).Value
 ' get frequency
 dFreq = portfolioRange.Offset(i, freqOffset).Value

j = 0
 dateRange.Offset(k, j).Value = pcdDate
j = 1
 dateRange.Offset(k, j).Value = ncdDate
j = 2
 nextDate = ncdDate
Do
 nextDate = [atpvbaen.xls].Edate(nextDate, 12 / dFreq)
' If nextDate <= MatDate Then
    dateRange.Offset(k, j).Value = nextDate
'    End If
    j = j + 1
```

```
  Loop While j <= 60

i = i + 1
k = k + 11


Wend


End Sub


Sub Generate_Rates()
Dim dateRange As Range
Dim portfolioRange As Range
Dim curveRange As Range
Dim curveDates As Range


Dim pcdDate As Double
Dim ncdDate As Double

Dim payDate As Double

Dim i As Integer
Dim j As Integer
Dim k As Integer
Dim df As Double
'


Set dateRange = Worksheets("QF Pay Assets CF").Range("D2")
Set portfolioRange = Worksheets("Inputs and Portfolio").
Range("B100")
Set curveDates = Worksheets("Curve").Range("h6:h43")
Set curveRange = Worksheets("Curve").Range("i6:k43")

i = 0
k = 2
j = 0

pcdDate = dateRange.Offset(k - 1, j).Value
While portfolioRange.Offset(i, 0).Value <> ""
' process all credits until a blank line
  ' get ncddate

j = 1
  Do
    ncdDate = dateRange.Offset(k - 1, j).Value
    df = MyexpInterp2(ncdDate, curveDates, curveRange)
    dateRange.Offset(k, j).Value = df
```

```
j = j + 1
Loop While j <= 60

i = i + 1
k = k + 11
```

```
Wend
```

```
End Sub
```

16.5.8 Curve Sheet

The rate generation function utilizes the linked curve data from the **Curve Sheet**. The linking also reduces the need for unnecessary recalculation. Data can easily be updated when and if required by using the Edit->Links commands on the Edit menu, which has sub-commands to open the linked file, update the linked file or change the linked status.

16.5.9 Collation

Two collation sheets are provided, **Qtrly Pay Assets Collated Sheet** and **Qrtly Pay Assets VBA Sheet**. The latter is the spreadsheet that is actually used, the former was included to demonstrate the collation process and to verify the VBA code was working correctly. It may be deleted if not required.

The "non-VBA" **Qtrly Pay Assets Collated Sheet** has a collation area in columns B, C, and D, a collection date range in column F and then, starting in Column G, three columns per asset to summarize interest, principal and defaults. Starting with the first asset, columns G, H, and I hold the interest by period, the principal repaid and the principal defaulted. All use a very similar function, SUMIF(), to sum collections less than the date in the collection date range in column F. For example, cell G7 contains the formula "=SUMIF(OFFSET('Qrtly Pay Assets CF'!$F$4,(G$5-1)*11+1,0,1,50),<"&$F7,OFFSET('Qrtly Pay Assets CF'!$F$4,(G$5-1)*10+5,0,1,50))-IF($E7>0,SUM(G$6:G6),0)", which indexes into the columns and sums payments less than the collection date. The last part of the formula subtracts payments collated in previous periods. The formulas for the default amounts and principal payments are the same, except the cell offset changes for the column. The total collation in, say, Column B, utilizes a simple form of tagging to conditionally sum only the interest collections. That is, above each interest payment column in row 2 is a tag, I for interest, P for principal or D for default. The collations say for interest make use of this tag with the formula "=SUMIF($G$2:$IU$2,B$4,$G7:$IU7)+...", for cell B7, the collated interest for the period. Principal and defaults are collated similarly.

The **Qrtly Pay Assets VBA Sheet** uses a similar approach and is called via the button "Collate" on the spreadsheet. The macro invoked is "Collate_payments_defaults" and is reproduced below.

```
Sub Collate_payments_defaults()
" " " " " " " " " " " " " " " " " " " " " " " " " " " " " "
' Routine to collect cashflows from the QF sheet
'
```

```vba
"""""""""""""""""""""""""""""
Dim dates() As Date
Dim interest() As Double
Dim principal() As Double
Dim defaults() As Double
'
' parameters
'
 Dim n As Integer
 Dim da As Date
 Dim ds As Date
 Dim ifreq As Integer
 Dim pDay As Integer
 '
 ' ranges
 '
Dim pRange As Range 'portfolio
Dim cRange As Range ' cashflows
Dim oRange As Range ' outputs
'
' counters
'
Dim i  As Integer
Dim j As Integer
Dim k As Integer
Dim l As Integer 'calculated index
Dim dl As Double

'
'
' read parameters
'

n = [vba_periods].Value
da = [first_date].Value
ds = da
ifreq = [vba_freq].Value

'
' redim parameters
'

ReDim dates(0 To n)
ReDim interest(0 To n)
ReDim principal(0 To n)
ReDim defaults(0 To n)

Application.Calculate
'
' Set the dates
'
```

```
i = 0
Do
 dates(i) = da
 da = [atpvbaen.xls].Edate(da, 12 / ifreq)

 i = i + 1
Loop While i <= n

Set pRange = Worksheets("Inputs and Portfolio").Range("B100")
Set cRange = Worksheets("QF Pay Assets CF").Range("d2")
Set oRange = Worksheets("Qrtly Pay Assets VBA").Range("B10")

i = 1
k = 1
j = 1
While pRange.Offset(i, 0).Value <> ""

 For j = 1 To n
  da = cRange.Offset(k, j).Value
  If da < ds Then
   l = 0
   GoTo Nextj
  Else
   dl = (da - ds) / 365.25 * ifreq
   If dl - CInt(dl) > 0.000001 Then
    l = CInt(dl + 0.5)
   Else
    l = CInt(dl)
    If da = dates(l) Then l = l + 1  'move payment into next
period if it matches record date
   End If

   If l = 0 Then l = 1
  End If
  If dates(l) < da Or dates(l - 1) > da Then
   ' search for l
   If dates(l + 1) < da Then
    While dates(l + 1) < da
     l = l + 1
    Wend
   ElseIf dates(l) > da Then
    While dates(l) > da
     l = l - 1
    Wend
   End If
  End If
  'recored data
 Nextj:
 interest(l) = interest(l) + cRange.Offset(k + 4, j).Value
 principal(l) = principal(l) + cRange.Offset(k + 6, j).Value
 defaults(l) = defaults(l) + cRange.Offset(k + 5, j).Value
```

```
  Next j
i = i + 1
k = k + 11
Wend

' now write outputs
  Set oRange = Worksheets("Qrtly Pay Assets VBA").Range("b10")
  oRange.Value = "Dates"
  oRange.Offset(0, 1).Value = "Interest"
  oRange.Offset(0, 2).Value = "Principal"
  oRange.Offset(0, 3).Value = "Defaults"
'

  For i = 0 To n
   oRange.Offset(i + 1, 0).Value = dates(i)
   oRange.Offset(i + 1, 1).Value = interest(i)
   oRange.Offset(i + 1, 2).Value = principal(i)
   oRange.Offset(i + 1, 3).Value = defaults(i)
  Next i

'

End Sub
```

16.5.10 Agency Simulations Sheet

The **Agency Simulations Sheet** loads the agency simulation data from files. The named ranges in column B determine the agency format of the data file (cell C3, or "sim_type"), the number of simulations to load (cell C4, or "no_sims" named range), the name of the file (in cell C4, via a lookup), and finally the directory in which to find it in cell (C5, or named range "fdir"). The macro, "Load_Agency_Sims", is called via the button "Load Agency Data", and will attempt to load the minimum number of simulations in the file and the available space in the worksheet. The code for macros is reproduced below.

```
Sub Load_Agency_Sims()
"""""""""""""""""""""
' Routine to collect simulation data from the Files
'
"""""""""""""""""""""
' declare variables
Dim fstring As String
Dim dstring As String
Dim nsims As Long
Dim agencyString As String
Dim fileString As String
'
' get data from the parameter block on the w/s
'
  dstring = [fdir].Value
  fstring = [fname].Value
```

```
    nsims = [no_sims].Value
    agencyString = [sim_type].Value
    fileString = dstring & fstring
'
' Call the appropriate routine
'
    If agencyString = "Moodys" Then
        Call readMoodys(fileString, nsims)
        ElseIf agencyString = "S&P" Then
      Call readSandP(fileString, nsims)
End If


End Sub

Sub readMoodys(fn As String, nsims As Long)
"""""""""""""""""""""""
' Routine to load the simulation data from a Moodys file
'
"""""""""""""""""""""""
' declare variables
Dim maxK As Long
Dim WholeLine As String
Dim lcount As Long
Dim tFields() As String
Dim i As Long
Dim j As Integer
Dim k As Long
Dim l As Long
Dim m As Long
Dim n As Long
Dim tArray() As Double


On Error GoTo endSub
n = 1000 'chunk it in blocks of 1000
ReDim tArray(n, 5)
i = 1
k = 0
l = 0
m = 0
Open fn For Input Access Read As #1

Worksheets("Agency Simulations").Range("B9:IV65536").ClearContents
[Simulation_Values].Offset(-1, m * 6 + 0).Value = "Simulation No."
[Simulation_Values].Offset(-1, m * 6 + 1).Value = "Anthithetic"
[Simulation_Values].Offset(-1, m * 6 + 2).Value = "Time to Default"
[Simulation_Values].Offset(-1, m * 6 + 3).Value = "Obligor"
[Simulation_Values].Offset(-1, m * 6 + 4).Value = "Recovery"

While Not EOF(1)
```

```
Line Input #1, WholeLine
' skip first 3 lines
If i > 3 Then

tFields = Split(WholeLine, vbTab)
j = UBound(tFields, 1)
For j = 0 To UBound(tFields, 1)
 tArray(k, j) = CDbl(tFields(j))
 If tArray(k, 0) > nsims Then
  GoTo endSub
 End If
Next j

k = k + 1
If k = 1000 Then
 For k = 0 To 999

  For j = 0 To 4
   [Simulation_Values].Offset(l * 1000 + k, m * 6 + j).Value =
   tArray(k, j)
  Next j
Next k
k = 0
l = l + 1
If l = 64 Then
 l = 0
 m = m + 1
 If m > 41 Then GoTo endSub

 [Simulation_Values].Offset(-1, m * 6 + 0).Value = "Simulation No."
 [Simulation_Values].Offset(-1, m * 6 + 1).Value = "Anthithetic"
 [Simulation_Values].Offset(-1, m * 6 + 2).Value = "Time to Default"
 [Simulation_Values].Offset(-1, m * 6 + 3).Value = "Obligor"
 [Simulation_Values].Offset(-1, m * 6 + 4).Value = "Recovery"


 End If
 End If
Else

End If
i = i + 1
Wend
endSub:
 maxK = k - 1
 For k = 0 To maxK
  For j = 0 To 4
   [Simulation_Values].Offset(l * 1000 + k, m * 6 + j).Value =
   tArray(k, j)
  Next j
 Next k
```

```
Close #1
End Sub


Sub readSandP(fn As String, nsims As Long)
""""""""""""""""""""""""""
' Routine to load the simulation data from an S&P file
"
""""""""""""""""""
' declare variables
Dim WholeLine As String
Dim lcount As Long
Dim tFields() As String
Dim tFields2() As String
Dim i As Long
Dim j As Integer
Dim k As Long
Dim l As Long
Dim m As Long
Dim n As Long
Dim tObligorArray() As Double
'
'set exit on error
'
On Error GoTo endSub
'
' initialise variables
i = 1
k = 0
l = 0
m = 0
'
' open file
'
Open fn For Input Access Read As #1
'
' Clear previous values
'
Worksheets("Agency Simulations").Range("B9:IV65536").ClearContents
'
' Read the file
'
If Not EOF(1) Then
Line Input #1, WholeLine
' skip first 3 lines
Else
 GoTo endSub
End If
'
  'Split the line as its tab delimited
  tFields = Split(WholeLine, vbTab)
```

```
 n = UBound(tFields, 1)
 ReDim tArray(0 To n)

 If Not EOF(1) Then
 Line Input #1, WholeLine
 tFields = Split(WholeLine, vbTab)
End If
'
For j = 1 To UBound(tFields, 1)
 tArray(j) = CDbl(tFields(j))
Next j
j = 1
' now skip the next n lines
While Not EOF(1) And j <= 24
 Line Input #1, WholeLine
 j = j + 1
Wend
'
' write headers
'
[Simulation_Values].Offset(-1, m * 4 + 0).Value = "Simulation No"
[Simulation_Values].Offset(-1, m * 4 + 1).Value = "Obligor"
[Simulation_Values].Offset(-1, m * 4 + 2).Value = "Default time"

k = 0
While Not EOF(1)
 Line Input #1, WholeLine
 tFields = Split(WholeLine, vbTab)

 For j = 1 To n
   If CDbl(tFields(0)) > nsims Then GoTo endSub
   If tFields(j) < 100 Then
     i = tArray(j)
     ' record the values
     [Simulation_Values].Offset(l * 1000 + k, m * 4 + 0).Value =
tFields(0)
     [Simulation_Values].Offset(l * 1000 + k, m * 4 + 1).Value =
tArray(j)
     [Simulation_Values].Offset(l * 1000 + k, m * 4 + 2).Value =
tFields(j)
     k = k + 1
     If k = 1000 Then
      k = 0
      l = l + 1
      If l = 64 Then    'move over m columns
        m = m + 1
        l = 0
        ' rewrite the headers
     [Simulation_Values].Offset(-1, m * 4 + 0).Value =
     "Simulation No"
     [Simulation_Values].Offset(-1, m * 4 + 1).Value = "Obligor"
```

```
      [Simulation_Values].Offset(-1, m * 4 + 2).Value =
      "Default time"
    If m = 64 Then GoTo endSub
   End If
  End If
 End If
Next j


Wend
endSub:

Close #1
End Sub
```

16.5.11 Driver Sheet

The **Sim_Results Sheet** is effectively the driver sheet for the *Cash Flow Model with Simulation Controls*. It basically does the following on both an individual and a range of simulations:

1. finds the default times and obligors for each run;
2. loads those default times into the default column on the portfolio sheet;
3. regenerates the cash flows by calling the "Collate_payments_defaults" routine
4. copies the result of step 3 to the simulation results area on the **collateral worksheet**;
5. runs the *Cash Flow Model with Simulation Controls*;
6. records the outputs on **the worksheet**

The inputs to the driver sheet are the:

- Model Name (cell C3);
- Model Directory (cell C4);
- Drive Principal (cell C5);
- Drive Interest (cell C6);
- Drive Default (cell C7);
- Start_Sim (cell C9);
- End_Sim (cell C10);
- simulation range (Sim Range) in the *Cash Flow Model with Simulation Controls* (cell C11);
- a named range (Model_Outputs, cells B13 to C18), which contain the name and the named range of the outputs of interest; and
- an individual simulation number (cell C19), the results of which are written to cells D13 to D18.

To operate the models, both the *Cash Flow Model with Simulation Controls* and the *Complex Warehouse Model* must be open at the same time. Currently the macros are geared to run Moody's simulations but can be readily adapted to run S&P as well. The Run Sims button calls the macro "run_moodys_sims", and records the results in cells D20 onwards. The Load Sim button will run the individual simulation number in cell B17 and record results as discussed above.

Table 16.4   Simulation controls

	A	B	C
87			
88		**Simulation Controls**	
89		Override Interest	TRUE
90		Override Principal	TRUE
91		Override Defaults	TRUE
92			
93			
94			
95			
96			

16.5.12 Modifications to the *Cash Flow Model*

There have been some changes to the *Cash Flow Model* from the previous chapters to allow generated cash flows to be applied directly to the model. Table 16.4 shows cells B92 to B99 on the **Inputs Sheet** of the main *Cash Flow Model with Simulation Controls*.

These inputs allow for the override of interest, principal and defaults on the **Collateral Sheet** in the *Cash Flow Model with Simulation Controls*.

The aggregate initial pools area on the **Collateral Sheet** has also been adjusted to switch between the generic rep line approaches to use the generated cash flows from the *Complex Warehouse Model*. For example, cell K105 which used to hold the formula `"=K205"`, now holds `"IF(OR(P_OR,D_OR),Collateral!S104,K205)"`, where "P_OR" is the principal override switch shown above and "D_OR" is similar to the default override. Similarly, the cell column M205, the default column, the formula is adjusted from `"=MIN(I218*IF(Default_Original_or_Outstanding,K$104,K218),K218+L218)"`, to `"=IF(D_OR,AV105,MIN(I205*IF(Default_Original_or_Outstanding,K$104,K205),K205+ L205))"`, for the default override. Principal cash flows are adjusted in cell P205, to `"=IF(P_OR,AU105,H205/((1-IF(B205>1,SUM(OFFSET ($H$205,0,0,B205-1,1)),0)+Epsilon))*(K205-M205))"`, to allow for principal overrides. The interest is overridden in U105, for example, to `"=IF(I_OR, Collateral!AT105,(L105+M105-N105)*(HLOOKUP (Interest_Vector,Interest _Rate_Vectors,$B105+2,FALSE)+(HLOOKUP(Init_WAS_Vector,Interest_Rate _Vectors,$B105+2,FALSE)/10000))*(D105))"`, to allow for interest income level overrides. There is also the range of cells AT104 to AV184 on the Collateral Sheet, named "Simulation Results", which is the target range for the copy from the *Complex Warehouse Model*.

16.6 TRANSITION MATRICES

16.6.1 Background

A further refinement on a single weighted average point estimate for default probability is to examine cohort transition performance. Moody's, for example, publishes annual studies with regard to credit performance (typically at least one for corporate obligors and another for structured finance issuers) which detail rating transition by year and type of issuer. For example, Moody's will bucket a particular set of issuers by type and year of issue ("a cohort"), and then track their performance until one of two events occur: maturity or default. Maturity is typically recorded as rating withdrawn, although it may also include corporate events such as merger, or less often a rating withdrawn request. Moody's will then typically provide a long-term average of the cohorts' performance and sometimes also idealize them by excluding outlier technical defaults, such as the Texaco defaults in the 1980s.

Rating agencies use transition matrices to meter their performance with regards to assignment and monitoring of issuer ratings. They typically do this on an actuarial basis by looking back at the "birth" of the rating, i.e., when it was issued and grouping ratings by vintage, type and initial rating into cohorts. Over time, these ratings will tend either to remain stable, migrate upwards (i.e., be upgraded), or migrate downwards (i.e., be downgraded) until they either mature or default. The agencies track both the default statistics and the migration statistics and use that to measure their own performance. The only major problem with this as the reader can most likely already see, is that it is a backward looking approach. Hence, if they get it wrong, it is only known after the event. Adjustments to rating methodologies therefore tend to be after the event and backward looking. It is the rating agencies' aim to do better in the future. That might be cold comfort to those investors who have bought an investment with a more volatile rating performance than expected. Looking at the performance of ratings in such publications as Moodys "Corporate Defaults, 1920-[various years]", series it can be seen that there have been several and almost regular episodes of above-average migration and default activity.

16.6.2 Generating defaults

As a first approximation to generating defaults, it is possible to apply the one year migration table and multiply it for each year to generate both migration and defaults. This is effectively 100% correlation and effectively assumes one obligor. If additional stress is desired, then rather than using the average it is possible, by looking at an individual cohort performance, to apply cohorts that have performed worse than average. However, when applied to a diversified portfolio and disparate portfolio, this could be considered too harsh and unrealistic. Hence it is more common to apply a multi-period Monte Carlo simulation to estimate the migration over the life of the CDO. The advantage of a multi-period transition matrix approach is that it will generate migration and distribution of ratings as well as defaults. As discussed in more detail below, this can be useful in accessing the risk of structural features in the transaction such as OC haircuts, EOD events and calls. Combining the ratings with a spread process such as a Cox-Ingersoll-Ross (CIR) to generate a stochastic process linked to the rating can help to estimate the value of the portfolio in liquidation, either forced or via the exercise of equity option. This approach was the one employed in the capital models used to address the market value and liquidation risk in SIVs and SIV-Lites.[6]

A basic approach is as follows:

1. obtain appropriate typical 1-year transition matrix/matrices (more than one may be required for different types of obligor, i.e., CLOs and corporates);
2. normalize the matrices to 100% to compensate for withdrawn ratings by pushing shortfall (i.e., the amount that a row does not total 100%) into the "stable" state;
3. scale the matrix/matrices (discussed further below);

---

[6] See, "The Moody's Capital Model", Moody's Investment Services, 28 January 2004.

4. convert the transition probabilities for each rating category to a cumulative normal distribution;
5. create correlation matrix;
6. create a Cholesky decomposition of the transition matrix.

For each simulation:

(a) draw a random number from a uniform distribution for each obligor;
(b) convert to a normal deviate;
(c) convert to a correlated normal deviate via a Cholesky matrix;
(d) check where normal deviate falls in the distribution;
(e) convert to the new rating; and
(f) record statistics for defaults, transitions and losses.

With heterogeneous pools, as discussed, different transition matrices may be required.

16.6.3 Evaluation

For each simulation it should be possible to apply the defaults via the ***Complex Warehouse Model*** with regard to timing and migration (i.e., to measure EOD risk or over-collateralization ratios), and record the losses and/or yields. In addition, it is possible, as discussed, to apply a forward market spread approach using a CIR to estimate future market spreads and values.

16.6.4 Importance

Many transactions incorporate haircuts to the over-collateralization ratios based upon the transition of the original credit to much lower credit ratings. These first manifested themselves in the form of CCC/Caa haircuts for CLOs. That is to say, most CLOs had very little room for CCC/Caa-rated assets initially. However, they were introduced as a mechanism to align risks between the senior and junior notes, and to dissuade the manager from reaching for yield by buying "cuspy" assets. "Cuspy" assets are those that yield more than a similarly-rated asset as they are soon expected to deteriorate in credit quality (i.e., be downgraded) but have not yet been put on watch or downgraded by the rating agencies.

CCC/Caa haircut buckets work by applying a haircut to the par value of CCC/Caa assets in excess of a maximum threshold amount. Typically a 5% bucket is the maximum amount of CCC/Caa assets permissible in a CLO before haircuts are applied. The excess notional above the threshold is subject to a haircut either at the market value or a fixed percentage. Variations of the market value haircut include haircutting at the average, the last or the worst. If no prices can be obtained, then a minimum agency recovery rate is applied, at least for a period, often zero after.

As OC haircuts are clearly advantageous to the senior classes and should act to deter the manager from buying high yielding "cuspy" assets, they were extended into investment grade structured finance CDOs and typically worked by applying fixed percentage haircuts based upon ratings to below investment grade assets. For example, these were typically 10% for BB/Ba assets, 20% for B/B assets and 50% for CCC/Caa assets or lower. However, haircuts were typically ignored by the rating agencies when evaluating and modelling the CDOs. Additionally, in some CDOs, language was added to the documents to effect an "event of default" (EOD) when certain asset-to-liability ratios were breached. Historically, these had been added for the benefit of financial guarantors and negative basis protection providers. As long as the trigger of these tests were through actual losses, i.e., excluding any haircuts for rating migration, and the threshold was above the attachment point of the tranche, then these EOD triggers had effectively no impact on the ratings. However, from 2005 through 2007, the agencies began to rate deals where migration haircuts were applied to the EOD triggers as well. This effectively implied that tranches were no longer rated to default or loss but to the point where the credit quality was lower than a threshold level, even if the underlying assets were still performing.

The effect of EOD depended typically on the type of transaction and the wording, but basically there were the following generic effects:

- soft restrictions;
- acceleration to the senior notes through a change in the priority of payments;
- liquidation; and
- counterparty or provider consequences, e. g., for derivatives or liquidity.

Soft restrictions included termination of the reinvestment period, restrictions on trading by the portfolio manager (typically restricting or forbidding discretionary sales), and termination of pro-rata payment schemes.

Acceleration (through changing the waterfall), typically diverted all cash to the senior most class/swap until it was paid off (or fully defeased in the case of an unfunded senior swap in hybrid transactions, i.e., cash was reserved in an account until it fully covered the exposure). This meant that second pay AAA/Aaa bonds and AA/Aa bonds could be potentially cut off from current payment for years, if not until the legal final maturity.

The most severe consequence was a liquidation scenario. Most cash CDOs restrict liquidation such that it can only occur if all the rated notes can be paid off. Otherwise the transaction is not rated to loss and has an implied market value risk embedded. Cash CDOs are typically rated to ultimate loss through default and do not address losses attributed to a decline in market value. However, many synthetic and hybrid transactions that were in breach of the EOD covenants provided for liquidation at the request of the controlling class to repay or terminate credit default swaps. Subordinated classes, including second and third pay AAA/Aaa bonds, consequently received very little with regard to interest and principal.

Finally, another consequence which also could prove harmful to the note holders was the potential for hedge and credit swap counterparties to terminate transactions on the occurrence of an EOD, often with significant termination payments being paid senior in the transaction waterfall to the detriment of all the note holders.

The consequence of these EOD events was a large rise in CDO defaults and/or downgrades of several notches for any transaction which had EOD events linked to collateral levels with rating haircuts. The degree of downgrade depended which of the above consequences arose, with the largest downgrades assigned to those transactions that allowed for unilateral liquidation at the behest of the controlling class, without the requirement to pay off the other rated notes.

16.6.5 Sources of transition matrices

As previously discussed, the agencies typically publish annual transition matrix studies as a demonstration of the robustness of their rating methodologies. Typically, for example in the Moody's studies, generic rating transitions are published that tend to average out transition volatility over time, but also individual cohort (by year formed) data is also presented. Typically, at least for each asset class, a 1 year transition is presented. The data usually includes a category for rating withdrawn, which usually implies that the instrument matured. These have to be factored back into the rating transition matrix, typically by adding the difference to 100% back to the leading diagonal (i.e., the stable state in the matrix).

16.6.6 Scaling the transition matrix

As discussed previously, the transition matrix usually has a 1 year transition horizon. If period by period simulation is desired, then the matrices need to be scaled accordingly to the desired fraction of a year. However, scaling matrices is not a trivial matter. The basis of the problem is taking the fractional root of the matrix.

To be considered a viable transition matrix, the row probabilities should total 100% and there should be no negative probabilities. In addition, one terminal state or absorption state is required. In order to take the fraction root of a matrix, the matrix must have a non zero determinant. One approach to scaling which the authors have used that tends to work well for semi-annual periods, and by extension to quarterly periods, is Denman and Beavers (DB) method[7] which is a matrix method using the Newtonian approximation for a square root. Another approach is to generate the eigenvalues and eigenvectors for the matrix and scale them accordingly. However, this does not always produce a viable transition matrix as negative probabilities can arise.

In order to generate the fraction root, the generic solution is to exp(1/t*log(A)). Where exp is the exponential function, log is the natural logarithm, t is the fractional root, and A is the transaction matrix, as discussed in Cheng et al.[8] This is generally only required when scaling for a high frequency sampling such as daily, weekly or monthly (typically for SIV-style capital models). The good news for less mathematical readers is that their best approach has been reproduced in Mathlab®, so purchasing a copy, while not cheap, will provide a quick method to calculate the matrix, particularly for fractions which are not a power of 2.

Even once the appropriate root of the matrix is obtained, it still may not be well conditioned as a transition matrix. The probabilities may not total 100% and there may be negative transistion probabilities. A paper by Kreinin and Sidelnikova,[9] discusses both root finding and regularization methods for transition matrices. An example is given in the *ScalingTM Model* of using the QOM, or Quasi-Optimization Method, for a year transition matrix being scaled to 6 monthly.

16.6.6.1 Example

An example is given in the *ScalingTM Model*. The initial matrix is a 1-year corporate transition matrix, already scaled to 100% per rating category. To determine the 6-month transition matrix, the square root is required. As discussed, this can be performed in a number of ways. This example will use the Denman-Beavers approximation to the square root. To find the square

---

[7] See E.D. Denman and A.N. Beavers, "The Matrix Sign Function and Computations in Systems", *Appl. Math. Comput.,* 2 (1976) pp 63–94.

[8] See S.H. Cheng, N. Higham, C.S. Kenney and A.J. Laub, "Approximating the Logarithm of a Matrix to Specified Accuracy", *SIAM Journal*, Matrix Analysis Applications, Volume 22, Number 4, pp 1112–1125.

[9] See A. Kreinin and Marina Sidelnikova, "Regularization Algorithims for Transition Matrices", *Algo Research Quarterly*, Volume 4, Numbers 1,2, March/June 2001.

root of matrix A, use:

$$Y_{k+1} = \frac{1}{2}\left(Y_k + Z_k^{-1}\right),$$

$$Z_{k+1} = \frac{1}{2}\left(Z_k + Y_k^{-1}\right)$$

$$Y_0 = A$$

$$Z_0 = I$$

where I is the identity matrix of the same order as A.

Cells C3 to T20 on the **D-B Square Root Sheet** contain the original matrix, i.e., matrix A, or Y_0. Cells W3 to AN20 on the **D-B Square Root Sheet** contain the identity matrix, i.e., matrix Z_0. Cells C22 to T39 and cells W22 to AN39 contain the first iteration of the method for Y and Z respectively. The formula in cell C22 is "`{=(C3:T20+MINVERSE(W3:AN20))*0.5}`", entered as an array formula, and it calculates the DB iteration for Y_1. Similarly, in the range W22 to AN39 is the iteration for Z_1. These iterations are repeated and within four iterations the result is converging with a difference of the order of 1e-9 between iterations.

However, the matrix has negative probabilities and consequently is not a well-conditioned transition matrix. The **QOM Sheet** performs the "Quasi-Optimization Method" as discussed by Kreinin and Sidelnikova. The following is a step-by-step use of the QOM method outlined in their paper.

Step 1: The projection of each row on the hyperplane is determined by creating first the lambdas in line with

$$\lambda = \frac{1}{n}\left(\sum_{i=1}^{n} a_i - 1\right)$$

and create for each row. Cells C3 to T20 on the **QOM Sheet** contain the scaled matrix. Cells X3 to X20 contain the calculated lambdas in line with the above equation.

Step 2: The next step is to create the projection on the hyperplane, i.e. the b_i in cells C22 to T39, in accordance with

$$b_i = a_i - \lambda$$

If the values in all the b_i vectors are non-negative then stop, otherwise proceed to step 3.

Step 3: Order each b_i in descending order using the sort function, but only as applied to each row, not to the whole matrix. Let this sorted array be a_i, a permutation of b_i that is in descending order, as in cells C41 to T58.

Step 4: Calculate the C_k in accordance with the formula below:

$$C_k = \sum_{i=1}^{k} \hat{a}_i - k\hat{a}_k$$

These are calculated in cells W41 to AN60. For example cell W42 has the formula "`=SUM($C41:D41)-X$40*OFFSET($B41,0,X$40)`".

Step 5: This step is to find the ordinal, k*, for each row, that the sum of the C_k is less than or equal to 1. This is calculated in cells A81 to A199, and the ordered numbers are presented in cells C81 to T99.

Step 6: Finally the reverse ordering is applied to generate the matrix transition. The transformation matrix is in cells C60 to T79. The ordering is found by matching each element in the original matrix to those in the ordered matrix. This ordering information is then used to reverse the conditioned matrix in Step 5. The final matrix appears in cells C103 to T120.

A final check is performed by squaring the matrix and comparing it to the original matrix, to check for differences. The squared matrix is in cells C122 to T139, the original matrix is in cells C141 to T160, and the difference is in cells C160 to T179.

16.6.6.2 *Transition matrix example*

A basic example of a transition matrix simulation is provided in the *Migration Simulation Model*. This provides a year-by-year simulation using the yearly matrix as discussed in the previous section. This can be readily scaled to six monthly by using the techniques above, or even quarterly by a repeat application of such techniques. The authors are aware that many readers may be unable to afford a high-end package such as Matlab. There are, however, good free-ware Excel XLAs available on the web, for example, MATRIX.XLA which was developed by the Foxes team at http://digilander.libero.it/foxes/index.htm. This is an XLA that performs a number of matrix functions including the exponential function. The site is unfortunately no longer active but the code is freely available for download. The authors have extended it to provide both a natural logarithm function and a DB function. This is available from the authors on request.

16.6.7 Inputs

The main inputs to the transition matrix simulation are:

- Number of years or periods (cell C2 on the **Correlation Migration Sheet**)
- Portfolio information (cells C5 to F105 on the **Correlation Migration Sheet**);
- Transition matrix (cells J5 to AA21 on the **Correlation Migration Sheet**)
- Correlation matrix input (cell C2 on the **Correlation Matrix Sheet**)

The correlation matrix assumes flat correlations between each obligor. Non-flat correlations could be used but may give rise to a non-positive definite matrix, i.e., non-invertible. Similarly to the QOM transformation for transformation matrix, there are "massaging" techniques to obtain a semi-positive definite matrix, the scope of which is beyond this book. However, all is not lost, as within the CDOROM^{TM} program, once the view/edit correlation matrix button is selected, there is a button option to make the correlation matrix positive definite.

The macro to run the simulation is called RunCorrelatedMonteCarlo. The basic algorithm is shown below:

- randomize timer;
- set up the probability thresholds;
- calculate the Cholesky matrix in order to correlate uncorrelated deviates;
- generate uncorrelated random numbers
- convert them to correlated numbers via Cholesky matrix;
- perturb the rating;
- check to see if it has migrated;
- record the ratings and losses.

```vba
Public Sub RunCorrelatedMonteCarlo()

    'on error resume next
    On Error Resume Next

    Dim i, j, k, m As Long
    'Dim inputrange() As Range
    Dim inputrange As Range
    Dim outputrange As Range
    Dim rating As Range
    Dim rLosses As Range


    Dim data() As Double
    Dim defaults() As oDefault
    Dim migration() As Double
    Static inputstring() As String
    Dim cholesky() As Double
    Dim random() As Double

    Static outputstring As String
    Static nsim As Variant
    Dim count As Long
    Dim maxCount As Long
    Static inputstringcounter As Long
    Dim stringreferences() As String
    Dim numbersim() As Long
    Dim nYears As Integer
    Dim notional As Range
    Dim maxYears As Long
    Dim maxSims As Long
    Dim recovery As Range
    Dim migrationOut As Range

    Dim letter() As Integer
    Dim zthreshold() As Double
    Dim defcnt As Double

    ReDim losses(1 To [CNYears].Value)


    Set rating = Range("CNRatings")
    Set rLosses = Range("CLosses")

    Set inputrange = Range("CCredits")
    Set notional = Range("CNotionals")
    Set recovery = Range("CRecovery")
    maxCount = WorksheetFunction.Max(inputrange.Rows.count,
inputrange.Columns.count)
    ReDim inputstring(1 To maxCount)
'
```

```
  count = 0
  nYears = [CNYears].Value

    count = count + 1
    'redimension array
    If count > UBound(inputstring, 1) Then
            ReDim Preserve inputstring(0 To UBound(inputstring, 1)
+ 1)
    End If
    'set input range and put string

    inputstring(count) = "'" + inputrange.Worksheet.Name + "'!" +
inputrange.Offset(count, 0).Address

  'set output range
  Set outputrange = inputrange.Worksheet.Range("P30")
  Set migrationOut = inputrange.Worksheet.Range("V30")

    outputstring = "'" + outputrange.Worksheet.Name + "'!" +
outputrange.Address


    'set number of simulations
    nsim = Application.InputBox(prompt:="Input number of
simulations", Default:=nsim, Type:=81)

    'redimension data storing array
    count = 0


  ReDim data(1 To nsim, 1 To maxCount, 1 To nYears)

  ReDim numbersim(1 To nsim, 1 To 1)
  ReDim stringreferences(1 To 1, 1 To maxCount)
  ReDim migration(1 To nYears, 1 To 18)
  ReDim letter(1 To maxCount)
  ReDim random(1 To maxCount)

    'freeze screen
    'Application.ScreenUpdating = False

    'now do montecarlo
    Randomize Timer

    StandardizedAssetThreshold [transitionmatrix], zthreshold()

    'calculate cholesky matrix
    CholeskyMatrix cholesky(), [correlationmatrix]

    For i = 1 To nsim
```

```
    'increment counter and shock sheets and set status bar
    count = 0
    Application.Calculate
    Application.StatusBar = "Percentage simulation complete:
" & WorksheetFunction.Round(100 * i / nsim, 1) & " %"
    'put data into numbersim array
    numbersim(i, 1) = i


    Simulate random(), cholesky()


  For k = 1 To maxCount
  letter(k) = rating.Cells(k + 1, 1).Value


  For j = 1 To nYears
     ' pertub rating
   letter(k) = FindNewRating(letter(k), zthreshold(), random(k))
   migration(j, letter(k)) = migration(j, letter(k)) +
notional(k, 1).Value
    ' defaulted?
    data(i, k, j) = letter(k)
   If letter(k) = UBound(zthreshold(), 2) Then
    'has defaulted
    losses(j) = losses(j) + notional(k, 1).Value * (1 -
recovery(k, 1))
    defcnt = defcnt + 1
    ReDim Preserve defaults(defcnt)
    defaults(defcnt).period = j
    defaults(defcnt).obligor = k
    defaults(defcnt).nominal = notional(k, 1).Value
    defaults(defcnt).sim = i
    Exit For ' do not count losses again
  End If


  count = count + 1




Next j
     'stringreferences(1, k) = inputrange.Worksheet.Name +
"Credit " + inputrange.Cells(k, 1).Value
     stringreferences(1, k) = "Credit " & inputrange.
Cells(k, 1).Value
  Next k

Next i


  count = nYears * nsim
```

```
maxSims = 2 ^ 16 - 2 ^ 5
If count > 2 ^ 16 - 32 Then
    maxYears = count / nsim
End If
count = 0
outputrange.Worksheet.Select

'summarise defaults
For i = 1 To defcnt
   outputrange(i, 0).Value = defaults(i).sim
   outputrange(i, 1).Value = defaults(i).period
   outputrange(i, 2).Value = defaults(i).obligor
   outputrange(i, 3).Value = defaults(i).nominal
Next i
'summarise losses

For i = 1 To nYears
  rLosses.Offset(i, 0).Value = losses(i) / nsim
Next i
'summarise migration

For i = 1 To nYears
  For j = 1 To 18
   migrationOut(i, j).Value = migration(i, j) / nsim
  Next j
Next i


 'unfreeze screen + status bar
  Application.ScreenUpdating = True
  Application.StatusBar = False

End
```

16.6.8 Outputs

Defaults and transitions can be fed into the *Cash Flow Model with Simulation Controls* as with the single period defaults. The advantages of using a transition matrix has been discussed as it can feed in haircuts for overcollateralization ratios and potentially EOD events as well.

16.7 CONCLUSION

This chapter aimed to introduce the concept of valuation of CDO tranches and the various approaches that can be adopted using an Excel framework to evaluate cash CDO tranches. As hopefully was demonstrated, cash CDO evaluation is not a trivial thing, and though conceptually simple, it is in practise quite complicated. The authors further hope that the reader was able to gain both an appreciation of the task and some useful approaches to the problem of CDO valuation. The authors would be happy to hear from readers about their efforts, including any alternatives. Contact details are provided at the end of Chapter 17.

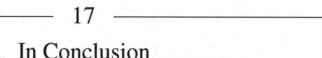

17
In Conclusion

Congratulations to all our readers who have made it this far. For those of you for whom cash flow modelling is a new experience, hopefully you now have the confidence and tools to tackle your own model, or at least be familiar enough with the model presented in this book to be able to adapt it to your needs. For those of you with some experience of modelling cash flow CDOs, hopefully the book has not been too dull and arduous, and we hope that there are at least some new ideas or tools presented that you can incorporate into your own modelling going forward.

As we stated at the beginning of the book, part of the purpose of the book is to stimulate discussion on the modelling and valuation of cash flow CDOs. To that aim we have established a website and look forward to receiving your feedback. In addition, errata and other resources will be posted there. The website name is www.cashcdo.com and you can reach us by emailing either darren@cashcdo.com or pamela@cashcdo.com.

Index

Printed in the United States
By Bookmasters